The Link That Divides

This important book illuminates the deeply intertwined histories of the Nicaragua Canal and the Afro-Indigenous Mosquito Coast, uncovering a compelling truth long overshadowed by the triumphalist narrative of the Panama Canal. Focusing on British and U.S. efforts to control the canal route through Nicaragua, Rajeshwari Dutt shows how imperial ambition, racial ideology, and local power struggles shaped one of Latin America's most contested infrastructure projects. She traces the role of racial language in imperial, colonial, and national agendas; the shifting dynamics of Anglo-American imperialism on the Mosquito Coast; and the violence embedded in the very pursuit of interoceanic connection. Methodologically, the book advances a practice of reading failure as a lens through which to understand the fragility of imperial projects and the contradictions that undermine their global ambitions. At its heart, *The Link That Divides* reveals a central paradox: that dreams of connection were built on – and undone by – the reality of division and exclusion.

Rajeshwari Dutt is Associate Professor in the School of Humanities and Social Sciences at the Indian Institute of Technology, Mandi. She is the author of *Maya Caciques in Early National Yucatán* and *Empire on Edge: The British Struggle for Order in Belize during Yucatán's Caste War, 1847–1901*.

Cambridge Studies in US Foreign Relations

Edited by

Ryan Irwin, *University of Albany*
Theresa Keeley, *University of Louisville, Kentucky*

This series showcases cutting-edge scholarship in US foreign relations that employs dynamic new methodological approaches and archives from the colonial era to the present. The series will be guided by the ethos of transnationalism, focusing on the history of American foreign relations in a global context rather than privileging the US as the dominant actor on the world stage.

Also in the Series

Mario Del Pero, *In the Shadow of the Vatican: Texan Evangelical Missionaries in Cold War Italy*

Andrew Johnstone, *Spinning the World: The Public Relations Industry and American Foreign Relations*

Pierre Asselin, *Vietnam's American War: A New History* (second edition)

Kuan-Jen Chen, *Charting America's Cold War Waters in East Asia: Sovereignty, Local Interests, and International Security*

David P. Fields and Mitchell B. Lerner (eds.), *Divided America, Divided Korea: The US and Korea During and After the Trump Years*

Talbot C. Imlay, *Clarence Streit and Twentieth-Century American Internationalism*

Susan McCall Perlman, *Contesting France: Intelligence and US Foreign Policy in the Early Cold War*

Pete Millwood, *Improbable Diplomats: How Ping-Pong Players, Musicians, and Scientists Remade US-China Relations*

R. Joseph Parrott and Mark Atwood Lawrence (eds.), *The Tricontinental Revolution: Third World Radicalism and the Cold War*

Aaron Donaghy, *The Second Cold War: Carter, Reagan, and the Politics of Foreign Policy*

Amanda C. Demmer, *After Saigon's Fall: Refugees and US-Vietnamese Relations, 1975–1995*

Heather Marie Stur, *Saigon at War: South Vietnam and the Global Sixties*

Seth Jacobs, *Rogue Diplomats: The Proud Tradition of Disobedience in American Foreign Policy*

Sarah Steinbock-Pratt, *Educating the Empire: American Teachers and Contested Colonization in the Philippines*

Walter L. Hixson, *Israel's Armor: The Israel Lobby and the First Generation of the Palestine Conflict*

Aurélie Basha i Novosejt, *"I Made Mistakes": Robert McNamara's Vietnam War Policy, 1960–1964*

Greg Whitesides, *Science and American Foreign Relations since World War II*

Jasper M. Trautsch, *The Genesis of America: US Foreign Policy and the Formation of National Identity, 1793–1815*

The Link That Divides

Race, Empire, and the Quest for the Nicaragua Canal in the Nineteenth Century

RAJESHWARI DUTT

Indian Institute of Technology, Mandi

CAMBRIDGE
UNIVERSITY PRESS

Shaftesbury Road, Cambridge CB2 8EA, United Kingdom

One Liberty Plaza, 20th Floor, New York, NY 10006, USA

477 Williamstown Road, Port Melbourne, VIC 3207, Australia

314–321, 3rd Floor, Plot 3, Splendor Forum, Jasola District Centre,
New Delhi – 110025, India

103 Penang Road, #05-06/07, Visioncrest Commercial, Singapore 238467

Cambridge University Press is part of Cambridge University Press & Assessment, a department of the University of Cambridge.

We share the University's mission to contribute to society through the pursuit of education, learning and research at the highest international levels of excellence.

www.cambridge.org
Information on this title: www.cambridge.org/9781009553322
DOI: 10.1017/9781009553315

© Rajeshwari Dutt 2026

This publication is in copyright. Subject to statutory exception and to the provisions of relevant collective licensing agreements, no reproduction of any part may take place without the written permission of Cambridge University Press & Assessment.

When citing this work, please include a reference to the DOI 10.1017/9781009553315

First published 2026

Cover image: col.illus.of River San Juan" in *Panama Canal Pamphlets* 1885-1890, Courtesy of Linda Hall Library of Science, Engineering & Technology.

A catalogue record for this publication is available from the British Library

A Cataloging-in-Publication data record for this book is available from the Library of Congress

ISBN 978-1-009-55332-2 Hardback
ISBN 978-1-009-55327-8 Paperback

Cambridge University Press & Assessment has no responsibility for the persistence or accuracy of URLs for external or third-party internet websites referred to in this publication and does not guarantee that any content on such websites is, or will remain, accurate or appropriate.

For EU product safety concerns, contact us at Calle de José Abascal, 56, 1°, 28003 Madrid, Spain, or email eugpsr@cambridge.org

For my darling Virangana, with all my love

Contents

List of Figures	*page* ix
List of Maps	xi
Acknowledgments	xiii
Introduction	1

PART I

1	Glimmers of a Canal	25
2	The British Conquest of San Juan del Norte	48
3	The Consolidation of Greytown	69

PART II

4	United States Enters the Canal Contest	97
5	The Rise and Fall of Greytown	120
6	Filibustering on the San Juan	150

PART III

7	The Road to Arbitration	185
8	Canal Dreams and the Fate of the Mosquito Reserve	216
9	Conclusion: The Turn towards Panama	255
Index		271

Figures

I.1	Map of Humboldt's proposed routes for passage between the Atlantic and Pacific Oceans	page 2
I.2	View of El Castillo	8
1.1	Mosquito national flag	30
1.2	H.M.S. *Tweed*	33
2.1	The Tehuantepec route	51
2.2	Map of San Juan del Norte showing in gray the possible position of British forces	60
3.1	Patrick Walker's map of May 20, 1847, with Mosquito territorial claim in black and Walker's own suggested boundary in the inset	78
3.2	Sketch of Christie's residence in Greytown	90
4.1	A depiction of a Miskitu "captain" in E. G. Squier's *Waikna*	115
5.1	Panorama of Greytown	125
5.2	Map of Greytown showing the area occupied by the transit company	137
5.3	Bombardment of Greytown by U.S.S. *Cyane*	142
6.1	Greytown, circa two years after the *Cyane* bombardment	152
6.2	River steamers plying Greytown c 1855	160
6.3	1856 Broadside with William Walker and Henry Kinney	170
7.1	Bedford Pim's proposed railroad	190
7.2	Nicaragua as the center of world commerce	191
7.3	Young Chief William Henry Clarence	200
8.1	Nicaragua Canal relief model at the Transportation Building of the Columbian World's Fair at Chicago, 1893	217

8.2	Eastern division of the canal route	224
8.3	Western division of the canal route	225
8.4	Ciudad América	230
8.5	British seamen from H.M.S. *Cleopatra* with Consul Bingham in a white shirt at the back	237
8.6	Robert Henry Clarence and Consul Bingham with officers of H.M.S. *Cleopatra*	244
9.1	Crowd gathered outside the *New York Journal* Building on Park Row to read the latest news of the Spanish–American War displayed on bulletin boards	260
9.2	The front page of the *San Francisco Call*, May 10, 1902	265
9.3	Illustration of volcanoes around the Nicaragua Canal route	266
9.4	"New United States of Central America"	270

Maps

1 Major proposed Nicaragua Canal routes through the San Juan River–Lake Nicaragua waterway in the nineteenth century   xv
2 The Mosquito Coast in the nineteenth century   xvi

Acknowledgments

While *The Link That Divides* explores the fraught connections that shaped imperial canal ambitions, its actual writing was sustained by links of a very different sort. Institutions, colleagues, friends, students, and family – sometimes from halfway across the globe – pitched in, helping me fill gaps, pushing me to ask hard questions, and making the writing of this book rewarding and enjoyable.

I am especially indebted to Paul Eiss, Eric Zolov, Matthew Restall, Leo Garofalo, George Reid-Andrews, Kris Lane, and Nico Slate for their continuous support of my work. Michel Gobat gave me generous feedback on a draft of this book that significantly helped to improve it. The Linda Hall Library (LHL) Fellowship, coming at a critical moment when I was trying to connect the story of the Nicaragua Canal to broader questions of empire and race, was truly transformational. Conversations with Benjamin Gross, then Vice President for Research and Scholarship at LHL, opened up new ways of conceptualizing the book and helped me see its potential beyond what I could have imagined on my own. Toni Betasso, Ben Gibson, and Jon Rollins of LHL provided indispensable help. I am especially grateful to David Díaz Arias, Justin Castro, Henry Jacob, Luciano Barraco, Matthew Dziennik, Mateo Jarquín, and Eline van Ommen for their advice and support at various points during the research and drafting of this book.

I am indebted to the many institutions and colleagues who helped me during my research for this book. I thank the staff of the Instituto de Historia de Nicaragua y Centroamérica (IHNCA) for helping me locate primary materials remotely before its closure. I want especially to give my heartfelt thanks to El IHNCA en el Exilio for giving me access to Nicaraguan materials under extremely difficult and complicated circumstances and for their work in preserving the history and memory of Nicaragua. I also thank Ariel Hamilton, who helped me share my work with *costeños* and the people of Bluefields. I owe special thanks to Kris Lane and his students, Victor Medina, Jason Bedolla and Andrés Vargas, who helped me access Tulane University's Latin American Library collections. I am grateful to the staff of the National Archives in Kew and Nick Dexter for making the process of data collection in the U.K. simple and efficient. I am indebted to Daniel Ugalde for his help in collecting materials from the Archivo Nacional de Costa Rica. I am also grateful to the Greenwich Maritime Museum, the Library of the Royal Geographical Society, the New York Historical Society, the Library of Congress, the John Hay Library at Brown University, the Spencer Library at the University of Kansas, the LHL, and the digital archive of the Biblioteca Enrique Bolaños for their collections, which greatly enhanced this book.

I thank the Transatlantic Studies Association for their early support of this project, when it first took shape as a study of the Mosquito Coast. I also thank the Indian Institute of Technology Mandi (IIT Mandi) for providing a conducive atmosphere for the writing of this book. I am grateful to Palvi Agarwal as well as my doctoral students Nupur Bandyopadhyay, Papari Saikia, Ritriban Chakraborty, and Gayathri Varier. Several undergraduate engineering students at IIT Mandi helped me understand the technological side of the canal story: Kshitiz Jain, Ishaan Dahiya, Saatvik Chugh, Balkar Singh, Chinmay Patil, and Surinderpal Singh. I am grateful to my editor at Cambridge, Cecelia Cancellaro, who was excited about this project from the very beginning and to Victoria Phillips, her editorial assistant. I am grateful to my cartographer, Joe LeMonnier, for the wonderful maps. Laura Blake, Philip Fernandes, and Magda Wojcik expertly shepherded the book through production.

Finally, my family has been the solid foundation on which this book was built. I am grateful to my brother, Nataraj Dasgupta, and my sister-in-law, Suraiya Nahar, for their steady support. My parents-in-law, Vijay Kumar Dutt and Poonam Dutt, have been constant sources of encouragement. My mother, Purabi Dasgupta, has been a pillar of strength and support, caring for my daughter during my archival trips and making this work possible in indispensable ways. My husband, Varun Dutt, lived through every rhythm of this project – its frustrations and its joys – and helped me emerge from the process intact. And my ten-year-old daughter, Virangana, who loves nothing more than editing my work, has pushed me to do better with every draft, reminding me, time and again, that my writing is still "not quite there."

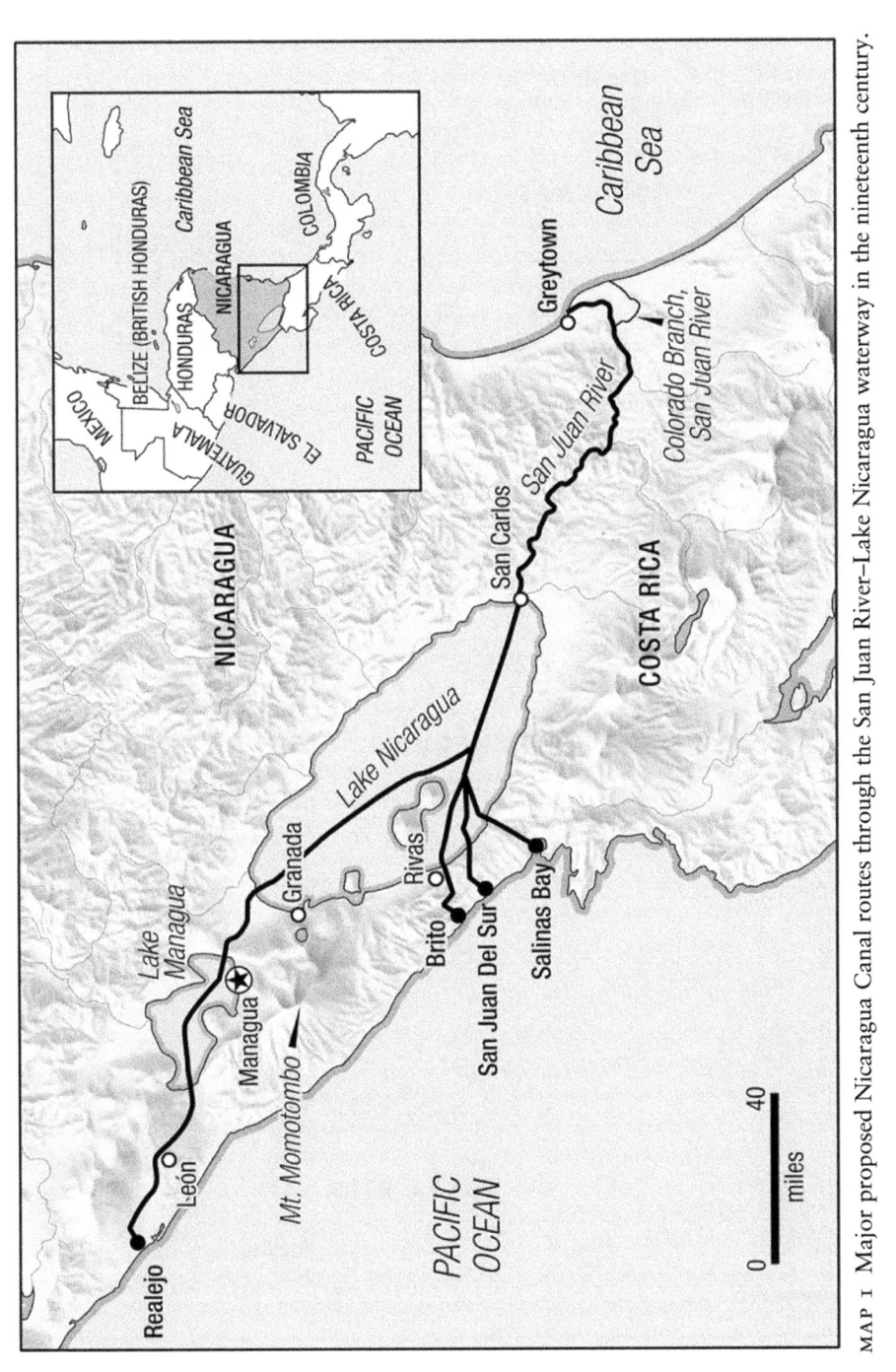

MAP 1 Major proposed Nicaragua Canal routes through the San Juan River–Lake Nicaragua waterway in the nineteenth century.

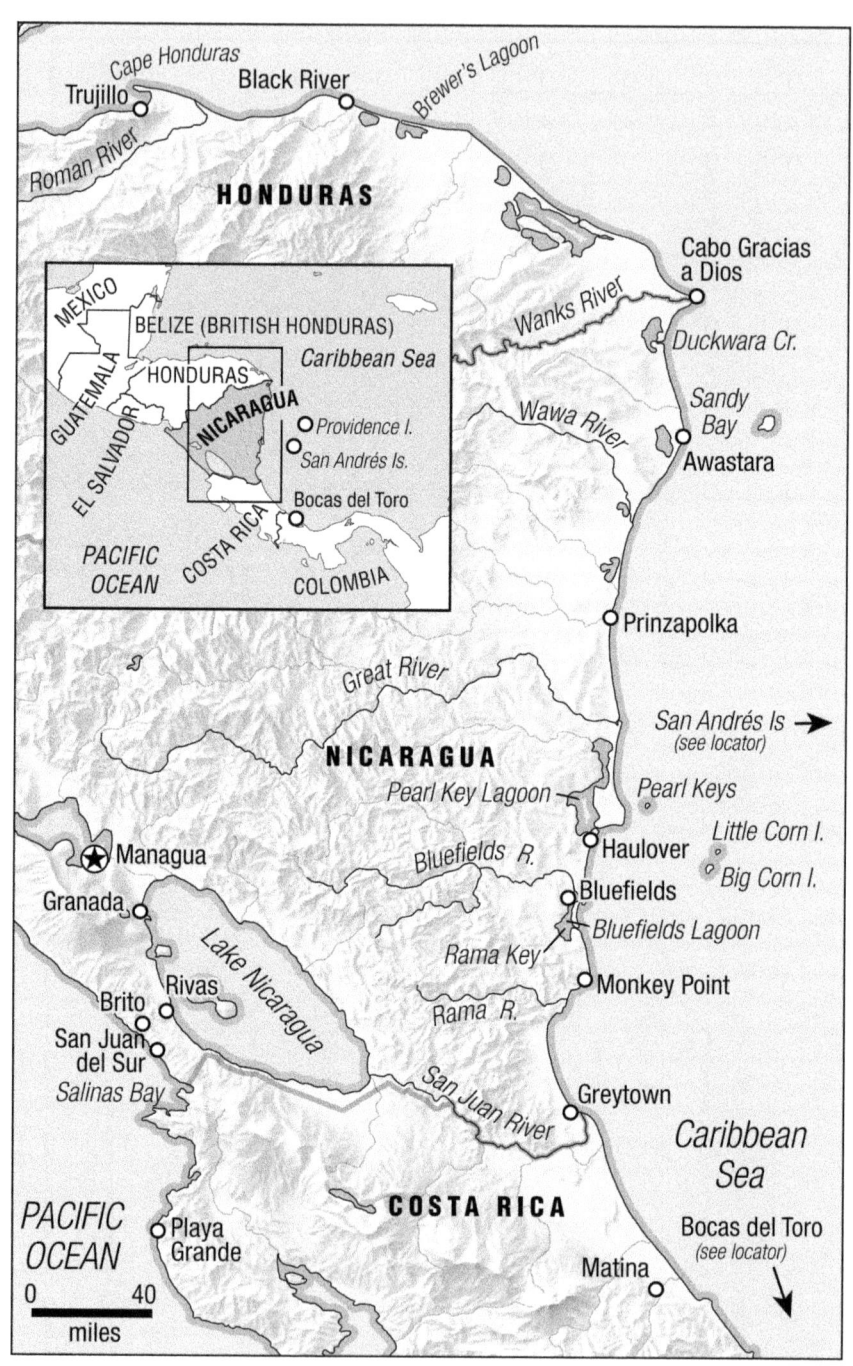

MAP 2 The Mosquito Coast in the nineteenth century.

Introduction

In 1804, Alexander von Humboldt's expedition to Spanish America seemed to open new ways of imagining not just geography but nature itself. Humboldt's travels helped him visualize nature as united, connected, one part linked to the other. It is perhaps not surprising that the Nicaragua Canal would find space within this Humboldtian "cosmic" vision of unity. The Nicaragua Canal appears in two of Humboldt's most widely read works: *Political Essay on the Kingdom of New Spain* and *Personal Narrative of Travels to the Equinoctial Regions of the New Continent during the Years 1799–1804*. In the first, he presented the Nicaragua route as one of nine possible routes for linking the Atlantic and the Pacific Oceans (see Figure I.1). In the second, he made his preference for Nicaragua clear. "It seems quite probable," he wrote, "that it will be the province of Nicaragua that will be chosen for the great work of uniting the two oceans."[1] In this, Humboldt was echoing the wisdom of over three centuries of explorations in the isthmus that saw Nicaragua as a prime locale for an interoceanic canal. A little over 100 years later, the construction of the Panama Canal would irrevocably change this narrative.

The story of the interoceanic canal linking the Atlantic and Pacific Oceans has been inextricably and almost exclusively tied to the

---

[1] *Viage á las regiones equinocciales del nuevo continente: Hecho en 1799 hasta 1804, por Al. de Humboldt y A. Bonpland / redactado por Alejandro de Humboldt; continuación indispensable al ensayo político sobre el reino de la Nueva España por el mismo autor*, vol. 5 (Paris: 1826), 30.

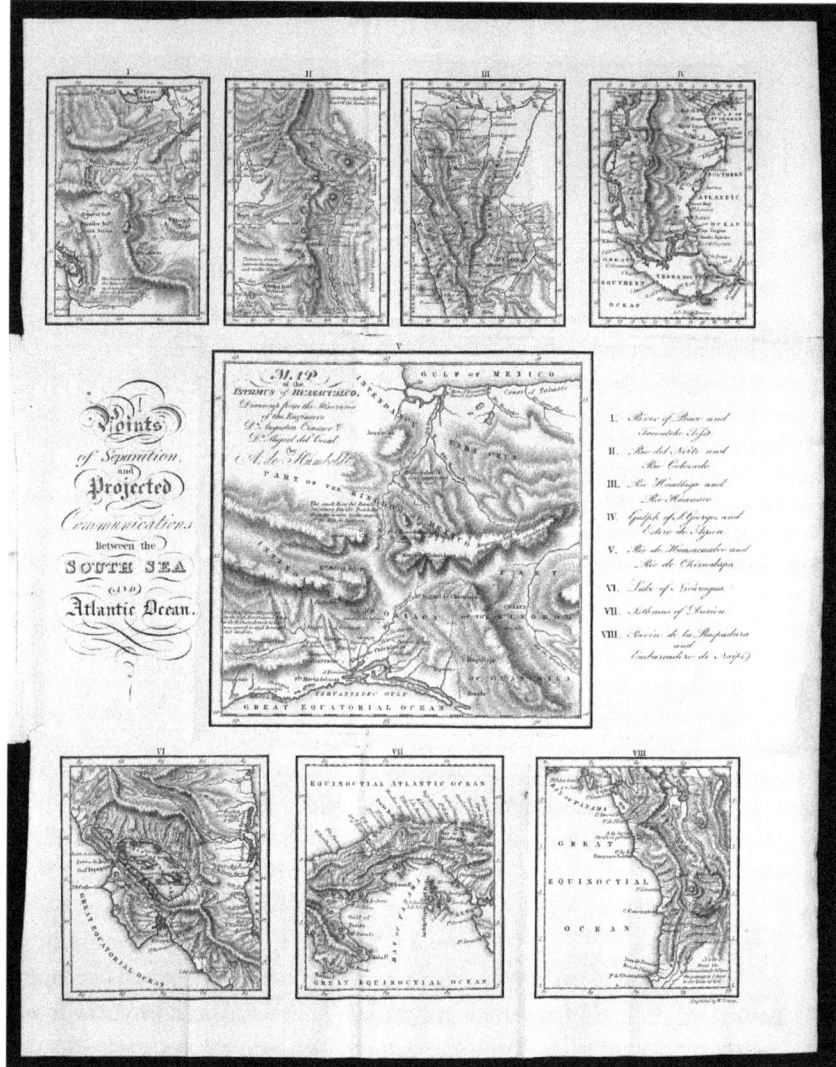

FIGURE I.I Map of Humboldt's proposed routes for passage between the Atlantic and Pacific Oceans. Image source: Alexander von Humboldt and John Black, *Political Essay on the Kingdom of New Spain*. 2nd ed. (English), *Atlas* (vol. 5). London: Longman, Hurst, and Brown (etc.), 1814, pl. 9. Courtesy of the Linda Hall Library of Science, Engineering and Technology.

triumphalist narrative of the Panama Canal. In this version of events, competing canal schemes of the nineteenth century are portrayed as mere byproducts or detours on a long and arduous journey, with Panama as the inevitable endpoint.² Yet such a narrative threatens to erase a 400-year-old historical trajectory where Nicaragua was widely regarded as a preferred choice for the location of a transisthmian route through Central America. In the nineteenth century, in particular, the Nicaragua route became a zone of active contestation between the imperial powers of Great Britain and the United States and the focal point of Nicaraguan national and Central American regional ambitions.

Recovering the interwoven histories of the Nicaragua Canal (see Map 1) and the Afro-Indigenous Mosquito Coast³ (see Map 2) in the nineteenth century, *The Link That Divides* complicates the received story of Panama as destiny. It charts the tensions that characterized the transatlantic quest for the Nicaragua Canal, revealing the central paradox of the interoceanic dream: that visions of connection and unity that drove canal ambitions stood on – and were, in turn, shattered by – the fractured foundations of rivalry, conflict, and exclusion.

A STORY OF ERASURES

Following the decision to build the canal in Panama in 1902, we find an erasure of the story of the Nicaragua Canal from the triumphalist narrative of the Panama Canal. The official narrative of the Panama Canal history portrayed the decision to build a canal through Panama as logical and cumulative. The construction of this narrative owes much to the efforts of Joseph Bucklin Bishop, who was the chief executive of the U.S. Isthmian Canal Commission (ICC) and its "unofficial propagandist."⁴ Bishop crafted a triumphalist narrative of the Panama Canal that presented it as the inevitable culmination of the historical quest for an interoceanic canal through the Central American isthmus. "The Panama Canal," wrote Bishop in the opening line of his book *Panama Gateway*,

---

² In recent years, there has been a growing scholarly effort to explore the lesser-known schemes for infrastructure projects throughout Latin America. See, for instance, Eric Rutkow, *The Longest Line on the Map: The United States, the Pan-American Highway, and the Quest to Link the Americas* (New York: Scribner, 2019); Nathanael Grimes and J. Justin Castro, "The Less Imperial Path: The Mississippi Valley, US Expansionism, and Engineer James B. Eads' Failure to Build a Ship Railway," *The Historian* 82:2 (2020), 156–181.
³ I use "Mosquito Coast" to refer to the broader Caribbean region historically inhabited by the Miskitu people, and "Mosquito Shore" when referring to the British protectorate, following the terminology used in nineteenth-century diplomatic and colonial sources.
⁴ Henry Jacob, "Reverse Engineering the Narrative: A. B. Nichols's Failed Attempt to Amend the Canal Zone's History," *The Latin Americanist* 65:1 (March 2021), 57.

"is the realization of an idea four centuries old."[5] In this narrative, the Nicaragua Canal appeared as a small step towards the natural and inevitable move towards Panama. For instance, in writing about the contest between the Nicaragua and Panama Canal routes, Bucklin suggested that the only reason for the ICC's positive report on Nicaragua was the unfavorable terms of sale offered at the time by the New Panama Canal Company. In Bishop's narrative, once these terms of sale were favorable, the U.S. government naturally gravitated towards the Panama Canal. In Bishop's view, the choice to build the canal at Panama was "beyond dispute."[6] Bishop's narrative would have a lasting impact on both academic and popular renditions of the story of the Panama Canal.[7] Writing about the congratulatory literature around the Panama Canal produced in the lead-up to the opening of the Canal, Sarah Moore described it as "a heroic account of the massive undertaking and technological accomplishments of the United States in building the canal."[8] Indeed, newspapers often described the Panama Canal as the eighth wonder of the world.[9] In later renditions as well, the story of the Nicaragua Canal was mostly invisible or subsumed to provide a touch of drama to the Panama Canal story. We can see this way of incorporating the story of the Nicaragua Canal into the Panama Canal narrative in almost all extant works on the history of the Panama Canal, including David McCullough's acclaimed *The Path between the Seas* and Matthew Parker's *Panama Fever*, in a chapter aptly titled "The Battle of the Routes." While there has been a plethora of popular and academic books on the Panama Canal, the Nicaragua route has received scant attention.[10]

---

[5] Joseph Bucklin Bishop, *The Panama Gateway* (New York: Charles Scribner's Sons, 1913), 3.
[6] Joseph Bucklin Bishop and Admiral Robert E. Peary, *Uncle Sam's Panama Canal and World History, Accompanying the Panama Canal Flat-Globe* (New York: World Syndicate Company, 1913), 22.
[7] Jacob, "Reverse Engineering the Narrative," 58.
[8] Sarah J. Moore, *Empire on Display: San Francisco's Panama-Pacific International Exposition of 1915* (Norman: University of Oklahoma Press, 2013), 44.
[9] See, for instance, *The Vidette*, May 27, 1915.
[10] Some popular works on the Panama Canal include: David McCullough, *The Path between the Seas: The Creation of the Panama Canal, 1870–1914* (New York: Simon and Schuster, 2004, reprint); Matthew Parker, *Panama Fever* (New York: Knopf Doubleday Publishing Group, 2009); Noel Maurer and Carlos Yu, *The Big Ditch: How America Took, Built, Ran, and Ultimately Gave Away the Panama Canal* (Princeton: Princeton University Press, 2023); Ashley Carse, *Beyond the Big Ditch: Politics, Ecology, and Infrastructure at the Panama Canal* (Cambridge, MA: MIT Press, 2019); Sylvia Engdahl, Building the Panama Canal (Detroit: Greenhaven Press,

In some ways, the erasure of the story of the Nicaragua Canal and the related preponderance of the Panama Canal narrative appear logical and natural. After all, the Panama Canal *exists*. Yet I would argue that despite the fact that the Nicaragua Canal was never built, it was patently *real* for imperial and national governments, for diplomats and soldiers on the ground, and for filibusters and local Miskitus, whose lives were forever upended as a result of the contest over the Nicaragua route in the nineteenth century. The quest for the Nicaragua Canal – even though it never finally transpired – irretrievably altered the course of imperial, regional, national, and local history in Central America. Moreover, the erasure of the Nicaragua Canal story is a denial of the very *real* trajectory of four centuries of canal exploration and diplomacy, where Nicaragua was widely considered to be a prime location for an isthmian canal through Central America. Focusing on developments in the nineteenth century, this book argues that the Panama Canal was not inevitable, the ultimate choice to build it, not simply a result of cumulative knowledge. The turn towards Panama was disruptive to the main flow of Anglo-American efforts to build a transisthmian canal, which throughout the nineteenth century had been largely concentrated in Nicaragua. This is not to deny the significance of the Panama Canal but rather to recover a longer, more complex history of the interoceanic canal, one in which the "unbuilt" had as much impact as the project that was eventually realized. The argument here is not that the Nicaragua Canal was central or inevitable but that contestation over it shaped imperial, national, and regional projects even in failure.

This book also attempts to recover the interwoven history of the Mosquito Coast and the Nicaragua Canal, which had significant

---

2012). However, there is a dearth of any serious treatment of the Nicaragua Canal in the extant literature. One of the earliest works on the Nicaragua Canal is Lindley Miller Keasbey's *The Nicaragua Canal and the Monroe Doctrine* (New York: G. P. Putnam's Sons, 1896). Following Keasbey, David Folkman's *The Nicaragua Route* (Salt Lake City: University of Utah Press, 1972) is the only English-language book that centers on the Nicaragua Canal. Craig Dozier's *Nicaragua's Mosquito Shore: The Years of British and American Presence* (Tuscaloosa: University of Alabama Press, 1985) is the single best account of the diplomatic contests among the United States, Britain, and Nicaragua over the Mosquito Shore and touches on the Nicaragua Canal; however, it does not take the Nicaragua Canal as its central focus. There have been some important Spanish language monographs on the Nicaragua Canal: JanGeert Van der Post, *El largo y sinuoso camino: Razones por las que no ha sido construido el canal de Nicaragua* (Managua: IHNCA-UCA, 2014); Frances Kinloch Tijerino, *El imaginario del canal y la nación cosmopolita: Nicaragua, siglo XIX* (Managua: IHNCA-UCA, 2015).

repercussions for Miskitu politics and Afro-Indigenous lives.[11] In the mid nineteenth century, the Mosquito Coast, a narrow strip of land on the Caribbean coast of Nicaragua, became the locus of the transatlantic contest among Britain, the United States, and Central American republics for control over a possible canal route linking the Atlantic and the Pacific Oceans. During this contest, the status of the Mosquito Kingdom as an "Indigenous" polity became a crucial linchpin around which the different transatlantic powers maneuvered to gain control over the Mosquito Coast's San Juan delta, including the harbor of San Juan del Norte (Greytown), the proposed Caribbean mouth of the interoceanic canal. The story of the Nicaragua Canal was intimately connected to the Mosquito question and had a real impact on the relationship between Nicaragua and the Mosquito Coast. Yet in none of the extant narratives of the Panama Canal that touch on the Nicaragua story, do we get any sense of these stakes on the ground. This book takes on the task of recovering this second erasure resulting from the narrative around the Panama Canal: the erasure of the story of the Mosquito Coast. Because the surviving sources are overwhelmingly imperial and colonial, this recovery is necessarily partial, reading both the traces and the silences they contain. By rendering the intertwined history of the Nicaragua Canal and the Mosquito Coast, I show that the deployment of the language of race, indigeneity, and exclusion was central to imperial, colonial, and national efforts to control the Nicaragua Canal route.

[11] There have been some critical studies on race and ethnicity in the Mosquito Shore (Michael Olien, "The Miskito Kings and the Line of Succession," *Journal of Anthropological Research* 39:2 (Summer 1983), 198–214; Michael Olien, "Micro/Macro-Level Linkages: Regional Political Structures on the Mosquito Coast, 1845–1864," *Ethnohistory* 34:3 (Summer 1987), 256–287; Michael Olien, "Were the Miskito Indians Black? Ethnicity, Politics, And Plagiarism in the Mid-nineteenth Century," *Nieuwe West-Indische Gids / New West Indian Guide* 62:1/2 (1988), 27–50; Karl Offen, "The Sambo and Tawira Miskitu: The Colonial Origins and Geography of Intra-Miskitu Differentiation in Eastern Nicaragua and Honduras," *Ethnohistory* 49:2 (Spring 2002), 319–372; Karl Offen, "Race and Place in Colonial Mosquitia, 1600–1787," in *Blacks and Blackness in Central America: Between Race and Place*, eds. Lowell Gundmundson and Justin Wolfe (Durham: Duke University Press, 2010); Karl Offen, "Mapping Amerindian Captivity in Colonial Mosquitia," *Journal of Latin American Geography* 14:3 (2015), 35–65; Charles Hale, *Resistance and Contradiction: Miskitu Indians and the Nicaraguan State, 1894–1987* (Stanford: Stanford University Press, 1994); Baron Pineda, *Shipwrecked Identities: Navigating Race on Nicaragua's Mosquito Coast* (New Brunswick: Rutgers University Press, 2006)), but there has been little work on how these preoccupations colored the contest over the canal route. However, neither the existing Spanish- nor English-language works connect the Indigenous history of the Mosquito Shore to the history of the Nicaragua Canal.

AN IMPERIAL STAGING ARENA

It is near impossible to tell the story of the Nicaragua Canal – or the Mosquito Coast – without recounting the impact of repeated imperial incursions on the region. Shortly after Vasco Núñez de Balboa's 1513 expedition opened the Pacific Ocean to Western imagination, in 1539 Captain Alonso Calero and Diego Machuca de Suazo conducted a significant exploration of the San Juan–Lake Nicaragua waterway. Their expedition mapped the topography of the San Juan River, including its multiple rapids, and confirmed its connection to the Atlantic Ocean, enhancing Spanish knowledge of the region's strategic waterways. While, like many conquistadores of the sixteenth century, Calero claimed that he had paid for his own armada to undertake this expedition, there is no doubt that this early exploration phase of the Nicaragua route was closely tied to Spanish conquest expeditions and as such was characterized by both the thrill of discovery and the specter of violence.[12] Calero and Machuca's expedition, for instance, was outfitted with a brigantine and a force of 200 Spaniards.[13] Not only was the San Juan River (the critical artery of the canal route) a base for conquest expeditions to "pacify" Indigenous groups, but it was also rife with piracy. In the seventeenth century, in a bid to retain control over the San Juan River, Spanish authorities erected the fort of El Castillo on the right bank of the river overlooking the Santa Cruz rapids (see Figure I.2). El Castillo was the largest defense structure built in Central America at the time and became a focal point of subsequent contests over the San Juan River and the canal route.[14]

However, the concentration of Spanish institutions on the Pacific side of Nicaragua meant that until the mid-seventeenth century, the Indigenous communities of the Caribbean coast – who would eventually constitute the Mosquito Kingdom – remained largely isolated from

---

[12] Matthew Restall argues that much of the early phase of conquest expeditions was carried out by Spaniards, who were not formally soldiers in the employ of the Spanish crown but had joined these expeditions in the expectation that they would later be rewarded by the crown with wealth and prestige (Matthew Restall, *Seven Myths of the Spanish Conquest* (New York: Oxford University Press, 2021)).
[13] David R. Radell, "Exploration and Commerce on Lake Nicaragua and the Río San Juan, 1524–1800," *Journal of Interamerican Studies and World Affairs* 12:1 (January 1970), 107–125.
[14] Max Harrison Williams, "San Juan River–Lake Nicaragua Waterway, 1502–1921," PhD thesis, Louisiana State University, 1971, 64.

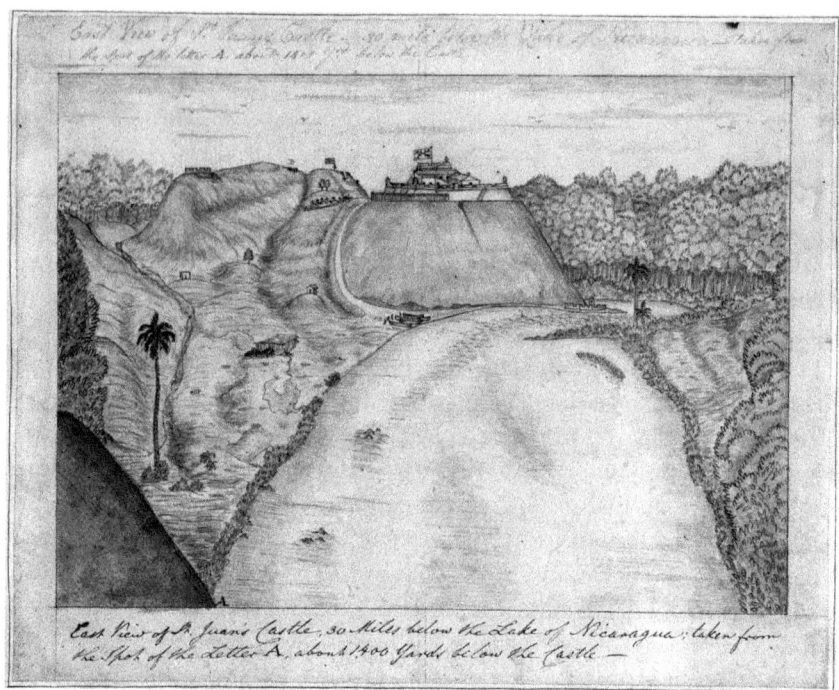

FIGURE I.2 View of El Castillo. Source: "East View of St. Juan's Castle, 30 miles below the Lake of Nicaragua; taken from the spot of the Letter A, about 1,400 Yards below the Castle," in Charles Napier Robinson, *A Pictorial History of the Sea Services: Or Graphic Studies of the Sailor's Life and Character Afloat and Ashore. Vol. X, Part 1: Nelson, 1758–1800* (London: n.p., 1911). Courtesy of John Hay Library, Brown University.

Spanish influence. As Daniel Mendiola writes: "Accordingly, no known sources referenced the Mosquito people by any name until the English settlers at Providence Island began trading with them in the 1630s."[15] These communities, however, soon began to engage in commercial relations with the English and even participated in raids on Spanish settlements in the interior of Nicaragua.[16] As these Amerindian groups became more closely integrated into the Caribbean world, new patterns of African admixture reshaped the Indigenous population, giving rise to communities identified as Tawira Miskitus, who emphasized Amerindian

---

[15] Daniel Mendiola, "The Rise of the Mosquito Kingdom in Central America's Caribbean Borderlands: Sources, Questions, and Enduring Myths," *History Compass* 16:1 (2017), https://doi.org/10.1111/hic3.12437.

[16] Williams, "San Juan River–Lake Nicaragua Waterway," 59.

descent, and Zambo Miskitus, who identified as Afro-Indigenous. These identities persisted in the Mosquito Kingdom, a confederation of Miskitu communities that developed into an important regional player.[17] Following the War of Jenkins' Ear (1739–1748), with the British installing a protectorate over the area, close relations developed between the Indigenous Miskitu leadership and the British settlers in the area. The Miskitu also developed a high degree of affinity for British ways, with prominent Miskitus acquiring English names and even royal coronations of Miskitu kings taking place amidst pomp in the neighboring British settlement of Belize.

Amidst growing Anglo-Spanish rivalry in the context of the American Revolution, the San Juan River became a critical staging point for imperial struggle in the Caribbean. By the 1760s, the Royal Navy's explorations on the Pacific Coast of Nicaragua had convinced the British government of the vital importance of the Lake Nicaragua–San Juan waterway to the Spanish Empire. Control of the San Juan River, which effectively connected the Lake to the Atlantic and Pacific coasts, could thus strategically cleave the Spanish empire into two, separating Central America from South America. Led by the legendary Horatio Nelson in what would become Britain's "most significant military intervention in interior Central America,"[18] British forces descended on the San Juan River with a view to capturing El Castillo, which became a battleground between British and Spanish forces. Though Nelson's victory was ultimately pyrrhic, the military engagement underscored the importance of the San Juan route to Anglo-Spanish rivalry and illuminated how the Mosquito Coast became a southern theater of war during the American Revolution.[19]

Following a treaty with Spain in 1787, the British protectorate came to an end, and most settlers, and their enslaved, evacuated to Belize. Although the Spanish returned to the Coast following the evacuation,

---

[17] Daniel Mendiola, "The Founding and Fracturing of the Mosquito Confederation: Zambos, Tawiras, and New Archival Evidence, 1711–1791," *Hispanic American Historical Review* 99:4 (2019), 619–647.

[18] Matthew P. Dziennik, "The Miskitu, Military Labour and the San Juan Expedition of 1780." *The Historical Journal* 61:1 (2018), 156.

[19] See Dziennik, "The Miskitu"; Nicholas Rogers, *Blood Waters: War, Disease and Race in the Eighteenth-Century Caribbean* (Woodbridge: The Boydell Press, 2021); Matthew Lockwood, *To Begin the World over Again: How the American Revolution Devastated the Globe* (New Haven: Yale University Press, 2019); Peter Linebaugh, *Red Round Globe Hot Burning: A Tale at the Crossroads of Commons and Closure, of Love and Terror, of Race and Class, and of Kate and Ned Despard* (Oakland: University of California Press, 2019).

they faced difficulties in exerting effective control over this frontier region. The Spanish continued to depend on the English settlers, who had stayed behind on the Coast, to mediate with the Miskitus. By 1800, the Miskitus had successfully repelled the Spanish from the Coast, and relations with the English in Belize gradually resumed. Miskitu Princes George Frederic[20] and Robert Charles Frederic traveled to Jamaica in June 1805 for their education, and in 1816, George Frederic's coronation ceremony took place in Belize.[21] While traditional views of Anglo-Miskitu relations portrayed the Afro-Indigenous groups as pliant "puppets" of British merchants and officials, a new spate of scholarship has successfully retrieved Miskitus as powerful and complex political agents.[22] While engaging closely with this work, this book does not

---

[20] Several Miskitu rulers shared similar names across generations. For clarity, I refer to George Frederic (r. 1801–1824) as George Frederic, and his later successor George Augustus Frederic (r. 1845–1865) as George Augustus. These simplified forms are used throughout the text.

[21] Damian Clavel, "The Rise and Fall of George Frederic Augustus II: The Central American, Caribbean, and Atlantic Life of a Miskitu King, 1805–1824," *Business History Review* 96 (Autumn 2022), 537–540.

[22] For older scholarship that viewed Miskitus as recipients of change see: Mary Helms, "The Cultural Ecology of a Colonial Tribe," *Ethnology* 8:1 (January 1969), 76–84; Troy Floyd, *The Anglo-Spanish Struggle for Mosquitia* (Albuquerque: University of New Mexico Press, 1967); Robert A. Naylor, *Penny Ante Imperialism: The Mosquito Shore and the Bay of Honduras, 1600–1914 – A Case Study in British Informal Empire* (London: Golden Cockerel Press, 1989). For scholarship that shows the complexity of Miskitu politics and highlights Miskitu agency, see: Philip A. Dennis and Michael D. Olien, "Kingship among the Miskito," *American Ethnologist* 11:4 (November 1984), 718–737; Michael Olien, "General, Governor, and Admiral: Three Miskito Lines of Succession," *Ethnohistory* 45:2 (Spring 1998), 277–318; Olien, "Were the Miskito Indians Black?"; Olien, "The Miskito Kings and the Line of Succession"; Frank Griffith Dawson, "William Pitt's Settlement at Black River on the Mosquito Shore: A Challenge to Spain in Central America, 1732–87," *The Hispanic American Historical Review* 63:4 (November 1983), 677–706; Karl Offen, "A Miskitu Critique of British Trade Practices," *Ethnohistory* 69:3 (July 2022), 313–323; Offen, "The Sambo and Tawira Miskitu"; Karl Offen, "Race and Place in Colonial Mosquitia, 1600–1787," in *Blacks and Blackness in Central America: Between Race and Place*, eds. Lowell Gundmundson and Justin Wolfe, 92–129 (Durham: Duke University Press, 2010); Karl Offen and Terry Rugeley, *The Awakening Coast: An Anthology of Moravian Writings from Mosquitia and Eastern Nicaragua* (Lincoln: University of Nebraska Press, 2014); Caroline A. Williams, "Living between Empires: Diplomacy and Politics in the Late Eighteenth-Century Mosquitia," *The Americas* 70:2 (October 2013), 237–268; Charles Hale, *Resistance and Contradiction: Miskitu Indians and the Nicaraguan State, 1894–1987* (Stanford: Stanford University Press, 1994); Baron Pineda, *Shipwrecked Identities: Navigating Race on Nicaragua's Mosquito Coast* (New Brunswick: Rutgers University Press, 2006); Daniel Mendiola, "The Founding and Fracturing of the Mosquito Confederation: Zambos, Tawiras, and New Archival Evidence, 1711–1791," *Hispanic*

attempt a comprehensive ethnohistory of the Miskitu. Rather, adding to this vibrant conversation, this book incorporates the Miskitu story within the history of the Nicaragua Canal, highlighting along the way the impact of competing projects of control over the canal route on Miskitu communities and documenting moments of resilience and resistance.

This book focuses on the Anglo-American quest for the Nicaragua Canal, which largely defined the contest over the San Juan River and the Mosquito Coast in the nineteenth century. It is important to mention at the outset that this book is not a study per se of Anglo-American relations; rather, it explores the nature and limits of both British and U.S. projects of imperialism in the context of the Nicaragua Canal. Since Gallagher and Robinson's assertion that the British "expanded overseas by means of 'informal empire' as much as by acquiring dominion in the strict constitutional sense," much of the British Empire's activities in Latin America in the nineteenth century have been understood through the trope of "informal empire." Looking beyond the focus on economics and trade that characterized Gallagher and Robinson's work, Robert Aguirre has successfully incorporated the role of culture within the notion of "informal empire." In an edited collection by Matthew Brown (2008), scholars have stressed the importance of culture in revitalizing the concept of "informal empire." In the context of the Mosquito Coast, Robert Naylor examines the British informal empire on the Atlantic coast of Nicaragua and argues that the British did not have a "grand design" in Central America. Charles Hale shows how the legacies of the British informal empire in Mosquito Shore affected Miskitu self-identity and consequently the Indigenous political position in the twentieth century. Recently, scholars such as Ann Stoler have questioned the term, pointing out that it is really a euphemism for imperialism. Adding to the historiography of "informal empire," this book suggests that there was a great deal of dissonance between British imperial/metropolitan policies and the

American Historical Review 99:4 (2019), 619–647; Clavel, "The Rise and Fall of George Frederic Augustus II"; Samantha Billing, "Indios, Sambos, Mestizos, and the Social Construction of Racial Identity in Colonial Central America," *Ethnohistory* 68:2 (April 2021), 269–290; Samantha Billing, "Indigenous Slavery in the Circum-Caribbean: The Miskitu's Slave Trade and Its Consequences," *Slavery & Abolition* 45:4 (2024), 758–782, https://doi.org/10.1080/0144039X.2024.2378476; Luciano Barraco, "Chief Robert Henry Clarence: The Last Hereditary Chief of the Mosquito Reserve," *AlterNative: An International Journal of Indigenous Peoples* 20:4 (2024), 649–657, https://doi.org/10.1177/11771801241263601; Luciano Baracco, "The Last Days of the Mosquito Reserve: The Mosquito Indian Diplomatic Mission to Restore the Mosquito Reserve, 1894-1907," *Ethnohistory* 71:3 (July 2024), 299–319.

actions of British officials on the ground in the Mosquito Shore. Thus, whereas British official policy regarding the Mosquito Shore was one of nonintervention, on the ground, colonial and consular officials were much more interventionist and, in some cases, did not balk from using military force to preserve British influence in the region.[23]

Studies of U.S. intervention in Latin America have traditionally focused on the early twentieth century. However, recent efforts of historians have begun to recognize the crucial importance of the nineteenth century in forging practices of U.S. imperialism. Michel Gobat (2005) has highlighted that since the mid nineteenth century, U.S. actions in Nicaragua were part of a broader project of U.S. imperialism in the Caribbean and, in his 2018 book, links William Walker's enterprise in Nicaragua to U.S. liberal imperialism in the nineteenth century.[24] Greg Grandin (2006) argues that from the mid nineteenth century onwards, Latin America constituted a "workshop" or "trial run" for U.S. imperialism that would later be deployed at a global level.[25] According to Alan Knight (2008), the circum-Caribbean was a "paranoid" concern for U.S. foreign policy since at least the early twentieth century, if not before.[26] Recently, Daniel Immerwahr (2019) has suggested that the U.S. logo conveniently "hides" an empire that was forged beginning in the nineteenth century and including parts of the Caribbean basin.[27] Aims McGuinness (2008) has highlighted the intertwined history of the Panama route and U.S. imperial expansion in the Gold Rush era.[28] Julie Greene (2009) has illuminated

---

[23] John Gallagher and Ronald Robinson, "The Imperialism of Free Trade," *The Economic History Review, New Series* 6:1 (1953), 1–15; Robert D. Aguirre, *Informal Empire: Mexico and Central America in Victorian Culture* (Minneapolis: University of Minnesota Press, 2005); Matthew Brown, *Informal Empire in Latin America: Culture, Commerce and Capital* (Oxford: Wiley-Blackwell, 2008); Naylor, *Penny Ante Imperialism*; Hale, *Resistance and Contradiction*; Ann Stoler, "On Degrees of Imperial Sovereignty," *Public Culture* 18:1 (2006), 136.

[24] Michel Gobat, *Confronting the American Dream: Nicaragua under U.S. Imperial Rule* (Durham: Duke University Press, 2005); Michel Gobat, *Empire by Invitation: William Walker and Manifest Destiny in Central America* (Cambridge, MA: Harvard University Press, 2018).

[25] Greg Grandin, *Empire's Workshop: Latin America, the United States, and the Making of an Imperial Republic* (New York: Picador, 2021).

[26] Alan Knight, "Rethinking British Informal Empire in Latin America," *Bulletin of Latin American Research* 27:1 (2008), 23–48, https://doi.org/10.1111/j.1470-9856.2007.00243.x.

[27] Daniel Immerwahr, *How to Hide an Empire: A History of the Greater United States* (New York: Picador/Farrar, Straus and Giroux, 2020).

[28] Aims McGuinness, *Path of Empire: Panama and the California Gold Rush* (Ithaca: Cornell University Press, 2008).

how the Panama Canal forged America's "new empire" in the post-1898 period.[29] This book contributes to this conversation by showing the United States' deep involvement in the Nicaragua Canal project – both officially, and through the actions of the "advance-men" of imperialism, the filibusters – and the importance of the Nicaragua Canal to U.S. geopolitical vision and imperial ambitions in the second half of the nineteenth century.[30] Thus while popular narratives have traditionally identified the wars of 1898 as the starting point of U.S. imperialism, the story of the Nicaragua Canal challenges this timeline, revealing an earlier trajectory of U.S. imperial efforts. The Nicaragua Canal story exemplifies how grand infrastructure projects, whether completed or not, often function as proxies for broader geopolitical influence, with competing powers using them to assert authority and secure strategic advantages. Indeed, it can be argued that the quest for the unbuilt Nicaragua Canal was deeply entangled with the United States' rise as the dominant influence in Latin America, effectively supplanting Great Britain by the dawn of the twentieth century.

According to historian Jay Sexton, the Monroe Doctrine (1823) became "American shorthand for a hemisphere (and, ultimately, a world) cleared of the British empire."[31] While scholars of Anglo-American relations have pointed to a period of "rapprochement" at the turn of the twentieth century[32] – marking the shift from rivalry to partnership and the ascendancy of U.S. power – this transition was neither inevitable nor

---

[29] Julie Greene, *The Canal Builders: Making America's Empire at the Panama Canal* (New York: Penguin Books, 2014).

[30] For other important (including recent) works on U.S. imperialism in Nicaragua, see Karl Bermann, *Under the Big Stick: Nicaragua and the United States since 1848* (Boston: South End Press, 1986); Daniel Kovalik, *Nicaragua: A History of US Intervention & Resistance* (Atlanta: Clarity Press, 2023); Eline Van Ommen, *Nicaragua Must Survive: Sandinista Revolutionary Diplomacy in the Global Cold War* (Oakland: University of California Press, 2024); Mateo Jarquin, *The Sandinista Revolution: A Global Latin American History* (Chapel Hill: The University of North Carolina Press, 2024). Notable works on U.S. imperialism in Latin America include Lars Schoultz, *Beneath the United States: A History of U.S. Policy toward Latin America* (Cambridge, MA: Harvard University Press, 1998); Alan McPherson, *A Short History of U.S. Interventions in Latin America and the Caribbean* (Chichester: Wiley/Blackwell, 2016).

[31] Jay Sexton, *The Monroe Doctrine: Empire and Nation in Nineteenth-Century America* (New York: Hill & Wang, 2012), 10.

[32] See, for instance, Bradford Perkins, *The Great Rapprochement: England and the United States, 1895–1914* (London: Gollancz, 1969); Kenneth Bourne, *Britain and the Balance of Power in North America, 1815–1908* (Berkeley: University of California Press, 1967); Howard Temperley, *Britain and America since Independence* (Hampshire: Palgrave, 2002).

uncontested. As this book demonstrates, the story of the Nicaragua Canal serves as a microcosm for understanding this imperial "changing of the guard" in the Western Hemisphere, as British influence waned and U.S. power rose to dominance. Contrary to the belief that the United States stepped into a power vacuum in Central America after Britain disentangled itself from the region in the 1860s, this book argues that the Nicaragua Canal was a crucial battleground in the shifting balance of power throughout the nineteenth century. Rather than depicting this transition as a seamless process, this book reveals how, at the local level, the Anglo-American contest was fractious and, at times, even violent. Treaties such as the Clayton–Bulwer Treaty – one of the only agreements of its kind in which the United States sought to limit its own future territorial expansion – further complicate the idea that U.S. imperialism was inexorable or inevitable. By incorporating the history of the Mosquito Coast, this book further challenges the notion of a two-way struggle by illustrating how regional and local actors shaped, resisted, and maneuvered within Anglo-American rivalries. Thus, rather than portraying the Anglo-American shift as a smooth and inevitable progression, this book highlights the spaces of contestation and struggle that defined the transition from British to U.S. dominance in the hemisphere.

While this book focuses on the nineteenth-century developments related to the Nicaragua Canal, it is important to acknowledge the legacy of imperial contests over the isthmian route. In recent years, China has shown its own interest in developing the interoceanic canal, raising fears of a shift in geopolitical equilibrium and U.S. influence in Central America. With the Panama Canal confronting dire technical challenges in the face of climate change, there are renewed hopes and prospects for building the Nicaragua Canal. As this book demonstrates, the Nicaragua Canal has long served as a testing ground for empires. Its story has powerful resonance in a geopolitical future where the Central American isthmus will continue to be a crucial fulcrum for newly emerging configurations of global superpowers.

HISTORIES OF FAILURE

The nineteenth century was an age of technological optimism. Newfangled inventions like steamboats, the telegraph, and automobiles revolutionized social and cultural life, and whether in the construction of the Eiffel Tower or the inauguration of the Great Exhibition of 1851, Western nations celebrated the scientific and technological progress of the era. The idea that technology could bridge geographical, social, and cultural divides imbued nineteenth-century imagination, leading to a proliferation of science fiction such as Jules Verne's *Around the World in Eighty Days* and *Journey to the Centre of the Earth*. Imperial powers such as Britain, France, and the United States viewed the Nicaragua Canal as the enterprise that would not only connect the Atlantic and Pacific Oceans but also Europe and the United States with their Asian economic interests. For an internally riven Nicaragua, the Canal presented a geographical destiny akin to the United States's own Westward expansion and held out the promise of making the young republic the center of global commerce. In the backdrop of the disintegration of the Central American Federation, the newly formed republics of Central America also saw in the Canal a way to rise above petty internal squabbles and move towards a new union of Central American republics.[33] The Nicaragua Canal would dash these hopes, becoming not the pinnacle but rather the graveyard of competing imperial, national, and regional political and technological projects.

The history of imperialism in the nineteenth century has generally been told as a history of success, and with good reasons. It was during this time that the British Empire reached its largest extent, so that the "sun never set" on its dominions. For the United States, this century marked both its successful consolidation as a continental nation and the beginning of international expansion and influence. These stories of success jump out of the pages of archival documents, often reported in multiple correspondences with copies across different folders. Yet what if we were to mine these archives for instances of failure? As this book shows, delving into cases of failure opens up new ways of visualizing the limits of imperial and national projects. Such instances allow us to uncover evidence of anxieties, dissonances, and conflicts that are more easily swept under the carpet in narratives of success. As Scott Sandage, in his acclaimed book on failure in the nineteenth-century United States, writes, "Failure stories are everywhere, if we can bear to hear them."[34]

---

[33] There is a rich literature on the role of science and technology in fostering national imagination in Central America. See, for instance, Sophie Brockmann, *The Science of Useful Nature in Central America: Landscapes, Networks and Practical Enlightenment, 1784–1838* (Cambridge: Cambridge University Press, 2020); Lina del Castillo, *Crafting a Republic for the World: Scientific, Geographic, and Historiographic Inventions of Colombia* (Lincoln: University of Nebraska Press, 2018).

[34] Scott Sandage, *Born Losers: A History of Failure in America* (Cambridge, MA: Harvard University Press, 2006), 9.

Ultimately, this book offers a methodological proposition for the study of imperialism and nation-making, which centers on mining for instances of failures to shed light on the shadowy limits of power and sovereignty.

As a society, we are obsessed with stories of technological success. But for every successful technological project, there are scores of undertakings that fail, go unfinished, or are never realized. We tend to ignore these failed attempts as the usual byproducts on the route to technological innovation and success. As Jonathan Coopersmith, one of the foremost historians of technology to talk about failure, wrote: "Histories of technologies usually focus on success, on the triumphant progress of a technology from a dream into a world-reshaping reality. These histories tend to minimize, if not exclude, failure."[35] Other historians of technology, such as Henry Petroski, have recognized the ways in which examining cases of failure can result in new insights on both the technology and the context in which it is deployed.[36] Focusing on the unrealized Central American Seaway proposal, Christine Keiner has illuminated the lasting legacies of unbuilt megaprojects.[37] In recent years, historians of technology have begun to move away from writing about shiny new inventions to the humdrum but equally vital issue of maintenance and repair – a crucial aspect of preventing failure.[38] Adding to this burgeoning conversation, this book suggests that failures can provide us a glimpse into the human condition and illuminate the complex play between human power and the natural environment that undergirds all technological interventions. It illuminates how official and imperial egos, racial politics, and local power struggles impacted one of the most important infrastructure projects in Latin American history.[39] In the process, it shows how the

---

[35] Jonathan Coopersmith, *Faxed: The Rise and Fall of the Fax Machine* (Baltimore: Johns Hopkins University Press, 2016), 2.

[36] Henry Petroski, *To Forgive Design: Understanding Failure* (Cambridge, MA: The Belknap Press of Harvard University Press, 2014).

[37] Christine Keiner, *Deep Cut: Science, Power, and the Unbuilt Interoceanic Canal* (Athens: University of Georgia Press, 2020).

[38] Lee Vinsel and Andrew Russell, *The Innovation Delusion: How Our Obsession with the New Has Disrupted the Work That Matters Most* (New York: Currency, 2020).

[39] This book adds to the emerging conversation on the politics of Latin American technology and infrastructure. See, for instance, Jonathan Alderman and Geoff Goodwin, eds., *The Social and Political Life of Latin American Infrastructures* (London: School of Advanced Studies, 2022); Diana Montaño, *Electrifying Mexico: Technology and the Transformation of a Modern City* (Austin: University of Texas Press, 2023); J. Justin Castro, *Radio in Revolution: Wireless Technology and State Power in Mexico, 1897–1938* (Lincoln: University of Nebraska Press, 2016).

study of failure can help us understand that technological projects are, at their heart, *human* problems.

Interestingly, recent studies on the history of the Panama Canal have significantly illuminated the human cost of large infrastructure projects in Latin America. Recent literature on the Panama Canal has highlighted not just the engineering and diplomatic dimensions of the canal story but also the impact of the canal on people on the ground, using race as a crucial analytical category. Scholars such as Velma Newton, Olive Senior, and Joan Flores-Villalobos have highlighted the role of West Indian immigrants and black labor in the building of this great infrastructure.[40] In her acclaimed book *Erased*, Marixa Lasso gives a powerful account of the untold human cost of the Panama Canal by recovering the history of displaced populations.[41] This book adds to this conversation on the racial dimensions of the transisthmian canal project by showing how racial concerns and the language of race – and more specifically, indigeneity – became crucial tokens through which the contest over the canal route was negotiated. By recovering the interwoven history of the Nicaragua Canal and the Afro-Indigenous Mosquito Kingdom, this work also adds to the conversations around the human fallout of the canal project on communities on the ground and recovers the Mosquito Coast as a revelatory site of imperial contradiction.

LIMITS OF TECHNOLOGICAL OPTIMISM

Between February and December 1915, the Panama–Pacific International Exposition in San Francisco witnessed a record crowd of over 18 million people who had gathered to celebrate the opening of the Panama Canal. The Expo, which celebrated the opening of the Panama Canal, was spread over 635 acres, which included a 5-acre model of the canal itself – a tribute to what was then widely considered the greatest American technological achievement to date. The Expo signified the world's limitless optimism about the potential of the interoceanic canal in the midst of the raging World War I that shattered the nineteenth-century aura around

---

[40] Velma Newton, *The Silver Men: West Indian Labour Migration to Panama 1850–1914* (Kingston: Ian Randle, 2014); Olive Senior, *Dying to Better Themselves: West Indians and the Building of the Panama Canal* (Mona: University of the West Indies Press, 2014); Joan Flores-Villalobos, *The Silver Women: How Black Women's Labor Made the Panama Canal* (Philadelphia: University of Pennsylvania Press, 2013).

[41] Marixa Lasso, *Erased: The Untold Story of the Panama Canal* (Cambridge, MA: Harvard University Press, 2019).

technological progress. As aircraft and machine guns underscored the grim fallout of a century of technological innovation and the world literally reached a breaking point, the idea of the Canal continued to be seen as a panacea for a war-torn world.

In a remarkable compendium of views gathered from people in all walks of life about the legacy of the Expo, contributors highlighted how the Panama Canal exemplified the "pursuit of peace" amidst the destructiveness of the war. As C. J. Bushnell, the president of Pacific University, Oregon, declared: "In these times, when the face of so large a part of the world has been miserably turned backward toward barbarism, I believe that the Panama–Pacific International Exposition has done much to turn the face of humanity toward the larger era of international cooperation and goodwill that is surely coming."[42] Similarly, a resident of Santa Rosa, California, wrote: "The trail of War leaves crime, poverty, misery, destruction and death. The Panama-Pacific International Exposition – most wonderful, beautiful, successful and most educational exhibit the world has ever seen – is a living demonstration that the path of Peace brings life, strength, health, courage, valor, harmony, happiness and prosperity."[43] Ironically, the Panama Canal and the Expo, which were heralded as harbingers of peace and cooperation, legitimized U.S. expansion in Latin America.[44]

As I pen these words, the Panama Canal has become the latest casualty of climate change. Record-setting droughts have severely hampered passage through this shipping artery that is a vital trading link between the Eastern and Western Hemispheres, giving fresh salience to a centuries-old question: Do we require an alternative route between the Atlantic and Pacific Oceans? For much of the nineteenth century, the answer to this question had been the Nicaragua route – a path through the seas that many contemporaries believed had unique advantages over the Panama route, including the existence of water bodies for almost the whole length of the proposed canal route, a shorter traveling distance between the U.S. Eastern and Western Coasts, and reportedly more favorable winds and climate. In fact, the idea of the Nicaragua Canal continues to persist. In 2013, the Nicaraguan President Daniel Ortega contracted a Chinese

---

[42] The Legacy of the Exposition: Interpretation of the Intellectual and Moral Heritage Left to Mankind by the World Celebration at San Francisco in 1915 (San Francisco, 1916), 30.
[43] Ibid., 32.
[44] Alexander Missal, *Seaway to the Future: American Social Visions and the Construction of the Panama Canal* (Madison: University of Wisconsin Press, 2009).

private company to build a canal through Nicaragua that would be longer, wider, and deeper than the Panama Canal. Briefly, Russia appeared to signal interest in lending its support to the Chinese-led canal. Indigenous groups protested this latest onslaught on their ancestral land and way of life since the canal would pass through the largely Indigenous Mosquito Coast. Although this latest plan to build the Nicaragua Canal eventually petered out, it raises uncomfortable questions. What would the proximity of a competing transisthmian canal controlled by Chinese and Russian interests mean for the United States and the post-Cold War world order?[45] And what would be the social and cultural fallout of a project that undermines local Indigenous interests?

The interoceanic canal project has always captured public imagination, and its physical act of linking hitherto separated oceans has served symbolically to exemplify the canal's potential for bridging social, cultural, and political divides. Although newspaper reports prior to the 1915 Expo noted Nicaragua's participation in the Fair, remarkably no mention of it appears in the documents publicizing the Expo, including the *Official Guide*. The Nicaraguan isthmian route that had fueled Anglo-American rivalry and dominated visions of interoceanic canals in the nineteenth century had been effectively erased from public imagination. Yet the pages in this book reveal how the Nicaragua Canal became a crucible of nineteenth-century dreams of technological progress – dreams that were spun through the webs of competing projects of expansion and unity.

Focusing on the Anglo-American contest over the Nicaragua Canal route in the nineteenth century, this book serves as a timely reminder that the canal has long been a testing ground for empires and a nemesis for grand ambitions of technological progress. Through exploring the deep rivalries, distrust, and even violent interventions that characterized the Nicaragua Canal project, *The Link That Divides* holds out the central paradox of the interoceanic dream: that visions of connection were built

---

[45] There is a growing literature on Chinese interest in Latin America. See, for instance, Li Xing and Javier Vadell, eds., *China–US Rivalry and Regional Reordering in Latin America and the Caribbean* (Oxon: Routledge, 2024); David Denoon, *China, the United States, and the Future of Latin America* (New York: New York University Press, 2017); Rhys Owen Jenkins, *How China Is Reshaping the Global Economy: Development Impacts in Africa and Latin America* (Oxford: Oxford University Press, 2022); Riordan Roett, Guadalupe Paz, and Theodore Kahn, eds., *Latin America and the Asian Giants: Evolving Ties with China and India* (Washington, DC: Brookings Institution Press, 2016).

on, and in turn, ruptured by the reality of division and conflict. Today, the Nicaragua route remains a locus of national and regional dreams and a geopolitical pivot point for imperial aspirations, just as it was 200 years ago. Such grand infrastructure projects, then and now, carry the potential to profoundly reshape local and Indigenous ways of life. Yet the persistence of the belief that technology can solve complex social and political problems reflects the enduring and dangerous naïveté of scientific optimism and the bureaucratic hubris that scientific knowledge and organization can overcome deep-rooted historical conflicts. As new configurations of global superpowers emerge, the Nicaragua Canal story offers a cautionary tale with renewed urgency.

BRIEF OVERVIEW OF THE BOOK

The Link That Divides revisits the long and often overlooked history of the Nicaragua Canal and its entanglement with the politics and sovereignty of the Mosquito Coast and the Mosquito Kingdom. The narrative of the book unfolds chronologically from 1837 to 1902 (the moment when there is a decisive shift toward the Panama Canal). Each chapter is centered on pivotal events and periods that shaped the interlinked history of the Mosquito Coast and the Nicaragua Canal in the second half of the nineteenth century.

Part I (Chapters 1–3) focuses on British efforts to control the canal route through the exploration of the tenures of three British officials, Belizean Superintendent Colonel Alexander MacDonald, his aide (later British consul) Patrick Walker, and British Consul William Dougal Christie, who sought to establish themselves as the central authority figures in the Mosquito Shore in the context of the breakdown of the Central American Federation and the emerging interests in the canal route.

As the early 1840s saw a growing rivalry between nascent Central American republics over the Mosquito Coast as a likely site for a transisthmian canal through Río San Juan, MacDonald and Walker justified British authority over the region by harking back to the historic ties between the Mosquito Kingdom and Great Britain even as, paradoxically, the actions of the British officials undermined the Indigenous Miskitu leadership. British Consul William Dougal Christie sought to settle territorial disputes over the Mosquito Shore with rival Central American republics and attempted to establish unchallenged British authority over the Nicaragua Canal route by shifting the capital of the Mosquito

Kingdom to the harbor of San Juan del Norte (renamed Greytown), the Caribbean mouth of the projected canal route. Even as policies of these British officials relegated Miskitus to the margins of governance, they reached back to a glorious Miskitu past to justify British involvement in the tussle over San Juan. As the possibility of a Nicaraguan canal loomed ahead, competing sovereign powers of Britain and Nicaragua converged on the authenticity of the Afro-Indigenous Mosquito Kingdom as the linchpin around which to settle their territorial dispute over the San Juan delta. Thus, from the very beginning of the contest over the Mosquito Coast in the nineteenth century, race and indigeneity were central to British efforts to control the Nicaragua Canal route.

Part II (Chapters 4–6) examines the escalating struggle over the Nicaragua Canal route, particularly the port town of Greytown. It explores the emergence of the United States as a rival to British interests in the region and the growing sentiment of unionism in Central America to counter perceived U.S. threats.

The 1850s saw the rise of U.S. interest in the Nicaragua Canal in the context of the Gold Rush as well as the beginning of a transatlantic rivalry between Great Britain and the United States over control of the canal route. The Gold Rush transformed Greytown and made the Nicaragua route a serious contender to Panama. However, increasing tensions between the local government at Greytown and Cornelius Vanderbilt's Accessory Transit Company ultimately led to the bombardment of Greytown and undermined dreams of the canal. In the mid-1850s, the canal route became central to American filibustering enterprises under Henry Kinney and William Walker. Throughout this decade, Nicaragua and Central America wrestled with the consequences of increasing American interest in the canal route and began to perceive the importance of national and regional unity as a counterweight to threats of U.S. influence in the region.

Part III (Chapters 7 and 8) illuminates the period of revival of international interest in the Nicaragua Canal, following the successful completion of the Suez Canal. It charts the efforts of Nicaragua to incorporate Mosquito territory within its nation, even as the post-Civil War United States increasingly sought to establish control over the canal route in a bid to carve out a position of leadership and rebuild its image as a global leader.

As Nicaragua attempted to consolidate and control the transit route, it pushed for greater incorporation of Greytown and the Mosquito territory (known as the Reserve) within the Republic, even as the Miskitu communities showed signs of internal splintering. Great Britain and the United States remained concerned with how Nicaraguan incorporation would affect their ability to retain neutrality of the route. In the 1880s, following the success of the Suez Canal, there was a revival of interest in the Nicaragua Canal. The latter became central to geopolitical identity both of the nascent Republic of Nicaragua and post-Civil War United States, even as the ideal of union that had nourished Nicaragua's relationship with the rest of Central America began to fracture. Espousing ideals of liberal nation-making, Nicaragua sought to assimilate the Miskitu by attempting to annex the Reserve to the Republic in 1894 and fulfill its vision of unbroken sovereignty from the Atlantic to the Pacific. Thus, the pursuit of the Nicaragua Canal was predicated on the elimination of the Mosquito autonomous territory.

Finally, the Conclusion (Chapter 9) focuses on the decisive moment that led to the creation of the Panama Canal and the waning of Nicaragua as the site of a potential transisthmian canal. The apparent abruptness of the decision to build the canal in Panama in 1902 belied the steady buildup of a new American way of looking at the world that was heavily informed by the American press. The final turn towards Panama profoundly altered the course of Nicaraguan history and effectively stymied dreams of regional unity.

PART I

I

Glimmers of a Canal

By 1834, the *Encyclopaedia of Geography*, published in London, held out the Nicaragua Canal as the most likely site of an interoceanic canal.[1] On May 9, 1836, Juan Galindo, an Irish-born citizen of the Central American Federation, described in one of several correspondences with the recently established Royal Geographical Society (RGS) the Edenic landscape of parts of Central America where "a perpetual spring and verdure ever exist and realize the dream of the ancient European poets who without experiencing it, imagined a similar climate for their favourite Elysian fields and the island of Calypso."[2] Yet while the United States seemed keen to find its own path between the Atlantic and the Pacific Oceans – the Lewis and Clark expedition under Thomas Jefferson was tasked with finding the "Northwest Passage" – Great Britain's efforts in the 1830s to cognize an interoceanic route isthmus seemed largely confined to the academic plane. While in the 1820s the private firm of Barclay, Herring and Richardson had offered a proposal to the Central American Federation to invest in the Nicaragua Canal, throughout the 1820s and 1830s, the British Foreign Office remained largely reluctant to involve itself in Central American affairs. Ironically, of all the powers of the day, Great Britain alone maintained a tangible foothold in Central

---

[1] Hugh Murray et al., *An Encyclopaedia of Geography, Comprising a Complete Description of the Earth, Physical, Statistical, Civil and Political, Exhibiting Its Relation to the Heavenly Bodies, Its Physical Structure: The Natural History of Each Country and the Industry, Commerce, Political Institutions and Civil and Social State of All Nations*, v. 3 (London: Green and Longmans, 1834), 305.

[2] "On Central America and the State of Costa Rica" by Colonel Juan Galindo, Journal Manuscripts, May 9, 1836, RGS.

America. And it would be the actions of its local colonial officials – often in contravention of broader British metropolitan intentions – that would see the entry of the British in the struggle over the Nicaragua Canal route in the nineteenth century.

On August 12, 1841, Alexander MacDonald, the Superintendent of British Honduras – the only recognized British settlement in Central America – embarked on a sloop of war. He had on board the Miskitu King Robert Charles Frederic and a British merchant named Thomas Haly. Both MacDonald and Frederic were united in their desire to map the boundaries of the disputed territory of the Mosquito Coast on the Caribbean coast of Nicaragua. Yet what began as a tour of legitimizing Miskitu claims to the Coast ended with an act of outright conquest: the sloop stopped at the port of San Juan del Norte, hauled down the Nicaraguan flag, and seized the Nicaraguan administrator of the port, Manuel Quijano. MacDonald's actions invited British castigation for exceeding the authority of his position and Central American outrage at what it saw as open British aggression. The Nicaragua Canal was still a distant prospect, and MacDonald's motives had much more to do with the interests of Belizean mahogany traders, who saw in the rich timber stands along the northern coast of the Mosquito Coast a way to compensate for the depleting mahogany cover of British Honduras at a time when the global demand for mahogany was skyrocketing. Yet MacDonald's actions inserted the British within a much longer and wider territorial strife between the Afro-Indigenous Miskitus and the surrounding Hispanic sovereignties, a tendency that would continue under subsequent British officials on the Mosquito Shore. The establishment of a British protectorate on the Mosquito Shore in 1844 and the arrival of Patrick Walker would mark a watershed, laying the path towards more direct British action with regard to the Nicaragua Canal route at the same time as undermining the authority of the Miskitu kingship. As Great Britain, the United States, and even European powers began to show interest in the Nicaragua Canal route, Central American leaders foreshadowed the war of narratives that would occupy the contest over the canal route in the nineteenth century by forwarding a narrative of the Nicaragua Canal as an authentically Central American project.

1.1 RENEWAL OF BRITISH–MISKITU RELATIONS

The beginning of the railway age in Britain, with the Liverpool–Manchester line opening in 1830, had important repercussions for the

British mahogany trade in Central America. The lucrative timber was already a popular material, serving the demands of luxury furniture on both sides of the Atlantic. British Honduras, as Britain's only settlement in Central America and blessed with a rich timber cover, was the main supplier of this coveted wood. By the 1830s, the construction of railway carriages in Britain drove up demand for mahogany at a time when merchants in Belize confronted the reality of the depletion of mahogany forests in Belize after decades of overexploitation. Belizean merchants soon began to push beyond the boundaries of the settlement in search of the valuable timber, eventually finding their way to the rich mahogany stands of the northern coast of Honduras. The Miskitu King Robert Charles Frederic claimed the entire region from Cape Honduras to the mouth of the San Juan River at the Nicaraguan border with Costa Rica to be part of the Mosquito Kingdom, and Belizean Superintendent Alexander MacDonald now sought to legitimize this claim as a way of guaranteeing Belizean access to Honduran mahogany. Of course, in finding common cause with the Miskitu king, MacDonald was following a longer tradition of alliance with the Miskitu leadership that dated back to the eighteenth century, when the British had exercised a protectorate over the Mosquito Shore. MacDonald was also shaped by a lineage of Belizean administrators who had cultivated close relations with the Mosquito Coast. Indeed, one of MacDonald's predecessors, Superintendent George Arthur, had been instrumental in securing the freedom of Mosquito Coast enslaved persons in Belize in the 1820s against strong settler opposition, and indeed, had it not been for the fact that George Arthur was reassigned to Van Diemen's Island in 1822, relations with the Mosquito Coast might have resumed much earlier.

However, it would be wrong to think that the initiative of renewal of relations between the Mosquito Coast and Belize emanated solely from the actions of Belizean officials. Rather, the fragmentary evidence surrounding the Indigenous leadership of the Mosquito Coast suggests that the Miskitu leadership itself may have taken the first steps towards forging an alliance with Belizean interests in the early nineteenth century. The first recorded direct contact between Miskitu leadership and Belizean officials in the nineteenth century is that of the delegation sent by the Miskitu King Robert Charles Frederic that arrived in Belize in December 1829. Of course, prior to this moment, West Indian merchants on the Mosquito Coast had served to link the Indigenous Miskitu leadership with British and even American interests in the Caribbean. Some merchants, such as Peter and Samuel Shepherd, were deeply embedded within the internal political dynamics of the Mosquito Kingdom, and some, such as Stanislaus Thomas Haly and Thomas Hedgecock, were important advisers to the Miskitu king. Yet this embeddedness did not necessarily mean – as much of the early historiography of the Mosquito Coast suggested – that the Miskitu kings were puppets of the British merchants. Rather recent scholarship on Miskitu kingship and the Mosquito Coast allows us to reconsider the evidence to craft a narrative of Mosquito history that underscores Miskitu agency in the renewal of relations with Belize in the nineteenth century.

Documentary evidence also suggests that it was the Miskitu King Robert Charles Frederic who sought MacDonald's help in thwarting Central American incursions on the territory he claimed to be part of the Mosquito Coast.[3] The dispute between the Miskitu leadership and Central American governments over the territory of the Mosquito Coast originated in the Spanish Royal Order of 1803, which placed the Mosquito Coast within the jurisdiction of the Viceroyalty of Santa Fé de Bogotá. The subsequent decree by the Republic of Colombia on July 5, 1824, claimed the Mosquito Coast as part of its territory.[4] In the 1830s, with the dissolution of the Central American Federation, the independent republics of New Granada and Costa Rica asserted their claims on the Mosquito Coast, motivated in part by the economic opportunities it presented. Alexander MacDonald calculated that a 5 percent duty on goods imported from the ports of Matina, Salt Creek, and Bocas del Toro could amount to nearly $140,000. Besides, the sea island cotton grown on the offshore Corn Islands was a lucrative export commodity. The Indigenous Miskitu leadership itself had a long history of regional attempts at territorial aggrandizement. Scholars of the eighteenth century have provided convincing evidence of a powerful Miskitu confederation that was an important regional power.[5] For the nineteenth century, there is an increasing focus on Miskitu kings as self-aware rulers who strategically used their connections to Belizean merchants and authorities to

---

[3] R. C. Frederic to H.M.S. King of Great Britain, January 25, 1837, Colonial Office Records at the National Archives, UK (hereafter CO), 123/50.

[4] "Decree of the Colombian Government, Declaring the Mosquito Shore to Belong to the Republick, and Prohibiting Settlements Thereon," July 5, 1824, British and Foreign State Papers, 1823–1824, vol. 11 (London: Ridgway and Sons, 1843), 816.

[5] See Mendiola, "The Rise of the Mosquito Kingdom"; Mendiola, "The Founding and Fracturing of the Mosquito Confederation."

further their economic and political ambitions.[6] In response to Colombian claims, a flag was adopted during King George Frederic's reign (Figure 1.1) to justify Miskitu claims on the Coast.[7]

The renewal of British–Miskitu relations in the early nineteenth century, therefore, can be seen as an alliance of convenience. Just as Belizean authorities and merchants hoped to benefit economically from a close relationship with the Miskitu leadership, so too Miskitu kings looked up to the British as powerful supporters of Miskitu regional ambitions and guarantors of Miskitu sovereignty in the face of Central American aggressions.

1.2 ALEXANDER MACDONALD AND THE *TWEED* VENTURE

With his characteristic zeal for independent action, Alexander MacDonald proved receptive to the appeals of the Miskitu king and British merchants on the Coast and supported the Miskitu king in his territorial disputes with Central American powers.[8] Determined to open up the mahogany reserves of the Mosquito Coast to Belizean interests, MacDonald did not shy away from challenging the claims of Central American leader Francisco Morazán and his partner Marshall Bennett to the northern Honduran coastline. The Miskitu king, at the behest of prominent merchant brothers Peter and Samuel Shepherd, had claimed the southern boundary of the Mosquito Kingdom to extend to Bocas del Toro (in present-day Panama).[9] This brought the Mosquito Kingdom into conflict with New Granada, which took possession of the disputed territory between 1836 and 1838. When New Granada attempted to gain control over the offshore Corn Islands in 1839 – a region that had resisted Spanish control even in the colonial period – the Miskitu king appealed to MacDonald for help. While the situation with New Granada worsened, Costa Rica laid claims to the regions of Salt Creek and Matina. The Mosquito Coast was suddenly poised at the precipice of an explosive regional conflict. If matters were not grave enough, news from the Mosquito Coast suggested an erosion

---

[6] See, for instance, Clavel, "The Rise and Fall of George Frederic Augustus II"; Rajeshwari Dutt, "The *Tweed* Venture: The Language of Freedom and British Informal Empire on the Mosquito Shore," *The Journal of Transatlantic Studies* 22:2 (2024), 81–102.

[7] George Frederic to Edward Codd, March 8, 1824, CO 123/35; see also Clavel, "The Rise and Fall of George Frederic Augustus II," 554.

[8] This section has been partly drawn from my published article, Dutt, "The *Tweed* Venture."

[9] Naylor, *Penny Ante Imperialism*, 101–102.

FIGURE 1.1 Mosquito national flag. Source: Enclosure in George Frederic to Edward Codd, March 8, 1824, CO 123/35.

of the Miskitu king's authority over the Indigenous inhabitants of the Coast.

The crisis on the Mosquito Coast came at an inauspicious moment. The end of slavery in the British West Indies had begun a restructuring of British imperial relations with the Caribbean, gradually reorienting the Empire away from the Caribbean and towards more remunerative sites of colonial expansion.[10] James Stephen of the Colonial Office, a noted antiexpansionist, summed up the economic rationale for such policy:

> every shilling which can be devoted to colonization and to the defence of New Colonies should be spent where the want is greatest, and where the probable returns on such expenditure greatest, and I should suppose that to starve the Public Service in New Holland or New Zealand, in order to strengthen ourselves on the Mosquito Shore will be a bad use of our money.[11]

The British Foreign Office on its part vacillated in its stance towards the Mosquito Coast, preferring to wait and watch rather than authorizing any sort of open intervention in Mosquitian territorial disputes.[12] With both the Colonial and the Foreign Office unwilling to commit resources to mitigate the crises on the Coast, MacDonald now acted autonomously, exceeding his sanctioned authority as superintendent.

In February 1840, Miskitu King Robert Charles Frederic appealed to MacDonald for assistance in countering what he saw as the depredations on the lives and properties of his subjects at the hands of interlopers from surrounding Central American republics.[13] He also requested MacDonald's help in regulating the internal affairs of the Coast, which he believed was witnessing an increasingly serious situation of crime and disturbance.[14] In response, MacDonald sent a notice to New Granada to confine itself within its own borders and formed a Commission in Belize of five officers and magistrates – including himself and his aide Patrick Walker – to regulate the internal affairs of the Mosquito Shore. The Colonial Office strongly disapproved of MacDonald's actions and by April 1841 had annulled the Commission. As Henry Taylor of the Colonial Office argued, MacDonald's actions in regulating the internal

---

[10] Christopher Taylor, *Empire of Neglect: The West Indies in the Wake of British Liberalism* (Durham: Duke University Press, 2018).
[11] James Stephen minute, January 29, 1841, CO 123/59.
[12] C. W. H. to Lord Stanley, September 22, 1841, CO 123/59.
[13] R. C. Frederic to Alexander MacDonald, Belize, February 13, 1840, CO 123/57.
[14] Alexander Macdonald to John Russell, February 29, 1840, CO 123/57; Residents of Gracias a Dios to R. C. Frederic, 1.1.1838, CO 123/57.

affairs of the Mosquito Shore without explicit sanction from the British colonial government were an act of unauthorized "conquest and colonization."[15] In August 1841, however, in direct contravention of British official policy of neutrality on the Mosquito Shore, MacDonald formed another commission, this time under the authority of the Miskitu king, independent of any approvals by the British government.[16] Even more radically, right after the formation of the new commission, MacDonald began his most open military actions against the Central American powers.

In August 1841, on board the sloop of war *Tweed* (see Figure 1.2), MacDonald set off with the Miskitu king on a whirlwind tour purportedly to announce freedom from slavery in the various parts of the Mosquito Shore, making stops at the Corn Islands, Bluefields, Bocas del Toro, Pearl Lagoon, and San Juan del Norte. In reality, given that New Granada had firm claims over places such as the Corn Islands and Bocas del Toro, the tour amounted to nothing less than an attempt at military conquest of these disputed regions. In Bocas del Toro, MacDonald even gave out muskets to the English settlers for use against New Granadian authorities.[17] But it was in San Juan del Norte that MacDonald took his most radical step against Central American claims. There he hauled down the Nicaraguan flag, hoisted the Mosquito standard in its place, and seized the Nicaraguan administrator of the port, Manuel Quijano. Reporting back to the governor of Jamaica, Charles Metcalfe, MacDonald declared, "If the weight of the explanation I have already tendered relative to the removal of Mr. Quijano from St. John's River is not conceded, I justify the act on the indisputable fact of his being an intruder on the territory of the King of the Mosquito nation."[18]

MacDonald's actions on the San Juan immediately sparked outrage among Central American powers. Protesting against the attack and the seizure of his person, Manuel Quijano, in a sharply worded message to MacDonald, denied British rights to dispose of Central American territory and described the rise of patriotism among Central Americans following the *Tweed*'s unprecedented aggressions in San Juan del Norte,

---

[15] Henry Taylor to James Stephen, April 28, 1840, CO 123/57.
[16] Robert Charles Frederic, Bluefields, August 9, 1841, CO 123/60.
[17] Edmund T. Gordon, *Disparate Diasporas: Identity and Politics in an African-Nicaraguan Community* (Austin: University of Texas Press, 1998), 42; Alexander MacDonald to John Russell, September 8, 1841, CO 123/60s.
[18] Alexander MacDonald to Charles Metcalfe, November 6, 1841, CO 123/62.

FIGURE 1.2 H.M.S. *Tweed*. Source: Sketch of the naval vessel *Tweed* entering Portsmouth, with figures in rowing boats and on the shore in the foreground, and women hanging out washing, with inscriptions, c 1823. PAE9943. © National Maritime Museum, Greenwich, London.

Salt Creek, and Bocas del Toro.[19] By December 1841, Guatemala had sent its representative, Alejandro Marure, to London to advocate for the interests of Central America following the assault on San Juan del Norte.[20] In the same month, a patriotic leaflet protesting British actions in the San Juan circulated in San Salvador.[21] In February 1842, the Legislative Chamber of Honduras expressed its indignation at MacDonald's actions on the San Juan and joined Guatemala in its representation in London.[22] In the aftermath of the San Juan incident, Nicaragua passed laws to strengthen its defense capabilities in the event of any future aggression,[23] and as retaliation for the San Juan assault, officials in San Juan del Norte seized five British merchants on the Bluefields River.[24]

Ironically, MacDonald's unauthorized assault on the San Juan forced the vacillating British metropolitan government to openly consider the possibility of extending a protectorate over the Mosquito Shore. Although Metcalfe cautioned MacDonald not to interfere in the Mosquito Shore and only act "mediatorially" in relations with its Central American neighbors,[25] Naval correspondence in the period following the San Juan incident suggests a growing consideration of the strategic nature of the Mosquito ports. Thus Commander Darley writing to Vice-Admiral Charles Adam described the utility of the port of Bocas del Toro that the Miskitu king claimed as part of his territory: "The Boca del Toro ... is a magnificent harbour capable of receiving the largest fleets, being 15 miles long and from 10 to 12 broad with a depth of water from 5 to 17 fathoms clean bottom both entrance are narrow and rather intricate but have sufficient depth of water through them for the largest vessels."[26] Writing to the governor of Jamaica, the Earl of Elgin and Kincardine, Charles Adam supported an increasing British role on the Mosquito Shore arguing for "a regular Government, equal laws and the means of public instruction" on the Shore.[27]

It is in the context of these debates around the British role in the Mosquito Shore that the question of the interoceanic canal first surfaces

---

[19] "Documento no. 2," Andrés Vega Bolaños, *Los atentados del superintendente de Belice, 1840–1842* (Managua: Editorial Unión, 1971).
[20] "Documento no. 54," ibid.   [21] "Documento no. 56," ibid.
[22] "Documento no. 80," ibid.   [23] "Documento no. 57," ibid.
[24] Jamaica Dispatch, October 28, 1841, CO 123/61.
[25] Charles Metcalfe to Alexander MacDonald, February 28, 1842, CO 123/62.
[26] Commander Darley to Charles Adam (n.d.), CO 123/63.
[27] Charles Adam to Earl Elgin, June 24, 1842, CO 123/63.

in Colonial Office documents. In 1841, Reverend John Prowett (son-in-law of the late superintendent of Mosquito Shore, Robert Hodgson) wrote to the Colonial Office: "Thro' one of its [Mosquito Shore's] rivers (the Bluefields) lies the only practicable communication with the Lake of Nicaragua and thence with the Pacific." While Prowett's letter had no date or address, it was carefully marked up and minuted on reaching the Colonial Office. Prowett's statement on the strategic location of Bluefields was underlined, and one of the minutes read:

> If it be really true that the River Bluefields has a practicable communication with the lake Nicaragua, and that it is the only chanel from the Gulf of Mexico to that Lake, there can been no doubt that a good and safe harbor on the mouth of that River must be one of the most if not the most important locality on the globe.[28]

Although Prowett had erred in thinking that the Bluefields River was connected to Lake Nicaragua, his letter and the accompanying minutes show that by 1841, the interoceanic canal was already within the radar of British metropolitan interests in the Mosquito Shore. Britain's interests in the interoceanic canal were sufficiently threatening at this point that in February 1842, the American agent in Central America W. S. Murphy wrote a detailed letter to U. S. Secretary of State Daniel Webster outlining the importance of entering a treaty with Central American states to retain American control over San Juan del Norte:

> The St. Johns offers to the U. States the greatest & most Singular Commercial advantages ... The additional distance by sea to this Port, is of very little moment, when we reflect, that it opens into so vast a region of uncultivated country, and is in reality, the only Key to the Pacific Ocean ... Here, at the Port, and on the River St. John, and on Lake Nicaragua, the United States should at once plant their flag of Commerce ... Delay to do this for a few more years, and British Commerce & British Manufacturers, will wear a channel too broad & too deep and run in flood too strong, for the infant effort of our country to cross, wade in, or oppose.[29]

As Central American states now sought to counter British interests on the Mosquito Shore by courting the United States, the Nicaragua Canal began to assume growing importance. Henry Savage, heading the legation of the United States to Central America, did not fail to note the strategic advantages of entering a treaty with the Central American states that would give the United States control over Nicaraguan ports, which would

---

[28] John Prowett to (?), n.d., CO 123/61.
[29] W. S. Murphy to Daniel Webster, February 4, 1842, William Manning, *Diplomatic Correspondence of the United States: Inter-American Affairs, 1831–1860*, vol. 3 (Washington, DC: Carnegie Endowment for International Peace, 1933), 176.

"in time, become of incalculable advantages to the commerce of the United States."[30]

Despite growing international interest in the interoceanic canal route through Nicaragua, the British metropolitan government appeared unable to take a clear stand regarding the status of the Mosquito Shore. Much of this can be attributed to the changes in key ranks of the Colonial and Foreign Offices, as well as the colonial governments of Jamaica and Belize. As Naylor points out:

> Lord Stanley replaced Lord Russell as Colonial Secretary in September 1841, at the same time that Lord Aberdeen succeeded Lord Palmerston in the Foreign Office. In March 1842, Lord Elgin followed Sir Charles Metcalfe as governor of Jamaica, and Colonel Charles Fancourt replaced Alexander McDonald as superintendent of Belize in June 1843. These changes led to delays and to continual reassessments of British policy for the area.

As a result, during the years between 1841 and 1843, the British government's policy towards the Mosquito Shore failed to solidify. It would be the internal breakdown of order within the Mosquito Kingdom – in the context of growing interest in the canal – that would finally force the British metropolitan government to cross the Rubicon.

1.3 MOSQUITO KINGDOM AND THE DESCENT INTO "CHAOS"

While traditional historical accounts of the Miskitu relations with British officials in the nineteenth century generally characterized Miskitu kings as puppets of British officials and merchants, recent scholarship offers us a new way of visualizing Miskitu kingship, where Indigenous leaders acted on their own political and economic ambitions. Damian Clavel, examining the figure of Robert Charles' half-brother and predecessor, George Frederic, has convincingly shown that the Miskitu king was driven by his own vision of Miskitu sovereignty. Elsewhere, in the context of slave emancipation, I have found that Robert Charles Frederic also acted out of his own understanding of broader currents of antislavery in the Caribbean.[31] Indeed, read against the grain, the fragmented documentary evidence surrounding the figure of Robert Charles Frederic suggests that he co-opted Belizean officials and British merchants into supporting his pre-existing claims on the territories of the Mosquito Coast that were

---

[30] Henry Savage to Daniel Webster, June 18, 1842, ibid., 195.
[31] See Dutt, "The *Tweed* Venture."

disputed by his Central American neighbors. Thus, the Miskitu authorities collected tribute from the offshore Corn Islands throughout the eighteenth and early nineteenth centuries, and it was only in the context of New Granadian claims on the Corn Islands that we find Robert Charles Frederic seeking out Belizean help in consolidating his hold over the islands. It is important to note that Robert Charles accompanied MacDonald on the *Tweed* venture and played a significant role in conveying his claims to the disputed territories to the inhabitants. Robert Charles Frederic thus used the *Tweed* tour to cement his alliance with the inhabitants of the disputed regions, landing muskets at Bocas del Toro and distributing gifts to the residents of Chiriquí Lagoon.[32] MacDonald estimated that the Indigenous persons who swore allegiance to the Miskitu king numbered up to 20,000 souls.[33]

According to Offen, between 1790 and 1830, the Zambo-Miskitus regularized a tributary relationship with neighboring Indigenous communities.[34] In fact, the efforts of Miskitu rulers George Frederic and Robert Charles Frederic in ending the practice of slavery in the Coast may have been as much a way to disempower Tawira Miskitus, who engaged in Indian slave raiding, as much as it was a way of gaining the sympathy of the British government. For the eighteenth century, historians have documented the Zambo–Tawira tensions culminating in a civil war around 1791, though recent evidence complicates that view. Signs of discord also appeared to surface well into the nineteenth century. In his narrative about his visit to the Mosquito Coast in 1820, Orlando Roberts noticed dissension between the Zambo king and the Tawira chief Clementi.[35] Roberts indicated the possibility of a future conflict between the two groups, writing that

> it is not improbable that their [Zambos'] vicious propensities, encouraged by the imprudent conduct, and imbecility of their head men, may shortly rouse the vengeance of the genuine Indians, who are by far the most numerous, and have only been kept in a kind of nominal subjection by their love of peace, fear of their common enemy the Spaniard; and, by the divisions which the Mosquito-men [i.e. Zambos] have artfully created, and take care to keep up amongst themselves.[36]

---

[32] Alexander MacDonald to John Russell, September 8, 1841, CO 123/60. [33] Ibid.
[34] Offen, "The Sambo and Tawira Miskitu," 344.
[35] Orlando Roberts, *Narrative of Voyages and Excursions on the East Coast and in the Interior of Central America: Describing a Journey up the River San Juan, and Passage across the Lake of Nicaragua to the City of León* (London: Hurst, Chance and Co., 1827), 137.
[36] Ibid., 153–154.

In the 1830s, George and Robert Charles Frederic's policies may have further alienated the other Indigenous communities from Zambo leadership. Orlando Roberts, for instance, noted that upon returning from his education in Jamaica, George Frederic felt himself a stranger in his Indigenous Mosquito Coast. Traveling to the Mosquito Coast in 1839, Thomas Young, the deputy superintendent of the British Central American Land Company, met Miskitu King Robert Charles Frederic, who was dressed in the uniform of a post captain in the British navy. Young witnessed the execution of an Indigenous prisoner, which Frederic proudly proclaimed had been carried out according to English law and warned his subjects from engaging in superstitions, declaring "that any of his people who did wrong, should be hung and warning them to beware of putting faith, or following the bad advice of the sookeahs."[37] The tendency of both George Frederic and Robert Charles to emulate what they saw as English values and an English way of living may have served to alienate the kingship from its Indigenous base.

The impact of these differences became apparent after the death of Robert Charles Frederic in October 1842, shortly after the *Tweed* expedition. Thus, Stanislaus Bell, commandant of the Mosquito Kingdom, reported that in the absence of any real Indigenous leadership and British inaction, Miskitus had taken to attacking neighboring Spanish settlements.[38] Miskitus also appeared to be assaulting Indigenous communities within the Coast, with Ramas "being the most exposed."[39] For his part, the new superintendent of Belize, St. John Fancourt, blamed MacDonald for precipitating this disorder by supporting the minor second son, Prince Clarence, as heir and thus effectively leaving the Mosquito Shore without a legitimate figurehead.[40] Fancourt was convinced that the Miskitu people regarded the king's eldest son, Prince George Augustus, as the lawful heir.[41] The governor of Jamaica, Lord Elgin Kincardine, felt that departing from the long-practiced principle of primogeniture would exacerbate the chaos into which the Shore had descended following the death of Robert Charles Frederic: "It is to be

---

[37] Thomas Young, *Narrative of Residence on the Mosquito Shore during the Years 1839, 1840 and 1841 with an Account of Truxillo and the Adjacent Islands of Bonacca and Roatan* (London: Smith, Elder and Co., 1842), 28.

[38] Stanislaus Bell to Earl of Elgin and Kincardine, North Bluefields, May 4, 1843, CO 123/65.

[39] Stanislaus Bell to Patrick Walker, North Bluefields, November 13, 1842, CO 123/65.

[40] St. John Fancourt to Lord Elgin, August 11, 1843, CO 123/65.

[41] St. John Fancourt to Lord Elgin, December 15, 1843, CO 123/67.

feared that any deviation from the line of Hereditary Succession may break the fragile bond of nationality which connects the Mosquito Tribes together."[42] Before leaving for England in the summer of 1843, MacDonald had authorized Patrick Walker to appoint acting regents during Prince Clarence's minority. Walker divided the Shore into three jurisdictions and named three Miskitu chiefs Lowrie Robinson,[43] Prince Wellington, and Colonel Johnson as regents with authority over the three districts. However, Robinson soon appeared to be colluding with the government of Honduras. In addition, the Miskitu people opposed the regency, as in Sandy Bay, where residents beat up Wellington.[44]

This discourse of disorder was of course not merely descriptive. Rather, it functioned as a narrative to portray the Mosquito Coast as unstable and justify imperial oversight. Writing about the failure of organizing an effective constabulary, James Stanislaus Bell – in strikingly racialized terms – wrote that the inhabitants of the area were incapable of self-government except "in the punishment and oppression of the class of free slaves and of the Indians."[45] More alarming still, in the eyes of British officials, was the news that neighboring republics had made decisive inroads into the Miskitu territory: by April 1843, the main commercial ports of San Juan, Salt Creek, and Bocas del Toro had been occupied.[46] Fancourt feared that Central American powers would exploit the divisions in Mosquito Shore to gain control over it at the detriment of British interests.[47]

Parallel to these developments on the Shore, the idea of an interoceanic canal was gaining more ground. Latin American independence was accompanied by a geographical reimagination, whereby the ruling elite embarked on the project of nation-making by a concerted effort to tap into the strategic and commercial value of their newly acquired territory, comprising both land and water bodies.[48] Even as early as 1813, Nicaraguan representatives at the Cortes of Cádiz had spoken in favor

---

[42] Lord Elgin to Lord Stanley, January 7, 1844, CO 123/67.
[43] Lowry Robinson was the son of General Lowry Robinson, a Zambo Miskitu. Some writers have confused them, thinking there was only one Lowry Robinson who lived for 100 years. Olien, "The Miskito Kings," 222.
[44] James Stanislaus Bell to St. John Fancourt, North Bluefields, October 21, 1843, FO 53/1.
[45] Ibid.   [46] James Stanislaus Bell to Walker, April 4, 1843, CO 123/67.
[47] Naylor, *Penny Ante Imperialism*, 150.
[48] See, for instance, Brockmann, *The Science of Useful Nature in Central America*; del Castillo, *Crafting a Republic for the World*.

of constructing an interoceanic canal through Nicaragua.[49] For the fledgling Central American Federation, the San Juan River delta in the Caribbean Coast of Nicaragua promised to be the gateway to modernity, and over time, the Central American government would invest significantly (including by hiring foreigners) to gain a better understanding of the topography of the region. Two of these foreigners – Irish-born Juan Galindo and English engineer John Baily – would communicate their findings to the RGS.

From its inception in 1830, the RGS, whose members included high-ranking government officials and naval and military men, was intricately tied to British imperial pursuits. While originally commissioned by Francisco Morazán to survey the Nicaragua Canal route, after the dissolution of the Federation, John Baily would reach out to the RGS in 1842, apparently under the advice of British consul in Central America, Frederick Chatfield. Thus, Chatfield's crucial role in bringing Baily's work to a British audience was arguably tied to the consul's imperial ambitions in Central America, where British naval expeditions had already charted the Atlantic and Pacific coasts of Nicaragua.[50] Baily's survey, which was one of the most detailed examinations of the Nicaragua route at the time, posited that despite topographical challenges like rapids, the San Juan River could be made navigable. He argued that the Nicaragua route, utilizing the San Juan River and Lake Nicaragua, was a viable – and in some respects superior – alternative to the Panama route. The presence of water bodies, for example, meant there was less excavation needed in Nicaragua and consequently made it less expensive to build, in addition to the Nicaragua route having suitable harbors at both ends of the canal.[51] Baily's proposed route extended from San Juan del Norte on the Atlantic Coast to the western terminus at San Juan del Sur on the Nicaraguan Pacific Coast. His work would serve as a critical foundation for all subsequent surveys and proposals for the Nicaragua Canal, shaping the discourse on interoceanic canal construction throughout the nineteenth century. In 1844, the same year that Baily's survey of the Nicaragua Canal route was published in the *Journal of RGS*, Foreign

---

[49] Ivan Escobar Fornos, "La constitución de Cádiz: Modelo del constitucionalismo," *Anuario Iberoamericano de Justicia Constitucional* 16 (2012), 165–189.

[50] Naylor, *Penny Ante Imperialism*, n. 267.

[51] John Baily, *Central America: Describing Each of the States of Guatemala, Honduras, Salvador and Nicaragua; Their Natural Features, Products, Population and Remarkable Capacity for Colonization with Three Views* (London: Trelawney Saunders, 1850), 127–149.

Secretary Lord Aberdeen named Patrick Walker as British agent and consul general on the Mosquito Shore, thus effectively establishing a British protectorate in the region.[52]

1.4 THE CORONATION OF KING GEORGE AUGUSTUS FREDERIC

Despite stationing Walker in Mosquito Shore, the Foreign Office still sought to maintain a stance of neutrality towards the region. In a vaguely worded letter, Lord Aberdeen instructed Walker as he assumed office:

> H. M.'s Govt. have decided ... to revert to the custom formerly observed of stationing a British resident in the Mosquito Country, who without directly interfering in the affairs of the Government, may be able when necessary to offer to the King and Chiefs such counsel and advice, under instructions from H. M.'s Govt. as will tend to support their legitimate authority, to promote civilization, and to develop the natural resources of the country.[53]

Walker's appointment elicited protest among the neighboring republics, particularly New Granada, which saw the act as British support for Mosquito claims of the disputed regions.[54] By the end of 1844, New Granada had moved decisively into Bocas del Toro, destroying property there and seizing the muskets landed there by the *Tweed*.[55]

By the late king's will, MacDonald was to function as regent during his sons' minority, and it was not until 1845 that the eldest son, George Augustus, was old enough to assume the role of king. For Walker, the internal conditions of the Shore were inextricably connected to its external defense. The power vacuum left by the death of Robert Charles Frederic had provided neighboring Hispanic republics with the opportunity to make inroads into the disputed regions of the Shore. By August 1844, Nicaragua, Costa Rica, and New Granada had made inroads into San Juan del Norte, Salt Creek, and Chiriquí Lagoon,

---

[52] John Baily, "On the Isthmus between the Lake of Granada and the Pacific; Being an Extract from a 'Memoir on the Lake of Granada, the River San Juan, and the Isthmus between the Lake and the Pacific Ocean, in the State of Nicaragua, Central America,'" The Journal of the Royal Geographical Society of London 14 (1844), 127–129; Naylor, *Penny Ante Imperialism*, 151.

[53] Lord Aberdeen to Patrick Walker, April 30, 1844, Foreign Office Records at the National Archives, UK (hereafter FO) 53/1.

[54] General Mosquera to Lord Aberdeen, July 1, 1844, CO 123/68; O' Leary to Aberdeen, July 27, 1844, CO 123/68.

[55] Patrick Walker to Lord Aberdeen, September 9, 1844, FO 53/1; Patrick Walker to Lord Aberdeen, December 12, 1844, FO 53/1.

respectively.⁵⁶ By September, Walker was writing to Aberdeen, calling for firm steps to stop Central American incursions.⁵⁷ It is in the backdrop of this growing external threat that Walker pushed for the coronation of the young King George Augustus in Belize. Requesting the coronation to take place at the earliest, Walker wrote to Aberdeen:

> It is of great moment that some importance should be attached to an act of so solemn a character and one calculated to make a very great impression on the minds of the neighboring states, whose serious attention will by this means be more called to the King's intimate relations with Her Majesty's Government than if the coronation were to take place in any obscure part of his own dominions.⁵⁸

Before the king's coronation could take place, however, the tension between New Granada and the Mosquito Kingdom boiled over in their tussle for control over the Corn Islands.

In March 1845, James Stanislaus Bell, sheriff and commandant of Mosquito Shore, informed Walker about an impending New Granada offensive. A New Granadian schooner named *Tescua* was heading for the Corn Islands with the commandant of San Andres, Antonio Escalona, on board with the purpose of hoisting the New Granadian flag on the island. According to Bell, New Granada intended to station the schooner among the islands for six months, presumably to make repeated visits to the area.⁵⁹ A day later, the matter assumed even greater gravity as Escalona abducted Judy Hunter, an emancipated, formerly enslaved woman from Corn Island, who had been living as a free woman in Bocas del Toro.⁶⁰ Bell boarded the *Tescua* as it lay anchored at the port of Bocas del Toro, attempting to obtain the release of Judy Hunter but was rebuffed by Escalona, who refused to recognize Bell's authority.⁶¹ Walker received the news on March 31 and immediately proceeded aboard the schooner *Scylla* towards the Corn Islands.⁶² On the way, the *Scylla* ran aground and damaged its keel, forcing Walker to abandon his mission.⁶³ Walker informed Aberdeen that the larger purpose behind *Tescua*'s expedition to the Corn Islands was "reimposing the fetters of slavery on all the slaves

---

⁵⁶ James Stanislaus Bell, August 16, 1844, FO 53/1. Chiriquí Lagoon was seen as a potentially valuable naval station; Patrick Walker to Lord Aberdeen, September 9, 1844, FO 53/1.
⁵⁷ Patrick Walker to Lord Aberdeen, September 9, 1844, FO 53/1.
⁵⁸ Patrick Walker to Lord Aberdeen, September 10, 1844, FO 53/1.
⁵⁹ James Stanislaus Bell to Patrick Walker, March 10, 1845, FO 53/2.
⁶⁰ James Stanislaus Bell to Patrick Walker, March 11, 1845, FO 53/2.   ⁶¹ Ibid.
⁶² Patrick Walker to Robert Sharpe, March 31, 1845, FO 53/2.
⁶³ Patrick Walker to Daniel O' Leary, April 7, 1845, FO 53/2.

emancipated by their legitimate monarch the Mosquito King in 1841."[64] He sent a sharply worded message to Escalona: "Your present intention in conjunction with certain individuals to attempt to reimpose the fetters of slavery ... leaves me only the alternative of demanding the immediate surrender of Judy Hunter and of warning you against any interference with the Corn Islands."[65]

Walker was convinced that the residents of the Corn Islands, whose enslaved people had been emancipated, had been complicit in Escalona's escapade. Following the emancipation in the Corn Islands in August 1841, the slave owners had demanded compensation for their loss of enslaved persons. But the continuing confusion over who bore the responsibility for paying the compensation – the British government or the Mosquito Kingdom – meant that in 1845, four years after the emancipation of the Corn Islands captives, the matter remained unresolved and the owners uncompensated. Walker informed Aberdeen that "certain parties in Corn Island actually did make overtures to the New Granadian to take possession of the Island – in the hope, if such a step was taken, of recovering the services of their slaves emancipated by the Mosquito king in 1841."[66] Walker's actions were reminiscent of MacDonald's bold expedition aboard the *Tweed*, and indeed, Walker may have been emulating his predecessor when he set off on the *Scylla*. In December 1844 Walker wrote to Aberdeen, "I am afraid New Granada will not be inclined, on the strength of official representations or diplomatic protests, to submit its pretensions ... unless, indeed, we repeat the unsuccessful demonstration affected on the lagoon by His Majesty's sloop *Tweed*."[67]

Walker's gallantry in setting off to rescue Judy Hunter, however, elicited disapproval among the ranks of the British government. Mr. O' Leary, the British chargé d'affaires at New Granada, asked Walker to adopt a conciliatory attitude towards New Granada and allow the matter to be resolved diplomatically.[68] Referring to Walker's request to the commander of *Scylla*, Captain Sharpe, to board the *Tescua* and seize Judy Hunter, Lord Aberdeen wrote: "I have now ... to caution you not to call upon the officers commanding H.M's Ships of War to act in any

---

[64] Patrick Walker to Lord Aberdeen, April 8, 1845, FO 53/2.
[65] Patrick Walker to Antonio Escalona, April 5, 1845, FO 53/2.
[66] Patrick Walker to Lord Aberdeen, July 19, 1845, FO 53/2.
[67] Patrick Walker to Lord Aberdeen, December 12, 1844, FO 53/1.
[68] Daniel O' Leary to Patrick Walker, May 13, 1845, FO 53/3.

manner against any foreign government in amity and friendship with H.M.'s govt. at the demand of the Mosquito magistrates, without the previous sanction and authority of H.M.'s govt."[69] Walker, on his part, defended his actions, writing to Lord Elgin that his timely actions had saved the Corn Islands from being invaded by New Granada.[70] Walker also argued that his position as a British representative would have been undermined by inaction on his part: "I cannot adequately convey to your Lordship of how insignificant I should have become in the eyes of these ignorant people [i.e. the Indigenous groups] had I stood tamely by and permitted, with power in my hands, any aggressive act on the part of New Granada."[71] Walker also justified his actions by pointing to the ill-treatment of Judy Hunter (whom Walker described with characteristic racialized paternalism as the "most comely black young woman I have seen on this coast"[72]), who had been flogged by Escalona after her seizure for refusing to return to slavery.[73]

While Walker – who would later apply for a British knighthood – presented his own actions as gallant and decisive, fragmentary evidence suggests the importance of Miskitu leadership in legitimizing and consolidating Walker's claims on the Corn Island. Immediately after the Corn Islands incident, Walker tried to stage a grand coronation for the young king, requesting Lord Aberdeen for a new crown, a scepter, and a sword. On April 17, 1845, a British sloop, the *Hyacinth*, arrived in Bluefields to convey the young king to Belize, where a coronation ceremony took place amidst pomp at St. John's Church.[74] A procession of the 2nd West India Regiment from Government House marched to the gate of St. John's, presenting arms as the king passed by, and a band played "God save the King," adding to the solemn atmosphere of the ceremony.[75] The superintendent of Belize, Fancourt himself, took special interest in the coronation, hosting a dinner party in honor of the young king. The ceremonial procession also consisted of Indigenous chiefs from Mosquito Shore, a practice that had also been followed by George's predecessors, and which aimed to legitimize the young king in the eyes of his compatriots.[76]

---

[69] Lord Aberdeen to Patrick Walker, October 16, 1845, FO 53/3.
[70] Patrick Walker to Lord Elgin, September 6, 1845, FO 53/3.
[71] Patrick Walker to Lord Aberdeen, September 29, 1845, FO 53/3.
[72] Patrick Walker to John Bidwell, December 20, 1845, FO 53/3.
[73] Patrick Walker to Lord Aberdeen, November 13, 1845, FO 53/3.
[74] Patrick Walker to Lord Aberdeen, May 10, 1845, FO 53/2.
[75] *Observer and Gazette*, May 10, 1845, FO 53/2.   [76] Ibid.

The young King George Augustus's first act after his coronation was to visit the contentious Corn Islands, where another ceremony was conducted. The five Indigenous chiefs, who had attended the coronation in Belize, accompanied the king and Walker to Great Corn Island, where the Mosquito flag was hoisted, and the *Hyacinth* gave a royal salute. For Walker, this demonstration of Mosquito legitimacy had the desired effect of discouraging what he saw as the "pretensions" of New Granada to the Corn Islands. Walker wrote to Aberdeen that the appearance of the *Hyacinth* "had the desired effect of inducing the New Granadians to desist, for the moment from their contemplated operations."[77] Occurring just a couple of months after Walker's *Tescua* expedition, the new king's visit to the Corn Islands shows that the Miskitu king was still an important figure and crucial to legitimizing the actions of the British resident. Ironically, it would be as a result of Walker's actions over the course of his tenure as British consul on the Shore that Indigenous Mosquito authority would begin to fray.

1.5 CONCLUSION: GLIMMERS OF A CANAL

On July 24, 1830, Mariano Gálvez, who would later become the chief of state of Guatemala within the Central American Federation, addressed the Congress of the Federal Republic on the subject of opening a canal through Nicaragua. A champion of the vision of a progressive and modernized Central America, Gálvez visualized the canal as a catalyst for Nicaraguan – and by extension, Central American – development and prosperity. In his vision, the canal would transform not just the prospects and the topography of the isthmus but also the very nature of Central America itself, turning barren lands into rich fields and awakening the region from indolence into industriousness. Nicaragua, he declared, was poised to become the center of world commerce and the most "abundant point on the globe."[78] In 1837, Francisco Morazán employed John Baily to survey the Nicaragua Canal route from the San Juan River in the Pacific through Lake Nicaragua to San Juan del Norte on the Atlantic coast. Even after the dissolution of the Central American Federation in

---

[77] Patrick Walker to Lord Aberdeen, June 18, 1845, FO 53/2.
[78] Mariano Gálvez, *Informe que presentó al congreso federal, el secretario de estado y del despacho de hacienda: Al dar cuenta del negocio relativo á la apertura del canal de Nicaragua – En la sesión pública ordinaria del sabado 24 de julio de 1830* (Guatemala: n. p., 1830), University of Kansas, Spencer Library, Griffith D418, 5.

1839 brought an end to Baily's expedition, the utopian vision of a Nicaragua Canal that had informed Gálvez continued to drive the ambitions of the newly formed Central American republics.

While the young Central American republics confronted the possibility of British dominance on the isthmian route following the establishment of a protectorate on the Mosquito Shore, the United States also began to feel its way into the canal question. In 1835, following a failed negotiation between Central America and the Netherlands for a canal contract, the U.S. Senate passed a resolution to begin negotiations with Central America and New Granada for the purpose of opening a ship canal between the Atlantic and Pacific Oceans. General Jackson sent a special agent to Guatemala to draw up a contract with Central America, but the agent died during the journey, leaving the task unfinished. In the late 1830s, American scholar and diplomat John Lloyd Stephens embarked on a journey through Central America that was almost Humboldtian in its scope and impact. Stephens' low-priced travelogs brought the beauty and allure of Central America to a broad U.S. audience. Preceding the annexation of Texas in 1845 and the subsequent beginning of U.S. imperial expansion in the Mexican–American War, Stephens' travels, which saw him bring ancient Mesoamerican artifacts to the United States (and a failed attempt to move an entire archaeological site to New York City), had undeniably imperialist overtones, not least because his travels were for the most part sponsored by the U.S. government. It is perhaps not surprising that the Nicaragua Canal occupied Stephens' imagination during his visit to Central America.

Drawing from Baily's earlier work, Stephens presented the Nicaragua Canal route with its eastern terminus on the San Juan harbor on the Atlantic coast as the most feasible route for an interoceanic canal. Reminiscent of Gálvez's eloquent exaltation of the geographical promises of the Nicaragua Canal, Stephens wrote:

> It will compose the distracted country of Central America; turn the sword, which is now drenching it with blood, into a pruning-hook; remove the prejudices of the inhabitants by bringing them into close connexion with people of every nation; furnish them with a motive and a reward for industry, and inspire them with a taste for making money ... A great city will grow up in the heart of the country, with streams issuing from it, fertilizing as they roll into the interior; her magnificent mountains, and valleys now weeping in desolation and waste, will smile and be glad.[79]

---

[79] John L. Stephens, *Incidents of Travel in Central America, Chiapas, and Yucatan*, vol. 1 (London: John Murray, 1841), 419.

Conclusion: Glimmers of a Canal

For Stephens, as it had been for Gálvez, the Nicaragua Canal was much more than a work of engineering. It had the transformative potential to change the very nature of Central America, bringing peace to the turbulent region and turning it into an earthly paradise ripe for U.S. enterprise.

In the context of growing British influence on the Mosquito Shore, the newly formed state of Nicaragua also began to make overtures to European powers, in particular, France, to take an interest in developing the interoceanic canal. Francisco Castellón, Nicaraguan envoy to Prince Philippe, communicated with Prince Louis Napoléon Bonaparte on the subject of the canal during the latter's stay in Ham. Ironically, Bonaparte would advocate for the route in London, presenting a case for the Nicaragua Canal at the Institution of Civil Engineers. In his book, *Canal of Nicaragua*, published in London in 1846, Louis Napoléon Bonaparte presented the Nicaragua route with San Juan del Norte as the eastern terminus as the superior route for the canal compared to Panama.[80]

Foreshadowing the war of narratives that was to follow in the subsequent years, in 1845, Guatemalan politician and historian Alejandro Marure presented a narrative of the Nicaragua Canal that posited the promised project as an authentically Central American – later, Nicaraguan – enterprise. As Brockmann writes: "He [Marure] pointed out that this was not a newfangled idea, the Spaniard Gil Gonzales Dávila having been the first person to survey the Pacific coast with this idea in mind in 1522."[81] Pointing to the Nicaraguan origins of the modern canal idea, Marure declared that "un hijo de Nicaragua," Manuel de Cerda, had been the first to promote the enterprise of the Nicaragua Canal.[82] In the following years, such narratives would form the linchpin around which the contest over the Canal would unfold.

---

[80] Louis Napoléon Bonaparte, *Canal of Nicaragua: Or a Project to Connect the Atlantic and Pacific Oceans by Means of a Canal* (London: Mills and Sons, 1846), 8.
[81] Brockmann, *The Science of Useful Nature in Central America*, 212.
[82] Alejandro Marure, *Memoria histórica sobre el canal de Nicaragua* (Guatemala: Imprenta de la Paz, 1845), 12.

2

The British Conquest of San Juan del Norte

> You have discovered a Mosquito nation which never existed, and an allied King whose creation was a fiction. You have also discovered that the Port of St. Juan ... has always belonged to the Mosquito nation, in order to contrive that it should now belong to Great Britain.
> — *Juan Bonilla, San Salvador, June 14, 1848*

While his predecessor, Alexander MacDonald, had felt no qualms about seizing the commandant of San Juan del Norte in a bid to thwart Central American designs on the Mosquito Shore, Patrick Walker's initial intent was to come to an amicable solution to the problems posed by the disputed boundaries of the Shore. The appointment of Patrick Walker to the post of consul general in the Mosquito Shore was intended in part to promote better relations between the Shore and its Hispanic neighbors. British Foreign Secretary Lord Aberdeen, for instance, had voiced the hope that the measure would prevent the continuation of Central American aggressions on the Mosquito Shore.[1] Walker himself, on assuming office, had expressed his desire to "cooperate in facilitating the settlement of all disputed points and promoting a good understanding between the inhabitants of the Spanish provinces and the people of the Mosquito territory." On the use of force, he maintained that he intended to avoid taking any military initiatives himself.[2] Ironically, however, the brief period of Walker's residency saw the beginning of one of the most contested struggles involving the Mosquito Shore: the clash over control of the harbor of San Juan del Norte. The eastern terminus of the projected

---

[1] Lord Aberdeen to Patrick Walker, April 30, 1844, FO 53/1.
[2] Patrick Walker to John Bidwell, February 26, 1844, FO 53/1.

transisthmian canal, the port would later figure prominently in the imperial rivalries of Great Britain and the United States.

As Walker sought to extend his control over the Shore's external relations, he simultaneously attempted to rein in what he believed to be the internal troubles of the Shore. The death of King Robert Charles Frederic had been followed by a power vacuum and, reportedly, a descent of the Shore into "lawlessness." Walker strove to restore order now by stripping off Indigenous governance of the Shore. His Council of State, composed almost entirely of Creole and white members, with a young King George Augustus as a figurehead, maintained the fiction of Miskitu rule but, in reality, gave Walker unprecedented authority over the internal matters of the Shore. Walker justified his actions by subscribing to a broader narrative of Miskitu decay and degradation. Ironically, even as the Miskitus became less important in the daily governance of the Mosquito Shore, the struggle between Britain and Nicaragua became expressed (on both sides) by heated arguments over the very existence of a Mosquito Kingdom. Paradoxically, as Walker's policies stripped the Miskitus of a role in governance, so also it became ever more important to project the legitimacy of the Mosquito Kingdom in the context of a growing interest in San Juan del Norte as the locale for the entry point of a transisthmian canal.

2.1 CHANGING BRITISH STANCE TOWARDS CENTRAL AMERICA

The period of Walker's tenure coincided with a shift in the British Foreign Office's attitude towards events in Central America and the British role in the region. The Foreign Office, which had hitherto been guided by a policy of nonintervention, now began to espouse a more active role in Central America, spurred on by its aggressive agent in the region, British Consul Frederick Chatfield. The latter was convinced that if the British government did not immediately stake its claim on the canal route, it would be out-beaten by other imperial powers, notably France and the United States. In February 1846, Chatfield received the intelligence that Prince Louis Napoléon Bonaparte was considering the possibility of establishing a monarchy in Mexico. The prospect of a French foothold in Central America, particularly in light of Bonaparte's well-publicized interest in a transoceanic canal, would have troubled the British consul. More worrying still was the unmistakable imperialist advance of the United States, which, since the spring of 1846, had been involved in a war of expansion against Mexico and had already annexed Texas to its territory.

The Mexican–American War was not only the United States' first major imperialist war of territorial expansion, but it was also widely seen as a prelude to American control over the transoceanic canal route. On March 16, 1847, U.S. Vice-President George M. Dallas spelled out the link between the two objectives. He wrote:

> It would seem understood that one of the objects at which the Government will aim when negotiating a peace with Mexico, is the purchase of so much soil, or the concession of so much irrevocable jurisdiction, as may enable us to unite by a canal or railway the Atlantic and Pacific oceans on the Isthmus of Tehuantepec. And this, I conceive, if promptly and vigorously carried out, must be followed by consequences whose vastness and beneficence cannot be easily exaggerated.[3]

Newspapers across the United States publicized the Tehuantepec route (see Figure 2.1) as a logical corollary to the impending American victory against Mexico. Following Commodore Perry's capture of Tabasco, the *Richmond Enquirer* gushed: "The [Tehuantepec] isthmus is now, or may be, to all intents and purposes, ours."[4] By July 1847, an American contingent of 500 men had arrived in Mexico to survey the Tehuantepec route.[5] The United States, moreover, appeared to be working on multiple fronts to realize its dream of a transoceanic canal. In December 1846, it concluded the Bidlack Treaty with New Granada that gave the United States right of way across the isthmus of Panama, and by August 1847, the U.S. consul in Granada, Francis J. Clark, arrived in Costa Rica in a likely attempt to explore the prospective Nicaragua Canal route.[6]

Chatfield adopted a two-pronged approach to what he saw as the U.S. challenge to British interests in Central America, both of which were ultimately predicated on gaining control over the Nicaragua Canal route. In the first place, Chatfield urged the Foreign Office to extend its control over the Pacific ports of Realejo and La Unión in the Gulf of Fonseca. The former, particularly, was important as a likely western terminus of the projected Nicaragua Canal route. In December 1847 – with the blessing of Lord Palmerston – the Admiralty sent a reconnoitering mission to the Gulf of Fonseca.[7] Secondly, Chatfield became more vocal about the need to take control of the port of San Juan del Norte, the Caribbean mouth of

---

[3] *Weekly National Intelligencer*, May 1, 1847.
[4] *Richmond Enquirer*, December 1, 1846.
[5] Mario Rodríguez, *A Palmerstonian Diplomat in Central America: Frederick Chatfield Esq.* (Tucson: University of Arizona Press, 1964), 293.
[6] Ibid. [7] Ibid., 283.

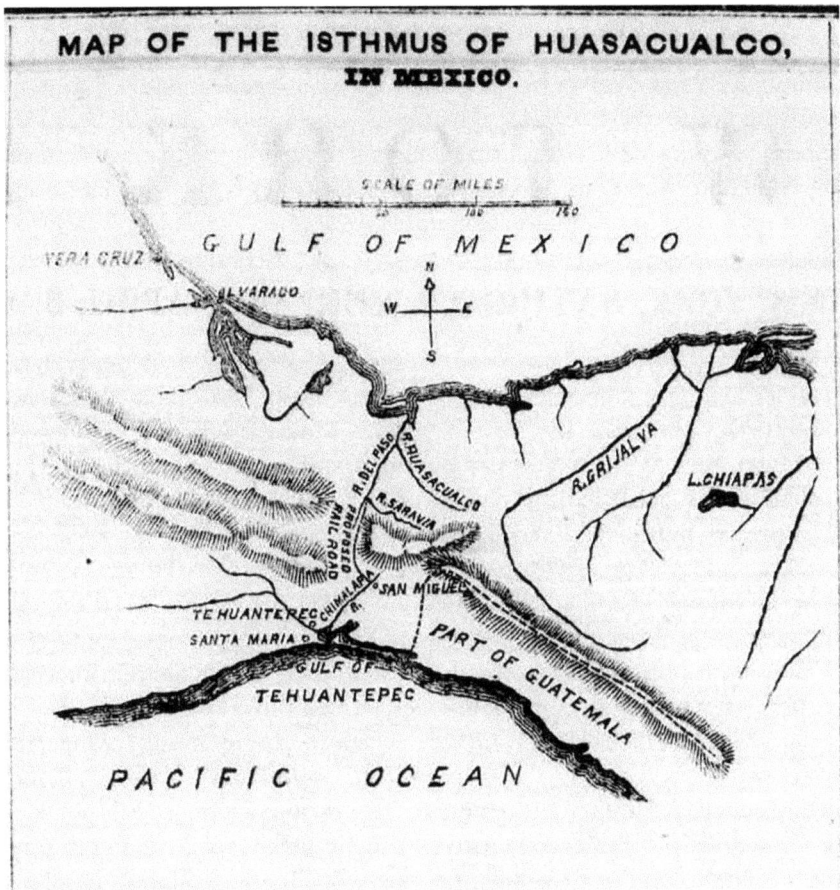

FIGURE 2.1 The Tehuantepec route. Source: *The New York Herald*, April 3, 1847.

the projected Nicaragua Canal.[8] Palmerston's concurrence with Chatfield on this issue can be seen through the Foreign Office's announcement in June 1847 declaring San Juan del Norte to be within the boundaries of the Mosquito Kingdom.[9] It is thus not surprising that whereas, the Foreign Office had condemned MacDonald's attempts to expand Miskitu territory through armed expeditions, it more explicitly supported Patrick Walker when he began to follow in the footsteps of his predecessor and cast his eyes on the Atlantic port of San Juan del Norte.

[8] Ibid., 281. [9] Ibid., 285.

2.2 INTERNAL MANAGEMENT OF THE MOSQUITO KINGDOM

Although Patrick Walker had begun his career as resident on the Shore by avowing not to interfere in local matters,[10] during his tenure, he began to subscribe to the view that a firm hand was needed in the management of the Mosquito Kingdom. Moreover, now that George Augustus had been crowned, the MacDonald Commission seemed irrelevant. Instead, Walker proposed a new body to govern the internal workings of the Kingdom – a Council of State. On September 10, 1846, George Augustus announced the Council and named the members. The Council consisted of both honorary and working members. MacDonald was retained as an honorary life member while Reverend Matthew Newport, Thomas Fox-Strangeways, Major William Hodgson Cadogan, and William Baron functioned as honorary councilors. The Council also consisted of paid working magistrates, including two Europeans (James Bell and James Green) and five Creoles (William Ingram, James Porter, George Hodgson Jr., Alexander Hodgson, and John Dixon).[11] The Council, while multiracial, was glaringly lacking in Indigenous or Miskitu representation. The Council of State provided Walker with broad and largely unchecked power in the Shore's internal matters as the councilors inevitably agreed to all his proposals.[12]

Surprisingly the Foreign Office, which had previously castigated MacDonald for creating the Commission, appeared to approve of the new Council. A Foreign Office note to Palmerston asserted: "Mr. Walker has had great difficulties to contend with, but he has succeeded in restoring a certain degree of order and regularity in the country. His late measures of inducing the King to name a Council of State for the govt. of the country cannot fail of producing the best results."[13] Part of the shift in Foreign Office's attitude must be attributed to the fact that now, as a protectorate, the Mosquito Shore was more firmly linked to Britain. More importantly, it appeared increasingly important to gain some control over the Shore, especially in the light of its strategic position. Nevertheless, the crowning of the new king and the fact that the Council had been formally constituted by the king allowed the British metropolitan government to maintain the fiction of noninterference.

---

[10] Patrick Walker to John Bidwell, February 26, 1844, FO 53/1.
[11] Ibid., 160. MoM Council of State, September 10, 1846, FO 53/5.
[12] Naylor, *Penny Ante Imperialism*, 160.
[13] "Lord Palmerston's Query," September 19, 1846, FO 53/5.

The Council of State gradually appropriated decision-making power on the most important issues related to the Shore. A month after the establishment of the Council, orders were issued for the raising of militias in various parts of the Kingdom. The regiments were to comprise all males between sixteen and forty-five years of age, who were deemed capable of bearing arms. Failure to attend the muster would result in fines: $1 for nonattendance of officers and $0.50 for noncommissioned officers and privates. Failure to keep arms and equipment in good condition was also liable to fines. Fines were also levied on officers disobeying orders of their superiors. This set of rules would have appeared draconian to the local population unaccustomed to military service. The broad levying of fines also made the system vulnerable to corruption. While ostensibly created to strengthen the "individual interests of every family," the main purpose of these new laws seemed to be to repel foreign aggressions. In perhaps one of the earliest articulations of citizenship in the Mosquito Kingdom, the Act for Raising and Training Regiments of Militia articulated that

The authorities trust that a feeling of personal honor and a sense of duty to the country of his birth or adoption, will prompt every individual to come cheerfully forward, and by zeal and obedience, the first qualities of a soldier, as well as a good citizen, raise and maintain the reputation of the inhabitants – repel foreign aggressions and secure the blessing of independence and the rights of freedom of their children.[14]

It is not hard to see in this case how Walker's ambitions relating to the external relations of the Mosquito Shore with respect to its Central American neighbors played a part in instituting an internal policy of militarization.

Another important area where the Council of State sought to extend its control was over the titles to land in the Shore. During the reign of erstwhile King Robert Charles Frederic, a great deal of territory of the Shore had been parceled out to private interests in the form of land grants. Haly and the Shepherds, for instance, were in possession of grants from the Grande River to Bocas del Toro.[15] In his will, penned on February 25, 1840, Robert Charles Frederic had entrusted MacDonald and a commission consisting of Rev. Matthew Newport, Patrick Walker, William Walsh, William Cox, and George Brown with the regency of the

---

[14] MoM Council of State, October 5, 1846, FO 53/5.
[15] Naylor, *Penny Ante Imperialism*, 161.

Kingdom. Following the death of Robert Charles, however, the commission had been annulled, and the new commission constituted in 1841 still lacked any real legitimacy or recognition from the metropolitan government.[16] The only act of the executors of the will prior to the departure of MacDonald from the Shore had been the appointment of commandants over different districts: Samuel Shepherd at Bocas del Toro, Peter Shepherd at San Juan, James Bell at Bluefields, S. T. Haly and Chief Wellington at Cape Gracias a Dios, and General Lowrie Robinson at Black River.[17] Eager to replace the old order with his own influence, Walker felt that the executors of the will should not interfere in local matters and "confine themselves to an approval of several of the appointments formerly made." Walker was also keen to reduce the power of the executors, some of whom like Messrs. Brown and Cox (part of the original commission of 1840 but removed from the 1841 commission) had direct interests in land grants.[18]

Walker was convinced that the extent of land grants already given severely undermined the Mosquito government and believed that "if the grants improperly given away by the late King could be sustained, neither his successor, Chiefs and people would have an acres interest in the country."[19] The Foreign Office on its part concurred with this assessment, with Frederick Chatfield asserting that the land grants rendered the young George Augustus' title of king "purely nominal."[20] On February 12, 1846, the executors of the late king's will issued a proclamation that would facilitate registering valid land grants in the offices of the government at Bluefields.[21] All land titles were to be presented for verification, after which they could be registered. The announcement of the proclamation was published in newspapers, and holders of the titles hurried to validate their titles.[22] However, before the proclamation could be carried into effect, Walker removed the power of the executors by replacing the commission with a Council of State in September 1846. The following month, a new proclamation by the Council of State effectively annulled all

---

[16] Unknown to Patrick Walker, June 2, 1846, FO 53/5.
[17] Patrick Walker to Lord Aberdeen, July 10, 1844, FO 53/44.
[18] Ibid.; also see Naylor, *Penny Ante Imperialism*, 132, 135.
[19] Patrick Walker to Executors of the Will of the King of the Mosquito Shore, November 26, 1845, FO 53/44.
[20] Frederick Chatfield to Lord Aberdeen, August 11, 1845, FO 53/44.
[21] Proclamation, February 12, 1846, FO 53/44.
[22] Geo. Upton to Lord Palmerston, December 26, 1848, FO 53/44.

land grants that had been obtained prior to October 8, 1841.[23] Another lucrative area brought under the purview of the Council of State was the mahogany works in the Shore. A bill passed by the Council on November 17, 1846, appropriated for the Council sole authority to give permissions for cutting mahogany and cedar within the Kingdom.[24]

Patrick Walker's policies effectively removed Indigenous authority from the governance of the Shore. On October 12, 1846, the Council passed an act abolishing Indigenous laws in the Shore. Instead, the laws of England would now be the basis for administering justice. This was, of course, not new. The erstwhile King Robert Charles Frederic had also established English laws in the Shore, but in practice the Indigenous system had continued to be followed. Now, the Council of State put in place stringent rules for adhering to English laws. Failure to administer justice according to the English law could result in fines or even lowering of rank for the culpable magistrates, headmen, and officers. Under the new system, the townships and rural districts would be subdivided into wards, which would be presided over by magistrates (appointed by the Council), who were to "take cognizance and punish by summary process all persons guilty of petty thefts, riots, assaults, violating the sabbath or neglecting to comply with the orders of the magistrate as to cleaning the bush and keeping his or her grounds in a cleanly state." The magistrate was also in charge of arbitrating disputes between servants and masters or laborers and employers. Magistrates were to hear and arbitrate felony cases in the "court of monthly sessions" to be held on the first Tuesday of every month in the respective township or rural district.[25]

One of Walker's main objectives was to regulate Indigenous labor, and he believed that the distribution of jobs rather than gift-giving would serve to promote more settled habits among the Indigenous communities. Writing to the Earl of Aberdeen, secretary of state for Foreign Affairs, in August 1844, Walker declared, "I do trust and with some confidence that in a very short time I shall obtain for the Indian fair value for his labor and the power to give or withhold it at his pleasure."[26] Walker thus proposed putting Indigenous residents to work on the construction of roads, bridges, churches, and other public works.[27] Walker's actions ran counter to the traditional informal mechanisms of patronage that had

---

[23] MoM Council of State, October 8, 1846, FO 53/5.
[24] MoM Council of State, November 17, 1846, FO 53/5.
[25] MoM Council of State, October 19, 1846, FO 53/5.
[26] Patrick Walker to Lord Aberdeen, Bluefields, August 1, 1844, FO 53/1. [27] Ibid.

allowed Miskitu chiefs and their king to hold on to power. Thus, to counter what he believed to be the oppression of Creoles and prominent Miskitus over other Indigenous communities, Walker created an office of registry for Indigenous employees. Any person employing an Indigenous would have to present themselves and the Indigenous people in their employment at the registry, whereupon "his treatment of them may be duly examined and seen into, and if just and satisfactory that he may receive a certificate in which the said terms may be narrated."[28] Henceforth, it became mandatory to hold a certificate in order to employ indigenous people. This bureaucratization effectively bypassed the Miskitu authorities and brought indigenous labor squarely within the purview of the British protectorate. By removing Indigenous labor from the ambit of Miskitu authority, Walker sought to reduce the exploitation that he felt characterized Miskitu influence over other Indigenous groups. Ending the custom of gift-giving was also meant to undermine Miskitu power, which had historically lubricated their own local patron–client networks and increased their prestige among other groups through their possession of European goods.

A parallel, but perhaps even more drastic method of stripping the Miskitus of governance was the move to shift the political center of the Kingdom from the centrally located Cape Gracias a Dios to Bluefields in the south. Until the late eighteenth century, Bluefields, located about 100 miles north of the mouth of the San Juan River, had a marginal existence in the Mosquito Kingdom. In 1770, Robert Hodgson Jr., the then superintendent of the Mosquito Shore, visited Bluefields, where he carried out a survey of Bluefields Bay. After being recalled to England and losing his position as superintendent in 1776, Robert Hodgson Jr. returned to Bluefields, which he "'governed' ... in the name of the Spanish crown,"[29] and profited from using the labor of black captives. Located in the region between Pearl Key Lagoon and Bocas del Toro, the Shepherd brothers controlled much of the trade of Bluefields in the 1830s and 1840s. By 1841 Bluefields was composed of 500 Creoles, including mainly descendants of Hodgson's settlement and some new immigrants from Jamaica and the Cayman Islands.[30] The Bluefields region was a site of constant dispute over competing land grants, until in 1841 Robert

---

[28] "Proclamation," North Bluefields, August 20, 1845, FO 53/3.
[29] William Sorsby, "Spanish Colonization of the Mosquito Coast, 1787–1800," *Revista de Historia de América* 73–74 (January–December 1972), 146.
[30] Naylor, *Penny Ante Imperialism*, 129.

Internal Management of the Mosquito Kingdom

Charles Frederic annulled land titles given before 1816 and confirmed the titles to land to Hodgson's descendants.[31] Finally, following Walker's proclamation of October 1846, nullifying land grants given before October 8, 1841, effectively invalidated land titles that had been acquired in Bluefields by the powerful triumvirate of the Shepherd brothers and Haly.[32] Still, the presence of James Stanislaus Bell, brother of George Bell – one of the original claimants of land in Bluefields – continued to complicate the picture, as James Bell sought to establish mahogany works in the region.[33]

For several reasons, Bluefields was a strategic location for Patrick Walker and the new Council of State. Describing Bluefields in 1845, Walker wrote that the region was "unsurpassed on this continent for richness of soil and healthiness of climate."[34] The presence of numerous water bodies, and in particular, Gunboat Creek, which was "capable at all times of the year of turning mills and other works,"[35] gave it an important commercial advantage. In addition, the region was home to a large reserve of valuable timber. Perhaps even more importantly for Walker, Bluefields was gaining strategic importance as one of the closest settlements to the San Juan River. Thus, even though Bluefields had only tenuous connections to other parts of the Shore, Walker established it as the headquarters of the new government and place of his own residence. Besides its Creole and black inhabitants, Bluefields by 1846 was increasingly multiracial, being a refuge area for both Hispanic migrants and escaped captives from neighboring republics.[36] Still, it was markedly lacking in any Miskitu population, leaving the young king without his Indigenous base of support.

While Walker's steps served to remove the Miskitu base of support for the kingship now operating from the largely Creole settlement of Bluefields, he justified his actions on moral grounds. Thus, the establishment of English laws in the Shore was meant to remedy what he saw as a condition of "immorality," which the Indigenous had slipped into due to the practice of customary Indigenous laws.[37] Right from the beginning of his term as consul, Walker was concerned with what he regarded as the "religious destitution" of the Shore. In a letter to the bishop of London in

---

[31] Ibid, 136. [32] Ibid., 163.
[33] James Stanislaus Bell to Magistrate North Bluefields, July 6, 1846, FO 53/5.
[34] Patrick Walker to Executors of the Will, November 26, 1845, FO 53/44. [35] Ibid.
[36] Patrick Walker to Executors of the Will, January 19, 1846, FO 53/5.
[37] MoM Council of State, October 19, 1846, FO 53/5.

September 1844, Walker lamented the "looseness and immorality" of the inhabitants of Bluefields and the surrounding regions. He felt this created problems even in courts, as the unbaptized inhabitants could not properly take an oath.[38] During his reign, Robert Charles Frederic had established the Anglican Church as the official religion of the Mosquito Kingdom. However, there had been no visits of clergymen or missionaries from the English Church since the eighteenth century.[39] In 1847, the Council of State pledged to set aside one-tenth of the revenue of the country towards supporting clergy and for religious instruction.[40] During Walker's term, a small Moravian mission was established in Bluefields.[41] While Walker couched his actions in the language of morality, his personal ambitions likely played a role in how he went about his functions as resident. Arguing that he "could compass a great deal more than I have already achieved if I was visited by a mark of favor from the Crown," Walker submitted his request for being considered for knighthood in 1846.[42]

2.3 WALKER AND SAN JUAN DEL NORTE

Ironically, even as the Miskitus became marginalized in the governance of the Kingdom, the historical claims of the Miskitus to the territory of the Shore became increasingly important in justifying the British position vis-à-vis Central American republics over the Mosquito Kingdom. Nowhere is this more apparent than in the tussle for the port town of San Juan del Norte. Even as Walker consolidated his hold over the internal government of Mosquito Kingdom in 1846, he was troubled by the apparent loss of control over San Juan del Norte, which faced competing claims of Central American republics. Nicaragua claimed San Juan del Norte at the mouth of the River San Juan. Costa Rica claimed the territory between San Juan River and Bocas del Toro. In 1843 New Granada claimed the whole territory from the River Chagres to Cape Gracias a Dios, thus encroaching on the rights to territory claimed by both Nicaragua and Costa Rica.

Still, Walker hoped for a diplomatic resolution of the question and in 1846 restrained the residents of Pearl Key Lagoon, who were unhappy

---

[38] Patrick Walker to Lord Bishop of London, September 11, 1844, FO 53/1.
[39] Minutes of Meeting of Council of State, February 12, 1847, FO 53/7.
[40] Minutes of Meeting of Council of State, July 7, 1847, FO 53/8.
[41] Naylor, *Penny Ante Imperialism*, 163.
[42] Patrick Walker to Viscount Palmerston, Bluefields, September 19, 1846, FO 53/5.

with their difficulties in accessing fishing grounds south of the river, from taking San Juan del Norte by force.[43] The Foreign Office and Walker recognized that San Juan del Norte was important not just from a strategic but also a commercial standpoint as the Atlantic port that could function as a British entrepôt of trade for Costa Rica and Nicaragua.[44] Reports to the Foreign Office suggested that Costa Rica might be agreeable to negotiation on British terms. The river San Juan entered Costa Rica through its connection with the river Sarapiquí, which lay about 20 miles from the mouth of the San Juan. Writing in September 1847, Alexander MacDonald noted that because of Costa Rica's need for an Atlantic port to export its products, including the lucrative coffee, it would likely cooperate with the British for access to the port of San Juan.[45] New Granada, on its part, focused its energy on trying to maintain control of Bocas del Toro, an area that had been claimed by the Mosquito government to lie within the Kingdom. This left Nicaragua as the major contender for control over San Juan del Norte.

From the very start, the Mosquito Kingdom based its claim on San Juan del Norte on, what it considered to be, its historical rights to the area. Thus, the Council of State writing to the government of Nicaragua on October 25, 1847, enunciated its claims to San Juan del Norte based on the Mosquito Kingdom's "ancient and hereditary rights."[46] On October 26, a British vessel *Alarm*, with Walker and King George Augustus on board, stopped at the northern bank of the San Juan, where they compelled a Nicaraguan officer to haul down the Nicaraguan flag from the custom house at the mouth of the San Juan. The Mosquito flag was then hoisted on the *Alarm*, and it received a royal salute. Following this, the *Alarm* set off for Jamaica, where it reached on November 8, 1847.

This visit to Jamaica was important on several counts. First, Walker sought Jamaican recognition of the rights of the Mosquito king since he counted on British support to press his claims on San Juan del Norte. Second, even though Walker's policies had stripped the Miskitus of much of their traditional authority in the Shore, the visit was meant to show

---

[43] Patrick Walker to Lord Aberdeen, July 20, 1846, FO 53/5.
[44] The efforts to make San Juan del Norte a second entrepôt (after Belize) failed after mid-century. Leslie Bethell, ed., *Central America Since Independence* (New York: Cambridge University Press, 1991), 27.
[45] Alexander MacDonald, September 4, 1847, FO 53/11.
[46] George Hodgson to Secretary of the Supreme Government of Nicaragua, October 25, 1847, FO 53/8.

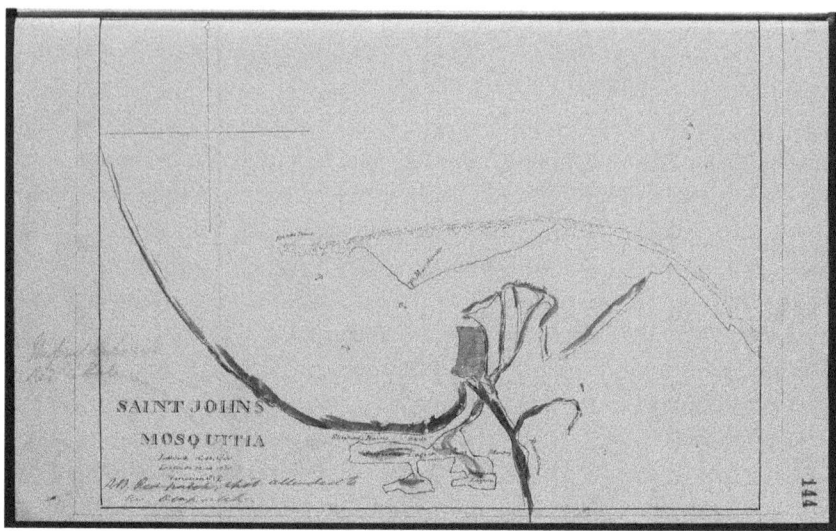

FIGURE 2.2 Map of San Juan del Norte showing in gray the possible position of British forces. Source: Enclosure 6 in Patrick Walker's Political No. 24, 1847, FO 53/8. Courtesy of the National Archives, Kew.

that the king was still an important figure mainly because, to stake a claim on San Juan del Norte, Walker (and indeed, the metropolitan government) needed to defend the legitimacy of the Mosquito Kingdom. In their despatch to the authorities of Nicaragua on October 25, the Council of State stipulated that Nicaragua needed to withdraw from the port of San Juan by January 1, 1848; failure to do so would result in British armed occupation of the region.[47] By the time of the Jamaica visit, Walker was already contemplating how to carry out this occupation. Shortly before reaching Port Royal, he communicated to Palmerston a sketch of San Juan del Norte showing possible positions a British force could take to defend the port from Nicaraguan aggression (see Figure 2.2).[48]

Already by the fall of 1847, rumors of an impending British invasion of San Juan del Norte had spurred on Central American states to make renewed efforts to form a union to resist British threats to the region, leading to the Pact of Nacaome of October 1847. However, within Nicaragua itself, the long-standing rivalry between León and Granada militated against a firm and cohesive stance against British interests. Even

---

[47] George Hodgson to Secretary of the Supreme Government of Nicaragua, October 25, 1847, FO 53/8.
[48] Patrick Walker to Viscount Palmerston, November 8, 1847, FO 53/8.

though Nicaragua sent envoys to the United States to appeal for help, divisions within Nicaragua were still too deep to surmount. Thus, conservatives in Granada and liberals in León diverged in their assessment of the situation and their position vis-à-vis the British threat. While León presented a bold front against British aggression, the conservatives were reluctant to enter into any conflict with the British. Moreover, a branch of the liberals under Francisco Castellón preferred to negotiate rather than take up arms. As Rodríguez points out, this lack of unity within Nicaragua weakened its response to the perceived British threat.[49]

On December 31, 1847, Walker and King George Augustus embarked on a cutter and headed towards the harbor of San Juan del Norte.[50] They were followed by the British steamer *Vixen*, which had on board sixty-five armed men of the Bluefields militia.[51] Both ships anchored at the San Juan harbor at 8 o'clock on the morning of January 1, 1848, to find that most of the Nicaraguan troops had already evacuated from San Juan and retreated to Sarapiquí. British forces then proceeded to haul down the Nicaraguan flag at the harbor while the Mosquitian flag was raised on the *Vixen* to the firing of a royal salute. When the Nicaraguan officers at the customs house in San Juan del Norte refused to recognize the rights of the Miskitu king, Walker ordered them to leave the port.[52]

The Nicaraguan administrator in San Juan, Patricio Rivas, was quick to condemn the occupation of San Juan del Norte. In a letter to Walker, he refused to recognize the validity of Miskitu claims on the port, describing it as a "pretended right which is sought to be alleged in favor of a chief of the tribes of Mosquitos who under title of King, without being recognized is supported by the English force."[53] In this, Rivas was echoing the Nicaraguan position, which was to deny the existence of the Mosquito Kingdom, a claim that would resurface throughout the contestation over San Juan del Norte in 1848. Despite rumors of possible Nicaraguan retaliation, the Nicaraguan officers of the customs house were evacuated in the first week of January 1848. A Mosquitian administration was left in charge of San Juan del Norte: George Hodgson as governor, Commander Little as captain of the port, and Captain Dixon as town

---

[49] Rodríguez, A *Palmerstonian Diplomat*, 289.
[50] Patrick Walker to Viscount Palmerston, January 15, 1848, FO 53/10.
[51] Patrick Walker to Captain Ryder, December 30, 1847, FO 53/10.
[52] Patrick Walker to Viscount Palmerston, January 15, 1848, FO 53/10.
[53] Patricio Rivas to Patrick Walker, January 3, 1848, FO 53/10.

major. Five men of the Bluefields militia were left as a police force to maintain order in the town.[54]

Anti-British feeling escalated in Nicaragua following the occupation of San Juan del Norte, and the Nicaraguan government solicited help from the French and U.S. governments to thwart what it perceived as British ambitions to monopolize the canal route.[55] There was some truth to this. While the Walker mission had been ostensibly to safeguard the interests of the Mosquito Kingdom, the Governor of Jamaica Charles Grey recognized that the broader objective was to fulfill the strategic interests of Britain in Central America. As the locale of a possible canal route, San Juan del Norte offered the prospect of unprecedented influence and profit, leading Charles Grey to comment that "an electric telegraph would enable an Admiral of the Harbor of Saint Juan to hold a conversation with an Admiral in the Pacific."[56]

On January 17, 1848, Walker received news that Nicaraguan forces from Sarapiquí under Colonel Salas had arrived in San Juan del Norte and hauled down the Mosquitian flag, replacing it with the Nicaraguan flag. More troubling still, they had taken Hodgson and Little as prisoners with them to Sarapiquí.[57] On February 8, Walker proceeded towards the mouth of the Sarapiquí with two British ships, the *Alarm* and the *Vixen*, with 200 seamen and 60 men of the 38th Infantry Regiment, with the principal object of obtaining the release of Hodgson and Little. This would be Walker's last action as consul general.[58] On the night of February 11, after a tiring journey of seventy hours amidst relentless rain, the British boats had anchored a mile below Sarapiquí when a lagging boat, *Bessie*, was hit by a bungo that had been cut adrift. In the pitch-darkness, the noise alarmed an officer, who immediately shouted to the men to stand to arms. In the confusion, Walker started up from his sleep, fell overboard, and drowned.[59]

Despite this setback, the fleet advanced the next morning towards the Nicaraguan post at Sarapiquí. The post, situated fifty feet high above the river, was surrounded by a dense forest in the rear and fortified by large, felled trees in the front forming an abatis, and its landing could only be

---

[54] Patrick Walker to Viscount Palmerston, January 15, 1848, FO 53/10.
[55] Naylor, *Penny Ante Imperialism*, 165; Patrick Walker to Viscount Palmerston, January (?), 1848, FO 53/10.
[56] Charles Grey to Earl Grey, March 8, 1848, FO 53/12.
[57] Patrick Walker to Viscount Palmerston, January 17, 1848, FO 53/10.
[58] Charles Grey to Earl Grey, March 8, 1848, FO 53/12.
[59] King George to Mr. Barrow, February 22, 1848, FO 53/12.

approached over a rapid that flowed at five knots an hour. Even though the British fleet carried a flag of truce, they were immediately fired on by Nicaraguan marksmen on both sides of the river and from the abatis. Despite this initial hurdle, the British forces soon regained ground and managed to drive Salas and his men into the woods. The final toll for the British force was two dead and thirteen wounded.[60] By March 1848, both Hodgson and Little had been released, and the *Vixen* and *Alarm* returned to Port Royal.[61]

2.4 WALKER AND THE NARRATIVE OF MISKITU DECAY

When Patrick Walker assumed the role of consul in the Mosquito Shore in the spring of 1844, he stepped into a world where the bonds of loyalty that tied the subjects to their king appeared to have eroded. In fact, Walker's correspondence indicates that he regarded the Miskitus as obstacles to progress, often citing their abuse of other Indigenous groups. In contrast, Walker tended to think of other Indigenous communities as more suited to the civilizing influence of the British. He regarded the Ramas and the Woolvas, for instance, as "peaceable and quiet" and felt that his policies would have the effect of transforming them into a valuable labor force.[62]

Even as Walker's policies undercut Miskitu influence, his correspondence highlighted a narrative of Miskitu decay. Thus, in Walker's estimation, while in the past the Miskitus had been a fierce and warlike race who had successfully defended the Kingdom against Spanish aggression, now they were reduced to a supine and indolent existence. Walker attributed this change to the debilitating influence of the Spanish after the British evacuation and the lack of proper British guidance. Thus, Walker wrote to Aberdeen, "At the close of our war with Spain the Mosquito tribes abandoned offensive operations against the Spaniards ... With the return of peace and the absence of inspiring influence and example of British cooperation and valor the warlike spirit of the people has declined and any system of union for common interest or defence has fallen into abeyance."[63] Walker believed that his own policies had had an

---

[60] Granville Lock to Francis Austen, February 20, 1848, FO 53/12; Charles Grey to Earl Grey, March 8, 1848, FO 53/12.
[61] Charles Grey to Earl Grey, March 23, 1848, FO 53/12.
[62] Patrick Walker to Lord Aberdeen, August 1, 1844, FO 53/1.
[63] Patrick Walker to Lord Aberdeen, December 31, 1844, FO 53/1.

ameliorating influence on the affairs of the Indigenous, promoting Indigenous loyalty and preventing the robbery and oppression, which he felt had characterized previous Miskitu relations with other Indigenous groups.[64] Documents suggest that Walker and the young king became increasingly dependent on Indigenous groups like Ramas and Woolvas – and even Caribs – thus further undermining the traditional reciprocal relation with the Miskitus. Thus, the Ramas were recruited to help build a house for the king's mother.[65] Similarly, Walker often called on the services of the Ramas, whom in one instance he described as "a small but excellent body of men."[66] The Council of State also appears to have gained assistance from the Carib chief, Sambolyer.[67] The location of the new government at Bluefields, far from Miskitu villages, exacerbated the process of distancing the administration from the Miskitu base.

While Walker made it a point to include the Miskitu king as part of his entourage in his visits to Jamaica or expeditions to the San Juan, read against the grain, the documentary evidence points to a growing disillusionment of the Miskitu base and even members of the Miskitu royal family with British actions and an erosion of the bonds of loyalty that tied the Miskitu king to his subjects. It is important to note, for instance, that on the eve of Walker's assault on San Juan del Norte, Princess Agnes, the sister of the Miskitu king, came to an understanding with the Nicaraguan government and supported its stance against British designs on San Juan del Norte, acknowledging the sovereignty of Nicaragua over the territory of the Mosquito Shore.[68] Similarly, General Lowrie Robinson, an influential chief of northern Mosquito Shore, had concluded an independent treaty with the Government of the State of Honduras prompting, Walker to describe him as a traitor. "He [Robinson] is," wrote Walker, "with a good deal of treachery in his disposition, a fine specimen of the Indian of this country who has received the benefit of a partial education."[69]

The narrative of Miskitu decay also found its echo in the Foreign Office, likely as a result of Walker's representations of the situation on the Shore. In a note accompanying a despatch from Walker, the Foreign Office noted, "The Mosquito Nation composed formerly of warlike

---

[64] Ibid. [65] George Augustus to William Dougal Christie, August 30, 1848, FO 53/10.
[66] Patrick Walker to Viscount Palmerston, October 20, 1846, FO 53/5.
[67] Clerk of Council to Sambolyer, June 1, 1847, FO 53/8.
[68] Naylor, *Penny Ante Imperialism*, 271.
[69] Patrick Walker to Lord Aberdeen, Bluefields, July 26, 1844, FO 53/1.

tribes, is now unable to defend itself."[70] Further, this notion continued to prevail even after Walker was succeeded by William Christie as consul general. The Miskitus, who had been recognized by the British from the eighteenth century as allies for their fighting prowess, were now regarded as unfit to form a defensive force in maintaining the sovereignty of their own Kingdom. In a Foreign Office draft (subsequently crossed out) on mustering a military force for defending San Juan, Palmerston wrote to Christie: "I conceive that the Mosquito militia, and the Indians generally, are not to be trusted nor fit by their habits for such an object."[71] While Walker and the Foreign Office's despatch suggest a growing perception of the Miskitu as a decaying race, there is also a sense of threat posed by the Indigenous people. In fact, the preoccupation with the trustworthiness of the Miskitu underlines not Miskitu decay as much as the erosion of the bonds of loyalty between the British and the Miskitu, likely as a result of Walker's policies that increasingly alienated them from a role in governance.

On September 5, 1848, William Dougal Christie, successor to Patrick Walker as consul general to the Mosquito Shore, sent a report to Palmerston detailing the condition of Bluefields and the port of San Juan. Christie's account shows with painful clarity the effects of Walker's policies on the Shore. Everywhere Christie found signs of decline of the Miskitu kingship. Although the young king still had some influence over the Indigenous groups, his connection with the Miskitus was eroding due to his location at Bluefields. "At Bluefields," wrote Christie, "there are no native Indians and he is there among strangers, who treat him with no respect." Not only so, but Indigenous chiefs, who had formerly occupied positions of authority, were now powerless: "The native Indian chiefs, through whom former Kings of Mosquito governed and received tribute, are altogether set aside and estranged from the King."[72] Walker had used the narrative of Miskitu decay to appropriate power instead in the body of the Council of State under his own control. While Christie arguably shaped his critique to show Walker in a negative light, there is enough evidence to suggest that Walker's policies may indeed have been a factor in eroding Miskitu authority.

---

[70] "Copy of Walker's No. 19 with Report on Mosquito Country and Its External Defences," June 4, 1845, FO 53/4.
[71] Draft of Viscount Palmerston to William Dougal Christie, June 16, 1848, FO 53/10.
[72] William Dougal Christie to Viscount Palmerston, September 5, 1848, FO 53/10.

2.5 THE CANAL AND THE PARADOX OF MISKITU "AUTHENTICITY"

Following the occupation of San Juan del Norte, the majority of Central American states came together to ratify the Pact of Nacaome, underlining the Central American response of uniting against the British threat.[73] Several Central American states, including Honduras and El Salvador, were vocal in their condemnation of British actions. In March 1848, the government of El Salvador declaring itself an ally of Nicaragua issued a decree, which declared that "The occupation of the Port of San Juan de Nicaragua affected by the English forces ... shall not be understood as an acknowledgment, direct or indirect, of the pretended right of the Mosquitos to the northern coast and the Port of San Juan, who are not recognized nor have ever been recognized as a nation."[74] With the concomitant rise of unionism and liberalism, Central American states now began to look at the United States as an important counterweight to the British threat in the region, creating a situation that was ripe for eventual U.S. intervention.

During his visit to Jamaica in December 1847, Walker, keen on proving that the English had historically been allied to the Miskitu, had examined the public records for evidence of Anglo-Miskitu ties. Walker's efforts paid off as he was able to gain access to several important documents. These included an extract from the House of Assembly of Jamaica ratifying a treaty between Mosquito King Jeremy and Governor Nicholas Lawes in 1720. Walker also consulted Edward Long's *History of Jamaica*, Sloane's *History of Jamaica*, Journals of the House of Assembly of Jamaica, and Parliamentary Debates of the House of Commons. Walker found evidence in all of this to suggest that the connection between England and the Mosquito Kingdom extended back to the early eighteenth century and sent copies of his findings to Palmerston.[75] The Foreign Office on its part also continued to assert the ancient rights of the Mosquito Kingdom in justifying its support of Walker's position. Thus, the Foreign Office noted: "It is easily to be collected from writers intimately acquainted with the Mosquito Shore ... that the Tribes under the Mosquito Kings have been

---

[73] Rodríguez, *A Palmerstonian Diplomat*, 292.
[74] "Decree of Salvador Government," May 31, 1848, Enclosure 1 in Frederick Chatfield to Viscount Palmerston, No. 22, July 10, 1848, FO 420/8.
[75] Walker to Palmerston, Queen's House, Jamaica, November 22, 1847, FO 53/8.

independent ever since the downfall of Montezuma."[76] By harking back to the ancient Aztec empire, the Foreign Office tried to imbue the Mosquito Kingdom with grandeur and legitimacy in a way that was quite similar to Walker's narrative (as in 1845, when Walker had compared Bluefields in the Mosquito Shore to that ancient Maya civilization site of Palenque[77]).

For its part, Nicaragua was quick to register its misgivings about British action, and it did so by questioning the very existence of the Mosquito Kingdom. On February 25, 1848, Pablo Buitrago, Nicaraguan minister of war, wrote to the captain of the *Alarm*, Granville Loch: "In reality, the Mosquitian nation does not exist, and consequently, it (Nicaragua) had no reason to consider the Mosquitians other than its own subjects, and the territory an integral part of Nicaragua."[78] Indeed, throughout the tussle over San Juan, Nicaragua consistently maintained that the Mosquito Kingdom was a fiction erected by the British to serve their own ambitions in Central America. In an address to the constitutional assembly of Nicaragua in December 1847, Buitrago asserted: "Honourable Representatives, you are aware that a youth of a nomadic tribe, exalted to the rank of King, to the derision of even those who profit by the counterfeit, serves for an excuse to a colossal foreign Power, for appropriating the northern extremity of the best known geographical line for the construction of the interoceanic canal."[79] While Nicaragua expressed its skepticism about the Mosquito Kingdom, the Foreign Office on its part defended British actions by asserting that the "aboriginal Mosquito Indians" had a greater claim to territory in the Kingdom rather than Nicaragua whose population was mestizo.[80]

Why did a diplomatic and political contest over a strategic location revolve around a seemingly abstract question about the nature of the Mosquito Kingdom? I would argue that it did for the same reason that the Foreign Office compared the Miskitus to the Aztec or Walker pored over the yellowing pages of the House of Assembly records of Jamaica from the 1700s: a search for legitimacy. For Nicaragua and its allies, the objective was clear: undermining the legitimacy of the Mosquito

---

[76] "Works Referred to in Mr. Walker's No. 15 of May 1847 Relative to the Extent and Boundaries of the Mosquito Kingdom," n.d., FO 53/8.
[77] Patrick Walker to John Bidwell, Bluefields, December 20, 1845, FO 53/3.
[78] Pablo Buitrago to Granville Lock, February 25, 1848, FO 53/12.
[79] "Report to the Nicaraguan Assembly," December 25, 1847, in Enclosure 1 in Frederick Chatfield to Viscount Palmerston, No. 14, April 19, 1848, FO 420/8.
[80] "Review," in Frederick Chatfield to Viscount Palmerston, No. 14, April 19, 1848, FO 420/8.

Kingdom would expose British pretensions on the Shore, particularly in the eyes of its imperial rivals such as the United States and France. This was the only way open for a struggling, internally riven Central American republic to challenge the power of one of the great empires of the world.

The Foreign Office continued to parry on this question as in June 1848, when Frederick Chatfield used a 1743 travel account of the Kingdom of Guatemala left by Don Luis Navarro to argue that "the Province of Tologalpa ... which we call Mosquito Territory, extends from the River Aguan to the River St. John."[81] This preoccupation with historical documents was not just idle academics, though. Rather, at stake was the validity of British involvement in the Mosquito Shore. The question of control over the possible Nicaraguan canal route raised the stakes even further. Lacking any real means to bolster their position as internal policies stripped the Miskitus of influence and members of the royal family began defecting to the side of Nicaragua, the British harkened back to the Miskitu past. Through proofs drawn from the brittle pages of century-old travel accounts and political treaties and the imagined connection to ancient Mesoamerican civilizations, the Foreign Office sought to justify its position on the Mosquito Shore. Paradoxically, even as the British reached back to a glorious Miskitu past to legitimize their involvement in the tussle over San Juan, the actions of local British officials on the ground fractured Miskitu society and relegated contemporary Miskitus to a narrative of decay.

[81] Frederick Chatfield to Viscount Palmerston, June 8, 1848, FO 420/8.

3

The Consolidation of Greytown

Following Patrick Walker's untimely demise, fears of Nicaraguan aggression on the San Juan and reports of lawlessness and anarchy on the Shore prompted the British metropolitan government to renew its official presence on the Shore through the appointment of William Dougal Christie as the new British resident and consul general in June 1848. Christie's time at the Shore was brief: he returned to Britain in the summer of 1849, although he continued to occupy the position of consul general till the autumn of 1851. Despite the brevity of his tenure on the Shore, Christie was remarkably active during his time as consul general, making diplomatic visits to Costa Rica and involving himself in the boundary disputes with Nicaragua and Honduras. On the domestic front, Christie sought to concentrate administrative authority in his own office. Importantly, Christie's tenure saw the establishment of British headquarters in the port of San Juan del Norte, the eastern terminus of the projected Nicaragua Canal route, and now referred to by the British as "Greytown" in honor of Governor Charles Grey of Jamaica. The move to Greytown undermined Miskitu authority as the young King George Augustus became increasingly isolated at Bluefields and dependent on Prussian settlers. Christie sought to build Greytown as a model British center, a process that was predicated on relegating Miskitus to the margins of governance as a "savage" race and populating the town instead with loyal British subjects from Jamaica – in time, altering fundamentally the demographics of this port town. Even as Christie sought to consolidate his hold over Greytown – and by extension, British control over the canal route – fragmentary evidence points to Miskitu resilience and efforts to counter official narratives of Miskitu savagery and decay.

3.1 AFTERMATH OF PATRICK WALKER'S DEATH

One of the main concerns of the Foreign Office following Walker's death was the situation in San Juan del Norte. In March 1848 Captain Loch had been successful in negotiating a treaty with Nicaragua that had at least temporarily caused a cessation of hostilities in the port of San Juan.[1] Governor Charles Grey worried that the treaty would not prevent Nicaragua from again holding a post at Sarapiquí, thus blocking off trade with Costa Rica. He also feared that the unsettled condition of Greytown might invite Central American interference. Writing to Palmerston in March 1848, Grey requested that a hulk outfitted with guns be stationed at the harbor of San Juan del Norte.[2] By April 1848, however, it was clear that help from the metropolitan government was not forthcoming: instead of stationing a ship of war at San Juan, Admiral Francis Austen agreed to an occasional visit by a British ship to the harbor.[3] To retain some semblance of control, Governor Grey instructed Major Sparks of the 38th West India Regiment to head to San Juan and "regulate" Mosquito Shore's relations with its Central American neighbors.[4] As Gavin Henderson points out "the government of Jamaica was naturally interested in the strategic position in the Caribbean Sea, and was anxious to maintain British claims on Mosquito Shore."[5] Governor Grey secured the services of fifteen men and a sergeant of the 1st West India Regiment and a medical officer to accompany Sparks.[6] Writing to Palmerston on April 20, 1848, Grey justified the need for a British show of support:

> If they [i.e. the Nicaraguan government] should learn that the British Government is determined not to post any troops at all on the Mosquito Coast ... they will at least threaten and disturb the Harbor of the St. Juan to such as an extent as to make the tenure of it by the Mosquito King insecure and hazardous ... and the transit to the Pacific will be more difficult than ever.[7]

Behind Grey's verve for protection of the Mosquito Kingdom thus loomed the larger question of the transisthmian canal.

---

[1] "Treaty between Great Britain and the State of Nicaragua," March 7, 1848, Enclosure 1 in Charles Grey to Viscount Palmerston, March 23, 1848, FO 420/8.
[2] Charles Grey to Viscount Palmerston, March 23, 1848, MS Corr 1, 2.
[3] Charles Grey to Viscount Palmerston, April 5, 1848, FO 53/13.
[4] Charles Grey to Major Sparks, April 14, 1848, FO 53/13.
[5] Gavin Henderson, "German Colonial Projects on the Mosquito Coast, 1844–1848," *The English Historical Review* 59:234 (1944), 259.
[6] Charles Grey to Viscount Palmerston, April 20, 1848, FO 53/13.   [7] Ibid.

It was not just the situation in San Juan that worried Grey. The death of Walker appeared to unleash a period of unrest in the Shore. Not only this, but the Council of State seemed inadequate to the task of administering the Kingdom in the absence of Walker. Writing to Governor Grey in February 1848 about the role of the Council, Stanislaus Bell expressed:

> I beg ... to state to your Excellency, unreservedly and emphatically that the aforesaid Council of State, now that it is deprived of the aid and support of Mr. Walker is utterly incompetent to administer the Government of this Country, even temporarily, and that disastrous consequences may be expected in the present situation of affairs if dependence be placed on it.[8]

News of Walker's death was met by shock and consternation in the Shore, with the young King expressing to Governor Grey that "it will be difficult to find any one so well qualified as Mr. Walker, was to advise upon all matters bearing upon the general welfare of the country."[9] At the initiative of Captain Loch, Dr. James Green, one of the members of the Council, was put in temporary charge of the young king and the management of the domestic concerns of the Shore, a move that was welcomed by King George Augustus as a means to provide some continuity from Walker's tenure.[10] Yet Grey was aware of the urgent need to appoint a new consul general on the Shore, writing to Palmerston that "the fate of the Mosquito King and Kingdom" depended on it.[11] While Grey sought to persuade the Foreign Office to act promptly in the matter, for the time being, reports from both James Green and Major Sparks provided steady information on the conditions on the Shore.

In the aftermath of Walker's expensive San Juan expedition, the Mosquito Shore government faced real economic hardships. In March 1848, James Green reported that the interference of Honduras in the mahogany cutting on the north coast of the Shore, and the requirements of defense for the Kingdom had resulted in "poverty of the exchequer in the country."[12] Major Sparks in his reports back to Governor Grey also conveyed the dire financial straits that the Shore had found itself in. Even the king lacked basic funds to defray his own personal expenses. "At present," reported Sparks, "the whole of the King's personal expenses, including the table, the rent of the house,

---

[8] Stanislaus Bell to Charles Grey, February 25, 1848, FO 53/13.
[9] George Augustus to Charles Grey, April 22, 1848, FO 53/13.
[10] Charles Grey to Major Sparks, April 14, 1848, FO 53/13.
[11] Charles Grey to Palmerston, March 9, 1848, FO 53/13.
[12] James Green to Charles Grey, March 22, 1848, FO 53/13.

occasional native followers of the King, boatmen, &c., have to be paid by Dr. Green, from his private means."[13] Major Sparks, like Green, attributed this want to the expenses incurred in the San Juan expedition and in the king's visit to Jamaica, as well as the patent impossibility of collecting revenue from the wood-cutting and fishing operations – including some illicit ones – on the coast. The lack of revenue was not only tied to domestic stability but also to external peace. The king's eldest sister, Agnes, had already defected to the Nicaraguan side, and Sparks worried that other members of the royal family might follow suit if the current problems in the Shore persisted. Writing about King George Augustus's eight-year-old sister, Victoria, Sparks expressed his apprehension that "It would be a great pity for her own sake, and would of course tend much to the King's injury, if from neglect, or want of proper care, she should be left to fall like her elder sister." The utter helplessness of the Mosquito government arising from this penury could be seen in the fact that it had been unable to meet the expenses of the only ship in the service of the Mosquito government, the cutter *Sun*. The *Sun* was sent to Belize to be sold off, and Sparks reported woefully that "The King, I suppose must recur to the method of his ancestors, and send canoes occasionally along the coast to look after his interests."[14]

Sparks' missives also provided important information on Bluefields, the center of the Mosquito government and Greytown, the strategic port of San Juan. Sparks, on his visit to Bluefields, was surprised by the presence of a small but apparently successful Prussian settlement. The enterprising Prussians (numbering 117) had arrived in Bluefields in 1846, where they had been provided asylum by Walker. Sparks was impressed with the Prussians' diligence, reporting to Grey that "By persevering industry and sobriety, these poor people have struggled through their difficulties, they have built good cottages, brought their allotments of land into cultivation, and seem contented."[15] Both Sparks and Green saw potential for prosperity in Bluefields. Green was convinced of the fertility of the soil in the land behind Bluefields and felt it could be an apt place for colonization if the British government could defray the cost of feeding settlers until the first crops were harvested. In sending Sparks to Mosquito Shore, Governor Grey had been careful in instructing him to desist from interfering in domestic matters. So there was little Sparks could do other than to report his observations in Bluefields. As he himself

---

[13] Major Sparks to Charles Grey, May 6, 1848, FO 53/13.   [14] Ibid.   [15] Ibid.

acknowledged, "these are matters lying quite beyond my province, as defined by your Excellency, and which demand particular consideration, much local inquiry, and study."[16]

While Sparks found the climate of Greytown to be salubrious, he was concerned about the lack of available labor and the absence of infrastructure to make it a British post. While the reports from Green and Sparks offered a glimpse into the conditions on the Shore, financial or defensive aid from the metropolitan government proved elusive. Writing to Major Sparks in June 1848, Governor Charles Grey conceded, "I should run the risk of misleading you and Dr. Green, if without instructions, I were to say even that I hope for any assistance from Her Majesty's Government."[17] Still, the reports appeared to have one desired effect: Governor Grey was now convinced that without proper government in place, Greytown would descend into further confusion and decay.[18] Finally on June 8, 1848, Palmerston appointed William Dougal Christie as the new consul general and British resident on the Mosquito Shore.[19] Dr. James Green was subsequently appointed vice-consul. Until Christie could reach the Shore, Major Sparks was left in command of Greytown.[20] Son of a British medical officer posted in India, Christie sat in the House of Commons from 1841 to 1847. Subsequently he entered the Foreign Service, and Mosquito Shore was his first posting. Christie was once described as an "impetuous and tactless man, ill-suited for diplomacy."[21] Despite his short stint in Mosquito Shore, Christie attempted to consolidate British control over the canal route by exploring an alliance with Costa Rica, actively remodeling the port of San Juan del Norte or Greytown and solidifying a narrative of Miskitu savagery that served to relegate the Miskitus to the peripheries of decision-making.

3.2 WILLIAM DOUGAL CHRISTIE IN CENTRAL AMERICA

Despite the short duration of Christie's tenure, he took an active interest in the pending disputes concerning the Mosquito Kingdom and its Central American neighbors. A short time after his arrival on the Shore, Christie started, on September 7, 1848, for Costa Rica. The Foreign Office had for

---

[16] Ibid.   [17] Charles Grey to Major Sparks, June 4, 1848, FO 53/13.   [18] Ibid.
[19] Viscount Palmerston to Acting Consul General, June 8, 1848, FO 53/12.
[20] Charles E Grey to King of Mosquito, July 14, 1848, FO 420/8.
[21] See William C. Lubenow, *The Cambridge Apostles, 1820–1914: Liberalism, Imagination, and Friendship in British Intellectual and Professional Life* (Cambridge: Cambridge University Press, 1998), 171.

some time considered Costa Rica as a valuable foil to Nicaraguan aggressions. In a draft to Christie in June 1848, Palmerston had recommended that Christie should proceed in person to San José and "endeavor to establish relations of the most friendly nature between the Government of Mosquito and that of Costa Rica."[22] Both the Foreign Office and Christie believed that Costa Rica, which lacked an Atlantic port, would be interested in trading through the port of San Juan del Norte. However, there were concerns that Nicaragua had already reached an agreement with Costa Rica before their expulsion from San Juan del Norte that, in return for Costa Rican exports passing through the port of San Juan del Norte duty-free, the two states would share the expenses of a customs house, which would be manned by Nicaraguans. Christie feared that Costa Rica, which was vulnerable to potential Nicaraguan incursion, might hesitate in joining hands with the British.[23] One of the major issues concerned a road from Sarapiquí that would connect to the port of San Juan, thus bringing lucrative Costa Rican commerce to Greytown and potentially offering Costa Rica a corridor to the canal route. An alliance with Costa Rica was desirable for opening the region south of the San Juan to British influence and the possible extension of Mosquito territory. Yet there were serious obstacles to reaching an agreement with Costa Rica. The internal politics of Costa Rica, where some interests looked to the Pacific rather than the Atlantic coast for a trading route, militated against constructing the Serapaquí road. Moreover, the tenuous hold of the British over the port of San Juan del Norte failed to inspire confidence in Costa Rica towards an alliance with the Mosquito Shore. As Major Sparks reported to Christie before his departure for Costa Rica,

> Everyone here who is connected with Nicaragua believed that we will give them back the Port. To tell them to the contrary is useless, and when they see that the crew of an armed boat might recapture the place at any moment, that there is not even a policeman, that the crew of the piraguas may be disorderly and that even thefts have been committed with impunity one can hardly wonder that the assertions of the Government of Nicaragua that we merely the Port "precariamente" [precariously] gains credit.[24]

Nevertheless, in September 1848 Christie made the difficult journey to San José, leaving the aging Peter Shepherd as temporary governor of Greytown in place of Sparks, who was scheduled to depart for

---

[22] FO draft to Patrick Walker, June 16, 1848, FO 53/10.
[23] William Dougal Christie to Viscount Palmerston, June 30, 1848, FO 53/10.
[24] Major Sparks to William Dougal Christie, August 4, 1848, FO 53/10.

Jamaica.[25] Having received an invitation from the president of Costa Rica to visit him in San José, Christie proceeded with understandable optimism.[26] By the fall of 1848, Nicaragua and Costa Rica had each sent diplomatic envoys – Francisco Castellón and Felipe Francisco Molina, respectively – to London to negotiate directly with the British government. While their immediate objective was to settle disputes over the Mosquito Coast and San Juan del Norte, as Robert Naylor notes, both missions carried "high expectations of a canal treaty."[27]

Christie's planned trip to San José led to a rise in expectations among those who hoped that the consul's visit to Costa Rica might help to sort out the difficult situation between Nicaragua and Costa Rica over the Sarapiquí road. Thus, Molina requested Christie to announce that the Nicaraguan attempt to thwart Costa Rican trade via San Juan would be seen as a hostile act by Great Britain.[28] The British vice-consul in León, John Foster, feared that the issue of Sarapiquí could threaten to become a full-blown contest of power between Nicaragua and Costa Rica: "The Province of Guana Casta, which included the Sarapiquí, has long been the bone of contention between Nicaragua and Costa Rica, and nothing but the want of means hinders these people from marching a force to take possession of it."[29] Foster hoped that Christie's visit might help to clarify the British position on the issue.[30] Palmerston would later nix Christie's ideas of extending British influence in Central America. However, for the time being, Christie proceeded to Costa Rica in an expectant mood.

Christie proceeded from Greytown on September 7, 1848, on an arduous eight-day journey to San José. The strong currents of the San Juan and Sarapiquí rivers slowed the boats of the entourage to an average of a mile an hour. From the landing at Sarapiquí, Christie rode on a mule through the dense forest path and passed over a steep mountain before reaching Alajuela. Not a soul could be seen on either bank of the Sarapiquí as the group proceeded, and it was only when they were about 12 miles from Alajuela that they spotted a few cottages, all in wretched

---

[25] Naylor, *Penny Ante Imperialism*, 172.
[26] President of Costa Rica to Mr. Christie, August 15, 1848, Enclosure 1, in Christie to Palmerston, September 6, 1848, FO 53/10.
[27] Naylor, *Penny Ante Imperialism*, 172.
[28] Felipe Molina to William Dougal Christie, August 15, 1848, Enclosure 3 in William Dougal Christie to Viscount Palmerston, September 6, 1848, FO 53/10.
[29] Vice Consul Foster to Major Sparks, August 10, 1848, Enclosure 7 in William Dougal Christie to Viscount Palmerston, September 6, 1848, FO 53/10.
[30] Ibid.

condition. Christie described his first view of Alajuela in romanticized terms, depicting a pastoral landscape dotted with maize, sugar, and coffee plantations with cattle grazing peacefully in the bucolic surroundings. At Alajuela, 15 miles from San José, Christie was greeted by an escort of a rider and two aides-de-camp, who had been sent by the president of Costa Rica The ride from Alajuela to San José charmed Christie, who nostalgically compared the landscape to his native England: "My today's ride from Alajuela to San José had been through a perfect garden; it has more the appearance of England not only than anything I have seen since I left home, but also than anything I have seen on the continent."[31] As Christie arrived at the president's house in San José, he was received by the president himself, along with officers of the government and members of the Costa Rican senate and assembly. Adding to the pomp, a military band played outside the house, and guns were fired. During Christie's stay in San José, he was honored by a dinner and a ball given by the president, as well as several other banquets by notable Costa Ricans. Christie reciprocated by throwing his own ball, where he invited "the largest number of people." Clearly enamored of his newfound fame, Christie wrote back to Palmerston, "I found all the people of Costa Rica prepared to receive me as a sort of Ambassador from England; they could not have made much more of the Queen herself if she had come here."[32]

While Naylor believed that the concurrence of the Castellón–Molina mission undermined the political impact of Christie's visit,[33] the available press coverage suggests that it nonetheless resonated symbolically within Costa Rica. On October 21, 1848, *El Costaricense* reported the details of Christie's visit on its front page, highlighting the grand balls and banquets held in his honor and suggesting that his presence would steer the negotiations in London in Costa Rica's favor. The visit also appeared to crystallize national aspirations around the canal project. As the newspaper declared: "The young Republic of Costa Rica, like the palm tree growing on the banks of the stream, will soon be flourishing, with one foot in the Atlantic and the other in the Pacific, greeting the future with modest confidence."[34]

Christie had arrived at an opportune moment: just weeks earlier, Costa Rica had officially declared itself a republic. Now he found the president

---

[31] William Dougal Christie to Viscount Palmerston, September 15, 1848, FO 53/10.
[32] William Dougal Christie to Viscount Palmerston, October 19, 1848, FO 420/9.
[33] Naylor, *Penny Ante Imperialism*, 172. [34] *El Costaricense*, October 21, 1848.

of Costa Rica eager to establish cordial relations with Great Britain. With Costa Rican exports fetching a lower price in the European markets, the Costa Rican government was eager to establish trading on the Atlantic coast via San Juan. Christie informed Palmerston that the President hoped to "place Costa Rica under the protection of and entirely at the disposal of Great Britain."[35] The Costa Rican government appeared eager to construct the Sarapiquí road and had already begun working on it. Christie, however, felt that more British support would ensure a speedier construction of the road.[36]

Despite Costa Rica's desire to establish friendly relations with the British, Christie noted that the threat of Nicaraguan aggression often prevented Costa Rica from publicly declaring its support for Great Britain. One of the major issues Christie tried to raise with the Costa Rican government concerned the status of the territory to the south of the San Juan River. The Mosquito Kingdom claimed that its territory extended from Cape Honduras in the north to King's Buppan in the south. This included the contested regions of Bocas del Toro, Matina, and Salt Creek within Mosquito claims. Walker's own view, conveyed in a map he sent to Palmerston in May 1847, was that the best interests of both the British government and the Mosquito Kingdom would be served by a boundary that extended from the Roman River till the mouth of the San Juan (see Figure 3.1).[37] While the Foreign Office, during Walker's time, had maintained that it only supported Mosquito claims till the left bank of the San Juan, the importance of the southern contested region grew because of its implications for British control over the canal route and trade in San Juan del Norte. Christie himself attempted during his visit to San José to come to an understanding with the Costa Rican government over the disputed region. Although worried that their stance might invite Nicaraguan hostilities, the Costa Rican government agreed to waive its claims to the region claimed by the Mosquito Kingdom south of the San Juan, leaving New Granada as the only rival claimant to Mosquito claims to the region.[38] Christie, on his part, assured Costa Rica that the British government would defend its interests, particularly in the free navigation of the San Juan River from Sarapiquí to Greytown.

---

[35] William Dougal Christie to Viscount Palmerston, October 14, 1848, FO 420/9.
[36] William Dougal Christie to Viscount Palmerston, October 19, 1848, FO 420/9.
[37] James Welsh to William Dougal Christie, August 11, 1849, Enclosure 1 in Christie to Palmerston, November 9, 1849, FO 420/9.
[38] William Dougal Christie to Viscount Palmerston, October 19, 1848, FO 420/9.

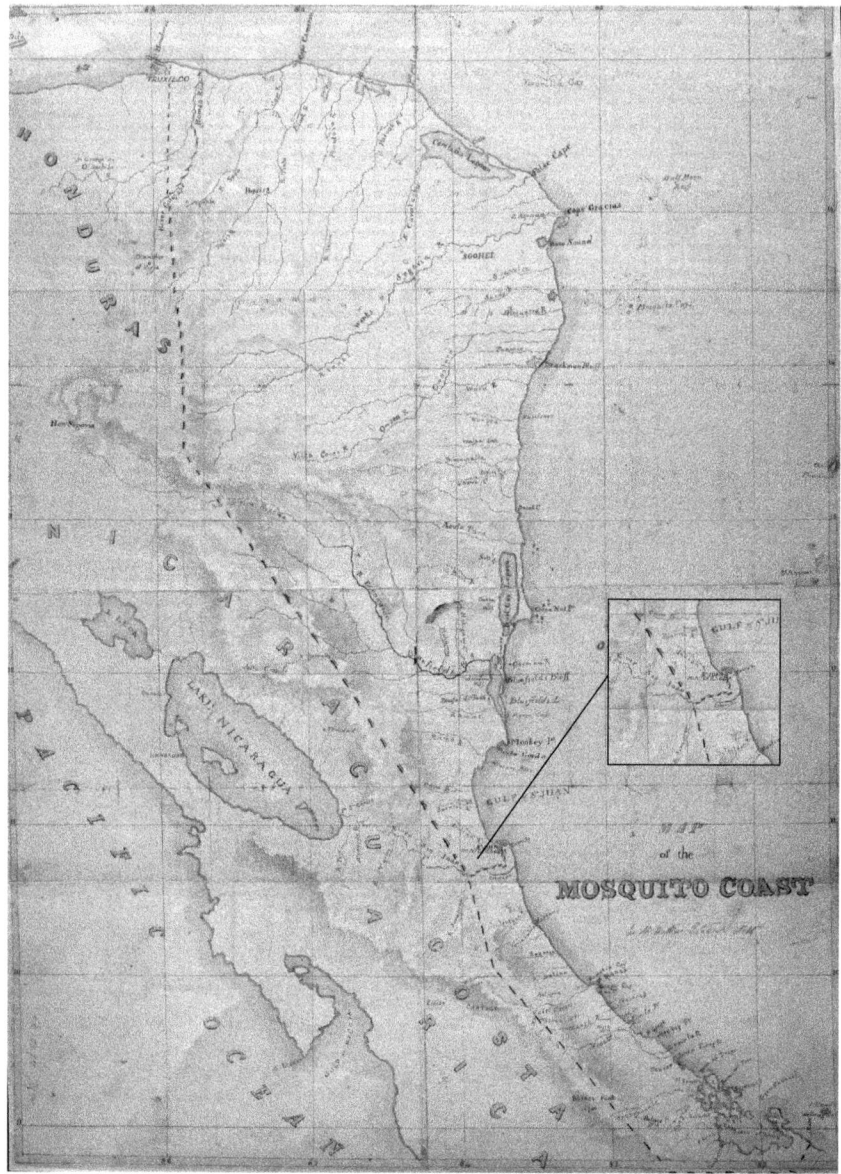

FIGURE 3.1 Patrick Walker's map of May 20, 1847, with Mosquito territorial claim in black and Walker's own suggested boundary in the inset. Source: MPK 1/199. Courtesy of the National Archives, Kew.

"However much it is to be hoped that their defence may never again involve the spilling of human blood," Christie wrote, "Great Britain would act as promptly and vigorously to punish any such interference as the lately acted with reference to the aggression of Nicaragua at St. Johns."[39] Christie encouraged the Costa Rican government to henceforth direct its trade with Europe through the San Juan River and promised to arrange duties at Greytown as "favorable as possible to Costa Rica."[40]

Aggravated by what he saw as Christie's overreach, Nicaraguan envoy Francisco Castellón voiced his disapproval of Christie's interference in the boundary question, writing scathingly to Palmerston: "With what right has Mr. Christie, in his character of consul general, interfered in the delineation of the limits in question?"[41]

The visit to Costa Rica also altered Christie's views on the Mosquito Shore, which he increasingly began to regard as a primitive region and a hindrance to British interests in Central America. Thus, Christie pushed for British colonization of Costa Rica arguing that: "The advantages which Mosquito offers to Great Britain are, in my opinion, quite insignificant in comparison with those of Costa Rica; and possessing Costa Rica, you may wait patiently for the development of Mosquito, which cannot be otherwise than slow and toilsome, and you will have a touch more favorable starting-point for the work of Central American civilization."[42] For Christie, Costa Rica with its bucolic and planned landscape and its Europeanized customs appeared to approximate his ideas of civilization. Even after his return from Costa Rica and throughout his short tenure in the Mosquito Shore, Christie would continue to cleave to a narrative of Mosquito primitiveness, which he had to redeem through measures of civilizing its people and landscape. Despite Christie's apparent success in Costa Rica, the Foreign Office did not share in the consul's assessment of British involvement in Central America. As Dozier points out, there is no

---

[39] William Dougal Christie to Minister Calvo, October 21, 1848, Archivo Nacional de Costa Rica (hereafter ANCR), Relaciones Exteriores, caja 16, expediente 3, sig. 17825, folio 12.
[40] William Dougal Christie to Minister Calvo, October 16, 1848, ANCR, Relaciones Exteriores, caja 16, expediente 3, sig. 17825, folio 8.
[41] Francisco Castellón to Viscount Palmerston, March 19, 1849, *U.S. Congress, House, Tigre Island and Central America Message from the President of the United States, Transmitting Documents in Answer to a Resolution of the House Respecting Tigre Island, etc., etc.*, 31st Cong., 1st Sess., H. Ex. Doc. 75 (Washington, DC: GPO, 1850), 254.
[42] William Dougal Christie to Viscount Palmerston, October 14, 1848, FO 420/9.

evidence that Christie's proposal for colonizing Costa Rica was ever seriously considered by the Foreign Office.[43]

At the end of October 1848, Christie left San José for Nicaragua, where he spent the first days of his visit in the town of Granada. If the visit to Costa Rica had enthralled Christie, he was dismayed at the conditions that greeted him in Nicaragua. Unlike Costa Rica, which welcomed Christie with great ceremony, the Nicaraguan minister Sebastián Salinas struck a markedly different tone. While assuring Christie that he would be treated with all due respect as a distinguished subject of the British Crown, Salinas firmly rejected his official status, declaring that Nicaragua could not recognize him as "consul to tribes living on the coast, who cannot form a nation, and who are an integral part of this very state of Nicaragua."[44] Still, Christie believed that it was important to establish friendly relations with Nicaragua, not least because no agreement with Costa Rica could really be effectively carried out without defusing the Nicaraguan threat.[45] "I would incur some inconvenience," wrote Christie, "to have the advantage of a personal communication with the rulers of Nicaragua, and of seeing with my own eyes the condition of that State."[46] Coincidentally, Christie visited Nicaragua at a time of great instability in that country. On August 10, 1848, Vice-Consul Foster informed Major Sparks that "The old quarrel 'Granada vs. León' has broken out again with fresh vigour." Eager to free itself from what it regarded as the tyranny of the Nicaraguan government in León, the wealthy city of Granada looked to the British for support.[47] While the Nicaraguan government under General Muñoz appeared interested in pressing its claims against Costa Rica on the boundary issue, Christie believed that the factionalism and instability in the country would prevent the Nicaraguan government from raising the funds needed for an invasion of Costa Rican territory. Summing up his perception of the conditions in Nicaragua, Christie reported to Palmerston, "The country is in a dreadful state."[48]

---

[43] Dozier, *Nicaragua's Mosquito Shore*, 63.
[44] *Gaceta del Gobierno* (León), November 4, 1848. See also William Dougal Christie to Viscount Palmerston, November 12, 1848, FO 420/9.
[45] William Dougal Christie to Viscount Palmerston, June 30, 1848, FO 53/10.
[46] William Dougal Christie to Viscount Palmerston, September 6, 1848, FO 420/8.
[47] Mr. Thomas to William Dougal Christie, August 20, 1848, Enclosure 8 in William Dougal Christie to Viscount Palmerston, September 6, 1848, FO 420/8; William Dougal Christie to Viscount Palmerston, November 12, 1848, FO 420/9.
[48] William Dougal Christie to Viscount Palmerston, November 12, 1848, FO 420/9.

Measuring the actual impact of Christie's visits to Costa Rica and Nicaragua is challenging. Felipe Molina, writing shortly after the event, mentioned the visit only in passing and chose not to emphasize its significance.[49] For Naylor, any potential diplomatic gains were undercut by the simultaneous Molina–Castellón mission.[50] Yet, as historian Clotilde Obregón observes, Christie's visit had an unintended legacy. Costa Rica's decision to receive him, despite Nicaragua's refusal to acknowledge the Mosquito Kingdom, had far-reaching consequences. It exacerbated tensions between the two republics and contributed to delays in resolving their disputes.[51]

Following his return from Nicaragua to Mosquito Shore, Christie continued to press for British support for Mosquito claims to territory south of the San Juan. Prior to Christie's arrival on the Shore, Major Sparks had conveyed to Governor Grey the importance of Bocas del Toro, describing it as "the most valuable part of the King's dominions."[52] Christie, too, was convinced of the benefits of gaining control over this region. Christie believed that a road from Bocas del Toro could cut across the isthmus connecting the Atlantic to the Pacific. Christie reported to Palmerston that coal might be found in the vicinity of Bocas del Toro, thus presenting the possibility of becoming a stopover for American steamers heading to Chagres.[53] With the Costa Rican government having promised Christie to waive its claims to the southern region, including Moin and Matina, Bocas del Toro remained the only region south of the San Juan claimed by the Mosquito Kingdom that was in dispute, and now Christie urged Palmerston to take up the issue with New Granada.[54] The Foreign Office, however, proved reluctant to act on Christie's urging, noting that any consideration of the issue would only follow after a formal cessation by Costa Rica to the Mosquito Kingdom of the territories to the south of San Juan.[55]

While Christie pressed for Mosquito claims to the south of San Juan, he was also confronted by border disputes in the north of the Mosquito

---

[49] Felipe Molina, *Bosquejo de la República de Costa Rica seguido de apuntamientos para su historia, con varios mapas, vistas, y retratos* (New York: S.W. Benedict, 1851), 110.
[50] Naylor, *Penny Ante Imperialism*, 172.
[51] Clotilde María Obregón, *El Río San Juan en la lucha de las potencias (1821–1860)* (San José, Costa Rica: Editorial Universidad Estatal a Distancia, 1993), 94.
[52] Major Sparks to Charles Grey, May 23, 1848, FO 420/8.
[53] William Dougal Christie to Viscount Palmerston, December 22, 1848, FO 420/9.
[54] Ibid.   [55] Viscount Palmerston to William Dougal Christie, April 16, 1849, FO 420/9.

territory. From Walker's period as consul general, mahogany cutters working in the northern border on the banks of the Roman (also known as Aguán) River had complained of Honduran disturbance of their mahogany works.[56] In particular, the mahogany camps on the Roman River, such as at Limas, remained under the constant threat of violence by Honduran officials at Truxillo. Matters were brought to the fore by the complaints of Messrs. Mathé & Co., a Belize firm that was backed financially by the Liverpool entrepreneur John Carmichael. Another Belizean, James Welsh, had in the 1830s received concessions for mahogany cutting in the hinterlands of Truxillo from Marshall Bennett, the business partner of President Morazán. By the 1840s, Welsh, working under the authority of the Honduras government, was the primary mahogany-cutting concern in the timber-rich Aguán Valley. In the mid-1840s, however, Mathé's firm had also begun to work in the Aguán Valley under Mosquito authority. The intense rivalry between the firms of Welsh and Mathé would eventually spill over into the dispute over the border between Honduras and the Mosquito Kingdom.[57] In July 1848, the firm of Mathé demanded compensation from the Honduras government for aggressions perpetrated by soldiers under the employ of the Commandant at Truxillo. Consul Chatfield, who received the complaint, was inclined to believe that Mathé and company had invited the aggressions by refusing to pay the Honduran government for cutting mahogany on the Roman River. Chatfield believed that the matter should have been resolved by the Mosquito government without involving the British government in the dispute. Instead, Chatfield informed Palmerston that "Messrs. A. Mathé and Co., were constantly urged to resist under promises of being supported and compensated by means of her Majesty's Government."[58] Once Christie had taken his charge at Mosquito Shore in autumn 1848, however, he appeared to champion the cause of Mathé and Co., urging Governor Charles Grey in November 1848 to "despatch a ship of war to Truxillo and the Roman and Limas rivers" to defend against Honduran aggressions.[59] Christie also felt that the northern boundary of the Kingdom should be extended to the dotted line at Truxillo in Walker's map of 1847 (see Figure 3.1).[60] While, for the time

---

[56] See, for instance, various correspondence in FO 53/7.
[57] See Craig Stephen Revels, "Timber, Trade, and Transformation: A Historical Geography of Mahogany in Honduras," PhD thesis, Louisiana State University, 2002.
[58] Frederick Chatfield to Viscount Palmerston, July 25, 1848, FO 420/8.
[59] William Dougal Christie to Charles Grey, November 10, 1848, FO 420/9.   [60] Ibid.

being, Palmerston was inclined to negotiate with Honduras to draw the boundary at Roman River, by November 1849 the British government had decided to stake the Mosquito claim all the way to Cape Honduras.[61] To what extent the British government's change in stance was owed to Christie's ardent championship of Mosquito claims is hard to say. But like Walker and Macdonald before him, Christie appeared to be personally vested in consolidating territorial gains in favor of the Mosquito Kingdom.

Regardless of Christie's efforts, however, the Foreign Office overall tried to maintain a stance of neutrality, rebuffing suggestions for more direct involvement in the affairs of Central America. Part of the reason for this certainly had to do with the perceived instability of the region and the fear that any involvement on the part of the British would not only be financially draining on the British government but also draw criticism from abroad. Christie's tenure also coincided with the outbreak of the Yucatecan Caste War (1847–1901), leading to considerable panic in the British settlement of Belize. In May 1848, Governor Grey lamented the "half-a-dozen" civil wars raging in the region.[62] Palmerston, too, proved reluctant to make any show of force in Central America, opting instead for the path of negotiation. The stereotypical view of Hispanic American states as immature and erratic was reflected in Chatfield's assessment: "The safe course with these people is to treat them as children when one has the power."[63] With the threat of the United States entering the disputes on the side of the Central American states and hostile Central American states uniting against the British looming in the background,[64] the Foreign Office opted for a policy of least intervention in spite of Christie's repeated appeals for British involvement on the Shore.

3.3 DOMESTIC AFFAIRS OF THE MOSQUITO KINGDOM

Christie's first point of arrival as he took charge as consul general on the Mosquito Shore was the town of Bluefields, where he arrived on July 30, 1848, aboard the ship *Daring*. The next day, he met the Council of State along with the Mosquito king.[65] The consul remained in Bluefields for

---

[61] William Dougal Christie to Viscount Palmerston, November 9, 1849, FO 420/9.
[62] Charles E. Grey to Palmerston, May 8, 1848, FO 420/8.
[63] Frederick Chatfield to William Dougal Christie, September 8, 1848, Enclosure 7 in Frederick Chatfield to Viscount Palmerston, September 8, 1848, FO 420/8.
[64] FO draft to William Dougal Christie, November 1, 1848, FO 53/10.
[65] William Dougal Christie to Viscount Palmerston, August 19, 1848, FO 53/12.

three weeks, after which he headed for Greytown, staying there for a fortnight. These initial visits created a strong impression in Christie's mind, and he sent a report back to Palmerston, which detailed his observations of the state of the country.[66] Christie was appalled at the administrative workings at the Mosquito Shore. He considered the Council of State – two of the members Christie described as "African" and the other two as "colored men" from Jamaica – to be an "absurdity." Christie reported the lack of legitimacy of the Council among the Indigenous chiefs, who "see no right to govern in these ignorant and needy African and Creole Councillors."[67] Christie felt that the lack of Indigenous representation on the Council was not merely a domestic issue. Rather, it had provided the justification for Nicaragua to portray the Mosquito Kingdom as a "mockery." One of Christie's first actions on his arrival in the Mosquito Shore was to stop the salaries of the councilors. He was determined to get rid of the Council – which he felt was the root cause of discontent in the Shore – by not renewing its term when it expired in September 1848. With the Foreign Office's concurrence, the Council was dissolved, resulting in consolidation of authority on the sole figure of Christie as consul general and British resident on the Shore.[68] Passing through Greytown in the fall of 1849, the new chargé d'affaires of the United States, Ephraim George Squier, characterized Christie as a "*de facto* dictator."[69]

One of Christie's most far-reaching actions during his time as consul general was to shift the center of operations of the Mosquito government from Bluefields to Greytown. During his first visit to Bluefields in July 1848, Christie found the town to be unsuitable from the point of view of shipping, trade, and commerce. Its harbor was inadequate for large vessels or exporting mahogany, and Christie observed that the town was in a "wretched condition." Greytown by contrast appeared to have the potential to be transformed into a great shipping port. The possibility of funneling Costa Rican trade through San Juan del Norte held out the hope of transforming the town into a wealthy port. Moreover, being on a possible canal route increased the value of Greytown tremendously. The

---

[66] William Dougal Christie to Viscount Palmerston, September 5, 1848, FO 420/8.
[67] Ibid.
[68] Viscount Palmerston to William Dougal Christie, November 16, 1848, FO 420/8.
[69] E. G. Squier to Mr. Clayton, June 10, 1849, *U.S. Congress, House, Tigre Island and Central America, Message from the President of the United States, Transmitting Documents in Answer to a Resolution of the House Respecting Tigre Island, etc., etc.,* 31st Cong., 1st Sess., H. Ex. Doc. 75 (Washington, DC: GPO, 1850), 135.

population of Greytown at the time of Christie's visit was a mere 129 people. Christie noted the lack of labor that might hinder the progress of transforming Greytown into a viable port and suggested the importation of convicts from other parts of the British Caribbean who would fill the labor gap.[70]

In December 1848, after a mere three months on the Shore, Christie decided to move his center of operations to Greytown, communicating to the young King George Augustus that the "convenient position of St. John's for receiving information from different quarters" had convinced him to make the move.[71] Considering the Indigenous inhabitants of the Shore to be unequal to the task, in January 1849 Christie traveled to Jamaica to procure convicts, as well as personnel for a police force, superintendent of port, and customs house at Greytown.[72] Apart from convicts, Christie was also keen to explore the emigration of skilled people – planters, laborers, and mechanics – to Greytown. Christie hoped that the emigration of skilled agriculturalists could reduce the dependence of Greytown on Nicaragua for basic food supplies.[73] Christie's plan for Greytown was thoroughly anglicized with squares and streets named after Queen Victoria, the reigning King of Mosquito Kingdom George Augustus, and other important figures in the Shore. Christie was at pains to show that the move to Greytown stemmed from his efforts to serve British interests rather than for any personal preference on his part, conveying to the Foreign Office that "Greytown is a more disagreeable residence than Bluefields, there is no medical man, and I lose Mr. Green's services as Secretary."[74]

While the move to Greytown marked a shift in British presence on the Shore, it also had implications for the Indigenous Miskitus, and especially King George Augustus. At the time of Christie's arrival on the Shore in the autumn of 1848, George Augustus was still a minor of around sixteen years of age. From the very beginning of his tenure, Christie regarded the Indigenous population as emotional and irrational. His perception of George Augustus was no different. Writing to Palmerston in September 1848, Christie averred, "His ancestors have all been men of violent passions; and Mr. Green tells me that this youth has often shown

---

[70] William Dougal Christie to Viscount Palmerston, September 5, 1848, FO 420/8.
[71] William Dougal Christie to King of Mosquito, December 25, 1848, FO 53/17.
[72] *The Antigua Observer*, May 3, 1849.
[73] William Dougal Christie to Viscount Palmerston, January 5, 1849, FO 53/17.
[74] William Dougal Christie to Viscount Palmerston, February 13, 1849, FO 53/21.

great waywardness when his pleasures have been interfered with."[75] Despite the fact that the young king was relatively isolated from his native base while living in Bluefields, Christie's move to Greytown threatened to further deepen the disconnection between the Mosquito administration and Indigenous leadership. The deterioration of the king's health worried Christie, particularly since the death of his brother, Clarence, had left his sister Agnes as presumptive heiress. Since Agnes had allied herself with Nicaragua, this boded ill for British interests on the Shore. As Christie wrote to Palmerston, "The King's life is a precarious one; if he lives his small and delicate frame renders it likely that he may not be able to procreate."[76] There was also a broader concern that bereft of the mentorship of Walker, George Augustus would tend towards dissolution. Palmerston agreed with Christie that the king should receive moral and religious instruction.[77] It is perhaps for this reason that in summer 1849, when James Green had to take charge at Greytown during Christie's absence from the Shore, Christie insisted that George Augustus stay with the head of the Moravian mission in Bluefields, Reverend H. G. Pfeiffer.[78] By attempting to import Jamaicans into Greytown and keeping the king at a distance in Bluefields, Christie's move to Greytown constituted a significant blow to Indigenous Miskitu authority on the Shore.

3.4 CHRISTIE AND THE NARRATIVE OF MISKITU SAVAGERY

While the practical measures undertaken by Christie served to undermine Miskitu power, his correspondence with the Foreign Office served to paint a picture of the Shore as primitive and its Indigenous inhabitants as savages in need of the civilizing influence of the British. Christie characterized the period following Walker's death as one of anarchy and lawlessness, a narrative that allowed Christie to portray the Indigenous Miskitus as irrational and uncivilized. On January 22, 1849, Christie forwarded reports of Miskitu "lawlessness" to the Foreign Office, including a description of the condition of Indigenous residents on the Shore penned by J. M. Daly. Describing the dissoluteness of Miskitu chiefs, Daly reported: "At the Cape there were great complaints; many complaining that the headmen were worse than the sailors or

---

[75] William Dougal Christie to Viscount Palmerston, September 5, 1848, FO 420/8.
[76] William Dougal Christie to Viscount Palmerston, April 7, 1849, FO 53/17.
[77] Draft FO to William Dougal Christie, September 25, 1849, FO 53/16.
[78] William Dougal Christie to Viscount Palmerston, May 21, 1849, FO 53/19.

soldiers, and that at a mushla drinking party when any of the men are drunk ... there is nothing else but maiming and shooting."[79] By February 1849, reports of Miskitu attacks on turtling vessels had caused consternation.[80] Christie also highlighted instances of Miskitu depredations on other Indigenous communities, evoking similar concerns that had arisen following the death of Robert Charles Frederic. Thus, in March 1849, Christie informed Palmerston of Miskitu cruelty towards the Valiente who lived near the Bocas del Toro.[81]

Reports of Miskitu lawlessness allowed Christie to justify his move to consolidate power in his own office. He wrote to Palmerston, "before such persons as composed the late Council, the chiefs of the Indian tribes should be the governors of the country, These, judging from the specimens I have seen, are even very wretched Indian chiefs." Christie built a narrative around Miskitu savagery that undergirded his own decision to exercise sole authority over the Shore: "Through them [the Indigenous chiefs] regular government and civilization are unattainable."[82] The idea of progress also formed the central argument that Christie presented to Palmerston for his unwillingness to create a system of government that gave Miskitu chiefs some modicum of control over the affairs of the Shore. "I have not however thought it expedient," wrote Christie, "to take any steps for organizing a government of the Indians on the plan carried out by the late king. Though by following that place an improvement on the present state of things could be effected, such a system of government will be a bar to progress."[83]

Christie's treatment of Miskitu King George Augustus was equally patronizing. In September 1848, Christie sent Palmerston a letter penned by the young king to "see how he writes English, left to himself."[84] In another despatch, Christie described the king thus:

The King and Mr. Green were here when I returned from Jamaica. I was able to give him a number of beads and gilt ornaments which I had brought out with me from England ... these gratified him very much and if I find that we can limit his generosity, I quite agree with Mr. Green that a few pounds a year will be well spent in this way to keep him in good humour.[85]

---

[79] "The Condition of the People etc," Enclosure in William Dougal Christie to [?], January 22, 1849, FO 53/17.
[80] R. Phelan to J. Mitchell Esq., February 17, 1849, FO 53/19.
[81] William Dougal Christie to Viscount Palmerston, March 8, 1849, FO 53/17.
[82] William Dougal Christie to Viscount Palmerston, May 12, 1849, FO 53/18.
[83] William Dougal Christie to Viscount Palmerston, June 15, 1849, FO 53/19.
[84] William Dougal Christie to Viscount Palmerston, September 5, 1848, FO 420/8.
[85] William Dougal Christie to Viscount Palmerston, April 7, 1849, FO 53/17.

Christie also seemed to be keen to keep the king at a distance from the new headquarters at Greytown purportedly to prevent any unpleasantness between the king and Nicaraguans at Greytown.[86] His despatches, however, reveal that Christie's poor estimation of the king may have been partly the reason for his insistence that the king reside in Bluefields. Christie wrote to Palmerston, "his chief occupation at present – running about the place with ragged boys, flinging stones and chasing cows. He was here [at Greytown] only a few days and I was very glad to get him away."[87] Reports that the king no longer enjoyed the loyalty of the Indigenous Miskitus also served to decrease his value in the eyes of Christie. J. M. Daly wrote to Christie about the condition of Miskitu chiefs: "I am told that they go so far as to say that they are all Kings, they have no King."[88] Thus, Christie felt that the late Robert Charles Frederic's formation of a largely non-Indigenous Council of State had loosened "the hold of the sovereign authority on the bulk of the population."[89] That Christie regarded George Augustus as a hindrance to British interests comes through in his suggestion to Palmerston that "If it suited the policy of England he might be easily shelved now; it may be much more difficult hereafter."[90]

With his perception of Indigenous Miskitus and their king as obstacles to progress, Christie turned to the possibility of importing Europeans into the Mosquito Shore. By April 1849, Christie felt that the English from surrounding Central American republics, who had fought for the cause of independence, might be induced to migrate to the Mosquito Shore by grants of land.[91] Mulling over the possibility of a Europeanized government of the Shore, Christie sent a list of the English and European residents of the Shore to Palmerston, inquiring: "The late Council and the Indian chiefs being out of the question, can any government be formed out of the European inhabitants of the country?"[92]

Christie's perception of Miskitus as savages also fed into his broader view that Britain should establish a formal protectorate over the Shore as had existed in the eighteenth century, rather than the loosely defined one

---

[86] William Dougal Christie to Mosquito King, May 11, 1849, FO 53/19.
[87] William Dougal Christie to Viscount Palmerston, April 7, 1849, FO 53/17.
[88] "The Condition of the People etc.," Enclosure in Christie to [?], January 22, 1849, FO 53/17.
[89] William Dougal Christie to Viscount Palmerston, June 15, 1849, FO 53/19.
[90] William Dougal Christie to Viscount Palmerston, September 5, 1848, FO 420/8.
[91] William Dougal Christie to Daniel O' Leary, April 7, 1849, FO 53/17.
[92] William Dougal Christie to Viscount Palmerston, May 12, 1849, FO 53/18.

it had exercised since 1844. In October 1849, he wrote to Palmerston in a lengthy despatch on the question of administering the Shore:

> It appears to me that the attempt to make a regular Kingdom of Mosquito is an unsuitable mode of dealing with barbarous aboriginal tribes and generates difficulties ... None of the Mosquito Indians are fit for soldiers; their fitness for civil employment is of course out of the question, the King being the only one among them who has any education; very few of them so far as I can judge, would at present be serviceable even as labourers.[93]

Christie also lamented the religious destitution of the Indigenous residents, quoting from a letter by Pfeiffer that read "the sight of the poor Indians makes my heart bleed."[94] Despite his poor estimation of the Indigenous Miskitus, however, Christie understood the strategic importance of maintaining influence over the Shore, which at the time promised to be the locale of a transisthmian canal. Christie suggested the outright colonization of the Shore was the only way to improve the conditions of the Mosquito Shore, including the moral conditions of the Indigenous residents through religious instruction.[95] Although in September 1848, Christie had made a similar suggestion of transforming the Shore into a British possession, it had been rejected outright by Palmerston.[96] Now, a year later, Christie reiterated his suggestion, carefully couching it in the narrative of Miskitu savagery and a British civilizing mission.

Christie's move to Greytown from Bluefields similarly relied on this narrative. That Christie regarded the move from Bluefields to Greytown as a means to promote English values and civilization and redeem the primitiveness that he felt characterized the Shore comes through clearly in his correspondence with the Foreign Office. Lamenting the lack of civilization at Bluefields, Christie wrote, "The African and Creole inhabitants of the place are a lazy apathetic set, content to live on plantations, and there is no one here to turn to recount, according to the modes of European civilization."[97] Distancing himself from both the Miskitu commoners and the king at Greytown, Christie sought to define the Englishness of the town by bringing in British subjects in the form of Jamaican immigrants. In the summer of 1849, Christie ordered a survey of Greytown, which revealed that out of a population of 209, there were 99 "Spaniards," 50 British subjects, 38 Germans, and 2 North

---

[93] William Dougal Christie to Viscount Palmerston, October 30, 1849, FO 53/20.
[94] Ibid.   [95] Ibid.
[96] Viscount Palmerston to William Dougal Christie, November 16, 1848, FO 420/8.
[97] William Dougal Christie to Viscount Palmerston, August 19, 1848, FO 53/10.

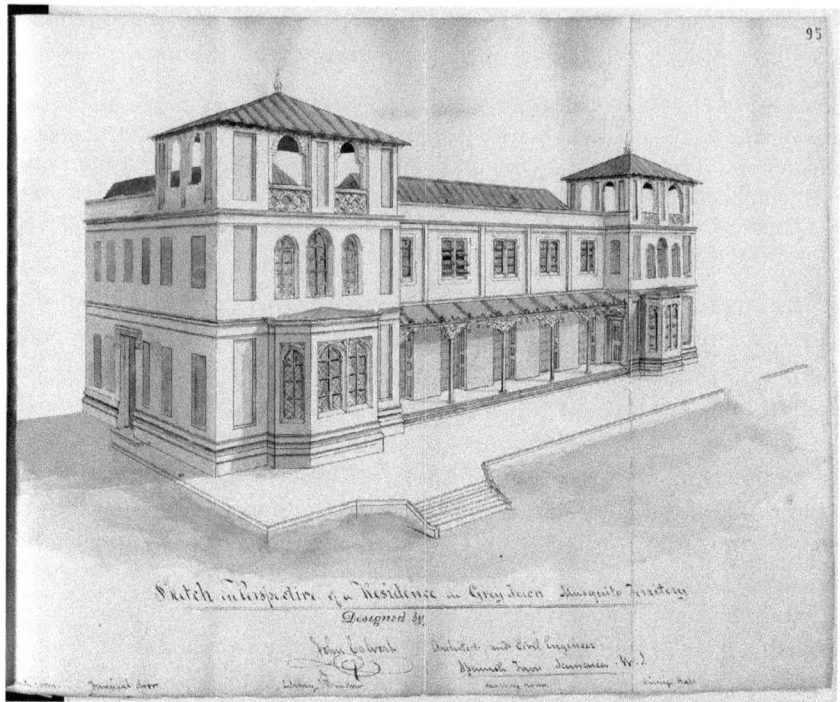

FIGURE 3.2 Sketch of Christie's residence in Greytown. Source: Enclosure in William Dougal Christie to Viscount Palmerston, April 17, 1850, FO 53/23B. Courtesy of The National Archives, Kew.

Americans. Thus, the makeup of the town was thoroughly non-Indigenous. Determined to promote order and cleanliness in the town, Christie created regulations for fencing in animals and instructed the inhabitants to build privies. Christie suspected that a lagoon behind the site of Greytown harbored malaria and suggested that it be cleaned and drained.[98] Christie even proposed to build a model English house in Greytown as part of his vision of creating a civilized and anglicized Mosquito Shore (see Figure 3.2).[99] Ultimately, Christie's narrative of Miskitu savagery was not merely incidental but emblematic of the deeply embedded racial logic at the heart of the imperial project.

[98] William Dougal Christie to Viscount Palmerston, June 20, 1849, FO 53/20.
[99] William Dougal Christie to Viscount Palmerston, February 13, 1849, FO 53/21. For a detailed discussion of Christie's plan for building his house, see Rajeshwari Dutt, "Christie's House: The Benefits of Mining for Failures in the Nineteenth Century," *Global Nineteenth-Century Studies* 1:1 (2022), 13–19.

Of course, in espousing the narrative of Miskitu savagery, Christie was echoing the argument made by Central American republics against Mosquito sovereignty. Throughout the dispute over San Juan del Norte, Nicaragua refused to recognize the Mosquito Kingdom on the grounds that the Miskitus were nothing more than a "savage tribe." In December 1847, for instance, Pablo Buitrago described Miskitus thus in the Nicaraguan assembly: "The Mosquitos were and are merely a savage fraction of Nicaragua."[100] In June 1848, Sebastián Salinas, minister for foreign affairs, communicated to Chatfield that the Nicaraguan government would not recognize the Mosquito Kingdom "The Director [of the state of Nicaragua] ... has directed me to say, that the dignity of the state that he rules does not permit him to recognize the sovereignty and independence of a savage and decaying tribe, which does not possess one of the attributes that constitute a nation."[101] Ironically, both Christie and republics like Nicaragua shared the belief that the Mosquito Kingdom could not exist as an independent sovereign power. While Nicaragua wanted to assert its own sovereignty over the Miskitus, Christie likewise made repeated suggestions to the Foreign Office of establishing a formal protectorate or colony over the Kingdom. Christie's suggestions were never entertained by Palmerston, however, who, despite believing in the British civilizing mission, did not want to needlessly become entangled in Central American affairs. Thus, in November 1848, Palmerston wrote to Christie:

With regard to your suggestions as to the possibility of converting the Mosquito Shore into a British possession, I have to state that Her Majesty's Government have no wish at present to increase the number of colonial possessions of the British Crown, and that their desire is, to assist the Mosquito Shore in its advance towards civilization, and to secure it against aggression and encroachment on the part of the neighbouring Spanish American Republics.[102]

There is no evidence that Palmerston ever wavered from this stance despite Christie's constant effort to gain greater involvement of the Foreign Office in the matters of the Shore.

3.5 GEORGE AUGUSTUS AND THE MYTH OF SAVAGERY

Although the voice of the Miskitus is notably absent from the colonial archives, careful reading of Christie's despatches allows us a glimpse into

---

[100] Pablo Buitrago, "Report to the Nicaraguan Assembly," December 25, 1847. Enclosed in Frederick Chatfield to Viscount Palmerston, April 19, 1848, FO 420/8.
[101] Sebastián Salinas to Frederick Chatfield, June 14, 1848, FO 420/8.
[102] Viscount Palmerston to William Dougal Christie, November 16, 1848, FO 420/8.

the efforts of the Miskitu King George Augustus to counter official narratives of Miskitu decay and savagery. Despite Christie's criticisms of George Augustus, the latter seems to have impressed Christie with his seemingly genteel ways, leading Christie to report to Palmerston that the British influence had given the young king "civilized tastes and habits" that set him apart from his fellow Indigenous residents.[103] Living in Bluefields, George Augustus faced his own struggles; the primary one being the lack of connection to his Miskitu base of support. As Agnes allied with Nicaragua and attempted to influence the rest of the Miskitu royal family, George Augustus increasingly became the only member of the royal family that the British could trust. His own poor health and the possibility that he might not survive for long or be unable to produce an heir worried the British, who rightfully saw him as their mainstay on the Shore.

One of the salient examples of the importance of George Augustus to British actions on the Shore, was Christie's decision to send him on a tour of the Shore to exhort Miskitus to abandon their "lawless" activities. In September 1849, the young king accompanied by the acting vice-consul for Bluefields, Robert Coates, left on an expedition to different Miskitu settlements along the Shore. He visited settlements along the Great River, Prinzapulka River, Haulover, Wawa River, Awastara, Sandy Bay, Ramona, Wanks River, and the Cape of Honduras. At each settlement, Coates assembled the Indigenous inhabitants, and the king addressed them. At Carata, a settlement next to Haulover, for instance, the king addressed the Miskitus,

> warning them against using any violence, committing robberies, or molesting in any way the vessels fishing for turtle at the Kays, also to pay all debts due by them, and fulfill all contracts, which they may have entered into with the various settlers on the coast, giving them notice that he should send to the public works at Grey Town those who did not behave properly.[104]

Still, even in this expedition, there were signs of erosion of the bond between the king and his subjects (and indeed, the narrative of "lawlessness" most likely reflected this erosion). Thus, the king suspended from authority a chief at Carata who had behaved "in a very disorderly and impertinent manner before the King."[105]

---

[103] William Dougal Christie to Viscount Palmerston, October 30, 1849, FO 53/20.
[104] Robert Coates to James Green, December 1, 1849, FO 53/23B.   [105] Ibid.

Part of the reason for the divide between George Augustus and the Miskitus no doubt stemmed from his living in Bluefields at a distance from Miskitu settlements. Yet, time and again, the young king demonstrated his connection to the Indigenous residents. Thus, he managed to get Rama and Woolva Indigenous laborers to build a house for himself in Bluefields. George Augustus also requested to live on his own in Bluefields, rather than with James Green, on the grounds that he "should be more independent, and would appear more manly, if he were living in his own house."[106] When ultimately, during Green's absence from Bluefields, George Augustus had to live with Reverend Pfeiffer, he appears to have embraced the new identity that working with the Moravian mission allowed him. George regularly attended the Moravian mission's Sunday school and evening meetings and helped to get Indigenous labor for the mission's construction of a chapel and mission house.[107] Still, the young king's life seemed to be marked by precarity. In May 1850 complaints reached the Foreign Office that the young king was starving due to a lack of food in Pfeiffer's establishment.[108]

Perhaps in no instance was George Augustus' efforts to counter the narrative of Miskitu decay and savagery more apparent than in his request to visit London for the Crystal Palace Exhibition set to take place from May to October 1851. The Exhibition, the first of its kind globally, was meant to display the achievements of British modernity, including industrial technology and craftsmanship. It was also meant to showcase the British Empire as a world leader. The "West India colonies" sent modest materials (mainly raw materials and agricultural produce) for exhibiting at the exposition and were given only a space of 403 feet out of over 1 million square feet that comprised the Crystal Palace.[109] In February 1851, Augustus wrote to James Green requesting to visit England, "having heard and read so much of the Exhibition that is to take place this year."[110] George Augustus presented himself not as a king of a savage group but as an educated man with an interest and awareness of the wider world. Green forwarded his request to Palmerston, suggesting that the king could visit England in a private capacity and stay with

---

[106] James Green to William Dougal Christie, December 20, 1848, FO 53/17.
[107] "Extract of a Letter from H. G. Pfeiffer," Offen and Rugeley, *The Awakening Coast*, 44.
[108] FO to James Green (?), May 16, 1850, FO 53/23A.
[109] Anthony Swift, "The Arms of England that Grasp the World: Empire at the Great Exhibition," *Ex Plus Ultra* 3 (April 2012), https://core.ac.uk/download/pdf/9995836.pdf.
[110] George Augustus to James Green, February 10, 1850, FO 53/26.

Green's family to minimize the expenses to the British government.[111] The response of the Foreign Office, however, betrayed the colonial government's espousal of the narrative of Miskitu savagery. In a draft of a despatch meant for Green, the Foreign Office noted:

> May I be permitted to suggest whether it might not be hazardous to bring the uncultivated sovereign of the Mosquito Indians too much into the public view, whether as a sovereign, or as a private individual? There seems also to be something anomalous, and rather ridiculous in the Mosquito Monarch boarding with the family of Green during his stay in England.[112]

By 1851, at the time of George's request to Green, Christie had already moved on from his position in the Mosquito Shore and from February 1851 took charge as the Secretary to Her Majesty's Legation to the Swiss Confederation.[113] Yet the persistence of the narrative forged during his tenure that relegated Miskitus to the ranks of savages could still be discerned in Foreign Office correspondence.

---

[111] James Green to Viscount Palmerston, February 16, 1851, FO 53/26.
[112] "Draft to Mr. Green Founded upon Lord Palmerston's Memorandum of March 30, 1851," FO 53/26.
[113] *The London Gazette*, February 25, 1851, www.thegazette.co.uk/London/issue/21185/page/488/data.pdf.

PART II

4

United States Enters the Canal Contest

In the spring of 1849, Roger Baldwin, a young Yale graduate, embarked on the *Mary*, a brig headed to San Francisco via the isthmian route of Nicaragua. Baldwin was traveling with Gordon's Passenger Line, which would first convey him on a brig from New York to San Juan del Norte, from there on a steamboat via Lake Nicaragua to Granada, thence on mules to the port town of Realejo, and finally from Realejo via the Pacific to San Francisco – completing the entire journey in two months. A month after sailing from New York, the *Mary* anchored at the harbor at the mouth of the San Juan on the Caribbean shore of Nicaragua. The young graduate's first view of Nicaragua left him breathless with wonder. Beyond the picture-perfect bay with its fine beaches and gleaming islands lay forests voluptuous in their abundance of fruits and game, while the distant summits of mountains framed the landscape. "I had expected it would be like Chagres," wrote Baldwin, "a collection of huts on some low, marshy point and utterly destitute of everything like beauty or interest; but I found it one of the prettiest and most charming little places it was ever my happiness to fall into."[1]

The news of the discovery of gold in California, corroborated by President James Polk's famous State of the Union address in December 1848, set off a frenzied movement of people to the West. The prevalent narrative of the Gold Rush emphasizes the long and laborious journeys of determined immigrants trudging westward on foot or on wagons along the Oregon Trail towards the promised lands of gold in California and the

---

[1] Roger Baldwin, "Tarrying in Nicaragua: Pleasures and Perils of the California Trip in 1849," *Century* 49:118 (1891), 912.

West. Yet, for the most part, the Gold Rush was a maritime venture. In the first few years of the Gold Rush, approximately 60,000 souls arrived by sea in the bustling port of San Francisco; each year, around half of them had made the arduous journey via the Central American isthmus.[2] In the early years of the Gold Rush, many Westbound immigrants had taken the long journey around Cape Horn along the southern coastline of South America to the Pacific Ocean. With the opening of the Panama route, however, most travelers preferred to take the Panamanian isthmian route, where they first arrived at the port of Chagres, going up the Chagres River to Gatun or Cruces, and then overland to Panama City on the Pacific coast, from where they could make the sea journey to the West Coast. Yet despite the traffic that plied this route – over 200,000 people crossed through this path to San Francisco in the first fifteen years of the Gold Rush – the route was infamous for its insalubrity. Henry Tracy, the U.S. Mail Steamship agent in Panama, wrote about Chagres in 1851: "I do not know anyone you can get to come here who will not be sick part of the time."[3] By contrast, the climate and surroundings of San Juan del Norte seemed veritably Edenic, leading Baldwin to assert that "I doubt if I ever was in better health in my life." In addition, the Panama route became notorious as a site of robbery and banditry.[4] The virgin route of Nicaragua, in contrast, looked increasingly appealing.

Baldwin's account highlights how the context of the Gold Rush led to the increasing international prominence of the interoceanic route through Nicaragua, particularly for Westward-moving Americans. As easterners rushed to reach the Western frontiers, there was a growing desire to speed up the journey to the West. Until the opening of the Panama route, the journey from the Atlantic to the Pacific coast of the United States could take between four and five months. The Panama route, regardless of its drawbacks, presented the quickest way West, completing the journey within six weeks under ideal conditions.[5] "Panama Fever" became so intense that passenger tickets from the isthmus to the West Coast were sold out months ahead, leading to agonizing delays for passengers stranded in the unhealthy environs of Chagres. Thus, for many adventurous travelers like Baldwin, the Nicaragua route, which promised a

---

[2] "Appendix Statistical," in *The San Francisco Directory for the Year 1852–53* (San Francisco, 1852), 26–28.
[3] *William Heilman versus Marshall O. Roberts Case* (New York: Wynkoop, Hallenbeck & Thomas, 1861), 272.
[4] McGuinness, *Path of Empire*, 75.   [5] Ibid., 38.

comparable economy and speed of travel as the Panama route, became an attractive option. Indeed, by the early 1850s, the Nicaragua route was steadily emerging as a rival to Panama, with 10,000 passengers making the trip through San Juan del Norte each year compared to 15,000 via the Chagres route.[6]

As the Nicaragua route through the Río San Juan emerged as a competitor to the Panama path across the isthmus for Westbound Americans, the U.S. government began to seriously consider the value of controlling the Nicaraguan transisthmian route. Historian Walter LaFeber has posited that the roots of U.S. imperialism could be traced to the projects of colonial expansion in the nineteenth century.[7] While traditional narratives of the history of the Gold Rush characterized it as a part of American domestic history, recent scholarship increasingly views American imperial expansion overseas as an integral part of U.S. policymaking as early as the 1840s. Such a view of U.S. history allows us to visualize Westward expansion, the Mexican–American War, and the efforts to control the transisthmian canal route as part of a common American imperial impulse through which these forces strengthened and fed into one another in the mid nineteenth century. The United States' imperial ventures in Mexico found a logical continuation in its pursuit of the Nicaragua Canal, pitting it against the interests of Great Britain, which was moving definitively towards consolidating its hold over San Juan del Norte, the eastern terminus of the projected canal route. As the United States entered the canal contest, its propagandists distorted Miskitu ethnohistory and produced a narrative that racialized Miskitus as "blacks" in order to undermine British claims to San Juan del Norte. Ratified in 1850, the Clayton–Bulwer Treaty achieved peace between the great powers but only through its silence on the Mosquito question, which would continue to be a divisive issue. Nicaragua, on its part, welcomed Americans with open arms, and the Nicaraguan elite saw in the dream of the interoceanic canal a way of finally uniting its fractious political landscape. Unlike other Central American states, where national projects emerged around domestic issues, the Nicaraguan national project forged in this critical period was centered on the promise of the interoceanic canal – a national project that, ironically, was predicated on the involvement of foreign powers for its fruition.

---

[6] Ibid., 69.
[7] Walter LaFeber, *The New Empire: An Interpretation of American Expansion, 1860–1898* (Ithaca: Cornell University Press, 1963).

4.1 THE U.S. DIPLOMATIC QUEST FOR THE NICARAGUA ROUTE

James Polk's term as U.S. president was characterized by a bold formulation of American expansionism that envisioned a continental nation that would extend from "sea to shining sea." Polk's attitude towards the transisthmian canal was a logical continuation of his efforts to expand the United States, which embroiled his administration in war with Mexico and a struggle with Great Britain over Oregon. While Polk's thrust towards controlling the Tehuantepec route did not materialize in the Treaty of Guadalupe Hidalgo that brought the Mexican–American War to an end, it would not be too far-fetched to say that the war fundamentally altered the U.S. vision of Latin America as a convenient backyard to enact U.S. imperial projects. Fueled by territorial acquisitions in the aftermath of the Mexican–American War, the United States turned to the Central American isthmus as a strategic point, which would allow access to trade, control of the Pacific, and consolidation of the continental United States in the context of the Gold Rush. The first concrete foothold came in Panama, where the Bidlack Treaty ensured the rapid establishment of U.S. interests. As Matthew Parker writes, "the acquisition by the United States of vast Pacific territories at the end of the Mexican War ... had inspired William Aspinwall and his partners to establish steamer service from Panama City to San Francisco and from New York to Chagres."[8]

In a report to the 30th Congress of the House of Representatives held on February 20, 1849, John Rockwell, a representative from Connecticut, presented an interoceanic route as a matter of national importance:

> The means of an easy and rapid communication between the oceans has heretofore been a subject of great interest to the United States in common with all civilized nations. It has now become a matter of the utmost practical importance, and the duty and necessity of uniting the remote and extended possessions of the country, is most obvious and undeniable.[9]

The report debated the various modes of traveling from the U.S. Atlantic to the Pacific coast and concluded that the most effective means would be a ship canal that could at the minimum accommodate 1,200 tons of shipping. The report presented information on three possible routes for

---

[8] Parker, *Panama Fever*, 42.
[9] "Canal or Railroad between the Atlantic and Pacific Oceans," February 20, 1849, 30th Cong., 2nd Sess., Serial Set Vol. No. 546 Sess., Vol. No. 2 H. Rpt. 145.

a large ship canal through the isthmus: the Panama route through Chagres, the Nicaragua route through San Juan del Norte, and the Mexican route through Tehuantepec. While all three routes seemed promising, the report did mention the insalubrity of the Panama path as a possible drawback of that route. While the first proper U.S.-sponsored survey of the Nicaragua Canal route – the Orville Childs' survey – would not take place until the fall of 1850, the diplomatic quest to gain U.S. control over the route would begin in earnest by the summer of 1849.

Since Patrick Walker's armed occupation of San Juan del Norte in January of 1848 – shortly before the signing of the Treaty of Guadalupe Hidalgo – public opinion in the United States framed British activities in Central America as an expression of its imperialist impulses. Through the summer of 1849, American newspapers attributed British interests in San Juan del Norte and the Mosquito Coast to their selfish desire to control the Nicaragua Canal route. Thus, the *Daily Union* published in Washington, DC, reported on May 15, 1849:

> It has long been supposed by knowing people that the real motive of the British government in pushing the alleged claim of its protégé, the King of the Mosquito Indians, to the line of the river San Juan de Nicaragua, was, by obtaining the command of that river and the harbor at its mouth, to lift the standard of British supremacy over the particular spot which has always been believed by some writers to offer the best route for opening a communication between the two oceans, whether by canal or railroad.[10]

Side by side with the recognition that British actions on the isthmus were linked to her canal ambitions was a growing anti-British propaganda in the U.S. press that vilified British actions as detrimental to the interests of Central America and the United States. The *New York Commercial Advertiser* denounced British actions in Nicaragua as "butchery,"[11] while the *Weekly Herald* highlighted the "deplorable state of things" in the Mosquito Coast.[12] These newspapers pointed to the elimination of Indigenous offices that had taken place during Consul William Christie's tenure and presented the Mosquito Kingdom as a façade for British imperialism.

In this atmosphere of growing suspicion of British intentions in Central America, the United States State Department sent Elijah Hise on a fact-finding mission to Central America. Born in Allegheny County,

---

[10] *The Daily Union*, May 15, 1849.
[11] *New York Commercial Advertiser*, April 27, 1849.
[12] *Weekly Herald*, May 19, 1849.

Pennsylvania, Hise's first major posting was as the chargé d'affaires to Guatemala in April 1848. While Hise's main responsibility was to secure treaties of friendship with Guatemala and El Salvador, the U.S. government also expected him to report back on British activities in the isthmus. The feeling in Washington was also that Hise should encourage Central American states to unite against British incursions.[13] Hise, recognizing the importance of the Nicaragua Canal route to U.S. interests, took the unprecedented step of concluding a treaty with Nicaraguan Foreign Minister Buenaventura Silva on May 31, 1849, exceeding the authority that had been granted to him by the U.S. government. The Hise–Selva Treaty conferred on the United States the exclusive right to build a passage between the Oceans via canal, railways, or roads through the Nicaraguan route. By the treaty, Nicaragua ceded to the United States all the land required for creating such a passage. The United States also gained the right to build fortifications along the route and deploy troops to protect them. In return, the United States guaranteed the territorial sovereignty of Nicaragua, thus allowing for Nicaragua to become a virtual U.S. protectorate. In its scope and commitments, the Hise–Selva Treaty exceeded the terms of all subsequent treaties between the two countries and soon became a source of embarrassment for the U.S. government.

By the time the Hise–Selva Treaty was penned, the Polk administration, which had appointed Hise, had already left office. The new government under Zachary Taylor had despatched Hise's replacement – Ephraim George Squier – to Nicaragua, and he arrived there in early June 1849, just as the ink was drying on the Hise–Selva Treaty. The Hise–Selva Treaty threatened to bring into conflict British and U.S. interests because of the unequivocal way in which the treaty monopolized the canal route for the U.S. and Nicaraguan governments. Ultimately, however, the Taylor administration rejected the treaty as unauthorized and because the U.S. government did not envisage creating a protectorate over Nicaragua. Instead, the rest of 1849 would see Squier attempting to secure a more acceptable understanding with the Nicaraguan government over the canal route.

Ephraim George Squier was an eager scholar-writer in his late twenties when he was presented with the opportunity to travel to Central America on a diplomatic mission under the Zachary Taylor administration.

---

[13] James T. Wall, "American Intervention in Nicaragua, 1848–1861," PhD diss., University of Tennessee, 1974, 36–37.

Following in the footsteps of the illustrious John Lloyd Stephens, who had also traveled to Mayan ruins on a diplomatic mission and become a sensationally successful writer, Squier's primary motives in accepting the mission may have been to visit archaeological ruins in the region. By the time Squier headed off to Nicaragua in 1849, he had already made a name for himself as an archaeologist, particularly through his 1848 publication of the *Ancient Monuments of the Mississippi Valley*.[14] Squier's journey to Central America also happened at a time that saw a surge in American popular interest in the region, and he quickly became a central figure in how the region became represented to the popular and academic public in the United States.

Squier arrived in León on July 5, 1849, to a remarkable reception. As Squier rode into the plaza on horseback, he was greeted by the sound of church bells, exuberant cries of "¡Viva los Estados Unidos del Norte!," and the thunder of cannons. Crowds of eager onlookers cheered as the alcalde mayor made a speech in honor of the American envoy. In the evening, the visitor was feted with fireworks and a serenade. On the following day, in his speech to Nicaraguan dignitaries, Squier put forth a vision of an American continent free of foreign influence:

> while we would cultivate friendly intercourse, and promote trade and commerce with all the world, and invite to our shores and to the enjoyment of our institutions the people of all nations, we should proclaim in language distinct and firm, that the American continent belongs to Americans, and is sacred to Republican Freedom.[15]

The response of the Nicaraguan President Norberto Ramírez to Squier's words was equally ebullient, emphasizing that "the friendliest feelings towards North America pervades every Nicaraguan heart."[16]

Newspapers in the city, like León's *Boletín Oficial* of July 5, 1849, gushed as it described Squier's visit: "Today is the great day of Nicaragua's grand hopes and those of America!"[17] The *Correo del Istmo* termed it "A New Era for Nicaragua" and described the visit as a "sublime picture that was presented for the first time to Nicaraguan eyes."[18] What made Squier's visit such a momentous occasion? Squier was the first U.S. diplomat assigned to Nicaragua. British actions in the

---

[14] E. G. Squier et al., *Ancient Monuments of the Mississippi Valley* (New York: Bartlett & Welford, 1848).
[15] E. G. Squier, *Nicaragua; Its People, Scenery, Monuments, and the Proposed Interoceanic Canal* (New York: Appleton & Co., 1851), 232.
[16] Ibid., 234.   [17] *Boletín Oficial*, July 5, 1849.   [18] *Correo del Istmo*, July 16, 1849.

Mosquito Coast in the preceding year, particularly Walker's seizure of San Juan del Norte, had aroused Nicaraguan fear and outrage. A small and young Central American state pitted against a great imperial power, Nicaragua, had been impotent to muster effective resistance. Now with the arrival of an American plenipotentiary, the possibility of gaining a powerful protector in the form of the U.S. government seemed within reach. To Nicaraguans wracked by internal instability and external threat, the moment truly beckoned as the dawn of a "new era."

While Squier's glamorous reception seemed to indicate a grand hemispheric alliance between the two American continents and Squier's own inclinations were towards understanding the ancient origins of the isthmus, the real motive behind the U.S. deployment of Squier in Nicaragua was more strategic and specific. This comes through clearly in the instructions conveyed to Squier by the secretary of state, John Clayton. There is some evidence that these instructions may have been drawn up by Clayton under the influence of Joseph L. White, the chief counselor of Cornelius Vanderbilt's American Atlantic and Pacific Ship Canal Company, which intended to gain a contract for the construction of the transisthmian canal. Indeed, the Canal was at the forefront of Clayton's instructions to Squier. He wrote to Squier: "A passage across the isthmus may be indispensable to maintain the relations between the United States and their new territories on the Pacific, and a Canal from Ocean to Ocean might and probably would empty the treasures of the Pacific into the lap of this country." Clayton instructed Squier to use his good offices to secure a contract for the construction of the canal for U.S. commercial interests.[19] Clayton also instructed Squier to secure a treaty with Nicaragua that would permit free transit across the transisthmian route for U.S. citizens.

Immediately following his successful reception at León, Squier employed his growing influence in Nicaragua towards securing a canal contract for the American Atlantic and Pacific Ship Canal Company. The contract granted the company exclusive rights to construct the ship canal through Nicaragua, and Squier ensured that the shares of the company would always remain predominantly in American hands. The contract would be valid for eighty-five years. In exchange for exclusive control over the canal route, the company pledged to pay the Nicaraguan government $10,000 every year until the end of the construction. Six days

---

[19] John Clayton to Ephraim George Squier, Washington, May 1, 1849, *Diplomatic Correspondence*, vol. 3, 38.

after securing the canal contract, Squier concluded a treaty of amity and commerce with Nicaragua. The treaty guaranteed U.S. citizens free transit across Nicaragua and exempted American goods from import and export duties. Both the governments of Nicaragua and the United States pledged to protect that canal, but U.S. protection was guaranteed only as long as the route remained in U.S. control. The United States also guaranteed the sovereignty of Nicaragua over the canal route. The Nicaraguan assembly unanimously ratified the treaty on September 27, 1849.[20] While primarily a treaty of commerce, the Squier Treaty created an uncomfortable situation for Anglo-American relations. The canal contract with Vanderbilt's company had already elicited protest in Britain. However, the Squier Treaty, which guaranteed Nicaraguan sovereignty over the canal route, appeared to directly contravene the British position in the Mosquito Shore and its claims on San Juan del Norte, which was a critical section of the canal route.

While Clayton's instructions to Squier regarding the canal had been clear and strategic, his directions as regards the British threat were more equivocal. From the outset, Clayton communicated Washington's displeasure with British actions in the Shore and encouraged Squier to promote Central American unity – presumably, to counter that British threat. At the same time, Clayton was at pains to emphasize to Squier that the United States did not want a monopoly over the canal route but rather equal rights of passage for all nations.[21] Clayton's vacillation between anti-British sentiments and a desire to maintain cordial relations made his instructions in this regard to Squier murky and open to interpretation. Part of this certainly stemmed from the position of the Whig administration under Zachary Taylor, which faced the opposition of a Democratic majority in Congress. The Taylor government's political weakness made a strong and unequivocal policy towards Great Britain impossible to muster.

Despite the government's vacillation, however, Squier from the outset maintained a critical stance towards the British protectorate over the Mosquito Kingdom. In his letters to Clayton, Squier presented the Mosquito government as a sham, being controlled not by Indigenous Miskitus but rather British agents and their allies. Squier was convinced that the open hostility between the British and Nicaragua would lead to a

---

[20] Squier, *Nicaragua*, 683–686; Charles Lee Stansifer, "The Central American Career of E. George Squier," PhD thesis, University of Kansas, 1959, 44–48.

[21] Stansifer, "The Central American Career of E. George Squier," 35–36.

war that would allow Britain to seize the entire country. For Squier, the situation could only be defused by a show of force by the United States, and he exhorted Clayton to station vessels of war at the San Juan. Following the Squier Treaty, both Britain and the United States recognized the possible repercussions of the treaty on Anglo-American relations. Clayton disapproved of both the Hise Treaty and the Squier Treaty. The former, Clayton believed, risked bringing Britain and the United States into collision "on account of this intrinsically worthless country."[22] The Squier Treaty, while more palatable, still contained articles whose conditions of exclusive rights for U.S. interests Clayton felt would be diplomatically divisive. On the British side, Palmerston felt that the Squier Treaty would bind the United States to compel Britain to deliver Greytown to Nicaraguan authorities, an action that would without doubt spark conflict between the two great powers.

At the crux of the dispute between Great Britain and the United States was the status of the Mosquito Kingdom. Official correspondence and press reports from the period suggest that the Mosquito question gradually became inextricably linked to the canal question. Clayton summed up the U.S. position on this issue when he told the British chargé d'affaires to the United States, John Crampton, "You affirm the Mosquito title; we deny it. There we are at issue; and if that controversy be not arranged amicably, the canal will probably never be made for either of us."[23] Indeed, as Crampton himself pointed out, the virulence of the hatred towards Britain spewed by the U.S. press increased substantially after the two hitherto-separate issues of the canal and the Mosquito question became connected. The *New York Herald*, for instance, described the Mosquito Kingdom as a British "pageant" and declared that "England has no ground whatever to stand upon except the *brutus fulmen* of her own imperious will."[24]

At the root of American distrust of the British over the Mosquito question was the young nation's specific trajectory in the nineteenth century. The mid nineteenth century was characterized by a belief in Manifest Destiny and a commitment to the process of Westward expansion. Memories of the War of 1812, the last major engagement between Britain and the United States, were still fresh in people's minds. A tussle over prestige rather than resources, the War of 1812 had seen the British

---

[22] Mr. Crampton to Viscount Palmerston, September 17, 1849, FO 420/10.
[23] Mr. Crampton to Viscount Palmerston, October 1, 1849, FO 420/10.
[24] Mr. Crampton to Viscount Palmerston, October 1, 1849, FO 420/10.

allying with Indigenous populations such as the Tecumseh Confederacy against the fledgling United States. Arguably, the success of the United States in resisting an Old-World power in the War of 1812 proved to be decisive in encouraging a spirit of expansionism. In the 1840s, the struggles over Texas and Oregon again brought to the fore the issue of Anglo-American rivalry. As Haynes and Morris write, "Anglophobia ... has been a missing ingredient in most discussions of Manifest Destiny."[25] The period of American expansionism in the mid nineteenth century went hand in hand with a new racial view of Indigenous people as inferior and destined to be replaced by the superior Anglo-Saxon race. Newly established anthropological institutes such as the American School of Ethnology forwarded ideas of racial hierarchies, and "scientific" studies of craniology appeared to support the division of mankind into a hierarchy of racial types.[26] By the Indian Removal Act of 1830, Andrew Jackson legalized the forced movement of countless Indigenous persons, many of whom became sick and died along the infamous Trail of Tears. As Reginald Horsman writes, "The experience of the United States with the Indians in the first half of the nineteenth century helped to convince many Americans that American expansion might mean the eventual extinction of inferior races that lacked the innate ability to transform their way of life."[27]

It is important to understand this context to appreciate the U.S. reaction to the British championship of the Mosquito Kingdom in Central America. For a burgeoning nation that regarded Indigenous populations as obstacles to progress, the British position on the Shore was doubly problematic: first, on a philosophical level on a distinct difference in attitude towards Indigenous populations; second, on a pragmatic level on what could be the repercussions in the United States of the precedent of Great Britain interfering in sovereign nations on the side of Indigenous populations. This comes through clearly in reports published in Whig newspapers like the *New York Courier and Enquirer*. In its October 25 edition, for instance, the newspaper reported on the Mosquito question,

---

[25] Robert Walter Johannsen, Sam Haynes, and Christopher Morris, eds., *Manifest Destiny and Empire: American Antebellum Expansionism* (College Station: Texas A & M University Press, 2008), 5.

[26] John Jackson and Nadine Weidman, *Race, Racism, and Science: Social Impact and Interaction* (Santa Barbara: ABC-CLIO, 2004).

[27] Reginald Horsman, *Race and Manifest Destiny: The Origins of American Racial Anglo-Saxonism* (Cambridge, MA: Harvard University Press, 2009), 207.

where the author compared British actions in India with those in Nicaragua and its possible impact on the United States:

> There [in India] we have seen ... entire kingdoms swallowed up and absorbed, until nearly the whole of the East has been stolen from its legitimate masters, and annexed to the British crown ... And how has all this been accomplished? How except under the specious plea of "protection" to the native chiefs? Such "protection" as the vulture gives to the dove, such "protection" as she will have right to offer to every Indian chief within our own territory, if the Government of the United States once submit to her preposterous claims to interference upon this continent.[28]

Indeed, the press reactions to the Mosquito question allow us to understand the deep-seated anxieties that informed U.S. perception of the situation in Nicaragua. The parallels between events in Mosquito Coast and the United States loomed large. Just as the expanding United States had displaced Native Americans on its way to becoming a continental nation, so too the Miskitus were increasingly seen as obstacles in the path of Nicaragua's quest to control the canal route. In light of this, the British championship of Miskitus had disturbing implications for American expansionism. Thus, the *New York Courier and Enquirer* warned:

> if we recognize the authority of England to make such Treaty, or give such "protection" to the Mosquito chief, as she claims to have made and given, in defiance of Nicaragua, we are equally bound to recognize her right to treat with and give similar protection to our own Indian chiefs. And once we concede this, and we shall soon have the "philanthropy" of England exhibited in treating with and giving protection to the Indian chiefs on the borders of our great lakes and rivers, and controlling our commerce and disputing our sovereignty from the banks of Lake Michigan to the shores of the Pacific.[29]

Thus, for the United States, the question of the Mosquito Coast was not simply a diplomatic issue but rather held the potential to shape the narrative of what was transpiring within the United States.

The Mosquito question was especially problematic, since from a diplomatic point of view, the United States and Great Britain appeared to agree on all other major points regarding the isthmian canal through Nicaragua. Both powers were keen on guaranteeing the neutrality of the proposed route. Both had much to gain from a canal connecting the Atlantic and the Pacific Oceans – for Britain, it would ease connection

---

[28] "The Mosquito Question," from the *New York Courier and Enquirer*, October 25, 1849, FO 420/10.
[29] Ibid.

to its Asian interests, for the United States, the canal was essential for connecting the newly acquired territories in the Western frontier, such as California, to the mainland. Both recognized the economic potential of the canal, but neither wanted exclusive rights of passage through it. Moreover, both powers had the capital at their disposal to undertake such a project. At the same time, discord between the two powers could potentially deter private capital investment in the project. And above all, as official correspondence makes clear, the governments of both countries balked at the idea of being drawn into a conflict with each other over a narrow strip of territory in Central America. There is also evidence that Britain and the United States toyed with the idea of an Anglo-Saxon alliance in Central America – a racial philosophy that had ironically been an outgrowth of Manifest Destiny in the United States.[30] At the same time, the action of agents on the ground in Central America increasingly threatened to bring matters to a head.

The spark that ultimately galvanized efforts of both Britain and the United States to come to a swift mutual understanding over the issue emanated from the misguided efforts of Squier and his British counterpart, Frederick Chatfield in Honduras. From the start, both British and American officials on the ground had recognized the importance of gaining the support and confidence of Central American nations in their position on the Mosquito question. While British agents like Consul Christie had attempted to establish convivial relations with Costa Rica, the efforts of Squier had been focused on reviving the Chinandega Pact. Although the Central American Federation had collapsed by 1841, the dream of uniting the Central American republics never really disappeared. In 1842, there was another attempt to create a federation comprising Nicaragua, El Salvador, and Honduras known as the Pact of Chinandega, which also failed by 1844. In 1849, Squier tried to revive this pact to challenge Mosquito sovereignty. As Squier tried to rally support among Central American nations, Frederick Chatfield, the British consul in Central America, took it on himself to frustrate Squier's designs. Indeed, the rest of the troubled year of 1849 would be an exercise in one-upmanship with both Squier and Chatfield attempting to carve a sphere of influence in the region.

Relations between the two agents would reach a breaking point in October 1849. On October 16, in an unprecedented show of recklessness,

---

[30] See Horsman, *Race and Manifest Destiny*.

Chatfield authorized the seizure of Tigre Island on the Gulf of Fonseca off the Pacific coast of Honduras. On that day, Chatfield arrived at Tigre Island accompanied by eighty armed men in five longboats. The boats proceeded to fire on the town, while the troops landed on the island with muskets over their shoulders. The British forces pulled down the flag of Honduras and hoisted the English standard. Outnumbered and outgunned, the paltry Honduran force at Tigre Island had no choice but to submit to this humiliation.[31] While Nicaragua disputed Mosquito authority on the southern part of the Mosquito Coast, Honduras denied it on the northern side. Moreover, on the Pacific side, Tigre Island had a strategic position as a possible western terminus of the projected transisthmian canal. While the British government immediately reprimanded Chatfield for his impetuous actions and withdrew from Tigre Island to defuse tensions, the damage had already been done. The American press immediately pounced on this latest British infraction and presented it variously as a precursor to an imminent war in Central America, as an expression of British high-handedness, and a portent of new difficulties between Great Britain and the United States.[32] While American newspapers generally presented British actions in Tigre Island in a negative light, some newspapers also took aim at the rivalry between Squier and Chatfield. The *Farmer's Cabinet* remarked sarcastically that "Here is not mere casus belli, but 'horrida belllli' ... Two great nations rushing into war to sustain the foolish actions of two men who ought to have been employed in planting potatoes."[33] In a similar vein, the *Salem Gazette* observed: "As the matter appears now, it looks very much as if these two gentlemen – Messrs. Squier and Chatfield – were 'fighting on their own hook.'"[34]

The U.S. government also reacted to the news of the seizure of Tigre Island by taking a firm stand against British actions. Clayton asserted his government's inflexible determination to protect the canal route:

We have not desired to annex or colonize any part of the country, but we shall not be restrained by any act of the British government from treating with Honduras or Nicaragua ... We have frankly avowed to Great Britain, and she must fully have understood it, that our object is to protect a canal across the isthmus. She is fully

---

[31] Vicente Lechuga to the General in Chief, October 16, 1849, Doc 75, *Tigre Island and Central America, Message from the President of the United States, Transmitting Documents in Answer to a Resolution of the House Respecting Tigre Island, etc., etc.* (Washington, DC: GPO, 1850), 219.
[32] See, for example, *Easton Star*, December 18, 1849; *Pittsfield Sun*, December 20, 1849; *Washington Reporter*, December 19, 1849.
[33] *Farmer's Cabinet*, December 20, 1849.   [34] *Salem Gazette*, December 14, 1849.

aware that the lakes of Nicaragua and León furnish the most eligible route and means for feeding such a canal; and whether the canal should terminate in the Pacific, at Realejo, within the confines of Nicaragua, or at the gulf of Fonseca, within those of Honduras, we mean to protect it, with the consent of the States through which it may pass.[35]

Squier on his part appears to have anticipated Chatfield's designs on Honduras and by September 1849 had already concluded a treaty with Honduras by which he had gained the cession of Tigre Island for the United States. For Squier, it was critically important to prevent Tigre Island from falling into British hands. "The Gulf of Fonseca," he wrote, "*must* be *free* or the Canal will be worthless, for it will inevitably terminate there."[36]

While the popular narrative in the United States saw Great Britain as an adversary, on the ground, diplomatic officials from both countries sought to find a way out of these increasingly hostile bilateral relations. Interestingly, the conflict generated by the Tigre Island incident may have hastened the process of arriving at a mutual understanding between the diplomats representing the two powerful nations. Chatfield's precipitate action in Tigre Island and the subsequent firm stand of the United States on the issue underlined the seriousness of both powers in protecting the canal route. It also showed with frightening clarity that the two great nations indeed could come to war over the canal question unless immediate steps were taken to resolve the mutual antagonism that had escalated over the past year. The two main figures who would attempt to resolve the situation would be Sir Henry Lytton Bulwer, British ambassador to the United States, and John M. Clayton. In December 1849 Bulwer arrived in Washington to begin negotiations with the United States over the canal question. The tenor of the first meeting between Bulwer and the American President Zachary Taylor was cordial and hopeful. Bulwer, on being presented to the president, expressed his belief that the two governments would act together "in extending the best interests of civilization through the two great divisions of the world."[37] Indeed, the trope of an Anglo-Saxon alliance between the United States and Great Britain to bring civilization to the backward and barbaric Central American nations

---

[35] John Clayton to Abbott Lawrence, December 29, 1849, Doc 75, *Tigre Island and Central America*, 315.
[36] Mary Wilhelmine Williams, "Letters of E. George Squire to John M. Clayton, 1849–1850," *Hispanic American Historical Review* 1:4 (November 1918): 428.
[37] *New Hampshire Sentinel*, January 3, 1850.

would mark subsequent rhetoric of the diplomats from the two nations as they attempted to smooth over the turbulent relations that had marked Anglo-American diplomacy for much of 1849.[38]

For Bulwer, the present situation in terms of the sentiment in the United States regarding Great Britain made a resolution of the differences between the two powers over the canal route of paramount importance. For one, the U.S. government under Zachary Taylor was politically weak, wrestling with a deeply divided Congress and strong opposition. Bulwer was aware that the opposition's clamor for a strong line with Britain would be difficult to resist in the Congress, especially if the national sentiment stoked by incendiary press reports also developed along the same line.[39] For Bulwer, the task of reconciliation could not be left to the agents on the ground like Hise, Squier, or Chatfield, who seemed motivated more by personal ambitions than national concerns. Rather, Bulwer found in Clayton someone who understood the need to restore normalcy in the relations between the two great powers, and the correspondence reveals a real sense of respect between the two diplomats. Both were also remarkably alike in their thinking, realizing that the source of contention between the two powers was not the canal so much as the position of the Mosquito Kingdom. Both agreed to exclude the contentious issues of disputes with Nicaragua and the question of the Mosquito Kingdom in framing a convention to resolve the canal issue. The resulting first draft of the Clayton–Bulwer Treaty focused exclusively on ensuring the neutrality of the canal route, making no mention of the Mosquito Kingdom, even though eventually the Mosquito Coast was included among the territories to be left uncolonized by either power.[40]

While the two diplomats tried to come to an amicable solution, the opposition-controlled Senate and House of Representatives demanded all the papers related to the dispute in Nicaragua. Bulwer saw this development with apprehension, observing to Palmerston that, "Were such papers laid before Congress, the discussions which would take place must, without any final arrangement of the whole matter being announced, lead to such angry discussions, and to the promulgation of such violent opinions on this side of the Atlantic, as would render subsequent understanding between the two governments of excessive

---

[38] Naylor, *Penny Ante Imperialism*, 183.
[39] Sir Henry Bulwer to Viscount Palmerston, January 6, 1850, FO 420/10.
[40] "Draft of Convention with Respect to the Isthmus Canal," Enclosure to No. 19, Sir Henry Bulwer to Viscount Palmerston, January 6, 1850, FO 420/10.

difficulty."[41] The British and U.S. governments thus tried to move quickly on finalizing the convention. While the final version of the Clayton–Bulwer Treaty included a nod to Squier Treaty with Nicaragua, in essence, it underlined the mutual understanding between the two powers by rejecting any exclusive control of the canal, guaranteeing neutrality of the canal, and stipulating never to "occupy, or fortify, or colonize, or assume or exercise any dominion over Nicaragua, Costa Rica, the Mosquito Coast, or any part of Central America." The last clause would be a source of future tensions between the two nations, but for the time being, the Clayton–Bulwer Treaty effectively halted the escalating tensions between the two great powers. The treaty was formally signed on April 19, 1850, and ratified by both the governments of Great Britain and the United States.

4.2 THE RACIALIZATION OF THE MOSQUITO QUESTION

While the Clayton–Bulwer Treaty provided a temporary plaster over the frayed relations between the great powers, on the ground, men like E. G. Squier continued their propaganda war. Often writing anonymously or under a pseudonym, Squier tried to mobilize American public opinion against British actions through a series of articles on the pages of periodicals and magazines like the *American Whig Review*, *Democratic Review*, and *Harper's New Monthly Magazine*. In these articles, Squier lampooned the Mosquito chiefs, presenting them as childlike savages who were essentially puppets in the hands of the British officials. In the February 1850 issue of the *American Whig Review*, Squier wrote an anonymous article where he described the Mosquito king as a "dog-eating potentate" and reprinted a description of a coronation ceremony that had appeared in a recent travelogue on Central America: "His Majesty seemed chiefly preoccupied in admiring his finery, and after his anointing, expressed his gratification by repeatedly thrusting his hands through his thick bushy hair and applying his finger to his nose; in this expressive manner indicating his delight at this part of the service."[42] In his other writings, including his later novel *Waikna* written under the pseudonym of Samuel Bard, Squier challenged the notion that there was anything Indigenous about these Mosquito chiefs. Rather, Squier

---

[41] Sir Henry Bulwer to Viscount Palmerston, February 3, 1850, FO 420/10.
[42] E. G. Squier, "British Encroachments and Aggressions in Central America: The Mosquito Question," *The American Whig Review* 26 (February 1850), 190.

presented the Miskitus as "blacks." In 1852, for instance, in the *Democratic Review*, he described the Mosquito Kingdom as a "negro monarchy," and in *Waikna*, Squier claimed that the Miskitus were all with few exceptions "unmitigated negros."[43] In *Waikna*, Squier described his first encounter with a fictitious Mosquito king, "George William Clarence": "I soon saw who was the real 'king' in Bluefields ... He is nothing more or less than a negro, with hardly a perceptible trace of Indian blood and would pass at the South for "a likely young fellow worth twelve hundred dollars as a body-servant."[44] Squier's depiction of "Captain Drummer" (see Figure 4.1), a barefoot Miskitu chief dressed in a plume hat and an ill-fitting British naval uniform, was meant to portray the incongruity and ridiculousness of British influence on the Shore.[45]

Squier was not alone in this scathing commentary on the Miskitu people. The Gold Rush gave rise to a slew of travelogues describing the adventures and experiences of traveling Westward. Almost a hundred travelogues were published in the second half of the nineteenth century. Among these was John M. Letts' *Illustrated California* (1853), describing his journey to California via the two canal routes of Nicaragua and Panama in 1849. Letts' travelogue reflected the contemporary American view of British involvement in Central America. Thus, he notes sarcastically in the travelogue, "The philanthropy of Great Britain has become proverbial ... Great Britain, in her superior wisdom, however, decided that as Nicaragua had no particular use for seaports, they would be better in other hands, even if *she herself* should be *compelled* to assume the protectorate." Letts' description of the Mosquito king was equally disparaging: "Here was a great man, a chief, In actual possession of the country, i.e. he had actually hunted 'possums there for a period of six months!"[46]

Whether in the annals of the Whig newspapers of the day or in novels and travelogues, contemporary American writers recognized that the crux of the dispute over the canal route between Britain and the United States lay in the question of the Mosquito Kingdom. The British argument for holding on to the critical area around the San Juan River along the Nicaragua Canal route had been the need to protect the sovereignty of

---

[43] Sam A. Bard, *Waikna: Adventures on the Mosquito Shore* (New York: Harper & Bros., 1855), 58.
[44] Ibid., 64. See also Olien, "Miskito Kings and the Line of Succession," 224–225.
[45] Bard, *Waikna*, 93.
[46] John Letts, *Pictorial View of California Including a Description of the Panama and Nicaragua Route* (New York: Henry Bill, 1853), 165.

FIGURE 4.1 A depiction of a Miskitu "captain" in E. G. Squier's *Waikna*. Source: Sam A. Bard, *Waikna: Adventures on the Mosquito Shore* (New York: Harper & Bros., 1855). Digitized by the Library of Congress.

the native Mosquito Kingdom. By publishing derogatory accounts of the Miskitu people and by claiming they were African rather than Indigenous, men like Squier hoped to undermine Mosquito claims to the region. "In his [Squier's] view," writes José Lara, "racial (blood) purity was a requirement for territorial claim." By presenting Miskitus as "Africans," Squier sought to challenge the Miskitu Indigenous identity and instead portray them as "interlopers."[47] According to anthropologist Michael Olien, Squier's writings impacted later scholarship on Central America, perpetuating a belief that the Miskitu chiefs were black and that they were puppets in British hands.[48]

The racialization of the Miskitu as "blacks" reflected the deep embeddedness of the question of race in nineteenth-century American expansionism. Writing about the Mexican–American War, Peter Guardino posits that "Expansionist Americans had to construe Mexicans as constituting an inferior race to justify taking their land, and racism was central to American nationalism during the war."[49] The question of slavery loomed large over the acquisition of territory during American Westward expansion, including that of Texas. By the 1850s, a "pervasive" antiblack attitude characterized the sentiment in America, even in free states.[50] As Pulitzer prize-winning historian Daniel Howe writes: "Above all, westward expansion rendered inescapable the issue that would tear the country asunder a dozen years later: whether to expand slavery."[51] In the context of American racial anxieties as it expanded Westward, thus, questions of race and indigeneity became paramount in canal rivalries. By presenting the Miskitu Indigenous as "blacks," Americans sought to bury the guilt of Indigenous removal in the Westward expansion and justify their actions both on their own soil and in the tropical environs of the Mosquito Coast. The narrative of Miskitus as "blacks" would be subsequently appropriated by the Nicaraguan government as it sought to wrest control of the Mosquito Coast from British hands.

---

[47] Jose Lara, "US Travel Writer E. G. Squier and the Construction of Racialised Geographies in Nineteenth Century Honduras," *Bulletin of Latin American Research* 38:2 (2018), 127.

[48] Michael Olien, "E. G. Squier and the Miskito: Anthropological Scholarship and Political Propaganda," *Ethnohistory* 32: 2 (Spring 1985): 125.

[49] Peter Guardino, *The Dead March: A History of the Mexican–American War* (Cambridge, MA: Harvard University Press, 2017).

[50] Horsman, *Race and Manifest Destiny*, 274.

[51] Daniel Walker Howe, *What Hath God Wrought: The Transformation of America, 1815–1848* (New York: Oxford University Press, 2007), 852.

4.3 THE CANAL AND THE NICARAGUAN NATIONAL PROJECT

Despite the incursion of the United States into Mexico following the Mexican–American War, many in the Nicaraguan elite remained enamored of the possibilities of an alliance with the United States, particularly in building its canal and resisting British designs on the isthmus. Frances Kinloch Tijerino writes: "While the North American guns roared on Mexican soil, the Nicaraguan newspaper *Registro Oficial* urged legislators to prove themselves "worthy disciples of the immortal Washington."[52] Nicaraguans saw in the United States a political model to admire and emulate. At the same time, the annals of Nicaraguan newspaper *Correo del Istmo* reveal a deep-seated anxiety permeating the Nicaraguan elite following the Mexican–American War. The proximity of the War and Nicaragua's own internal political fragmentation and the inability to dislodge the British from Mosquito Shore perturbed Nicaraguans, who saw in the Mexican–American War lessons for their own sovereignty.

For the Nicaraguan elite, the message of the War was clear: Central America needed to unite internally, as did Nicaragua. The *Correo del Istmo* of March 7, 1850, raised a clarion call:

Ask the gentlemen of the opposition: If because the Mexicans have followed an erroneous conduct, and by it have lost a part of their territory, suffered so many misfortunes, damages and humiliations, are we Central Americans obliged to follow this conduct; or if it is prudent to draw experience from our neighbor and avoid in time the evils that are being prepared?

As Central American nations such as Costa Rica sought to forge closer ties with the British government, the *Correo* lamented: "Instruments in the hands of the strongest, against ourselves, even the most incredible efforts have been made to divide us, to annihilate us, and to deliver us into the power of the enemy."[53] In looking at a Central American Federation to counter the perceived threat to its sovereignty, the Nicaraguan elite played into the ambitions of Ephraim Squier, who had instructions to promote the unification of Central America as a counter to the British threat in the region.

For the moment, the Nicaraguan elite also looked inward, finding within its own internally riven nation the fault lines that compromised

---

[52] Tijerino, *El Imaginario del canal y la nación cosmopolita*, 226.
[53] *Correo del Istmo*, August 1, 1849.

sovereignty. Not only did the rivalry of León and Granada weaken a united Nicaraguan front, but also the year 1849 was rife with conflict, with uprisings in Rivas and a riot in León. "Until when, then, Nicaraguans," asked the *Correo del Istmo* of July 1, 1849, "until when, Central Americans, will you be divided and stubborn?" In 1849, the answer appeared to be the Nicaragua Canal. As in the past, the dream of the canal had the effect of bringing together a temporary unity so that elites from León and Granada set their differences aside to welcome Ephraim George Squier during his visit to Nicaragua. The mid nineteenth century was a period of liberal nation-making in much of Latin America, with many countries redirecting themselves towards an export-oriented economy and attempting to shape their national identities, often along a racial line.[54] For the Nicaraguan elite, it was not social or economic reorganization that emerged as the basis of a national program but rather the all-consuming ambition to build an interoceanic canal. Even as Squier was welcomed into León in July 1849, the *Correo del Istmo*'s call for national unity was based largely on promises of the canal under the aegis of the United States:

Let us now set our sights from milestone to milestone on the canal work, let us pay attention to the noise it has produced throughout the world, and since we are sought, enlightened and protected by the sons of immortal Washington, we will take advantage of the opportunity, verifying that indissoluble union, without which the work that would make us immortal could not be proposed.[55]

According to Salvador Martí Puig, it was this orientation of the Nicaraguan nationalist project that distinguished it from its Central American neighbors and set it on a path of recurrent American intervention:

Unlike the neighboring elites, the attention and dreams of the Nicaraguan ruling class revolved around another endeavor: the building of the interoceanic canal. It was precisely because of this that there was no appeal to any social entity during the building process of the national imaginary (as the Guatemalan elites did with the hispanized collectives of the isthmus or the Costa Ricans did with the relatively homogenous population) but rather to a geographic singularity.[56]

---

[54] Brooke Larson, *Trials of Nation Making: Liberalism, Race, and Ethnicity in the Andes, 1810–1910* (Cambridge: Cambridge University Press, 2008).
[55] *Correo del Istmo*, July 16, 1849.
[56] Salvador Martí Puig, "Nicaragua: The Difficult Creation of a Sovereign State," in *State and Nation Making in Latin America and Spain: Republics of the Possible*, eds. Miguel Angel Centeno and Agustín Ferraro (Cambridge: Cambridge University Press, 2014), 139.

And yet, the reality was that Nicaraguan society did not itself have the means to achieve the dream of a canal without foreign intervention. Nicaraguan institutions in the mid-1840s were characterized by oligopoly and "bred anarchy."[57] Historian Pedro Francisco de la Rocha, referring to the outmoded education system in Nicaragua, lamented that there was not a single person in the country who could draw up a topographic plan capable of making sense of the possibilities of the interoceanic canal.[58] Moreover, in order to realize its ambitions for the canal, Nicaragua would first have to wrest control of the critical Mosquitian port of San Juan del Norte, which was increasingly becoming a British stronghold. The canal at the center of the Nicaraguan national project was thus predicated on gaining foreign assistance, a condition that made Nicaragua ripe for U.S. enterprise and intervention in the mid nineteenth century. In the long run, however, the unity imagined by the Nicaraguan elite around the canal project proved illusory. As Bradford Burns writes, "The economic vision of a transisthmian route, commerce, and agrarian exports guided the otherwise fractious patriarchal elites through destructive decades as they fumbled to forge the Nicaraguan nation."[59] The factionalism and disunity inherent in the Nicaraguan political structure would finally descend into outright civil war by 1854.

---

[57] E. Bradford Burns, *Patriarch and Folk: The Emergence of Nicaragua, 1798–1858* (Cambridge, MA: Harvard University Press, 1991), 37.

[58] Pedro Francisco de la Rocha, *Revista política sobre la historia de la revolución de Nicaragua: En defensa de la administración del ex-Director Don Jose León Sandoval* (Granada: Imprenta de la Concepción, 1847), reprinted in the *Revista del Pensamiento Centroamericano*, 180 (July–September 1983), 44.

[59] Burns, *Patriarch and Folk*, 36.

5

The Rise and Fall of Greytown

> Our pleasant little town [now] lies a heap of smouldering ruins.
> — Alexander Wood, July 15, 1854[1]

The U.S.S. *Cyane* sailed into the harbor of Greytown on July 11, 1854. The square-rigged, 132-foot corvette had played a significant role in the engagements of the Mexican–American War, capturing key locations like California, San Diego, and La Paz. Captain George Hollins, who commanded the *Cyane* and had previously served with distinction in the Barbary Wars, was instructed by the naval department to protect the interests of American citizens. These citizens, particularly those with investments in the Accessory Transit Company (ATC) – a venture created by American magnate Cornelius Vanderbilt to oversee the transport of passengers across the isthmus of Nicaragua – had seen their property threatened by the residents of Greytown. On the same day, the U.S. commercial agent in Mosquito Coast, Joseph Fabens, issued a statement in concert with Hollins demanding reparations for damages caused by residents of Greytown to the persons and properties of American citizens, particularly in the possessions of the ATC, amounting to a total of $24,000. At the noncompliance of the Greytown residents, on July 12, Hollins issued a proclamation: "I shall, at 9 a.m. of tomorrow, 13th instant, proceed to bombard the town of San Juan del Norte aforesaid, to the end that the rights of our country

---

[1] Alexander Wood to Samuel Smith Wood, July 17, 1854, *Samuel Smith Wood Papers, 1849–1920*, Howard Tilton Memorial Library, Tulane University.

and citizens may be vindicated, and as a guarantee for future protection."[2] One of the river steamers owned by the transit company landed armed marines from the *Cyane* at Greytown, who then proceeded to the town's police station and seized its muskets, cutlasses, and other weapons. On the afternoon of July 12, one of the transit company steamers towed the *Cyane* into position for bombarding the town. The commander of the British schooner *Bermuda*, which was anchored at Greytown at that time, entered a protest against Hollins' actions and proceeded to board forty to fifty British and French citizens of Greytown, mostly women, and loaded on the British consular papers. The rest of the Greytown residents retreated into the forests surrounding Greytown. On July 13, with the Mosquito flag still flying above the besieged harbor, the *Cyane* commenced its operations. From 9 a.m. to 3 p.m., the *Cyane* fired relentlessly at the town with shots and shells. After three to 400 rounds of ammunition had been fired, the marines landed from the *Cyane* into the city and proceeded to break into houses, looting and setting fire to them. The commander of the *Bermuda*, Lieutenant Jolly, reported that only three or four small houses were left standing; the rest of the town, including all the houses together with their contents, was reduced to ashes. He estimated a loss of property exceeding $500,000.[3] The inhabitants of Greytown scattered into the surrounding forests, bereft of shelter and supplies, exposed to the elements during the unhealthiest season on the coastline. The *Bermuda* immediately headed for Corn Island to find shelter for its passengers and dispatch news of the outrage to the British command in Jamaica.

The bombardment of Greytown was a turning point. The fledgling port town, which had managed to eke its way into rivaling Chagres as the entryway into a major transisthmian route, had literally gone up in smoke. The meteoric rise and the equally dramatic destruction of Greytown reveal the layers of conflict and violence underlying the Nicaragua Canal project in the mid nineteenth century. The moment laid bare the central contradiction of the interoceanic dream, where visions of connection rested on the fractured grounds of division and conflict. While on the one hand, it reflected the failure of the Clayton–Bulwer Treaty to

---

[2] George Hollins, "Proclamation," July 12, 1854, enclosed in *Message from the President of the United States Communicating, in Compliance with a Resolution of the Senate, Information Respecting the Bombardment of San Juan de Nicaragua*, Ex. Doc. 85, 33rd Cong., 1st Sess.

[3] Captain Jolly to Thomas Henderson, July 14, 1854, FO 53/34.

resolve the Mosquito question between Great Britain and the United States, on a deeper level the *Cyane* bombardment revealed the tensions at the local level in Greytown that had resulted from the town's transformation as the entry point of a transit line as well as the failure of the weak Nicaraguan state to maintain control over the canal route. While the *Cyane* bombardment exemplified U.S. gunboat diplomacy, the context of U.S. expansionism under the Pierce government added a veneer of legitimacy to the act of destruction, while the independent actions of American citizens in Greytown presaged the later phase of filibustering. In the aftermath of the *Cyane* bombardment, Nicaragua, which had entered the mid-century with dreams of a canal supported by American enterprise and money, plunged into a period of deep disillusionment and civil war. Paradoxically, this would result in an even more insidious phase of American intervention.

5.1 THE TRANSFORMATION OF GREYTOWN

Although British consular agents such as William Dougal Christie had early on recognized the crucial importance of Greytown as a strategic port town, the condition of the town prior to the Gold Rush had little to recommend it to sojourners. The skyline of Greytown consisted of a scattering of poorly built thatched huts. There were no hotels, no bars, no grocery stores, and no amenities to attract travelers. Two overworked police officers provided the only modicum of security in a town that for every real purpose existed outside the reach of British laws. The California Gold Rush was not just transformative for the United States; it also irrevocably changed the landscape and trajectory of Greytown. As impatient gold seekers from the East Coast of the United States sought to find the quickest route to get to the West Coast, many of them made the shrewd calculation that they would save time and money if they traveled through the isthmus of Nicaragua rather than through the unhealthy environs of the Panama route or, worse, on bumpy wagons across the breadth of the North American continent. The resulting influx of adventurous travelers had far-reaching consequences for the physical layout, demographics, governance, and character of Greytown.

The British consul, foreseeing the potential of this sleepy port, had shifted his headquarters to Greytown in 1849 from the town of Bluefields, which, despite also having a negligible Miskitu Indigenous population, continued to function as the residence of the Miskitu king. Lacking a reliable local labor pool, Christie made costly visits to Jamaica in the hope of attracting willing migrants who could populate Greytown. Christie even pushed for Jamaican convicts to be imported into the town. Christie, whose belief in British superiority neatly echoed the racist stereotypes that informed British policymaking in Central America, conveniently overlooked the local poor Nicaraguans or Indigenous Miskitus in this quest to populate Greytown and transform it into an oasis of British civilization in the corner of an unstable and "ungovernable" Hispanic mainland. Even as Christie sought to anglicize Greytown by importing Jamaican colonial subjects, the force of the Gold Rush itself was contouring Greytown in unanticipated ways.

In the context of the Gold Rush, the United States sought to come to an understanding with Great Britain, which already had a presence in Greytown and the Mosquito Shore, in order to ensure neutrality over the proposed transoceanic canal linking the Atlantic and Pacific Oceans through Nicaragua. The resulting Clayton–Bulwer Treaty (April 1850) guaranteed neutrality but omitted any mention of the contentious issue of the British protectorate over the Mosquito Kingdom, which claimed the strategic port of Greytown as part of its own Indigenous territory. In the aftermath of the signing of the Treaty, the American magnate Cornelius Vanderbilt – who, like many Americans, assumed the agreement signaled British withdrawal from the Mosquito Shore – threw himself into the gargantuan task of realizing the dream of a Nicaragua Canal. Initial reports on the canal route through Nicaragua seemed promising: one report from 1850 suggested that the Nicaragua route would save a week's journey over the Panama route.[4] Convinced that the Nicaragua route would prove to be a profitable enterprise and buoyed by the signing of the Clayton–Bulwer Treaty, Vanderbilt and his associates commissioned Colonel Orville W. Childs to complete a survey of the canal route. By 1851, Vanderbilt also sought to divide his operations by creating another organization, the ATC, which he was able to establish after obtaining a concession from the Nicaraguan government to start transit operations on the canal route.[5] While the American Atlantic and Pacific Ship Canal Company would be responsible for building the canal, the ATC would focus its operations on ensuring the smooth functioning and transit of passengers over the Nicaragua route.

---

[4] Folkman, *The Nicaragua Route*, 23.
[5] Mario Rodríguez, "The 'Prometheus' and the Clayton–Bulwer Treaty," *The Journal of Modern History* 36:3 (1964), 264.

On August 27, 1850, Childs and his team of fourteen engineers arrived at San Jorge on Lake Nicaragua to begin the work of the survey. While the report, which would finally be presented in 1852, identified the San Juan River valley–Lake Nicaragua waterway as the only feasible route from the Atlantic mouth of Nicaragua, during the survey, the engineering team confronted the geographical obstacles to navigation presented by the rapids on the San Juan River. Three major rapids – Machuca, Castillo, and El Toro – on different points of the San Juan made navigation challenging. The high velocity of water at these points and the presence of large rocks made navigation over these difficult. The San Juan River flowed in several channels to its Caribbean mouth. The main branch, Colorado, however, was impassable due to sandbars at its entrance. Although the branch connecting to the harbor of San Juan del Norte or Greytown carried only half the water as Colorado, it thus proved to be the only feasible entrance to the canal route. Even then, steamers often had difficulty passing through this point at low tide. Childs recommended that the harbor at Greytown be enlarged by jetties and excavation to deal with this problem. Despite the shortcomings, however, in his report submitted in March 1852, Childs pointed to the practicability of constructing a canal through the San Juan–Lake Nicaragua waterway to the harbor of Brito, north of San Juan del Sur. He estimated the total length of the canal at 194.4 miles, encompassing both natural waterways and artificial cuts. However, his recommended dimensions of the canal – 17 feet deep, 50 feet wide at the bottom, and 118 feet wide at the top – did not provide provisions for larger vessels, which often required depths of between 25 and 30 feet. Childs calculated that the canal could be built in 6 years at a cost of $31,538,319. Childs' recommendations received the approval of the Corps of the United States Topographical Engineers.[6]

Despite initial enthusiasm over the report, which resulted in a substantial rise in the price of shares in the ATC, Vanderbilt was unable to raise sufficient funds for the canal project.[7] Investors were particularly worried that the relatively shallow depth of the proposed canal would make it unworkable for large vessels, which were crucial for long-distance trade. The cost of increasing canal depth was prohibitively expensive at around

---

[6] Orville Whitmore Childs, *Report of the Survey and Estimates of the Cost of Construction the Interoceanic Ship Canal, from the Harbor of San Juan del Norte, on the Atlantic, to the Harbor of Brito, on the Pacific, in the State of Nicaragua, Central America, Made for the American Atlantic and Pacific Ship Canal Co. in the Years 1850–51* report (New York: W.C. Bryant, printers, 1852), 137; Folkman, *The Nicaragua Route*, 35.

[7] Folkman, *The Nicaragua Route*, 36.

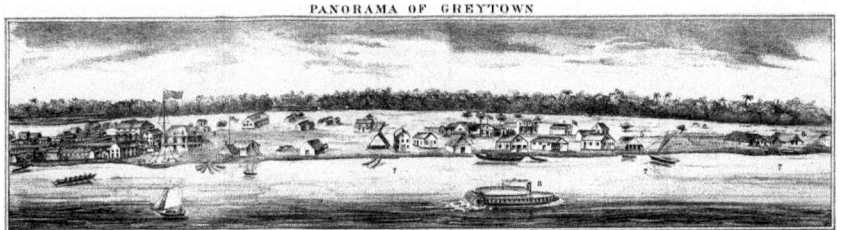

FIGURE 5.1 Panorama of Greytown. Source: British Library.

$100,000,000.[8] As hopes of realizing the dream of building a canal became increasingly out of reach, Vanderbilt – ever an astute businessman – now focused his energies on providing transit services to passengers who needed to cross the isthmus. The Nicaragua route thus steadily transformed from a site of a canal route to that of a *transit* route. During the period 1850–1851, the cost of a transit ticket across the isthmus on Vanderbilt's transit route was $40. Despite the attempts by Panama transit interests to create bad press for the Nicaragua route, Vanderbilt's line grew in popularity, and by the end of 1851, he was operating the line with a range of steamships, including the *Prometheus*.[9]

Greytown, that humble port town, which had become the headquarters of the British consul on the Mosquito Shore, soon began to assume a critical importance as the entry (and waiting) point for the transit down the San Juan River. Considered more habitable than the corresponding port of Chagres in Panama, Greytown's population soon became an eclectic mix of Americans, Europeans, Nicaraguans, and black Jamaicans. With the opening of Vanderbilt's transit line, a veritable transformation affected this once sleepy harbor. American-style wooden houses with verandas began to appear along the central square of the town, as did two-storied hotels and other buildings for administration and business. To cater to the steady influx of travelers, the town now offered recreational facilities and grocery stores with imported foodstuffs. An image of Greytown from 1851 suggests a bustling port of whitewashed houses and a harbor busy with the traffic of bungos, yachts, and steamships (see Figure 5.1). A Mosquito flag – a visible sign of the claims of the Mosquito Kingdom to this port – fluttering above the main plaza at the entrance to the town welcomed weary travelers as they made the long trip between the coasts of the United States.

[8] Ibid.   [9] Ibid., 33.

While port cities and termini have historically been locales of cosmopolitan, multiethnic cultures, the mixed population of Greytown presented a specific threat to both British and U.S. dreams of a transoceanic canal route. For the British, the increasing Americanization appeared to undermine the British character of Greytown. This was significant as one of the main ways in which the British entrenched themselves in the Mosquito Shore was through the local acceptance and even imitation of British ways. On the other hand, the presence of a large population of black Jamaicans in Greytown seemed to challenge U.S. ideals of a progressive "white" terminus for a project that ultimately epitomized nineteenth-century innovation and modernity. Time and again, thus U.S. interests in Greytown attributed lawlessness in the port not to the actions of white Americans – although they were the vast majority of newcomers in the town – but to the unbridled passions of black immigrants.

By 1851, the population of Greytown was only 500 – including a large percentage of Americans – but on the rise.[10] By 1853, there were more Americans resident in Greytown than in the employment of ATC.[11] Despite the strategically important location of Greytown at the mouth of a potential canal route, the British metropolitan government proved reluctant to provide any real defensive aid or pecuniary support to the government of Greytown under British Consul James Green. While the British sought to station warships in Greytown following the signing of the Clayton–Bulwer Treaty, practical considerations, including the cost of stationing a warship and the propensity of officers to fall sick after a stay at the harbor, made many naval commanders reluctant to send their ships to Greytown. Indeed, many commanders feared that the very presence of warships in Greytown could precipitate conflict with the United States. The situation proved untenable in the face of the threat from Nicaragua, where political instability fed into desperation, opportunism, and a desire to wrest Greytown from the grasp of the Mosquito Kingdom.

The vacillation of the British government on the question of Mosquito sovereignty and claim to Greytown certainly added to the vulnerability of

---

[10] George de Gerning to Sir Henry Bulwer, September 15, 1851, Inclosure in No. 171, Sir Henry Bulwer to Viscount Palmerston, October 25, 1851, FO 420/10.

[11] T. J. Martin to U.S. Secretary of State, March 3, 1853, enclosed in *Message from the President of the United States Communicating in Compliance with a Resolution of the Senate, Information in Relation to the Transactions between Captain Hollins, of the United States Ship Cyane, and the Authorities at San Juan de Nicaragua*, Ex. Doc. 8, 33rd Cong., 1st Sess.

Greytown. The Clayton–Bulwer Treaty deliberately omitted any mention of the Mosquito Kingdom in its agreement over the canal route, although the Mosquito Coast itself had been included. Following the signing of the convention, this issue reared its head in the U.S. Senate, which was especially critical of what it perceived to be the continuance of British presence on the Mosquito Shore and its support for the Mosquito Kingdom. The Senate believed that the British maintenance of a protectorate on the Mosquito Shore was a contravention of the Clayton–Bulwer Treaty, which stipulated that neither nation would establish dominion or control over any part of Central America. In fact, the British government was also more and more inclined towards washing its hands off the Mosquito protectorate. On April 28, 1850, just nine days after the signing of the Clayton–Bulwer Treaty, Henry Bulwer, the British minister to Washington and a key negotiator of the Treaty, expressed to Viscount Palmerston, the secretary of state of Britain for Foreign Affairs, that "we have no longer any interest in maintaining the Mosquitos."[12] Palmerston, on his part, clearly felt that protecting the Mosquito Kingdom was increasingly inconvenient and potentially a source of distrust with the United States.

On the status of Greytown, Great Britain felt that an amicable withdrawal was on the cards, although Palmerston voiced concerns about leaving Greytown to be governed by the Mosquito Kingdom. Palmerston firmly believed, as a port of strategic and international importance, that Greytown should be under the control of an efficient and organized government – something he was convinced was patently impossible for the Indigenous chief of the Mosquito Kingdom to provide. The terms of the Clayton–Bulwer Treaty clearly eliminated either Great Britain or the United States from assuming administrative control over the port. As the British government toyed with the idea of transferring sovereignty of Greytown to the friendly – and relatively stable – republic of Costa Rica, Greytown became the target of Nicaraguan reprisals.

In April 1850, at the instigation of a Nicaraguan commander of the San Carlos fort on the San Juan River, 100 Nicaraguan bungo men stormed into Greytown armed with long Spanish knives, demanding that Greytown be returned to Nicaragua. The Mosquito authorities at Greytown managed to rebuff the attack by charging at the bungo men with their bayonets. On the following morning, the Greytown authorities

---

[12] Henry Bulwer to Viscount Palmerston, April 28, 1850, *British and Foreign State Papers 1850–51*, vol. 40, 1031.

decided to make an example of one of the captured boatmen by flogging him at the Mosquito flagpole. In retaliation in May 1850, a band of armed Nicaraguans set fire to three bungos belonging to the Greytown merchant Mr. Bescher on Lake Nicaragua and began to proceed towards the port town with the intention of attacking and burning it. Helpless to defend Greytown without an armed force beyond a handful of policemen, Green appealed to Captain Nolloth of the British ship *Plumper*, which was fortuitously passing through the Greytown harbor at that time. While the immediate threat was averted, in the absence of a permanently stationed ship of war, Greytown was still easy prey. By June 1850, rumors circulated of Nicaraguans strengthening their forts and garrisons on the upper San Juan River at San Carlos and Castillo Viejo.[13] Taking things into his own hands, Green sought to increase the police force in Greytown to twelve men and acquired a howitzer and some arms and ammunition from the British warship *Trincomalee*. The lack of metropolitan aid had one important consequence. For better or worse, the British consuls stationed in the Mosquito Shore had since the early 1840s begun to operate with considerable autonomy from the British Foreign Office. At this important juncture in Greytown history, when the port was poised to play a prominent international role, the indifference of the British government to the security and pecuniary needs of Greytown allowed for Green to follow the tradition of independent action that had characterized his predecessors. Frederick Chatfield, the British agent in Central America – who, like other agents on the ground, maintained an independent streak – also encouraged Green to increase the hold of the Mosquito Kingdom on Greytown.[14] It was this increasing self-reliance that would prove to be the proverbial tinderbox.

Even before the signing of the Clayton–Bulwer Treaty, Frederick Chatfield had urged James Green to draw up a schedule of tariff duties payable by vessels at the harbor of Greytown to offset the expenditures of administering the port. On April 15, 1850, the port collector of Greytown, J. M. Daly, issued a public notice, which enumerated the duties payable by ships plying the harbor. Any disobedience of port regulations or lack of payment of these duties was now punishable by monetary fines or seizure of goods and cargo. Vanderbilt's American Atlantic and Pacific Ship Canal Company soon began to run into trouble with the port authorities at

---

[13] Charles Grey to Earl Grey, June 7, 1850, Enclosure in No. 85, FO 420/10.
[14] Frederick Chatfield to Viscount Palmerston, Nos. 30–36, plus Enclosures, April 8–10, 1850, FO 15/64.

Greytown. While the Clayton–Bulwer Treaty promised to establish free ports at both ends of the Nicaragua canal route, the status of Greytown and the question of whether Greytown should be made a free port became hotly debated, with Palmerston expressing his worries that a "free" Greytown would ultimately become a U.S. stronghold. When the representative of the American Atlantic and Pacific Ship Canal Company, Joseph White, complained to Henry Bulwer about port duties at Greytown, the British minister advised him to exercise discretion, remarking that until the status of Greytown was fixed, the British Agent James Green was "entirely independent." To be fair, Bulwer followed up by issuing a request to Green to conduct himself in a conciliatory manner with the representatives of the company: "You should ... endeavour to avoid, as far as is consistent with your duty, every unpleasant difference with the citizens of the United States."[15] By September 1850, the Foreign Office insisted that all vessels connected to the project of the canal should be exempted from duties at Greytown.[16]

While diplomatically, a free Greytown was desirable, the situation on the ground became increasingly untenable. Faced with threats from Nicaragua and internal lawlessness, Green authorized the purchase of building materials and labor for the erection of a police station in Greytown. Green also ordered the clearing of land in the areas surrounding the port in order to reduce the prevalence of mosquitos and sandflies around Greytown and make it more habitable. With profits from mahogany cutting having dried up since 1848, the tariffs on goods and duties on vessels were now the only source of income to offset what Green considered to be necessary expenses for the improvement of the port.[17] Mr. Livingstone, the U.S. consul in Nicaragua, while passing through Greytown, urged the agents of the Canal Company and other American citizens in the town to disregard Mosquito authorities. As a result, American vessels increasingly refused to pay duties or comply with Greytown regulations. More worrying still, American travelers passing through Greytown also reportedly disregarded the Mosquito authorities, "acknowledging no authority but force." This troublesome attitude was also reflected in the behavior of the employees of the Ship Canal Company, who consistently refused to adhere to the laws and regulations of Greytown.[18]

---

[15] Henry Bulwer to James Green, June 29, 1850, Inclosure 3 in No. 80, FO 420/10.
[16] Viscount Palmerston to Henry Bulwer, September 11, 1850, FO 420/10.
[17] James Green to Viscount Palmerston, April 18, 1850, FO 53/23B.
[18] James Green to Robert Smart, September 13, 1850, FO 53/23B.

Despite the differences with the authorities of Greytown, by spring 1851, it was becoming clear to Vanderbilt that if the Nicaraguan project was to stand a chance against the Panama route, he would need to take swift and decisive action. By April 1851, the task of building a transit line through the San Juan–Lake Nicaragua waterway, leading up through a road to the Pacific port of San Juan del Sur, was butting up against problems of manpower and engineering. Writing to Chatfield, Vice-Consul Foster lamented,

> In the neighborhood of San Juan [de Sur], there is not even a hut, and the small indenture in the coast is scarcely sufficient for shelter for even a few fishing-boats, but they talk of running out of a sort of jetty to facilitate landings; it can never, however, be made available for sailing vessels from want of its capacity, and the strong northeast winds of the Papaguayo.[19]

While twenty men were initially assigned to work at the rapids of the San Juan to make them navigable, most fell sick, bringing the work to a halt. In contrast, the Panama route appeared to be flourishing with its railroad in an advanced stage. Steamers, which were already making good business ferrying people to Panama, were reluctant to make the detour to Nicaragua. It began to look like Vanderbilt had little chance to compete against the firm of Howland and Aspinwall, which owned eleven steamers running between California and Panama and did swift business. Sensing this as a do-or-die moment, Vanderbilt sprang into action, establishing a "temporary depot" in Punta Arenas across from Greytown for assembling river steamers and working on the transit line. By May 1851, word had gone around that Vanderbilt intended to commence the transit line from July.

The opening of the Vanderbilt transit line in August 1851 was greeted with enthusiastic reports in the American press. One correspondent, Smith Crane, who had embarked from San Francisco, then proceeded on mule from the Pacific terminus of the Nicaragua transit route to the Lake Nicaragua–San Juan waterway, described the journey in idyllic terms. Río San Juan, he gushed, was "the most romantic and beautiful river I have ever seen." On August 12, Crane reached New York from Greytown with 360 other passengers on board the steamship *Prometheus*, completing the entire coast-to-coast journey between San Francisco and New York in twenty-two days. Even Mr. Stout, another correspondent, who experienced some bone-chilling moments on the treacherous rapids

---

[19] Vice-Consul Foster to Frederick Chatfield, April 15, 1851, FO 420/10.

on the San Juan River, praised the transit service: "With good swift boats, gentlemanly commanders, and with a scenery to attract the eye studded with banana, orange, lemon, palm, and a thousand varieties of other trees, what shall deter the traveller from the United States in making a choice of this sure and practicable route."[20] Vanderbilt erected a wharf, offices, shelters, and a coaling station at Punta Arenas to service the transit operations.

Despite the excitement associated with the opening of the Vanderbilt line, public opinion in the United States continued to be critical of the status of Greytown and, in particular, the British protectorate over the Mosquito Kingdom, which effectively controlled the port. A derisive press account published right after the opening of the Vanderbilt line, for instance, remarked, "The [Miskitu] Prince Consort is now in this town making a fence for a friend of mine ... British means to civilize these numerous tribes of Indians to subserve purposes of her own, to carry out her own deep subtle policy."[21] Similarly, the *New York Herald* of October 3, 1851, described the "Mosquito farce" as "disgusting and intolerable."[22] While Mosquito authorities faced open disobedience from the company employees, the political instability in Nicaragua also added to the urgent need to fortify Greytown's defense. Since its independence from the Federal Republic of Central America in 1838, Nicaragua had been plagued by internal rivalry and dissension between the Liberals in León and the Conservatives in Granada. While in 1849, the two factions briefly set aside their differences as Nicaragua signed the first canal contract with Vanderbilt's company, by 1851 the political instability in Nicaragua had led to a coup d'état by the Liberal leader General José Trinidad Muñoz, who overthrew the ruling Pineda government. News that Muñoz intended to attack Greytown led the residents to seek permission from Green to form their own national guard.[23]

Meanwhile, Green had been busy restructuring the administration of Greytown, granting exceptional powers to its leading citizens. On April 15, 1851, the residents of Greytown assembled at the behest of British Agent James Green and resolved to form a town government by electing five of the residents as aldermen, who, along with Green and the acting

---

[20] "Our Nicaragua Correspondence," J. F. Stout, July 29, 1851, FO 420/10.
[21] "Our Nicaragua Correspondence," August 3, 1851, FO 420/10.
[22] Extract from the *New York Herald*, October 3, 1851, Inclosure in No. 170, FO 420/10.
[23] Mr. George de Gerning to Sir Henry Bulwer, September 15, 1851, Inclosure in No. 171, FO 420/10.

magistrate, would constitute a council board. The council was vested with wide-ranging powers, including forming the laws and regulations of Greytown, electing officers and magistrates, and collecting taxes and revenues of Greytown and its port. In his letter to Palmerston on May 16, 1851, James Green justified the modification of Greytown's mode of government: "It [is] appearing to me very necessary as the Town is rising to some prominent, that the inhabitants should have a voice and responsibility in the construction and carrying out all Regulations for the Government of the Port and Town."[24] Now all at once, the stage was set for a confrontation between Vanderbilt's company now apparently poised to become the chief engine of Greytown's success and the newly minted and eager-for-action authorities of Greytown. The visible presence of company employees in Punta Arenas, who were viewed as usurpers of Mosquito territory, and the continued flouting by their vessels of port regulations at Greytown were quickly creating a pressure cooker situation that was about to explode.

5.2 THE *PROMETHEUS* INCIDENT

On November 21, 1851, the steamship *Prometheus* stood basking in the afternoon sun as it lay anchored in the harbor of Greytown. According to Greek mythology, Prometheus had brought the knowledge of fire to mortals against the wishes of the other gods. While humans prospered as a result, Prometheus was punished in the most macabre way: he was chained to a craggy mountain top, where every day an eagle swooped in to rip out his liver, which again regenerated until the eagle returned the next day. The steamship *Prometheus* was Cornelius Vanderbilt's passion project. He himself designed the engine of the 1,200-ton, triple-decker steamship. Prior to the construction of *Prometheus*, most oceangoing vessels had their machinery deep in the hull to avoid exposure to the elements. The "sidelever" engine, which was required to sail this type of ship, operated using a complex system of gearing that made the ship itself fuel inefficient. In February 1851, when Vanderbilt sailed the *Prometheus* from Nicaragua to New York, the vessel consumed just a third of the coal usually required of vessels of the same size and accomplished the voyage in just nineteen days.[25] As a harbinger of technology, *Prometheus* certainly lived up to its name. But it is the story of how the *Prometheus*

---

[24] James Green to Viscount Palmerston, May 16, 1851, FO 53/26.
[25] T. J. Stiles, *The First Tycoon* (New York: Vintage Books, 2013), 246.

ultimately resulted in a painful and long-drawn-out struggle over Greytown – a narrative with all the makings of classical retribution – that really underscores the human core of the technological saga of the Nicaragua Canal project.

On that winter afternoon, brimming with 500 Californians bound for the East Coast, the *Prometheus* readied to set sail. As Captain Churchill gave the signal and the boilers fired up, the ship was rattled by the force of a round shot fired over its stern. Passengers of the steamship watched helplessly as smoke billowed from the gunports of the British brig of war *Express*, which had closed in. The captain of the brig threatened to fire a bombshell at the *Prometheus* unless the steamer anchored immediately and ordered his crew to load the guns with grapeshot and canister. Indignation and anger erupted among the passengers. Firing on an unarmed civilian ship with passengers on board was nothing short of a violation of the basic norms of marine engagement. Californians on board, bristling with fury and injured pride, urged Churchill to resist the demand to anchor the ship. Vanderbilt, who had previously refused to recognize the authority of Greytown to levy duties on his vessels, now directed Churchill to return to the harbor, likely because even the shrewd businessman could no longer tell if the brig would carry out its threat. Churchill paid the amount under protest, and the steamer, now released by Greytown authorities, resumed its voyage to the United States, with a story that would ignite the American public and have far-reaching consequences on Greytown's bid to rival Chagres as the port of entry to a Central American transoceanic route.

The news of the attack on *Prometheus* caused international outrage. For one, the act of violence appeared to be intended to sabotage the construction of the proposed Nicaraguan Canal. As Joseph White, counsel of the Canal Company, pointed out, the *Prometheus* had been engaged in ferrying workers, engineers, and supplies for the work of canal construction. The money earned from ferrying passengers was meant to mitigate the expenses of the construction.[26] Secondly, the fact that a British warship had fired on an unarmed American vessel seemed to underline the threat that the British continuation of the Mosquito protectorate held for American interests in Central America. Even the British metropolitan government was aghast at the independent action taken by James Green in violently apprehending an American vessel, an

---

[26] Joseph White to Mr. Webster, December 2, 1851, Inclosure 1 in No. 179, FO 420/10.

act that was a flagrant violation of both the Clayton–Bulwer Treaty and British foreign policy towards the United States. The United States government responded by immediately despatching the warship *Saranac* to protect the interests of American citizens and commerce in Greytown. This would mark the beginning of the expansion of the U.S. presence in Greytown. By 1852, the United States would also station a commercial agent in Greytown to oversee its economic interests in the harbor.

On December 5, 1851, the American residents of Greytown wrote a letter justifying the actions of the Mosquito authorities against *Prometheus*. In it, they argued that the port duties charged had been moderate and were consistent with those levied on other vessels plying the port. Moreover, the residents asserted that the *Express* had only resorted to firing two rounds of shots at the vessel, after the *Prometheus* had ignored its warning shots fired using blank cartridges. In an apparent attempt to appeal to the irate U.S. public, the residents wrote,

> Nearly one-half the improved property is held, and more than one-half the business is done [in Greytown], by Americans. For good order and for safety of life and of property Greytown will compare favorably with any town in the country, and while Chagres has established an enviable reputation, and San Juan del Sur and Virgin Bay are following the same track, Greytown or San Juan del Norte presents the singular contrast of good order and safety, while almost surrounded by Spanish American anarchy.[27]

The residents of Greytown were not alone in defending the actions of the Mosquito government. George Law, for instance, who owned and contracted the U.S. Mail line steamers to Chagres, asserted that his vessels had always paid the harbor dues at Greytown, which he considered "just and moderate."[28] All the same, the damage was done. The British government disavowed the actions of the commander of the *Express* and issued an apology for the firing on the *Prometheus*. Green was sharply reprimanded for exceeding his authority and putting Great Britain in an embarrassing position. In his defense, Green reminded the Foreign Secretary Earl Granville that the British Foreign Office had never instructed either him or his predecessors, Patrick Walker and William Dougal Christie, to treat their duty as anything other than protecting the interests of the Mosquito Kingdom, which was what had essentially

---

[27] Letter Signed by American Citizens at Greytown, Respecting the *Prometheus*, December 5, 1851, Inclosure in No. 190, FO 420/10.
[28] John Crampton to Viscount Palmerston, December 15, 1851, FO 420/10.

motivated him to take action against *Prometheus*.[29] In 1851, following Palmerston's resignation as foreign minister and the recall of Chatfield, the British government continued to shift towards a peaceful resolution with the United States concerning the Mosquito Coast, a process that had already begun with the Clayton–Bulwer Treaty of 1850.

5.3 THE BOMBARDMENT OF GREYTOWN

Following the firing on *Prometheus*, Greytown achieved a semblance of calm with the great powers having apparently peacefully resolved their differences. But soon, cracks began to show, mainly as a result of developments in Punta Arenas and the growing divide between the town and the company. In the months following the *Prometheus* incident, the transit company transformed Punta Arenas into a self-sufficient unit, complete with hotels and barracks. As the entry point of passengers going Westward through Nicaragua, one of the main sources of income for Greytown had been the business created as a result of some 400 to 500 people disembarking from each steamship that stopped at Greytown and making their way Westward. The development of Punta Arenas threatened this source of livelihood. As the company infrastructure improved, the passengers disembarking from steamships went directly to Punta Arenas, from where, after availing the local services in the company enclosure, they embarked on transit company vessels to go up the San Juan River. The result was that Greytown was completely cut off from the profits of the transit route. One of the underlying reasons for this development was the shifting of focus from the ship canal route to the transit activities as a source of profit for the company. Lack of investment in the ship canal meant that by February 1853, the company had scrapped plans for the original ship canal and was proposing a smaller canal. Realizing the patent impossibility of profiting from a ship canal that seemed to resemble more and more a pipe dream, Vanderbilt sought to make the transit activities profitable enough to offset the difficulties with the ship canal. With stakes thus raised, it is no surprise that the company employees tried to monopolize the business of passengers who arrived at the port.

The U.S. government, determined to protect its commercial interests in Nicaragua in the wake of the *Prometheus* incident, despatched the frigate

---

[29] James Green to Earl Granville, March 6, 1852, FO 53/29.

U.S.S. *Saranac* under Commander Parker, which arrived in the harbor of Greytown on New Year's Day 1852. From the beginning, Parker assumed a firm stance, warning the commander of H.M.S. *Express*, which was also anchored at the port at the time, that he would not tolerate any British interference with the commercial interests of the United States on the Nicaraguan coast.[30] He alienated the Greytown leadership as well, referring to Greytown as "San Juan del Nicaragua" and rousing the anti-British sentiments of the disgruntled Nicaraguans. Thus writing to Palmerston on January 6, Green lamented, "The appearance of this American vessel has given spirit to the disaffected and the Nicaraguan cause; that there is an idea of endeavoring to restore this place to that territory."[31] Reprimanded for overstepping his authority in the *Prometheus* case, it was now Green's turn to retort, "I beg most respectfully to state the inutility of my remaining here to any good purpose to exercise any authority or to feel that my life is the least secure; for as certain as England wavers, so certain does anarchy and confusion, even to bloodshed, fully manifest itself in this town."[32] On March 29, 1852, Green withdrew from his position as chairman of the Greytown city council, and in the following month, the government of Greytown was reconstituted with a new constitution that claimed it as a free town. The new city government was dominated by American citizens, with an American as the city mayor.[33] In 1853, Samuel Smith Wood, an American merchant, was the president of the Greytown city council.[34] As the *New York Herald* reported, following the establishment of the new council, Greytown "became to all intents and purposes American."[35] At the same time, buoyed by the presence of U.S. warships and the arrival of a U.S. commercial agent, the ATC arrogantly denied the authority of Greytown over Punta Arenas, going so far as referring to the land as a territory under Costa Rica.[36] With canal hopes dashed, the stakes around transit activities (that now offered the only means of deriving profit from the route) heightened, leading to a tense situation on the ground.

Things finally came to a head in the spring of 1853 over the issue of quarantine land. In 1851, the transit company had been granted a spot of

---

[30] Earl Granville to Mr. Crampton, February 20, 1852, FO 420/10.
[31] James Green to Viscount Palmerston, January 6, 1852, FO 420/10.   [32] Ibid.
[33] Robert Walsh to Daniel Webster, May 28, 1852, Manning, Diplomatic Correspondence, vol. 4, 279.
[34] *Samuel Smith Wood Papers, 1849–1920*, Howard Tilton Memorial Library, Tulane University.
[35] *New York Herald*, July 26, 1854.
[36] James Green to Viscount Palmerston, January 6, 1852, FO 420/10.

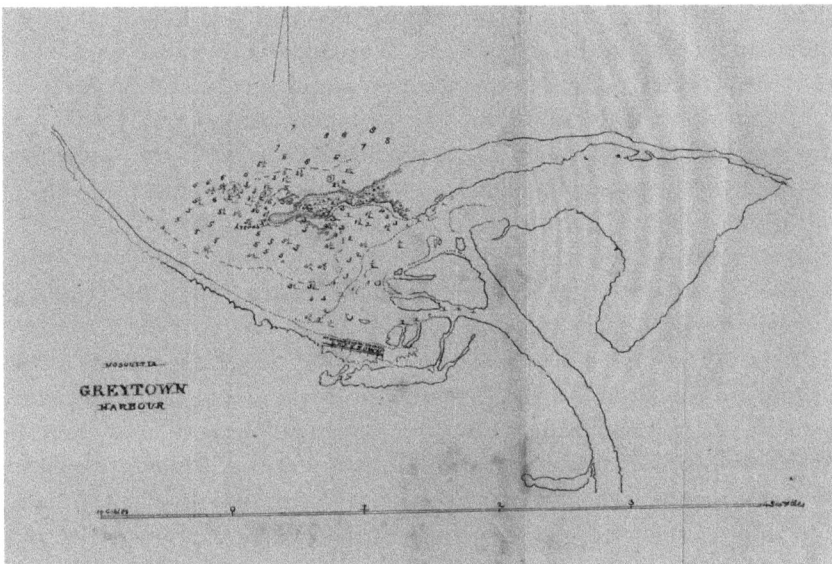

FIGURE 5.2 Map of Greytown showing the area occupied by the transit company. Source: Enclosure in James Green to John Russell, February 24, 1853, FO 53/31. Courtesy of the National Archives, Kew.

land in Punta Arenas measuring 200 by 400 feet on a monthly lease of six pence. The condition of the lease had been that the company would have to vacate the land on one month's notice should the Mosquito government require the spot for quarantine or other purposes. Neither did the company have the right to erect any buildings or extend its operations beyond the limits of that land. Sometime afterwards, however, the company began to erect hotels and houses in contravention of the prior understanding and refused to acknowledge the authority of the Mosquito government (see Figure 5.2). As the "sick" season of the spring approached, the Mosquito authorities demanded that the company vacate the land so that it could be used for quarantining sick people. They also issued an ultimatum: unless the company removed the buildings, which they had illegally erected, the city authorities would pull them down. When the company refused to give in to these demands, the Greytown government despatched a force of constables to Punta Arenas, where they proceeded to destroy some of the buildings.[37]

---

[37] Acting Consul Foote to Mr. Crampton, February 18, 1853; extract from the *National Intelligencer* of March 17, 1853, Inclosure 2 in No. 283, FO 420/10.

On February 18, 1853, Acting Consul Foote alerted John Crampton, the head of the British mission to Washington, of rising tension in Greytown, where citizens had started arming themselves in preparation for a showdown with the employees of the transit company.[38] By March, the situation seemed to be rapidly deteriorating, with the Greytown residents openly desecrating the American flag in Punta Arenas and infuriating public opinion across the Atlantic in the United States.[39] The agent of the company, Thomas Baldwin, immediately issued a protest, which was conveyed to the U.S. Secretary of State Edward Everett by the acting vice-commercial agent of the United States in Greytown, Henry Stevenson.[40] In his letter to Everett on March 2, Stevenson painted a dire picture of conditions in Greytown as a result of the open hostilities between the city authorities and the company employees: "The interests of this company in this country are in a very critical situation being in dispute – indeed at open warfare almost, with the local government here, and with the state of Nicaragua from whom they derive their charter and who will very soon seek to annul it."[41] On the afternoon of March 10, the U.S.S. *Cyane*, under Commander Hollins, arrived at the port of Greytown and by evening had landed a company of armed marines at Punta Arenas to defend the property of the ATC. The *Cyane* towed into position along Punta Arenas and established a blockade compelling all boats from Greytown to pass under its stern. In his ultimatum to the Greytown authorities on March 11, Hollins declared, "I have to state, most respectfully, that I cannot permit any depredations on the property of the Accessory Transit Company, whose depot is located upon Punta Arenas."[42] In a surprising turn of events, the Greytown mayor and authorities resigned their offices, describing Hollins' actions as an act of invasion and conquest, and hauled down the Mosquito flag under a twenty-one-gun salute.[43] Foote, who at the time had been visiting Bluefields for a "change of air," returned on the 14th, immediately re-

---

[38] Acting Consul Foote to Mr. Crampton, February 18, 1853, FO 420/10.   [39] Ibid.
[40] Henry Stevenson to Edward Everett, February 12, 1853, *Despatches from U.S. Consuls in San Juan del Norte, Nicaragua, 1851–1906*, U.S. State Department (hereafter *Despatches*), roll 1.
[41] Henry Stevenson to Edward Everett, March 2, 1853, *Despatches*, roll 1.
[42] Geo. Hollins to the Mayor of Greytown, March 11, 1853, enclosed in *Message from the President of the United States Communicating in Compliance with a Resolution of the Senate, Information in Relation to the Transactions between Captain Hollins, of the United States Ship Cyane, and the Authorities at San Juan de Nicaragua*, Ex. Doc. 8, 33rd Cong., 1st Sess.
[43] Acting Consul Foote to Mr. Crampton, March 18, 1853, FO 420/10.

hoisted the flag, and persuaded the Greytown city council to resume its functions.

The British Foreign Office understandably saw Hollins' actions as high-handed, considering that if a similar outrage had been perpetrated by the commander of a British ship, "but one voice of condemnation of such a proceeding would have resounded from one end of the United States to the other."[44] The United States government, on the other hand, gestured towards not just acknowledgment of but rather full support towards Hollins' actions with the President considering it the "unquestionable duty" of the commander of the *Cyane* to protect the ATC in the manner he had done."[45] While the damage due to Hollins' actions had been little in real terms – by March 1853, for instance, Consul James Green reported that the "best understanding" existed between Hollins and the British consular agents in Greytown[46] – it was an ominous sign of things to come.

Despite U.S. support of Hollins, the U.S. official presence in Greytown remained weak. In June 1852, the first commercial agent of the United States stationed in Greytown, Mr. Boone, had noted that what was needed in San Juan del Norte was a consular agent equal in power to its British counterpart.[47] He noted his own lack of authority as a mere commercial agent in a place that was wholly under British influence. Even American steamships that passed through Greytown paid little heed to the agent, often ignoring his requests for depositing their ship's papers with him. In September 1852, Boone would lament that although he had been called to protect American interests in Greytown, his situation as a commercial agent without even a vessel of war at his disposal meant that he was not even in a position to protect himself.[48] By January 1853, he had reached the end of his tether. He resigned, citing as his reason that he had "suffered so much in that country [Mosquito Coast]."[49] Vice-commercial agent, Henry Stevenson, who now took charge at Greytown, echoed Boone's concerns, writing to the U.S. secretary of state, Edward Everett, in March 1853 about the lack of respect accorded in Greytown towards the commercial agent.[50] Stevenson, as the only U.S.

---

[44] Earl of Clarendon to Mr. Crampton, April 29, 1853, FO 420/10.
[45] Mr. Marcy to Mr. Ingersoll, June 9, 1853, FO 420/10.
[46] James Green to Mr. Crampton, March 30, 1853, FO 420/10.
[47] Mr. Boone to Daniel Webster, June 5, 1852, *Despatches*, roll 1.
[48] Mr. Boone to Daniel Webster, June 5, 1852, September 23, 1852, *Despatches*, roll 1.
[49] Mr. Boone to Edward Everett, January 12, 1853, *Despatches*, roll 1.
[50] Henry Stevenson to Edward Everett, March 2, 1853, *Despatches*, roll 1.

official on the ground during *Cyane*'s first altercation with the Mosquito authorities in March 1853, expressed his concern with Captain Hollins' aggressive stance. On March 16, Stevenson wrote to Everett that

> the public feeling has been so exasperated by the Arbitrary, unwise and imprudent conduct of the commander of the *Cyane*, that I verily believe that had it not been for the strong personal regard entertained for the incumbent of this office that this agency would have been destroyed and its incumbent accommodated with a coat of tar and feathers by Americans – his own countrymen.[51]

Two months later, when Joseph Fabens succeeded Stevenson as agent, things were beginning to spiral out of hand. Unlike his predecessors, who had pressed for more local power to the agency, Fabens believed that the only solution was U.S. metropolitan action. On June 16, Fabens in the backdrop of increasing tension between Greytown and ATC, wrote to U.S. Secretary of State William Marcy that "I am of an opinion that no suitable indemnity can be obtained from the parties now in possession of affairs except by taking possession of, and holding the territory of Mosquito, so called, beneath whose flag the outrages in question were perpetrated."[52] With the U.S. commercial agency lacking in authority and resources on the ground, ordinary Americans of both Greytown and in the employ of ATC prepared to take up arms.

Over the spring and summer of 1854, Greytown apparently began to descend into chaos, with increasing reports of murders, robberies, and kidnappings in the port as well as destruction of ATC property. In this context, the strained relations between the ATC and the Greytown council precipitated an incident involving Solon Borland, the U.S. minister to Nicaragua. Borland, on board the steamer *Northern Light*, witnessed the American captain of another steamer shoot and kill a Nicaraguan bungo man on the San Juan River. The incident was precipitated by a growing conflict between local bungo boatworkers and American steamships over the changes wrought in sailing and working on the San Juan ever since the opening of the ATC.[53] Borland offered his protection to the captain, telling the Greytown leaders that they did not have any authority to arrest an American citizen. An irate mob of Greytown residents accosted Borland, and one of the crowd hurled a

---

[51] Henry Stevenson to Secretary of State, March 16, 1853, *Despatches*, roll 1.
[52] Joseph Fabens to William Marcy, June 16, 1854, *Despatches*, roll 1.
[53] See Miguel Angel Herrera C., *Bongos, bogas, vapores y marinos: Historia de los "marineros" en el río San Juan, 1849–1855* (Managua: Centro Nicaragüense de Escritores: 1999).

broken bottle at his face. In the aftermath of the Borland episode, a voluntary force of fifty armed guards under the command of Tennessee resident Crawford Fletcher pledged to defend American interests in Greytown. In this, Greytown created a precedent that would have significant future repercussions: the tendency of American citizens to take matters into their own hands in the absence of a strong U.S. official presence on the ground. Borland managed to return to Washington on board the *Northern Light*, where he reported the "insult" to his superiors. Washington responded with vehemence, sending the *Cyane* once more to Greytown to extract reparations and apologies from the Greytown authorities both for their continued theft and destruction of ATC property and their conduct towards a minister of the United States. The people of Greytown refused to accede to the demands. Instead, as U.S. commercial agent in Greytown, Joseph Fabens informed Hollins, "the chief actors and instigators [against ATC] are now in undisputed possession of the town, its arms and ammunition."[54] The battle lines, thus drawn, at 9 a.m. on July 13, the *Cyane* opened fire on the town (see Figure 5.3).

The bombardment of Greytown was a watershed moment. The unprecedented act of violence and the scale of destruction prompted widespread protests and calls for retribution against U.S. actions. Business interests, such as the representatives of the firm Messrs. Montgomery and Co., wrote to the Earl of Clarendon, asking, "What measures will be taken up against United States for the enormous crime perpetrated by the *Cyane*? The total amount of losses is one million dollars."[55] News of the bombardment rippled through Central America, the British Caribbean, and beyond. The *Gaceta de Guatemala* criticized U.S. action and attributed the bombardment to American corruption.[56] Governor Henry Barkley described the anxiety in Jamaica over the developments in Greytown: "A most painful sensation has been created in Jamaica by the news of the destruction of Greytown, no less on account of the violence of the act, and the proximity of the scenes, than of the long and intimate connection which has subsisted between the parts of the Mosquito Coast and this

---

[54] Joseph Fabens to Geo. Hollins, July 12, 1854, *Message from the President of the United States Communicating in Compliance with a Resolution of the Senate, Information Respecting the Bombardment of San Juan de Nicaragua*, Ex. Doc. 85, 33rd Cong., 1st Sess.
[55] Messrs. Montgomery and Co. to the Earl of Clarendon, August 31, 1854, FO 53/34.
[56] Documento 10, "Moralidad en Los Estados Unidos," Andrés Vega Bolaños, *1854: Bombardeo y destrucción del puerto de San Juan del Norte de Nicaragua* (Managua: Editorial Unión, Cardoza y Cía. Ltda., 1970).

FIGURE 5.3 Bombardment of Greytown by U.S.S. *Cyane*. Source: *L'Illustration, Journal Universel*.

Island."[57] M. Marcoleta, the Nicaraguan minister in Washington, immediately entered a protest demanding compensation and indemnification to Nicaraguan citizens and the government for the act of destruction.[58] Newspapers in Great Britain condemned the *Cyane*'s actions, detailing the scale of destruction and the wanton behavior of the instigators; the *Westmorland Gazette* reported:

> He [Hollins] fired about 200 shots, but, not burning up the town as he desired, he sent ashore a launch with a lieutenant and about twenty-five men, who proceeded to set on fire all that remained of Greytown. While doing so they are said to have inspected the interior of the buildings rather closely, and pillaged as much as they pleased. Before finishing this work they were pretty thoroughly intoxicated with wines and liquors and were constantly cheering. The amount of property destroyed by this bombardment is stated at 500,000 dollars. San Juan, or Greytown, on the 13th, was entirely destroyed.[59]

Following the bombardment, Fabens packed up the agency papers and prepared to head back to the United States with Captain Hollins.

The decline of Greytown had repercussions for Miskitu leadership as well. The bombardment of the town arguably reflected the failure of both the British and U.S. governments to satisfactorily resolve the "Mosquito question," which had been the main bone of contention in the Clayton-

---

[57] Henry Barkley to Sir George Grey, July 22, 1854, FO 53/34.
[58] "Abstract of a Correspondence between Mr. Marcoleta, the Nicaraguan Minister at Washington and the United States' Govt. in Consequence of the Proceedings of the Ud. States' Sloop of War '*Cyane*' and Greytown in July Last," October 26, 1854, FO 53/34.
[59] *Westmorland Gazette and Kendal Advertiser*, August 12, 1854.

Bulwer Treaty. Neither government was willing to include the Kingdom itself in the discussions around the fate of Greytown. Local Miskitu fishers and turtlers were increasingly displaced by the arrival of steamships on the San Juan.[60] By spring 1854, the Miskitu king appeared to reach a breaking point. On March 4, 1854, a proclamation by the Miskitu king, George Augustus, was pasted up in Bluefields announcing that henceforth he would, in his own person, assume "the supreme power in all matters connected with the government of this our Kingdom of Mosquito which has hitherto been exercised by Her Britannic Majesty's Consuls."[61] By 1854, there was evidence of increasing involvement of the Miskitu king in Moravian mission activities. In March 1854, for instance, the Miskitu king accompanied Brother H. G. Pfeiffer to Pearl Cay Lagoon to establish a church, and by 1855, Moravian missionaries appeared to provide counsel to the king in matters of internal law and discipline in the Miskitu territory.[62] Thus, as dreams of the interoceanic canal shattered in the wake of the *Cyane* bombardment, the Miskitu leadership also increasingly divorced itself from British influence and gravitated towards the Moravian mission.

5.4 UNITED STATES EXPANSIONISM AND LATIN AMERICA

Newspapers in the United States covered the dramatic incident, with New York-based newspapers taking a particularly critical stance towards the actions of the *Cyane*. Thus, describing the bombardment of Greytown as "the destruction of an American town by Americans," the *New York Herald* of July 26, 1854, wrote:

> The proximate cause of this bombardment and destruction of San Juan, it is said was a refusal on the part of the town to comply with certain demands made on behalf of the Nicaragua Transit Company ... the public, we think will agree with us in the opinion, that the refusal of San Juan to comply with their demands, afforded no adequate justification for the punishment inflicted upon the place. The civilized world will require to know if those demands were really just, before it can listen to any apology for the barbarity of the act, or relieve its perpetrators from the odium which rests upon them.[63]

---

[60] Herrera C., *Bongos, bogas, vapores y marinos*, 95
[61] Proclamation of King George Augustus Frederic, March 4, 1854, FO 53/34.
[62] H. G. Pfeiffer et al., "Extract of the Diary of Bluefields for the Year 1854," *Periodical Accounts Relating to the Missions of the Church of the United Brethren, Established among the Heathen* 22 (1856), 242–248.
[63] *New York Herald*, July 26, 1854.

Other U.S. newspapers, while reporting the incident in detail, remained cautious about overtly condemning the actions of the *Cyane*, especially in the face of the apparent official approval of Captain Hollins' actions. On September 4, a U.S. naval inspection of the *Cyane* turned into a quasi-celebration of Hollins' actions with the national brass band performing *Hail, Columbia!* and Lieutenant C.W. Pickering reading aloud a communication from the Navy "expressing unqualified approval" of Captain Hollins' actions in Greytown.[64] In his annual message to the Senate in December 1854, President Franklin Pierce placed the blame for the events in Greytown on the "heterogeneous assemblage gathered from various countries, and composed for the most part of blacks and persons of mixed blood" and justified the bombardment of Greytown, arguing that the alternative would have been to allow the "offenders" in Greytown to "persevere with impunity in a career of insolence and plunder."[65]

In the early 1850s, the Young America movement gained significant influence within the Democratic Party in the United States with an avowed belief in territorial expansion. Pierce, in his inaugural address, firmly espoused expansionism, averring that "the policy of my Administration will not be controlled by any timid forebodings of evil from expansion."[66] As Lars Schoultz points out, the logical zone of expansion was Southward, and therefore, "the politics of expansion became alloyed with the politics of slavery."[67] The Democratic Party favored Southern interests and was openly racist.[68] Under the Pierce administration, the 1854 Congress passed the Kansas–Nebraska Act, which repealed the Missouri Compromise and opened those territories to slavery. For Pierce, expansion into Latin America held the promise not only of territorial aggrandizement but also of expansion of slavery at a time when sentiments in the United States balked at domestic slavery expansion. For historian Robert May, vital to the Southern dream of an

---

[64] *Washington Sentinel*, September 8, 1854.
[65] "Second Annual Message," December 4, 1854, *A Compilation of the Messages and Papers of the Presidents / Prepared under the Direction of the Joint Committee on Printing, of the House and Senate, Pursuant to an act of the Fifty-Second Congress of the United States (with additions and encyclopedic index by private enterprise), Volume V, Part 3: Franklin Pierce*, Project Gutenberg.
[66] "Inaugural Address," March 4, 1853, *A Compilation of the Messages and Papers of the Presidents, Volume V, Part 3: Franklin Pierce*, Project Gutenberg.
[67] Schoultz, *Beneath the United States*, 40–41.
[68] Net Brandt and Yanna Brandt, *In the Shadow of the Civil War: Passmore Williamson and the Rescue of Jane Johnson* (Columbia: University of South Carolina Press, 2007), 41.

empire in the Caribbean and Latin America "was the expectation that slavery would be intrinsic to its realization."[69] In the 1850s, the project of extending slavery within the United States seemed like an impossible prospect. On the other hand, free states were regularly inducted into the union. As Southern states sought to maintain sectional balance, they looked southward to the Caribbean and Central America areas that had suddenly become open to American expansionist imagination, following the Mexican–American War.

Cuba, which – unlike other Caribbean and Central American nations in the mid nineteenth century – still practiced slavery, soon became a prime region for expansionist ambitions. An important region for U.S. trade and a significant source of sugar imports, Cuba's geographical proximity to the United States made it a vital territory to control. The fear of Cuba falling into the hands of Great Britain, thereby threatening U.S. regional dominance and potentially curbing the expansion of slavery, prompted calls for the annexation of the island.[70] The 1854 Ostend Manifesto, which outlined the Pierce administration's objective to buy or – failing that – seize Cuba, posited Cuba as being a "natural" part of the United States.[71] For Northerners, the annexation of Cuba was a "Southern plot" to expand slavery and representation in the Congress.[72]

The turn towards Nicaragua was a logical extension of Democratic and Southern preoccupations in the mid nineteenth century. Viewed in popular American newspapers as a Caribbean paradise,[73] Nicaragua teemed with possibilities as the likely site of a transisthmian canal. For Pierce, it was part of the broader expansionist agenda of his administration. As the *New Orleans Delta* remarked, "The fate of Cuba depends upon the fate of Nicaragua, and the fate of the South depends upon that of Cuba ... We must do or die."[74] Hollins' heavy-handed actions in Greytown and the Pierce administration's subsequent support of the bombardment must be seen in this context. Foreshadowing the gunboat

---

[69] Robert May, *The Southern Dream of a Caribbean Empire, 1854–1861* (Gainesville: University Press of Florida, 2002), 9.
[70] Alan McPherson, *Encyclopedia of US Military Interventions in Latin America* (Santa Barbara: ABC-CLIO, 2013) 54.
[71] McPherson, A Short History of U.S. Interventions, 26.
[72] Piero Gliejeses, "Clashing over Cuba: The United States, Spain and Britain, 1853–55," *Journal of Latin American Studies* 49:2 (2016), 24; Jules Benjamin, *The United States and the Origins of the Cuban Revolution: An Empire of Liberty in an Age of National Liberation* (Princeton: Princeton University Press, 2020), 11.
[73] May, *The Southern Dream of a Caribbean Empire*, 8.
[74] Quoted in McPherson, *A Short History of US Interventions*, 25.

diplomacy that would characterize U.S. interventions into Latin America in the second half of the nineteenth century, the *Cyane* bombardment was an integral part of U.S. expansionist ambitions rather than an aberration in its foreign policy. With the British mired deeply in the Crimean War, Pierce could condone the wanton destruction without fear of reprisals.

5.5 NICARAGUA: DISILLUSIONMENT AND DESCENT INTO CIVIL WAR

When Vanderbilt's 120-ton steamship *Director* sailed through Lake Nicaragua on January 1, 1851, it was greeted by a crowd of spectators on the Granada beach. Awash with the promise of American enterprise and technology, the *Correo del Istmo* gushed that a "new era" had begun in Nicaragua's march towards prosperity.[75] Yet Vanderbilt's formation of the ATC and the consequent transformation of the canal route into a transit route worried Nicaraguans, who soon began to realize that the American-controlled transit activities would bring little to no benefit to Nicaragua. More troubling still, in forming the transit route, the Canal Company had obtained favors from Granada, thus inflaming the government in León.[76] Under the ATC, the transit soon assumed the characteristics of an American enclave. This was more so because Vanderbilt's transit route bypassed the populous heart of Nicaragua, skipping Realejo and instead taking a southern route through mostly uninhabited terrain to the "empty beach" of San Juan del Sur.[77] Henceforth, the influx of Americans through the transit route would bring little economic advantage to Nicaragua – the profits and businesses being dominated by U.S. enterprises. As Bradford Burns writes: "Menial service jobs went to the Nicaraguans; the profits went to the Americans."[78] San Juan del Norte, the most important port terminus for the canal route, became dominated by foreigners with Americans in positions of authority. For the Nicaraguan government, the ATC was nothing short of a betrayal of Nicaragua's canal dreams, transforming "the vastest commercial enterprise of the nineteenth century ... to a common transit route."[79]

---

[75] *Correo del Istmo*, January 9, 1851.
[76] J. Estanislao Gonsáles to John Bozman Kerr, September 18, 1851, Manning, *Diplomatic Correspondence*, vol. 4, 240.
[77] Gobat, *Empire by Invitation*, 38.   [78] Burns, *Patriarch and Folk*, 184.
[79] J. Estanislao Gonsáles to John Bozman Kerr, September 18, 1851, Manning, *Diplomatic Correspondence*, vol. 4, 240.

The Orville Childs' survey had recommended the canal path terminate at the harbor of Brito on the Pacific coast, thus bypassing Salinas in Costa Rica –another widely acknowledged possibility of the western terminus – and placing the canal route firmly within Nicaraguan territory.[80] As the prospect of a transisthmian canal captured attention both in the isthmus and around the world, the boundary dispute between Costa Rica and Nicaragua assumed significance. Costa Rica maintained that its territory began at the mouth of the San Juan River and continued along the southern bank of the river up to a point near Lake Nicaragua. Costa Rica also claimed the district of Guanacaste, which had seceded from Nicaragua and joined Costa Rica in 1824.[81] This extended Costa Rica's territory to a point opposite the river La Flor, on the Pacific coast. While Nicaragua claimed exclusive rights over Lake Nicaragua and the San Juan River, Costa Rica demanded joint rights of navigation on these water bodies. The Webster–Crampton Treaty, drawn up in April 1852, aimed to settle various issues related to the construction of a transisthmian canal and the boundary disputes between Costa Rica and Nicaragua.[82] The treaty – which proposed concessions to both countries but ultimately pleased neither – was rejected by Nicaragua. The United States maintained the position that it would not proceed with the project of building the canal until the boundary dispute had been resolved. Private interests balked at the prospect of building a canal in a disputed area. As Kerr observed, "So long as the boundary question between Nicaragua and Costa Rica remains in litigation ... it is not to be expected that prudent capitalists will be ready to advance the necessary millions for the commencement and prosecution of such a work."[83]

Even as prospects of the canal dimmed, Nicaragua's own journey towards sovereignty seemed to push it closer to U.S. dependence. On November 8, 1849, Nicaragua entered into a pact with Honduras and El Salvador to form a union, the *Representación Nacional de Centro-América*. By the summer of 1851, with the seat of the federal government in León, the *Representación* had reportedly taken over the foreign affairs

---

[80] John Bozman Kerr to Francisco Castellón, June 23, 1852, Manning, *Diplomatic Correspondence*, vol. 4, 287.
[81] See Felipe Molina, *Memoir on the Boundary Question Pending between the Republic of Costa Rica and the State of Nicaragua* (Washington, DC: Gideon and Co., 1851), 4.
[82] Daniel Webster to John Bozman Kerr, April 30, 1852, Manning, *Diplomatic Correspondence*, vol. 4, 18–23.
[83] John Bozman Kerr to Francisco Castellón, June 23, 1852, Manning, *Diplomatic Correspondence*, vol. 4, 287.

of Nicaragua.[84] John Bozman Kerr, United States chargé d'affaires in Nicaragua described the union in skeptical terms: "The National Representation of Chinandega, though for some months at León, consists of four persons, at present, with six votes – two for Honduras, cast by a proxy in this City, two from Salvador & two for Nicaragua."[85] Internal turmoil within Nicaragua and a Liberal military coup in August 1851 brought the *Representación* in Nicaragua – which Kerr described as "a hot-bed of revolutionary mischief" – to an end, with the convention now moving to Teguzigalpa in Honduras.[86] By autumn of 1852, Kerr reported the failure of unionism in Central America: "Each State evidently prefers to manage its own affairs; & having reserved a right to accept or reject the project of the Constituent Assembly now in fact, after many false rumors, united at Teguzigalpa, we can scarcely expect any substantive Act from its deliberations."[87] By 1854, U.S. Secretary of State William Marcy reported that "after repeated and earnest efforts on the part of Nicaragua to secure the reestablishment of the Centro-American Confederation, which efforts had entirely failed, the Constituent Assembly had erected that part of Central America into a free, sovereign, and independent Republic."[88] As Nicaragua sought to define itself as a republic, moving farther away from ideals of a Central American Union, it paradoxically became more and more dependent on the United States.

As the dreams of a Central American Union and the prospects of an interoceanic canal began to fall apart, some Nicaraguans saw the internal structure of their country as the root of their weakness. Arguably, the weakness of the Nicaraguan state had allowed for the ATC to breach contracts.[89] Fruto Chamorro, the Nicaraguan supreme director, viewed the constitution of 1838, which granted the executive only a two-year term with no reelection, as a "guaranteed recipe for anarchy."[90]

---

[84] Justo Chamorro to Daniel Webster, June 4, 1851, Manning, *Diplomatic Correspondence*, vol. 4, 210.
[85] John Bozman Kerr to Daniel Webster, August 4, 1851, Manning, *Diplomatic Correspondence*, vol. 4, 229.
[86] John Bozman Kerr to Daniel Webster, March 15, 1852, Manning, *Diplomatic Correspondence*, vol. 4, 264.
[87] John Bozman Kerr to Daniel Webster, October 27, 1852, Manning, *Diplomatic Correspondence*, vol. 4, 312.
[88] William Marcy to José de Marcoleta, April 27, 1854, Manning, *Diplomatic Correspondence*, vol. 4, 58.
[89] Herrera C., *Bongos, bogas, vapores y marinos*, 95.
[90] Arturo Cruz, *Nicaragua's Conservative Republic, 1858–93* (New York: Palgrave, 2002), 34.

As Chamorro attempted to cement his control over the country, he not only promulgated a new constitution declaring Nicaragua a republic and strengthening the executive, but he also confronted the ATC over the company's actions that siphoned off all transit profits to American hands.[91] Paradoxically, Chamorro's efforts to strengthen Nicaragua internally rekindled León–Granada rivalries, and the young republic spiraled towards a civil war. The *Cyane* bombardment, following soon after the declaration of Nicaragua as a republic, underscored the weakness of the internally riven country as well as the terrifying outcome of Nicaragua's policy through the years of canal fever of opening the fledgling republic to U.S. enterprise and intervention.

[91] Burns, *Patriarch and Folk*, 184–185; Cruz, *Nicaragua's Conservative Republic*, 37.

6

Filibustering on the San Juan

> It is only to be regretted, in fact, that the countries which we call "Spanish America" are not capable of a confederation of purpose & strength, and hence the responsibilities of the continent thrown on the United States.
> — William Carey Jones, special agent of the United States to Central America, August 3, 1857

In the aftermath of the *Cyane* bombardment, Greytown became ripe as a refuge and breeding ground for filibustering enterprises. As early as 1851, Liberals in León had reached out to American citizens transiting through Nicaragua to join in the Leónese military forces against Granada. The potential of the Nicaragua Canal and the strategic importance of the San Juan River and Greytown attracted prominent filibusters, such as Henry Kinney and William Walker, whose actions transformed these locations into crucial battlegrounds between filibusters and their opponents. The transit route became a focal point in the struggle for control, and by 1856, the United States formally recognized Walker's regime, marking a turning point in American foreign policy towards the region. As Walker's regime became identified with U.S. imperialism, Central America briefly turned to Europe as a counterweight to American ambitions in the region. By the end of the decade, the Frenchman Félix Belly had drawn up a contract with Nicaragua for building the Nicaragua Canal.

Historians Michel Gobat and Aims McGuinness have traced the origins of the idea of Latin America to the 1850s, with Gobat linking it to reactions against Walker's filibustering and McGuinness emphasizing the role of interoceanic transit routes.[1] As this chapter shows, Central American republics framed their resistance to Walker as a regional struggle rather than a defense of individual nation-states. While the Nicaragua Canal was not the primary cause of aspirations for unity, it remained a key strategic concern for both Walker and the Central American republics. This was reflected in its centrality to the military engagements of the *guerra nacional*, during which a coalition of Central American forces converged to end Walker's regime. Ultimately, the period of filibustering in Nicaragua had several enduring consequences both for the fate of the canal route and the "Mosquito question." While the war disrupted transit activities and temporarily undermined dreams of a Nicaragua Canal, it also paradoxically speeded up the process of settlement of the Mosquito question as metropolitan governments realized that the longer the status of the Mosquito region remained unresolved, the more prone it would be to filibustering enterprises.

6.1 GREYTOWN ON THE EVE OF AMERICAN FILIBUSTERING

The condition of Greytown following its bombardment certainly played a role in fomenting disruptive behavior. Decimated in the wake of the *Cyane* bombing, Greytown made feeble attempts to recover but was unable to return to its previous flourishing condition (see Figure 6.1). New buildings rose from the rubble, but many were crude, lacking even basic features like ceilings or kitchens. Life in Greytown was now characterized by instability.[2] There was no real authority in the town and no reliable government. While previously, the British had enjoyed a great deal of support from the Greytown residents, including American citizens who had benefited from land grants, the inability of the British to prevent the destruction of the town and their perceived indifference to the fate of the residents resulted in a significant undermining of British influence in the town. The lack of resolution of the factors that had precipitated the *Cyane* bombing – including the relationship between the town and ATC – meant that tensions continued to simmer. The ATC had already shown a

---

[1] Michel Gobat, "The Invention of Latin America: A Transnational History of Anti-imperialism, Democracy, and Race," *The American Historical Review* 118:5 (December 2013), 1345–1375; Aims McGuinness, "Searching for 'Latin America': Race and Sovereignty in the Americas in the 1850s," in *Race and Nation in Modern Latin America*, eds. Nancy Appelbaum, Anne S. Macpherson, and Karin Alejandra Rosenblatt, 87–107 (Chapel Hill: University of North Carolina Press, 2003).
[2] Dozier, *Nicaragua's Mosquito Shore*, 90.

FIGURE 6.1 Greytown circa two years after the *Cyane* bombardment. Watercolor by Godfrey T. Vigne. Source: Paul Mellon Collection, B1975.3.179. Yale Center for British Art.

propensity for independent action to secure its own interests. Indeed, the militarism of individual employees of ATC and American citizens of Greytown foreshadowed the shift to filibustering that would characterize the political scenario of Nicaragua in the mid-1850s.

While the *Cyane* bombardment cast a long shadow over Greytown's development, the ethnic and racial makeup of the city's residents and persons in authority also played a role in priming the area for filibustering. William Walker's intervention, for instance, benefited from the political leanings of African Americans in the port town. African Americans who saw in Nicaragua, and in particular, in Greytown, the chance to rebuild their lives and gain the citizenship that they were denied in the United States, formed a sizable proportion of the residents of Greytown by the mid nineteenth century. As Michel Gobat writes, "The sudden interest of African Americans in Nicaragua resulted from the rise of the transit. It led many to view the resource-rich isthmus as the new El Dorado, while some hoped the region's proximity would facilitate the armed struggle against slavery in the United States itself."[3] Some of these immigrants even rose to prominence in the port town and in the political shift of 1852, when American citizens took control over the city council and governance of Greytown. African Americans found themselves in leadership positions, with a few even forming political links with the Nicaraguan Liberal Party. The new constitution of Greytown enshrined the rights of its multiracial population and the doctrine of equality: "All men are, by nature, possessed of certain inalienable rights, among which are those of enjoying and defending life and liberty,

---

[3] Gobat, *Empire by Invitation*, 52.

acquiring and protecting property, and securing happiness."[4] Thus, the U.S. antislavery newspaper, *Frederick Douglass' Paper*, described Nicaragua as "the most beautiful, freest and happiest region on the face of God's earth, where black and white interchange all the civil and social relations on the same platform."[5] As Michel Gobat has shown, William Walker's filibustering enterprise, though later associated with the expansion of slavery into Nicaragua, initially promoted republican ideals that attracted a diverse following, including Greytown's African Americans. León, the bastion of the Liberal Party, was itself a multiracial cosmopolitan city.[6] With Nicaragua descending into civil war in 1854, it was the Liberal Party of León, with its large multiracial following, that "invited" William Walker into Nicaragua.

The conservative newspaper *El Defensor del Orden*, based in Granada, lamented the arrival of foreign adventurers, accusing Nicaraguans themselves of betraying the nation.[7] "Peoples, know well," it thundered in July 1855, "those who shamelessly sell you to foreign peoples who have neither religion nor humanity, and who, to satisfy their insatiable greed for gold and more gold, are capable of savagely tearing apart the very womb that gave them life."[8] It was a final clarion call: *El Defensor* ceased publication just two months later, with Walker's seizure of Granada in October 1855. Greytown, as Nicaragua's Atlantic gateway, would go on to play a vital role in facilitating these filibustering expeditions – serving as Walker's logistical lifeline in his bid to dominate Nicaragua and, ultimately, Central America.

6.2 HENRY KINNEY IN GREYTOWN

While William Walker remains the most famous of the mid nineteenth-century filibusters, Henry Kinney was the first to use Greytown as a base of operations. Like Walker after him, Kinney understood the importance of allying with particular racial and ethnic groups, and he appears to have secured support from the Indigenous Miskitus in the area to legitimize his filibuster government. Greytown, a crucial point on the transit route connecting the Atlantic to the Pacific, became the focal point of

---

[4] *Frederick Douglass' Paper*, July 16, 1852.
[5] *Frederick Douglass' Paper*, January 15, 1852.   [6] Gobat, *Empire by Invitation*, 55.
[7] *El Defensor del Orden*, June 11, 1855, Instituto de Historia de Nicaragua y Centroamérica en El Exilio (hereafter *El IHNCA en el Exilio*).
[8] *El Defensor del Orden*, July 10, 1855, *El IHNCA en el Exilio*.

Kinney's ambitions. Although Kinney's stated aim was to develop the economy of the Mosquito Coast, his actions contributed to the instability of Greytown and were emblematic of the centrality of the canal route to filibustering ambitions in the mid-century.

Henry L. Kinney was born in 1814 in Pennsylvania but moved to Chicago as a teenager, where he rose to prominence as one of the wealthiest men in Illinois. He participated in the Mexican–American War and maintained a small army, which he employed against both Native Americans and Mexicans. The *Colonial Standard* of January 6, 1855, asserted that "the gentleman comes from Texas ... and understands thoroughly the process of annexation."[9] In 1839, the Mosquito King Robert Charles Frederic had made a grant of territory amounting to 22,500,000 acres near the mouth of the San Juan River to residents Peter and Samuel Shepherd. Although the British government later denied the validity of these land titles, the Shepherds offered to sell the concessions to Kinney for $500,000. Kinney sought to find financial backers for the grant and formed the Central America Land and Mining Company, issuing 225,000 shares in its name. The cost of each share was $25 and promised the buyer 100 acres of land in the Mosquito Coast.[10] The Kinney expedition was originally backed by the directors of the ATC, leading to accusations by the Nicaraguan government that the ATC was using Kinney to take control over the territory of the Mosquito Coast. Kinney's avowed purpose was the colonization of the Mosquito Coast and the development of its resources, and he personally invested $52,000 to equip the colonists in his expedition to carry out his plan.[11] As the neutrality of Great Britain and the United States became important in the context of the Crimean War, President Pierce ordered the arrest of Kinney, whose plan to colonize the Mosquito Coast threatened to undermine American neutrality in Central America. Kinney and his partner, the former U.S. commercial agent in Nicaragua, Joseph Fabens, were finally released on a bond of $10,000.[12] Kinney blamed the ATC for this reversal, highlighting the fact that he meant to pressure the company to recompense the people of Greytown for its role in the *Cyane* bombardment.

---

[9] "Supplement to the New Orleans Picayune," January 20, 1855, FO 53/36.
[10] Jonathan D. Del Buono, "The Business of Empire: American Capitalists, the Nicaraguan Canal, and the Monroe Doctrine, 1849–1858," MA thesis, University of Montana, 2017, 48.
[11] Wall, "American Intervention in Nicaragua," 116.
[12] Del Buono, "The Business of Empire," 50.

From the very beginning, Kinney and Fabens maintained that their expedition was a peaceful one, meant for the settlement of immigrants and development of agriculture and mining in the area under the land grants and Fabens' own landholdings in the Chontales region.[13] Yet Kinney's own personal letters suggest that he planned for a military takeover. In a letter to a resident of Montgomery, Alabama, for instance, Kinney wrote: "Every emigrant in Central America, who engages to be established there, in a military capacity, should it be required, for twelve months (as the militia of any country,) will receive a grant of land of 640 acres, and officers in proportion to their rank."[14] On September 6, 1855, Kinney and his followers successfully took control of the administration of Greytown, with Kinney styling himself "Civil and Military Governor" of the city. Following the *Cyane* bombardment, there had been a lack of government in Greytown, with the councils unable to deal with the strained relations between the city and ATC. This power vacuum provided Kinney with the opportunity to wrest control of the city without any opposition. In a proclamation issued to the people of Greytown, Kinney promised to bring resolution to the long-standing dispute between the town and ATC. He also assured the residents and traders in Greytown that he would seek monetary settlement for the damages suffered because of the bombardment of 1854.[15]

Fragmented evidence also points to Kinney's efforts to shore up support for his regime from among the Indigenous Miskitu in the area. His partnership with the Shepherd brothers may have facilitated this, even though his rule was never sanctioned by the Mosquito government under the British.[16] A letter from a Greytown resident thus described Kinney granting concessions to the Miskitus:

> Colonel Kinney yesterday concluded a grant treaty with the various Mosquito tribes of Indians and indeed it was a grand sight to see the weather-beaten Indians smiling and rejoicing in spirit, to think that the great deliverer had at last come and they called him a second "Penn." The contents of the treaty was that the Indians shall occupy their lands peaceable and that they will in no wise molest any person connected with the Kinney expedition.[17]

---

[13] Joseph Fabens to William L. Marcy, April 26, 1855, *Despatches*, roll 1.
[14] Henry Kinney, January 14, 1855, newspaper clip enclosed in *Report to the Treasury*, FO 53/36.
[15] Henry Kinney, "Proclamation," September 8, 1855, *Despatches*, roll 1.
[16] Olien, "Micro/Macro-Level Linkages," 277.
[17] J. R. Swift to William Sydney Thayer, October 18, 1855, *Letters from Henry Lawrence Kinney and Others Regarding Central America* (William Sydney Thayer Papers, Box 1, Folder V), Library of Congress, Washington, DC.

The *Central American*, the mouthpiece of California filibusters in Greytown, reported that Kinney had bestowed on an "Indian" the title of *comandante* besides signing a paper "guaranteeing to all the tribe having claims to land or improvements upon lands within the bounds of his purchase a full right to hold, or dispose of the same, and that their rights should at all times be respected."[18] Despite the fact that later historians assumed that Kinney did not have any local Miskitu support, fragmentary evidence suggests that to a degree Miskitus rallied to Kinney's cause. The Venezuelan newspaper *Diario de Avisos* thus reports: "The Indian tribes, out of gratitude for the benefits that the new Government has given them, have entered into a treaty with him and assumed the name 'Indians of Kinney.'"[19] Similar sentiments are echoed in the *Central American*, which describes how an Indigenous – possibly Miskitu – man declared that "*Indian* would live and fight for him [Kinney] if necessary to the death."[20] Central American newspapers also reveal the general understanding that Kinney had come to power with Miskitu support.[21] Collectively, these fragments of evidence suggest that Miskitu communities may have actively participated in early filibustering ventures and navigated the aftermath of the destruction of Greytown, following the *Cyane* bombardment, in ways that advanced their own interests.

The Nicaraguan Minister Marcoleta maintained that Kinney had been elected not by popular suffrage but by the "pirates" who had accompanied him to the isthmus and those of the residents of Greytown who had already been reprimanded for their involvement in the hostilities with the ATC.[22] Immediately after the "election," Captain Tarleton of the H.M.S. *Eurydice*, which was stationed at Greytown, complained against Kinney's takeover, asserting that the majority of Greytown residents had entered a protest against Kinney's election, which seemed to have been carried out in the presence of only twenty men, most of whom were part of Kinney's expedition.[23] Tarleton also questioned the legality of Kinney's election since a "provisional municipal administration" was still in force, having been unanimously supported by the governments of Great Britain and the United States. Moreover, the laws of Greytown stipulated that a mayor or

---

[18] *Central American*, October 27, 1855.   [19] *Diario de Avisos*, December 19, 1855.
[20] *Central American*, October 27, 1855.
[21] See, for instance, Costa Rica's *Boletín Oficial* for February 3 and 7, 1855.
[22] José de Marcoleta to William Marcy, Doc. 1310, October 8, 1855, Manning, *Diplomatic Correspondence*, vol. 4.
[23] Captain Tarleton to James Geddes, September 13, 1855, FO 53/36.

chief magistrate should have been resident in the town for at least six months in order to be elected to that position. Kinney's election violated all of these terms. Despite these criticisms, in the short term, Kinney's election seemed to have jump-started the economic and social life of Greytown with the prompt opening of schools, rebuilding of the decimated town and a new flurry of gold seekers through the transit route. By the end of September, however, Kinney had decided to acquiesce to Tarleton's demands for his resignation. On September 23, 1855, Kinney resigned, declaring that he would only accept the office of governor if it was "conferred on him by the unanimous choice of the people" of Greytown.[24] Likely, part of the reason for Kinney's resignation too was the wider disapprobation of his actions by the governments of Great Britain and the United States. While the U.S. government had already expressed its unwillingness to recognize "adventurers," the British consul James Geddes pointed out that Kinney's actions contravened the neutrality of the great powers established in the Clayton–Bulwer Treaty.[25] The involvement of Fabens in Kinney's schemes had already caused the U.S. government to revoke his position as U.S. commercial agent, and the new incumbent, Squire Cottrell, complained that the archives of the U.S. agency had been compromised, having been in the possession of Kinney's men.[26]

Yet, ironically, the main challenge to Kinney's influence over Greytown came in the form of another American adventurer, William Walker, who in October 1855 used ATC steamers to attack and capture Granada. Although initially he rejected the presidency, preferring instead to operate through a provisional government under President Patricio Rivas, Walker gained both power and popularity in Granada, where the elite hoped that Walker's rule would serve to garner U.S. support for the canal construction and undermine British control over San Juan.[27] Hoping for an alliance with Walker, who now styled himself as "General in Chief of the Nicaraguan Army," Kinney sent a contingent of his followers to meet with Walker in Granada. If Kinney had hoped that the commonalities that the two men shared would prove to be a foundation for a harmonious relationship, he was sorely mistaken. The

---

[24] Henry Kinney to the People of San Juan del Norte or Greytown, September 23, 1855, FO 53/35.
[25] Wall, "American Intervention in Nicaragua," 139.
[26] Squire Cottrell to William Marcy, October 12, 1855, *Despatches*, roll 1.
[27] Gobat, *Empire by Invitation*, 67–69.

New York Herald reported Walker's response to Kinney's contingent: "Tell Governor Kinney, or Colonel Kinney, or Mr. Kinney, or whatever he chooses to call himself, that if I ever lay hands on him on Nicaraguan soil I shall surely hang him."[28] Shortly after Walker's seizure of Granada, his men attacked Fort San Carlos on the San Juan River, forcing the commandant of the garrison at San Carlos to flee to Greytown. As Walker began to appear as a stronger, more successful leader, Kinney's own men, who had hitherto supported him in Greytown, left to join Walker's forces in Granada in November 1855.[29] Several ATC employees also left with the defectors for Granada.[30]

The instability among the ranks of Kinney's men in the latter part of 1855 and the early months of 1856 also resulted in violence and lawlessness in Greytown. Kinney himself was short on funds, and his men owed large sums of money to various people in the town. Writing to U.S. Secretary of State William Marcy in November 1855, Cottrell described Kinney's men in Greytown as: "Generally very dissipated young men, out of employment and devoid of principle or self-respect, with no prospect of earning for themselves a livelihood."[31] On December 30, two of Kinney's men, an American named Marshall and a British citizen, James White, got into a fight, leaving one of them severely wounded.[32] The cause of the dispute stemmed from Marshall's claim that "Kinney was the best man in the world and he [Marshall] was the next."[33] Matters worsened as a result of the continuing arrival of ships from the United States carrying passengers keen to join the filibusters in Nicaragua. Immigrants from New York and New Orleans arrived in Greytown in such destitute condition that it was apparent that they would live on debts, straining the resources of the port town. In April 1856, Tarleton pointed to the lawlessness resulting from this movement of people, which had led to a great surge in cases of assault and loss of life in Greytown.[34]

Kinney, on his part, seemed to still cling to the hope that he would find favor with Walker despite all the evidence to the contrary. On February 8, 1856, Walker issued a proclamation claiming the territory of the

---

[28] Quoted in Wall, "American Intervention in Nicaragua," 143, n. 71.
[29] "Extract of a Letter from Comm. Ogle of HMS [?] to Admiral Fanshawe," November 19, 1855, FO 53/39.
[30] Squire Cottrell to William Marcy, November 29, 1855, *Despatches*, roll 1.   [31] Ibid.
[32] Squire Cottrell to William Marcy, January 1, 1856, *Despatches*, roll 1.
[33] "Copy of Affidavit Made by James White against Marshall," December 30, 1855, *Despatches*, roll 1.
[34] Captain Tarleton to James Green, April 5, 1856, FO 53/39.

Mosquito Coast as an integral part of Nicaragua. The proclamation also directly threatened Kinney, decreeing that "the right upon which the said Kinney pretends to claim in and upon the said territory, are null, void, and of no effect, the same being the property of the Republic of Nicaragua; and consequently, every alienation made by the said Kinney is also void." The proclamation named Kinney as guilty of infringing on the integrity of Central America.[35] Still, Kinney, rather than giving up on hopes of an alliance with Walker, surprised the Granadians by arriving in a steamer to speak personally with Walker. However, after a disastrous interview with Walker,[36] Kinney was made a state prisoner, and newspapers reported that he was "drummed beyond the limits."[37] Kinney returned to Greytown but still refused to give up his dreams of colonizing the Mosquito Coast despite the lack of men and funds, staying on until July 1857, when he sailed for Corpus Christi.

6.3 WILLIAM WALKER AND THE TRANSIT ROUTE

Far more than Kinney, the Nicaragua Canal route lay at the heart of Walker's ambitions in Central America. As Bradford Burns writes: "Given his ambitions, Walker wisely understood that his future ... depended on the power he would gain from the transit route to the southeast, an umbilical cord to North American money, supplies, and recruits. If he were to control Nicaragua, he must dominate that route."[38]

It is not a coincidence that the very first article of the very first edition of Walker's newspaper *El Nicaraguense* laid out his visions for the canal and transit route:

> The whole civilized world demands a short, prompt and reliable communication between the Atlantic and the Pacific; two will be established ultimately. A railroad from San Francisco to St. Louise will be one; the other will be a railroad and steamboat line from Realejo, via Granada, to San Juan del Norte. Both lines will be the source of incalculable wealth to the districts through which they pass, especially the latter.[39]

By proposing a transit route through the populous regions of Realejo and Granada, Walker aimed to garner the support of Nicaraguans who had been disillusioned by Vanderbilt's line, which bypassed this densely populated heartland and excluded ordinary Nicaraguans from sharing in the

---

[35] *Plain Dealer*, March 3, 1856.   [36] Ibid.   [37] *Irish American*, March 8, 1856.
[38] Burns, *Patriarch and Folk*, 197.   [39] *El Nicaraguense*, October 20, 1855.

FIGURE 6.2 River steamers plying Greytown c 1855. Source: *Frank Leslie's Illustrated Newspaper*, vol. 1, no. 2 (December 22, 1855), 21. Courtesy of The Huntington Library, San Marino.

economic benefits of the transit trade. As historian Michel Gobat writes, "[Walker's] interest in the region had everything to do with how the Gold Rush intensified U.S. efforts to build an interoceanic canal through Nicaragua."[40] Indeed, the broader acceptance that Walker enjoyed in Nicaragua can also be attributed to the local belief that U.S. support could help Nicaragua gain control of the canal route from the British, who still held on to Greytown and part of the transit route. The importance of the transit route to Walker's bid for power in Nicaragua can be seen in the fact that Walker's first military actions in Nicaragua were on or near the transisthmian route. But it was not just that the canal fueled Walker's ambitions; the transisthmian route and the steamers that plied across it were also the crucial lifeblood of Walker's enterprise, allowing passage for men and supplies (see Figure 6.2). Indeed, an important aspect of Walker's expeditions in Nicaragua was his collusion with employees of the ATC, including in the very first attack on Granada, which Walker conquered using ATC steamers in October 1855.

In the summer of 1855, Walker's invasion of Nicaragua began with his seizure of San Juan del Sur and Rivas, on the Pacific side of the proposed transisthmian canal route. By October, he had closed in on Granada, which he entered with 400 men and took after only a fifteen-minute standoff with Granadian forces.[41] The complicity of the ATC with this

---

[40] Gobat, *Empire by Invitation*, 13.
[41] Mr. Wheeler to Mr. Marcy, October 14, 1855. *Message of the President Communicating Sundry Documents in Relation to the Affairs with the Government of Nicaragua, and*

invasion became apparent through the fact that the steamers used by Walker and his men to enter Granada belonged to that company. Gobat argues that while the ATC directors viewed Walker as a "marauder," the local ATC agents secretly colluded with him, and once Walker had gained control of the transit route, the ATC steamers became "his lifeline to U.S. recruits."[42] Luis Molina, the Costa Rican chargé d'affaires, lamented that "the facility which the steamers of the Nicaragua Transit Company afford for infringing the law is voluntary and culpable."[43] With the Pacific side of the transit route in his control, Walker now set his sights on San Juan del Norte and the transit on the Atlantic side. Shortly after taking Granada, Walker's men proceeded on the steamship *La Virgen* to San Carlos on the San Juan River, where they threatened the commander of the fort of San Carlos that unless he surrendered the fort, 200 California riflemen would descend on the fort and take it by force. The commander responded by firing cannons at *La Virgen*, and a timely thunderstorm that prevented the assailants from firing back helped the commander at San Carlos to prevail.[44]

But military actions were not the only means that Walker employed to get the transit route under his control. In February 1853, Vanderbilt recruited Cornelius Garrison (later the mayor of San Francisco) as the San Francisco agent of the ATC for a two-year period.[45] Garrison in turn entered a partnership with Charles Morgan, a railroad and shipping magnate who was already involved in the transit route through Panama. In the same year, while Vanderbilt was vacationing, Morgan deposed him and was installed as the president of the ATC.[46] However, Vanderbilt remained director of ATC, holding a significant portion of the company stocks. At the end of 1855, Walker entered into a cabal with Garrison and Morgan to remove Vanderbilt completely from the transit company and take the route under his control. The fact that Vanderbilt had not fulfilled his financial obligations stipulated as part of his agreement with Nicaragua as director of ATC – including nonpayment of $10,000 as well as 10 percent of profits –

Information that the New Minister from that Government Has Been Accredited by This Government, 34th Cong., 1st Sess., S. Exec. Doc. 68, 1856.

[42] Gobat, *Empire by Invitation*, 66.
[43] Mr. Molina to Mr. Marcy, December 20, 1855, 34th Cong., 1st Sess., S. Exec. Doc. 68, 1856.
[44] Squire Cottrell to William Marcy, October 21, 1855, *Despatches*, roll 1; Scott Martelle, *William Walker's Wars: How One Man's Private American Army Tried to Conquer Mexico, Nicaragua, and Honduras* (Chicago: Chicago Review Press, 2019), 155.
[45] Stiles, *The Last Tycoon*, 276.   [46] Ibid., 283.

made it easier for Walker to justify this coup. Walker pressured President Rivas to annul Vanderbilt's contract, which he did in February 1856 – the same month in which Walker issued a proclamation claiming the Mosquito Coast as an integral part of Nicaragua. Walker promised to give Garrison and Morgan a new charter with exclusive rights to the transit route as well as all ATC property in return for their support of the coup.[47] The result was a colossal miscalculation. Henceforth, Vanderbilt would mark Walker out as an opponent and lend his resources to Walker's Central American enemies in order to oust the filibuster from Nicaragua.

The United States had thus far distanced itself from the actions of the filibusters, declaring their expeditions to be illegal. However, in a remarkable volte-face, President Franklin Pierce, in his address to the Senate in the 1st session of the 34th Congress on May 15, 1856, extended his support for Walker and recognized the Rivas government as legitimate. That Pierce's actions were determined in part by his desire to secure access to the interoceanic canal and transit route comes through clearly in his address. On opening his address, Pierce declared:

> To us, on account of its geographical position and of our political interest as an American State of primary magnitude, that isthmus is of peculiar importance, just as the isthmus of Suez is, for corresponding reasons, to the maritime powers of Europe. But, above all, the importance of the United States of securing free transit across the American isthmus has rendered it of paramount interest to us since the settlement of the Territories of Oregon and Washington and the accession of California to the Union.[48]

Even though Pierce's support temporarily strengthened the Walker regime, it also caused an enormous backlash against U.S. imperialism. As Gobat writes, "It also triggered one of the first anti-U.S. moments in world history."[49] Both Europeans and Latin Americans now saw Walker's regime as an extension of U.S. imperialism, and the fear that the United States had cast its eyes on the entire isthmus created a fertile ground for Central American republics to join hands against a common enemy.

6.4 THE NICARAGUA CANAL ROUTE IN THE *GUERRA NACIONAL*

The Nicaragua Canal and transit route became central to the military and political strategies of both William Walker and the Central American

---

[47] Robert E. May, *Manifest Destiny's Underworld: Filibustering in Antebellum America* (Chapel Hill: University of North Carolina Press, 2004), 176–177.
[48] Franklin Pierce, May 15, 1856, 34th Cong., 1st Sess., S. Exec. Doc. 68.
[49] Gobat, *Empire by Invitation*, 76.

forces opposing him. The canal route, as the primary artery for transporting troops, supplies, and reinforcements, became a crucial battleground in the struggle for control of the region. For Walker, the route represented his "lifeline" to maintain dominance over Nicaragua and expand his influence in Central America. For the allied Central American republics, severing Walker's control over this vital corridor was the key to dismantling his power and safeguarding their independence from U.S. imperialism. It is no surprise that the San Juan River and the transit route became the focal points of intense military engagements during the *guerra nacional*.

As soon as Rivas had revoked the charter of Vanderbilt's American Atlantic and Pacific Canal Company, Costa Rica moved to restrain Walker's control over the transit route. On March 1, 1856, the Costa Rican President Juan Rafael Mora prepared to attack Nicaragua, making it clear that the enemies he sought to overpower were not native Nicaraguans but the American filibusters.[50] Describing the Costa Rican advance to Nicaragua, U.S. Consul Hine wrote:

A body of 3,500 troops are marching for the frontiers of Nicaragua. The president will take command personally. No declaration of war will be made, upon the ground that no government exists in Nicaragua, and the only object avowed is the extermination of the "filibusteros." It is said that no quarter will be given, and that all prisoners will be shot.[51]

Two days later, on March 3, 1856, the Costa Rican government issued orders to suspend ATC steamer service through the San Juan River and Lake Nicaragua on the grounds that these vessels were being used for the recruitment and passage of "bandits" who supported Walker's filibustering ambitions.[52] At the root of the Costa Rican decision to take up arms against the filibusters was no doubt the genuine fear that their country would be the next prey for Walker's filibustering band.[53] The Costa Rican government maintained that their army was acting in the interests of all of Central America, who were united in the resolve to drive out the filibusters.[54]

Walker retaliated by ordering his forces to invade Costa Rica. By mid-March, his forces were advancing on the Sarapiquí, a tributary of the San

---

[50] *Boletín Oficial de Costa Rica*, March 1, 1856.
[51] Marquis L. Hine to William Marcy, March 9, 1856, 34th Cong., 1st Sess., S. Exec. Doc. 68, 78. For the public notice of this order, see *Boletín Oficial de Costa Rica*, April 2, 1856.
[52] Ibid., 77 [53] Wall, "American Intervention in Nicaragua," 278.
[54] Señor Calvo to US Consul in San Juan del Norte, March 3, 1856, *Despatches*, roll 2.

Juan River, flowing through Costa Rica.[55] Shortly thereafter, Walker's men were forced to retreat back to Nicaragua after being routed at the battle of Santa Rosa.[56] On April 7, a Costa Rican army descended on Virgin Bay, destroying a $120,000 wharf belonging to the ATC and, according to the American Minister to Nicaragua John Wheeler, slaughtering unarmed Americans with impunity and taking possession of the transit route.[57] Shortly thereafter, a Costa Rican army of 150 men went down the Sarapiquí River just 8 miles shy of the junction of the tributary with the San Juan River, where an equal number of Walker's men waited, cannons at the ready.[58] President Rivas accused Costa Rica of using the filibusters as a pretext to attack Nicaragua.[59] Walker's army defeated the Costa Rican forces on April 10, although the next day the filibusters suffered reverses in Rivas.[60] Ultimately, however, it was nature that had the last say. By April 11, cholera had broken out in the Costa Rican camps, forcing them to withdraw.[61] Writing about the decision to retreat, President Mora wrote: "You cannot imagine the horror of the contagion; only by seeing it can it be understood."[62] Soldiers carried the disease back to their home country, resulting in the death of 10 percent of Costa Rica's population.[63] Buoyed by this reversal, the Rivas government framed the outbreak as divine justice. "The cholera epidemic, the morbid fever, and the desertion of their soldiers brought them back to their homeland in endless misery, shame, and disgrace," it declared, "teaching the world an important lesson: that a people who know their rights and know how to defend them cannot be conquered."[64]

[55] Squire Cottrell to William Marcy, March 17, 1856, *Despatches*, roll 2.
[56] Gobat, *Empire by Invitation*, 70.
[57] Mr. Wheeler to Mr. Mora, April 15, 1856, 34th Cong., 1st Sess., S. Exec. Doc. 68, 127–130.
[58] Squire Cottrell to William Marcy, April 18, 1856, *Despatches*, roll 2.
[59] "Proclamas de Señor Presidente," March 10, 1856, Boleiín Oficial no. 1, *El IHNCA en el Exilio*.
[60] Mr. Wheeler to Mr. Marcy, April 17, 1856, 34th Cong., 1st Sess., S. Exec. Doc. 68, 125–126.
[61] John J. Mangipano, "The William Walker and the Seeds of Progressive Imperialism: The War in Nicaragua and the Message of Regeneration, 1855–1860," PhD thesis, University of Southern Mississippi, 2017, 134.
[62] Juan Rafael Mora to Ministro de la Guerra, May 7, 1856, ANCR, Guerra y Marina, 8827, f 16 f y v.
[63] Gobat, *Empire by Invitation*, 72.
[64] Salinas to Prefectos departamentales, May 3, 1856, Boletín Oficial no. 5, *El IHNCA en el Exilio*.

While nearby Sarapiquí witnessed pitched battles between Walker's forces and the Costa Rican army, Greytown did not remain untouched by the violence surrounding it. The disturbed conditions of Nicaragua and Costa Rica undermined the economic viability of Greytown, where business had taken a hard hit. Worse was the crowding of immigrants coming into the port of Greytown from the United States, who, now that transit connections with the interior had broken down, had to stay on in Greytown. Cottrell, for instance, highlighted the inability of Greytown to maintain such a large population of mostly destitute travelers, especially since trade with Nicaragua and Costa Rica, which had been an important source of earnings for the port, was now at a standstill.[65]

Following the Costa Rican retreat, Guatemalan and Salvadoran forces marched on Nicaragua.[66] By the fall of 1856, an allied army of Guatemalan, Salvadoran, and loyal Nicaraguan troops confronted the filibusters, with the allies occupying Masaya, only a day's march from Walker's stronghold at Granada, by October.[67] Fighting on the San Juan and the transit route intensified as a Costa Rican force descended on canoes and bungos and forcibly took possession of Punta Arenas, including the steamers of the ATC, in December 1856.[68] This move by the Costa Rican government was a blow to Walker, who – now left with less than 900 armed troops – was waiting for reinforcements to reach him through the Greytown–San Juan route.[69] Perhaps more importantly, the seizure of Punta Arenas stemmed from the bitter split within the ATC between Cornelius Vanderbilt's original board ("the Old Company") and the new leadership headed by Charles Morgan. The point is underscored by the choice of Sylvanus Spencer – a Vanderbilt agent – to command the Costa Rican detachment. Eyewitnesses described Spencer's behavior as harsh and menacing and reported that he had declared that he had been sent by the Old Company and had Costa Rican President Mora's orders to lead the expedition and take control of the steamers. Cottrell

---

[65] J. L. Martin to James Green, April 18, 1856; Squire Cottrell to Captain Tarleton, May 1, 1856, *Despatches*, roll 2.

[66] "La Marcha de las fuerzas Guatemaltecas y Salvadorenas," no. 9, *Boletín de Noticias*, Cojutepeque, June 27, 1856, Angelita García Peña, ed., *Documentos para la historia de la guerra nacional contra los filibusteros en Nicaragua: Contribución a la historia de Centro América* (San Salvador: Editorial Ahora, 1958), 63.

[67] Guadalupe Saenz to José Maria Cañas, November 2, 1856, ANCR, Relaciones Exteriores, caja 26, expediente 5, sig. 17965.

[68] Squire Cottrell to William Marcy, December 28, 1856, *Despatches*, roll 2.

[69] Manuel del Bosque to President Mora, Liberia, January 12, 1857, ANCR, Secretaría de Guerra y Marina, sig. 13444.

insinuated in a letter to Marcy that the English officers in Greytown had assisted in Spencer's takeover. Testimonies suggest that Spencer had threatened to burn down the steamers if he did not receive assistance from the British officers, and one of the officers, Captain Wood, assisted Spencer by bringing him an anchor. Justifying the lack of a more forceful British stance against the Costa Rican army, Captain Erskine of the British naval forces at Greytown wrote,

> With respect to the participation of a force of Costa Ricans in the seizure and transfer of the steamers alluded to, I must observe that these steamers having been for some months past employed in embarking at this port and conveying to the parties with whom Costa Ricans now carrying on active hostilities, men and munitions of war; it appears to me that as a non-belligerent I am prohibited by the law of nations from preventing the execution of such an operation by a belligerent party.[70]

The San Juan River transformed into the locus of the contest between the Costa Rican forces and Walker's army. By the beginning of January 1857, Costa Rica had captured steamers anchored at the Castillo rapids and succeeded in taking the garrison at Fort San Carlos. With their 1,000-strong force stationed at various points on the river from Sarapiquí to Lake Nicaragua, Costa Rican forces under General Mora were determined to root out the filibusters. Walker's men, now in control of only one steamer, the *San Carlos*, were facing imminent defeat. On January 11, General Mora declared to the citizens of Costa Rica that his army had severed the filibuster route and that the Costa Rican army was now the master of the San Juan River and Lake Nicaragua.[71] Letters from Walker's aide-de-camp, Callender Fayssoux, suggest that there were also desertions from Walker's army at this point.[72] As the garrison at San Carlos fell to Costa Rican forces, Walker's men hurried to Greytown – which by January 4, 1857, was a point of refuge for forty of Walker's men. Mr. Harris, the agent for Morgan, responded to the Costa Rican threat by organizing a force under one of Walker's men, Colonel Lockridge, to defend their transit property at Punta Arenas. By February, Lockridge was joined by arrivals from New York and

---

[70] John Erskine to Squire Cottrell, December 23, 1856, *Despatches*, roll 2.
[71] "El Presidente de la República a los Costaricenses," *Boletín Oficial de Costa Rica*, 14.1.1857; see also, "The President of the Republic to All Costa Ricans," January 11, 1857, *Despatches*, roll 2.
[72] Callender Fayssoux to William Walker, February 8, 1857. Callender I. Fayssoux Collection of William Walker Papers, 1856–1860, folder 25, Howard Tilton Memorial Library, Tulane University.

New Orleans, but, as Cottrell wrote to Marcy, "there has been but little accomplished towards raising the blockade of the San Juan river."[73] Caught between the warring parties, residents of Punta Arenas requested Captain Erskine to assist them in evacuating back to the United States, a request that Cottrell opposed, explaining to Erskine that these residents were not considered to be U.S. citizens.[74]

Meanwhile, Costa Rica's chokehold on the transit route continued, making the situation in Greytown economically untenable. On April 12, 1857, George Canty, commander of the Costa Rican forces, addressed the inhabitants of Greytown, announcing that the blockade on the river would be lifted as soon as the filibusters had been removed. Canty also warned the residents of Greytown that anyone found assisting Walker and his men would be considered an enemy of the allied Central American republics.[75] Aware that as long as the disbanded soldiers of Walker's army stayed in Greytown and the surrounding region, British interests would continue to face difficulties, the captain of the British ship *Orion* offered to remove Lockridge's band to Aspinwall, from where they would be able to find passage back to the United States.[76] Leaving Lockridge and three others in Punta Arenas, British ships began evacuating the rest of the band by mid-April 1857, bringing an end to filibustering dreams.[77]

On May 27, 1857, Walker returned to New Orleans on a steamer via Panama, leaving a large band of destitute followers still in Nicaragua. According to Gobat, "many [of Walker's men] resented how their return to the United States was more arduous than Walker's."[78] Writing in June 1857, Cottrell lamented the deplorable state of Walker's disbanded men, most of whom were in destitute conditions in various locations, including San José and Greytown.[79] In the same month, the United States, which had so far been reluctant to get involved, despatched the U.S.S. *Cyane*, which evacuated 100 of Walker's men who had surrendered at

---

[73] Squire Cottrell to William Marcy, February 10, 1857, *Despatches*, roll 2.
[74] Robert Ellis et al. to Captain Erskine, April 9, 1857; Squire Cottrell to Captain Erskine, April 10, 1857, *Despatches*, reel 2.
[75] George Canty to the Inhabitants of Greytown, April 12, 1857, *Despatches*, roll 2. Also enclosed in "Correspondencia varia sobre la Compañía del Tránsito y la Campaña Nacional," Secretaría de Guerra y Marina, sig. 009930, April 14–July 15, 1857, ANCR.
[76] Captain of the Ship Orion to [?], April 13, 1857, *Despatches*, roll 2.
[77] Squire Cottrell to Lewis Cass, April 18, 1857, *Despatches*, roll 2.
[78] Gobat, *Empire by Invitation*, 276.
[79] Squire Cottrell to Lewis Cass, June 3, 1857, *Despatches*, roll 2.

Rivas.[80] As the evacuation began, Greytown functioned both as a refuge point and a rendezvous for filibusters.[81]

Still, the evacuation was at best disorderly and at worst, oppressive. Disbanded Americans complained that they had been forced to serve the Costa Rican army and treated as slaves.[82] Cottrell claimed that the Costa Rican army had sent back to the interior U.S. citizens who were trying to find a passage back to the United States.[83] By July 1857, Greytown was a refuge to 250 disbanded men who had arrived there in a destitute condition from San José, awaiting a passage back to the United States.[84] Life in Greytown was harder than ever, with Costa Rica showing no intention of lifting the blockade. Rather, in October 1857, the Costa Rican army under Canty blockaded Fort San Carlos, effectively cutting off Greytown from any communication through the San Juan River. Canty justified this move by asserting that the blockade had been instituted because Nicaragua was not able to guarantee that the San Juan River would be free from filibustering.[85] The effect of this prolonged period of blockade on Greytown was devastating. By October 1857, Cottrell reported that the cost of living in Greytown was double that of any town or city in the United States. It was impossible to get any merchandise beyond the most common. Houses were below par but charged enormous rent. The cost of basic services like laundry and boat services was exorbitantly high.[86]

While filibustering is often popularly seen as the product of individual ambition – figures like Kinney and Walker chasing personal glory – contemporary observers recognized its deeper entanglement with U.S. sectional and imperial interests. According to the mid-century French journalist, Alfred Assollant, Walker's enterprise in Nicaragua was intricately connected to Southern interests, where the establishment of a slave state in Nicaragua and control of the canal route were not separate agendas but one rooted in a shared racialized, expansionist impulse. He writes:

Those who had pinned their hopes of acquiring great wealth on this conquest – who had dreamed of owning vast tracts of land in Nicaragua, like in Texas and California, of building a canal and reaping enormous profits, of securing a monopoly on transit between two worlds, of establishing a slave state to be

---

[80] Squire Cottrell to Lewis Cass, June 18, 1857, *Despatches*, roll 2.
[81] FO, May 8, 1857, FO 53/41.
[82] Protest of David M. Beau, June 10, 1857, *Despatches*, roll 2.
[83] Squire Cottrell to George Canty, June 9, 1857, *Despatches*, roll 2.
[84] Squire Cottrell to Lewis Cass, July 29, 1857, *Despatches*, roll 2.
[85] George Canty to T. J. Martin, October 13, 1857, *Despatches*, roll 2.
[86] Squire Cottrell to Lewis Cass, October 31, 1857, *Despatches*, roll 2.

incorporated into the Union – these men, in Kentucky, Tennessee, Alabama, Arkansas, Mississippi, Louisiana, Georgia, and the Carolinas, held mass meetings, recruited men, raised money, and operated with the energy and audacity of a regular government to send reinforcements to Walker and secure his conquest.[87]

The *New York Herald* of November 19, 1856, pointed to private interests in securing the Nicaragua route as the "real origin" of Walker's "invitation" to Nicaragua.[88] The links between filibustering and canal ambitions are evident in a 1856 broadside that featured portraits of Kinney and Walker alongside a map of Nicaragua. The map emphasized the strategic appeal of the Nicaragua transit route, noting that it was 650 miles shorter than the Panama route (see Figure 6.3).

6.5 THE RETURN OF FILIBUSTERS

Despite the ignominious way in which Kinney and Walker's filibustering expeditions had been thwarted, the end of the 1850s would see a last-ditch effort by filibusters to regain power in Nicaragua.

In November 1857, Walker sailed from Alabama with 200 followers and arrived in Greytown, landing his men at the mouth of the Colorado River and entering the bay at Punta Arenas. Even now, at the lowest point in his expeditions, Walker maintained that he was the president of Nicaragua and had the Nicaraguan flag flying over Punta Arenas. However, Walker's attempt on Greytown would be short-lived; he was captured shortly after his landing in Greytown in December 1857 by U.S. Naval Commodore Hiram Paulding and forced to depart for a final time from Greytown on board an American steamship bound for New York via Aspinwall.[89]

By this time, Walker was increasingly seen as a U.S. foreign policy liability, particularly in light of the fragile Anglo-American balance of power in Central America. Crucially, the U.S. government's shift away from Walker reflected a broader reorientation in its canal policy.[90] In November 1857, the United States negotiated the Cass–Yrisarri Treaty that aimed to guarantee the neutrality of the Nicaragua transit route while quietly expanding U.S. naval access to it. In a fiery speech

---

[87] "Walker en Nicaragua – por Alfred Assollant," Peña, ed., *Documentos para la historia de la guerra nacional contra los filibusteros en Nicaragua*, 77.
[88] *The New York Herald*, November 19, 1856.
[89] Squire Cottrell to Lewis Cass, December 11, 1857; Squire Cottrell to Lewis Cass, December 26, 1857, *Despatches*, roll 2, 634–635.
[90] Del Buono, "The Business of Empire," 73–77.

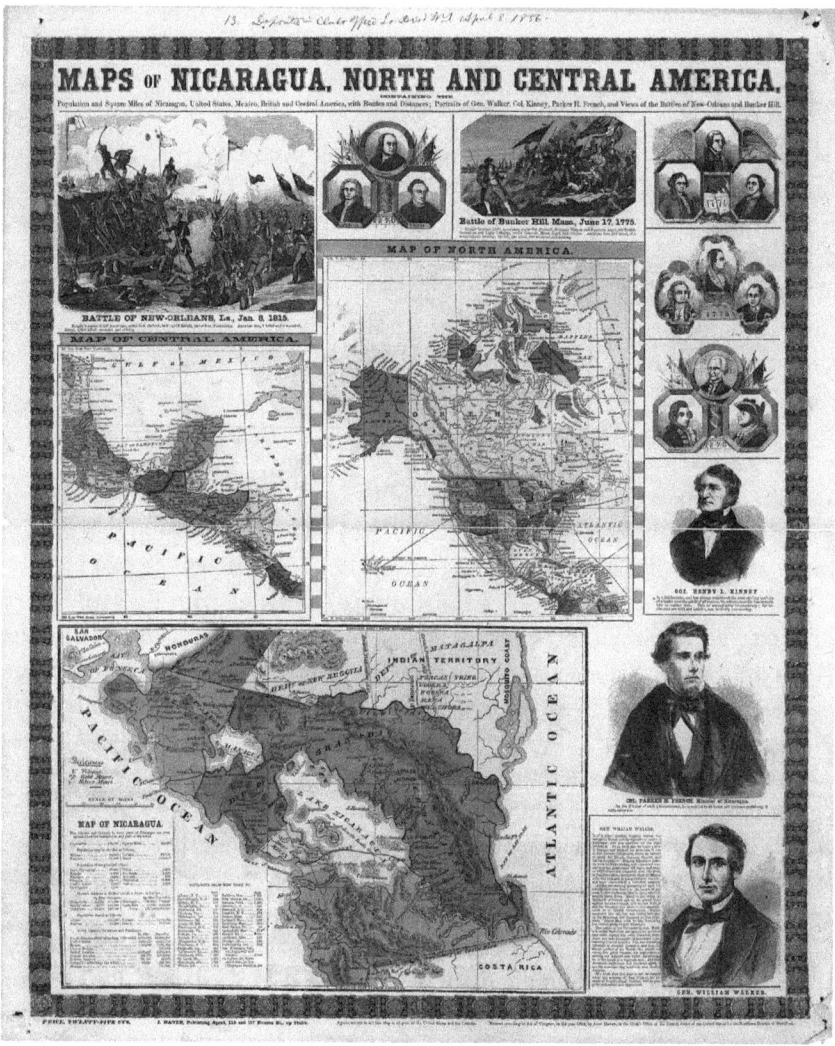

FIGURE 6.3 1856 Broadside with William Walker and Henry Kinney. Maps of Nicaragua, North and Central America: population and square miles of Nicaragua, the United States, Mexico, British, and Central America, with routes and distances; portraits of Gen. Walker, Col. Kinney, Parker H. French, and views of the battles of New Orleans and Bunker Hill. New York: J. D. Haven, 1856. Source: Library of Congress.

delivered in Mobile, Alabama, Walker accused "corrupt" politicians and New York businessmen of orchestrating a "monstrous" conspiracy to seize control of all three major transit routes – Nicaragua, Panama, and Tehuantepec – arguing that this explained the government's abandonment of his cause. Claiming that difficulties in Tehuantepec had shifted the United States' focus to the Nicaragua route, Walker thundered: "When the Tehuantepec project is defeated, then it is that the Nicaraguan policy is changed."[91] While Walker's conspiracy theory was exaggerated, his underlying point was not unfounded: the Nicaragua Canal and transit route were central to U.S. strategic and commercial ambitions in Central America. Filibustering, while ultimately disavowed by the U.S. government, was certainly one of the means through which those ambitions were pursued in the mid nineteenth century.

Throughout the long-drawn-out contest between Costa Rican forces and Walker's band of filibusters, control of the transit route through the San Juan River remained the decisive element for both sides. It explains why so many of Walker's military targets were located along the San Juan River, just as why the blockade of the transit route became the war strategy for the Costa Rican forces under Mora and Canty. With the transit route as the main artery of supplies and recruits, a stranglehold on the route was the only viable way to weaken Walker's enterprise. The effects on Greytown were largely detrimental, and in a town already devastated by the *Cyane* bombardment, the possibility of recouping losses and rebuilding became increasingly a distant dream.

But Walker's final escapade was not Greytown's last encounter with filibustering. On April 25, 1858, Kinney arrived with some of his followers on a barque from Aspinwall and proceeded to haul down the Mosquito flag in the Greytown plaza and raise the Nicaraguan flag in its place. Kinney's followers then proceeded to the home of the mayor of Greytown, Mr. Wolff, and attempted to arrest him. Wolff resisted keeping his doors barred against the men who were armed with pistols and guns. However, when his son later opened the door, Kinney's men overpowered the boy and entered the residence, after which they dragged Wolff to the station house where Kinney was waiting. Kinney demanded that Wolff resign, claiming that he was acting with the authorization of Captain Kennedy of the U.S. warship *Jamestown*. A considerable crowd of townspeople had gathered around the station house, and they now voiced their protests, urging Wolff not to resign. Wolff's account of the incident suggests that the townspeople were ready to take matters into their own hands to drive out the filibusters at this point. This is indicative of the exhaustion of the townspeople with filibustering attempts and a

---

[91] *New York Herald*, February 2, 1858.

determination to resist a return to the filibustering regimes of the recent past. Wolff, however, realizing that the fury of the crowd would not be satiated by a simple arrest of the intruders, urged the crowd to be patient. In the end, Wolff returned to his house – still the mayor of the town. The next day, the crowd assembled at the British consulate and drew up a protest that was signed by the British authorities and the Greytown residents before being presented to Captain Kennedy. The latter denied any involvement in Kinney's attempted takeover. On April 27, Kinney and his associates were arrested, bringing an end to this final attempt by a filibustering group to take control of Greytown and the transit route.[92]

Despite the success of Greytown in thwarting Kinney's attempted takeover, fear of further filibustering ventures continued to plague both the authorities and the people of Greytown. Writing in June 1858, Captain Wainwright, commander of the British ship *Leopard*, reported to Vice Admiral Sir H. Stewart that "all is at present quiet at Greytown, although the people seem apprehensive lest another attack, such as Colonel Kinney's should be made upon them."[93] By October the British government received intelligence that a new filibuster expedition was being organized at the behest of the Panama Railway Company to descend on Punta Arenas in order to obstruct the transit line through Nicaragua.[94] By November, rumors abounded that filibusters were gathering on the southern seaboard of the United States in preparation for an imminent descent on Nicaragua. Reports to British envoy Lord Napier suggested that these freebooters were proceeding to Nicaragua in the guise of traders and immigrants but that they intended to ally with a faction in Nicaragua before carrying out their plans for taking over the government of Nicaragua.[95] Consequently, the commander of the U.S. ship *Roanoke* complained that British officers were boarding American vessels at Greytown harbor in search of filibusters.[96] Throughout the rest of 1858 and into 1859, British vessels continued to patrol the harbor of San Juan del Norte, and some officers floated the idea of stationing Costa Rican forces along the Colorado River.[97]

---

[92] Squire Cottrell to Lewis Cass, May 3, 1858, *Despatches*, roll 3.
[93] Captain Wainwright to H. Stewart, June 17, 1858, FO 420/14B.
[94] Mr. Hammond to Secretary to the Admiralty, October 11, 1858, FO 420/14B.
[95] Lord Napier to the Officer Commanding Her Majesty's Vessels of War at Greytown, November 17, 1858, Inclosure in No. 179, Lord Napier to Earl of Malmesbury, November 20, 1868, FO 420/14B.
[96] Captain of *Roanoke* to Commander of *Valorous*, November 26, 1858, FO 53/43.
[97] Pedro Porras to Ministro de Guerra y Hacienda, January 14, 1859, "Informes al General José Marín Cañas sobre movimientos de filibusteros, Campaña Nacional, salida de

6.6 FILIBUSTERING AND CENTRAL AMERICAN UNITY

From the beginning of Central American retaliation against Walker, the young republics argued that they were taking up arms not in the name of a single nation but all of Central America. The leaders of the Central American states issued declarations and decrees to mobilize popular support for united action against Walker.[98] The National Congress of the Republic of Costa Rica announced by its decree of February 26, 1856, that the object of the war was "to protect the inhabitants of Nicaragua against the ominous oppression of the freebooters, and to drive them from the face of the soil of Central America."[99] In July 1856, when Guatemala, Honduras, and El Salvador signed a formal alliance to oust Walker, their intended purpose was to "throw out the adventurers who have tried to usurp the public power in Nicaragua and which oppress that Republic, threatening the independence of the remaining states."[100] Walker's proslavery decree, issued in September 1856, which appeared to relegalize slavery, galvanized Central American republics, who saw in Walker's regime both a mortal and a moral threat to Central American life.[101] The allied forces sent an unprecedented combined military force of 6,650 troops into Nicaragua in 1856.[102] Luis Molina, the Costa Rican chargé d'affaires at Washington, expressed a common sentiment when he wrote that "the war is not between Costa Rica and Nicaragua but between the united people of the two States, or rather, of Central America against a band of unauthorized adventurers who are impoverishing and oppressing the inhabitants of Nicaragua and who are threatening to impose the same yoke upon the rest of Central Americans."[103]

Walker also viewed himself as a catalyst for the unification of Central America, though under his own leadership and on terms dictated by his

---

William Walker a Honduras, Campaña de Tránsito, ayuda de franceses," Secretaría de Guerra y Marina, 1858–1859, sig. 012294, ANCR.

[98] Marco Antonio Soto Valenzuela, *Guerra nacional de Centroamérica* (Guatemala City: Editorial "José de Pineda Ibarra," 1975), 65–80.

[99] Lewis Cass to William Carey Jones, July 30, 1857, Doc. 1081, Manning, *Diplomatic Correspondence*, vol. 4, 96.

[100] Ralph Lee Woodward, *Rafael Carrera and the Emergence of the Republic of Guatemala, 1821–1871* (Athens: University of Georgia Press, 2008), 290.

[101] Gobat, *Empire by Invitation*, 249–250.

[102] Henry Savage to William Marcy, December 30, 1856, Doc. 1375, Manning, *Diplomatic Correspondence*, vol. 4, 581.

[103] Luis Molina to William Marcy, May 6, 1856, Doc. 1340, Manning, *Diplomatic Correspondence*, vol. 4, 524.

regime, and he considered Nicaragua as his "adopted homeland."[104] The pages of *El Nicaraguense* illuminate Walker's dreams of both Central American unity and the hoped-for centrality of Nicaragua within that union. On June 28, 1856, thus an editorial philosophized the Americanization of the isthmus under Walker:

> The movement has commenced for regeneration. The slow frontier increase has been discarded, and the southern extremity of the continent is now hemmed in. Americans surround it on all sides. They bend towards the centre. The circle narrows, and we can almost see the lines of force that draw Central America and Mexico into another Union, under a new power.[105]

El Nicaraguense thus predicted that under Walker's rule, "Nicaragua shall marshall her sister States in a nobler career than intestine broils."[106] In an editorial on May 24, 1856, the newspaper touched on Walker's role in Central America: "But, in truth, the only real sensible solution to the Central American difficulty is to be found in the continued presence and guidance of Gen. Walker. The people are too feeble to protect themselves from the constant revolutions planned and carried out by rival factions."[107] Under Walker, the newspaper averred, "Nicaragua will not only bloom as a garden, but she will control the destinies of Central America."[108] As Michel Gobat writes, Walker's goal was "forging a Central American empire in the name of spreading U.S.-style democracy and progress to a 'down-trodden and oppressed' people."[109] Walker dreamt of uniting Central America under his leadership – a goal exemplified by his flag, which depicted a star with five points representing the five Central American republics.[110]

Historians such as Michel Gobat and Aims McGuinness have traced the idea of "Latin America" to the decade of the 1850s. While Gobat locates it in the reaction to William Walker's exploits in Latin America, Aims McGuinness points to the violent struggle over the interoceanic canal and, particularly, the Panama route as being pivotal to the

---

[104] "Nicaraguenses," William Walker, June 4, 1856, *Boletín Oficial*, no. 9, *El IHNCA en el Exilio*.
[105] "Central America," *El Nicaraguense*, June 28, 1856, vol. 1, no. 34, 3.
[106] "Nicaragua and Costa Rica," March 1, 1856, *El Nicaraguense*, vol. 1, no. 19, 2.
[107] "The Central American Question," May 24, 1856, *El Nicaraguense*, vol. 1, no. 29, 2.
[108] "Servilism in Nicaragua," May 24, 1856, *El Nicaraguense*, vol. 1, no. 29, 2.
[109] Gobat, *Empire by Invitation*, 2.
[110] "Decrees of the Government," September 13, 1856, *El Nicaraguense*, vol. 1, no. 45, 3; Gobat, *Empire by Invitation*, 18.

development of the idea of a Latin American identity.[111] Historian David Díaz Arias notes that in the context of U.S. expansionism and manifest destiny, a distinct "Hispanic" identity developed in Latin America as a counter to the "Anglo-Saxon" identity of North America.[112] As this chapter shows, an expression of the aspirations for this common identity was in the joint military efforts of Central American republics in the *guerra nacional* during which time Central American leaders repeatedly asserted that they were taking up arms not for the provincial interests of their individual nation-states but in the interests of all of Central America. That control over the Nicaragua Canal played a crucial strategic role in this military struggle can be seen from the centrality of the transit route to the military engagements during the filibuster wars. While not a causal factor in the aspirations for Central American unity, control over the canal – both for Walker and Central American republics – arguably played a crucial role in their respective ambitions.

Central American presses during the period of the *guerra nacional* grappled with the idea of a common identity both for Central Americans and for the larger Latin American subcontinent. From the very beginning of the filibuster wars, newspapers in Central America saw Walker as a threat to the entire region. Thus, the *Gaceta de Guatemala* of November 9, 1855, opined:

> The example of the events that are taking place today in Nicaragua should not go unnoticed in the other states of Central America, and even in other Spanish-American republics, if internal tranquility and the preservation of independence and nationality is valued.[113]

The press saw in the *guerra nacional* a mandate for a Central American union, with the anti-Walker newspaper *Telégrafo Septentrional* based in Granada calling for "libertad de Centro-América" and "libertad de la América del Sur."[114] Central American newspapers of this time also show an attempt to articulate the idea of a "Latin American race." The *Boletín Oficial de Costa Rica*, for instance, saw the development of such a Central American race in opposition to what it saw as the Anglo-Saxon threat of

---

[111] Gobat, "The Invention of Latin America," 1345–1375; McGuinness, "Searching for 'Latin America,'" 87–107.
[112] David Díaz Arias, "Ensayo y conceptos políticos en Centroamérica, 1770–1870," in *Historia global y circulación de saberes en Iberoamérica: Siglos XVI–XXI*, eds. David Díaz Arias and Ronny Viales Hurtado, 99 (San José: CIHAC, 2018).
[113] *Gaceta de Guatemala*, November 9, 1855.
[114] *Telégrafo Septentrional*, April 25, 1857.

American filibusters.[115] Calling the filibusters "enemies of our race," the *Boletín Oficial de Costa Rica* averred that the war against Walker was a "noble cause ... not that of one people, nor two, nor only of Central Americans: it is the just cause of the entire great Hispanic–American family."[116] The Central American press, thus, voiced the need for rallying and uniting not just Nicaragua or Central America but rather signaled towards a united Latin American identity to counter the filibusters. It is no surprise that the first literary work to articulate the idea of "Latin America" was written in the context of the filibuster war in Nicaragua and ended with the clarion call to unite:

Everything calls those young nations

United and united to live.

South America! ALLIANCE, ALLIANCE![117]

The emergence of a Central American and Latin American identity (though mainly aspirational at this point) became a recurring theme in editorials across the region's newspapers, gaining new momentum during the filibustering era in Nicaragua.

6.7 NICARAGUA CANAL AND THE EUROPEAN INTERLUDE

The end of the phase of filibustering in Nicaragua was followed by a period of relative stability both within Nicaragua and among Central American republics. The old rivalries between León and Granada temporarily subsided with Conservatives and Liberals signing a pact on September 12, 1856, and joining hands to oust Walker and his men from Nicaragua.[118] The transitional government that took power in June 1857 embodied this spirit of unity and consisted of a diumvirate of leaders representing the two factions – Máximo Jerez and Tomás Martínez – who expressed a strong commitment to the idea of unity.[119] Martínez, galvanized by his firm belief that Central American unity was the only way to "command the respect of those foreign powers which have belittled us until now," played a significant role in settling Nicaragua's boundary dispute with Costa Rica.[120] The resulting Cañas–Jerez Treaty – signed

---

[115] *Boletín Oficial de Costa Rica*, January 26, 1856.
[116] *Boletín Oficial de Costa Rica*, March 8, 1856.
[117] Torres Caicedo, "Las Dos Américas."   [118] Burns, *Patriarch and Folk*, 221
[119] Antonio Irisarri to Lewis Cass, August 24, 1857, Doc. 1385, Manning, *Diplomatic Correspondence*, vol. 4, 592.
[120] Burns, *Patriarch and Folk*, 224.

just months after Walker's final departure from Nicaragua – included a firm nod to Central American unity. Thus, the first article of the treaty averred that:

peace, happily re-established, may be every day more and more consolidated between the two Governments, and the two nations, not only for the benefit and advantage of Nicaragua and Costa Rica, but likewise for the welfare and prosperity which must certainly accrue to our sister States, the rest of the Republics of Central America.[121]

This new spirit of Nicaraguan and Central American unity had another unexpected consequence. In the years immediately following the end of filibustering, Nicaragua turned more and more towards European powers and evaded U.S. influence, particularly in its schemes for the transit route and plans for the Nicaragua Canal.

The war against Walker disillusioned most Central Americans about the role of the United States in the region. Nicaragua and Costa Rica increasingly looked towards Europe to counter the filibustering threat and signed a convention with the Frenchman Félix Belly – who had been instrumental in securing the Cañas–Jerez Treaty – to open the Nicaraguan interoceanic canal.[122] In an extraordinary agreement reached in Rivas in May 1858, the two republics pledged to put the "foregoing convention, relative to the canal of Nicaragua, under the patronage of civilized Europe."[123] Belly, who had been a vocal critic of American filibustering and U.S. policies in the region, was popular in Central America, where many believed that he would deliver on his promise to open the transit and canal route through Nicaragua free of American influence.[124] On March 15, 1859, Belly arrived in Greytown with forty-five engineers and workmen to commence work on the canal route.[125]

---

[121] "Treaty of Territorial Limits between Costa Rica and Nicaragua," April 15, 1858, *British and Foreign State Papers, 1857–58* (William Ridgway: London, 1866), 1049.

[122] Antonio Irisarri to Lewis Cass, June 16, 1858, Doc. 1439, Manning, *Diplomatic Correspondence*, vol. 4, 736.

[123] "Declaration of Tomás Martínez and Juan Rafael Mora, Presidents of Nicaragua, and Costa Rica Respectively," May 1, 1858, enclosure in Mirabeau Lamar to Lewis Cass, July 26, 1858, Manning, *Diplomatic Correspondence*, vol. 4, 693.

[124] Cyril Allen, *France in Central America: Félix Belly and the Nicaraguan Canal* (New York: Pageant Press, 1966), 7, 66.

[125] Pedro Porras to Ministro de Guerra y Hacienda, March 15, 1859, "Informes al General José Marín Cañas sobre movimientos de filibusteros, Campaña Nacional, salida de William Walker a Honduras, Campaña de Tránsito, ayuda de franceses," Secretaría de Guerra y Marina, 1858–1859, sig. 012294, ANCR; "By Telegraph," *Boston Daily Advertiser*, February 19, 1859.

For a time, this Central American turn towards Europe troubled U.S. diplomats, who rightly worried that they were losing control over the interoceanic route. As Alexander Dimitry, United States minister resident to Nicaragua and Costa Rica, lamented, "The policy of the Government of Nicaragua in reference to the Transit, and the rights growing from it, has been to wrest the route, if possible, from the hands of American citizens."[126] It was a combination of factors – including Belly's increasing ineptitude in securing the means to open the canal and transit routes, the decline of the pro-European regime of General Mora in Costa Rica, and the beginning of French intervention in Mexico – that finally reversed the tide. With the departure of U.S. minister to Nicaragua and Costa Rica, General Mirabeau Lamar, widely considered proslavery and pro-filibuster,[127] the United States appears to have begun recalibrating its policy towards Central America. This shift arguably paved the way towards a gradual thaw in U.S.–Nicaragua relations after nearly a decade of tensions and upheavals.[128] Nicaragua's renewal of relations with the United States reflected, as Gobat argues, the elite belief that Nicaragua's "manifest destiny – the canal – was tied with that of the United States."[129]

Yet, ironically, the period of filibustering had taken a costly toll on the prospects of the Nicaragua Canal. Nicaraguan authorities were wary of reopening the transit route lest it leave the country vulnerable to renewed filibustering. The war itself had damaged the transit route as well as its related infrastructure and facilities. Félix Belly's inability to shore up funds and support for the canal and Nicaragua's vacillation in entrusting the route to U.S. capitalists further delayed work on the route. By 1863, a massive earthquake increased the silting in the harbor of Greytown, making it increasingly unnavigable for ocean steamers and large vessels.[130] By 1866, the Panama route had decisively overtaken the traffic over Nicaragua: in 1866, around 8,000 people crossed through Nicaragua compared to more than 35,000 through Panama.[131] Despite this setback, Walker's failed attempt to carve a Central American empire established a troubling precedent for future U.S. intervention in the region.

---

[126] Alexander Dimitry to Lewis Cass, April 30, 1860, Doc. 1553, Manning, *Diplomatic Correspondence*, vol. 4, 903.
[127] Allen, *France in Central America*, 42. [128] Allen, *France in Central America*, 133.
[129] Gobat, *Confronting the American Dream*, 45.
[130] Folkman, *The Nicaragua Route*, 115. [131] Ibid., 119.

6.8 THE PROTRACTED SETTLEMENT OF THE MOSQUITO QUESTION

The repeated filibustering expeditions of the late 1850s had a paradoxical effect on the settlement of the Mosquito question. On the one hand, it prompted Britain to seek to extricate itself from its involvement in the Mosquito Coast, where British vessels stationed in Greytown were often the only defense against freebooting expeditions. While the cost of defense may have been one factor that played into this, there was a larger desire of the British metropolitan government to settle its differences with the United States over the Mosquito protectorate following the Crimean War. More and more, even on the domestic front in Britain, public support for a British protectorate in Central America was increasingly tenuous. The filibustering attacks and the subsequent hostilities between Nicaragua and Costa Rica had also rendered the idea of an interoceanic canal through Nicaragua a distant dream. Blockade of the San Juan, in particular, had dealt a death blow to the business of providing transit for passengers across the isthmus. More and more, Greytown and the Mosquito Coast appeared as a costly liability. Additionally, the lack of clarity over the position and administration of Greytown made the town ripe as a breeding ground for piratical ventures.

On the other hand, Nicaragua, which had previously been strongly desirous of annexing the Mosquito Coast to its own territory, became increasingly apprehensive about acquiring responsibility for a region rife with filibusterism and seemingly, a constant target for freebooters from the United States. In a letter to the Earl of Malmesbury, Lord Lyons wrote, "the great difficulty in concluding the Treaty for the abandonment of the Mosquito Protectorate lies in the fear of Nicaragua that she will be unable to defend Mosquitia and Greytown from filibustering attacks when the British protection is withdrawn."[132] British agents charged with effecting a treaty with Nicaragua to settle the Mosquito question lamented that the fear caused by the repeated incursion of filibusters was the root cause of the delay in reaching an agreement.[133] As Great Britain despatched its agents to treat with representatives from Nicaragua and Honduras over disputes in the Mosquito territory, landed residents of Greytown appealed for Greytown to be recognized as a "free port" on the

---

[132] Lord Lyons to Earl of Malmesbury, June 21, 1859, FO 420/14B.
[133] W. G. Ouseley to Earl of Malmesbury, February 3, 1859; W. G. Ouseley to Earl of Malmesbury, April 2, 1859, FO 420/14B.

grounds that its citizens were foreigners.[134] Later, the clause in the draft treaty to keep Greytown a "free port" would prompt Nicaraguan protest on the grounds that it was the lack of jurisdiction over Greytown that made it a prime spot for filibustering enterprises and threatened the safety of the surrounding region.[135] Another important point of contention was regarding the position of the Mosquito Kingdom. Great Britain sought to protect the position of the Mosquito King by providing a clause for his economic upkeep. This was contested by both Nicaragua and the United States – both of whom maintained that they had never recognized the sovereignty of the Mosquito Kingdom.[136]

The Zeledón–Wyke Treaty (also known as the Treaty of Managua) resolved the long-standing Mosquito question in January 1860, recognizing Nicaraguan sovereignty over the Mosquito Coast while allowing the Miskitu people to maintain their customs and laws within a self-governing district known as the Mosquito Reserve. The treaty left open the possibility of the Mosquito Reserve's future integration into Nicaragua. Greytown (San Juan del Norte) was designated a free port under Nicaraguan sovereignty to facilitate international trade.

Not surprisingly, in all of these negotiations, neither party attempted to take any real consensus from the Indigenous Miskitus themselves regarding the settlement of their territorial claims. While official documents mention that opinions were being gathered from the Indigenous people, the documents are largely silent on what kinds of opinions were expressed or whether, or if at all, they were taken into consideration during the finalization of the treaty. Clause VI of the Zeledón–Wyke Treaty stipulated that "Her Britannic Majesty engages to use her good offices with the Chief of the Mosquito Indians, so that he shall accept the stipulations which are contained in this Convention."[137] An earlier correspondence reveals that the British stance towards the Mosquito Kingdom in terms of convincing them to go along with the treaty was couched in threats:

Sir Ouseley was told to take measures for apprising the Mosquito chief of what we were going to propose on his behalf, and for obtaining his assent thereto. He was

---

[134] W. G. Ouseley to Earl of Malmesbury, November 30, 1858, FO 420/14b.
[135] Pedro Zeledón to W. G. Ouseley, June 15, 1859, FO 420/14b.
[136] Lord Lyons to Lord J. Russell, September 22, 1859, FO 420/14b.
[137] "Treaty of Managua, 1860," in *The Nicaraguan Mosquitia in Historical Documents, 1844–1927*, eds. Eleonore von Oertzen et al. (Berlin: Verlag, 1990) (hereafter *Historical Documents*), 317.

at the same time told to give the Chief clearly to understand that if he were to refuse to accept them, he must not look to Her Majesty's Government for support in any more extended claims, and that his position and independence will be in danger of becoming more and more precarious every day.[138]

As noted earlier, some evidence points to Miskitu support for Kinney in Greytown. However, the available, albeit fragmentary, records indicate that Indigenous groups largely resisted the transformations brought about by Walker's rule and Nicaragua's subsequent annexation. We know that at least one filibuster expedition was repelled by a Miskitu force. In a letter from Ouseley to the Earl of Malmesbury, we find this rare glimpse into how the indigenous populations may have dealt with the filibuster threat:

> Subsequently a combined [filibuster] attempt on a larger scale was made ... The plan was frustrated by the wreck of the "Susan", and the probable total failure of the attempts to pass through Mosquitia, anticipated by those who best know the nature of the country and the difficulties which want of roads, insalubrity of climate, as also the hostility of the Mosquito Indians [in asterisks: "on whose aid the filibusters counted, mistakenly supposing that they could be induced to join them in attacking Nicaragua"] whose resistance would have been a serious obstacle to the advance of the invading forces into Nicaragua.[139]

Some documents report a rise in lawlessness in Indigenous communities[140] at this time, but it is arguable that what the colonial officials termed "lawlessness" was actually the legitimate resistance of indigenous Miskitus to both filibustering and the broader attempt to annex their Indigenous territory to Nicaragua.

---

[138] "Memorandum on Objections Raised by General Cass to Draft of Treaty about Mosquito Territory, Which Sir W. Ouseley Was to Propose to Nicaragua," Inclosure in No. 398, October 8, 1859, FO 420/14b.
[139] W. G. Ouseley to Earl of Malmesbury, June 28, 1859, FO 420/14b.
[140] James Stanislaus Bell to Earl of Clarendon, July 15, 1857, FO 53/41.

PART III

7

The Road to Arbitration

In 1853, the Nicaraguan Juan Francisco Irias had pointed to the rich resources of Mosquitia during his travel to Rio Coco: "It abounds in fish, and the forest is rich in honey, as also in valuable woods, the supply of which could not be exhausted in many years."[1] In the aftermath of William Walker's filibuster wars, Nicaragua – long divided within itself along Granada–León rivalries – began to espouse a new vision of modernity, one that saw geographical unity as the necessary precursor to national sovereignty. Following the Treaty of Managua (1860), the special status of the Mosquito Reserve as a self-governing enclave presented an obstacle to Nicaraguan dreams of unifying its territory from the Atlantic to the Pacific and, in the process, gaining control over the Nicaragua Canal route and the untapped riches of the nation's Caribbean coastline. Nicaragua's efforts to push for greater incorporation of the harbor of Greytown and the Reserve within the Republic brought it into conflict with the Reserve, which, under Moravian influence, was establishing its own autonomous and separate character from the Republic. Using the language of race to justify its encroachment into the Reserve, Nicaraguan officials challenged the Mosquito Reserve on the grounds that it was a black polity that existed not because of Indigenous support but through the machinations of foreigners. Despite Britain's avowed desire to remain neutral, British officials on the ground, such as Consuls James Green and Alexander Gollan, expressed their support of

---

[1] "Rio Wanks and the Mosco Indians: A Letter from Don Juan Francisco Irias," *Transactions of the American Ethnological Society*, vol. 3, pt. 1 (New York, Putnam: 1853), 162.

Miskitu autonomy and sought out greater British metropolitan intervention. Even as the conflict between Nicaragua and the Mosquito Reserve escalated, the opening of the Suez Canal sparked renewed American interest in the Nicaragua Canal. As the Nicaragua–Reserve struggle over the canal route became an international issue, years of war and instability threatened the vaunted geographical advantage of the Mosquito Coast, with the local conditions of Greytown making the entry point of the proposed canal route increasingly unnavigable. Ironically, Nicaragua's efforts to leverage U.S. interests in the canal led to conflict with Guatemala's aggressive unionism, undermining the ideals of regional unity that had sustained Nicaragua's relations with its Central American neighbors since the Mexican–American War.

7.1 THE TREATY OF MANAGUA

The Treaty of Managua brought the British protectorate over the Mosquito Kingdom to an end, transferring the sovereignty of the newly demarcated territory assigned to the Indigenous Miskitus, known as the Mosquito Reserve, to Nicaragua. The inhabitants of the Reserve would enjoy the right of self-governance and customary laws without interference from Nicaragua. By the Treaty, Nicaragua agreed to pay an annual sum of $5,000 to the Indigenous authorities of the Reserve for a period of ten years. Greytown was constituted a free port under the sovereign authority of the Republic of Nicaragua. The Treaty prohibited the imposition of duties or charges on vessels arriving in or departing from Greytown, except what was essential for maintaining the port.[2] Great Britain had also already signed a treaty with Honduras on November 28, 1859, with similar stipulations to protect the Miskitu Indigenous communities in Honduran territory.[3]

Even though the Miskitus or their chief were not consulted in the process of drawing up these treaties, Article VI of the Treaty of Managua stipulated that Great Britain should ensure Miskitu acceptance of the convention.[4] In fact, following the ratification of the treaties, on September 18, 1860, the British consul in Greytown, James Green, and the Miskitu king embarked on the British steamship *Racer* to visit the

---

[2] "Treaty of Managua, 1860," *Historical Documents*, 317
[3] "Treaty between Her Majesty and the Republic of Honduras," Inclosure in Lord John Russell to Consul Green, June 16, 1860, FO 881/4013.
[4] "Treaty of Managua, 1860," *Historical Documents*, 317.

various Miskitu settlements on the coast that had been affected by the terms of the Treaty. The two men visited Bluefields, Cape Cameron, which lay 8 miles west of Black River, Cape Gracias a Dios, and Corn Islands, before finally returning to Greytown. Commander Lyons of the steamship *Racer* reported the positive outcome of the king's visits: "The different Mosquito Chiefs with whom we communicated are, I fancy, without an exception, disposed to follow their King into the new limits of his territory agreed upon in the Treaties."[5]

By the terms of the Managua Treaty, the southern portion of the Mosquito territory, including Greytown, was transferred to Nicaragua, and on January 1, 1861, the flag of Nicaragua was hoisted over Greytown and saluted.[6] The occasion also underscored the end of British official presence on the shore, with Consul Green remarking on "the absence of an English ship-of-war on the occasion."[7] The Nicaraguan commissioner, Don Ramon Saenz, eager to conciliate the inhabitants of Greytown, met with the municipal authorities of Greytown and in concert with them drew up a provisional government constituting a magistrate, a clerk, and two policemen. Saenz issued a notice, decreeing that all merchant vessels would be charged 15 cents per ton, and a duty of 5 percent would be imposed on all goods imported for consumption in the port of Greytown for the upkeep of the port.[8] Despite this initial enthusiasm over achieving a consensus through the treaties, however, storm clouds were already gathering and would before long begin a two-decade-long period of struggle over the terms of the treaty.

7.2 NICARAGUA AND THE TRANSIT ROUTE

The period of filibustering under William Walker had an unexpected outcome in Nicaragua. Following the war against Walker, Nicaragua sought to bridge its internal discord between León and Granada and move towards a more unified national government. As Nicaragua attempted to consolidate, it was also haunted by the specter of invasion,

---

[5] Commander Lyons to the Senior Officer, Jamaica, October 12, 1860, FO 881/4013.
[6] After 1861, the name "San Juan del Norte" became the official designation for the town, particularly in Nicaraguan government records and local usage. However, "Greytown" continued to be used, especially in British and American diplomatic, commercial, and maritime circles.
[7] Consul Green to Lord J. Russell, January 10, 1861, FO 881/4013.
[8] "Notice," Enclosure 5 in Consul Green to Lord J. Russell, January 10, 1861, FO 881/4013.

particularly in the context of European intervention in Mexico, which culminated in the period of the French intervention and the installation of the Austrian Archduke Maximilian I as the ruler of Mexico.[9] Efforts to consolidate the nation were mirrored in Nicaragua's renewed efforts to control the canal route. According to Karl Offen, the national project of Nicaragua after 1860 consisted of unifying the natural resources and geography of the Mosquito Coast with the modernizing vision of the Pacific side of Nicaragua. He writes: "Based on visions of a unified national territory, the unlimited potential of tropical nature and the shortcomings of resident 'races,' the state sought to do three things: establish its civil and military authority over the new space; unite natural resources with progressive industry; and civilise and assimilate Mosquitia indigenes."[10] It is in this context of Nicaragua's vision of modernization that we must place its attempts at control over the Nicaragua canal route.

In April 1860, the directors of the American Atlantic and Pacific Ship Canal Company obtained a charter from Nicaragua. Recognizing the company under the name of Central American Transit Company, Nicaragua granted it the privilege of transit for a period of fifty years. The years of war, however, had greatly damaged the transit facilities along the Nicaragua Canal route, and the Transit Company faced an uphill battle to restart the transit route. When the company finally reopened the transit for passengers in October 1862, it was a dismal scene with passengers forced to walk for miles in the absence of sufficient steamers. The Nicaraguan government issued a decree that forfeited the company's charter and gave it a period of three months to wrap up its operations. On February 20, 1863, the company's charter was annulled, and the Nicaraguan Congress announced that it would take possession of the transit route on March 2.[11] On March 11, Nicaraguan forces proceeded to seize the company steamers and other property. The Nicaraguan governor of Greytown, Ramon Saenz arrived at the company's works, arresting its employees, ordering the American flags to be hauled down from the top of the buildings, and stationing guards on the river steamers, eliciting protests from the company's agents, who

---

[9] Tijerino, *El imaginario del canal y la nación cosmopolita*, 326.
[10] Karl Offen, "The Geographical Imagination, Resource Economies, and Nicaraguan Incorporation of the Mosquitia, 1838-1909," in *Territories, Commodities and Knowledges: Latin American Environmental Histories in the Nineteenth and Twentieth Centuries*, ed. Christian Brannstrom, 63 (London: Institute for the Study of the Americas, 2004).
[11] Folkman, *The Nicaragua Route*, 107-110.

addressed a memorial to the president of the United States against this act of outrage against American people and property.[12]

Internal political chaos in Nicaragua soon reopened space for the Company to regain the transit route. In early 1863, Liberal General Máximo Jerez invaded from Honduras. Later that year, insurgent activity reached San Carlos on the lake–river corridor, briefly disrupting transit before government forces reasserted control. Rumors of renewed invasions and fear of losing the transit route again to revolutionaries and filibusters led to Nicaragua renegotiating the contract with the Central American Transit Company, which was ratified in February 1864. The new charter was geared towards turning the transit route into an immediate source of revenue for the war-depleted government of Nicaragua and steamship service with a regular monthly schedule reopened in August 1864.[13] President Martínez's 1865 message to the Nicaraguan Congress not only highlighted his recent military victory over Jerez but also emphasized the optimistic outlook for the transit route, giving an account of the $100,000 contribution to the treasury from the transit company.[14] Indeed, for a brief period, Greytown flourished under the Transit Company's business. Writing in January 1865, the U.S. commercial agent, Squier Cottrell, observed, "The business of this Port, and likewise of the interior, has increased one hundred percent or more during the past year, and it is not unreasonable to attribute the cause in a great degree to the successful operation of the Central American Transit Company."[15]

Negotiations with the Central American Transit Company were only one of several possibilities explored by the Nicaraguan government in the early 1860s to secure profits from the transit route and explore possibilities of connecting the two oceans across the isthmus. One of the most well known of these ventures was Nicaragua's negotiations with Captain Bedford Pim to create a transoceanic railway line across the isthmus. Pim himself authored two books: *The Gate of the Pacific* (1863) and *Dottings on the Roadside, in Panama, Nicaragua, and Mosquito* (with Seeman, 1869), which give us a unique window into his proposed railway project and the local-level complexities in the Mosquito Coast.

---

[12] Squier Cottrell to William H. Seward, March 16, 1863, *Despatches*, roll 4.
[13] Folkman, *The Nicaragua Route*, 110–114.
[14] Cruz, *Nicaragua's Conservative Republic*, 56.
[15] Squier Cottrell to William H. Seward, January 18, 1865, *Despatches*, roll 4.

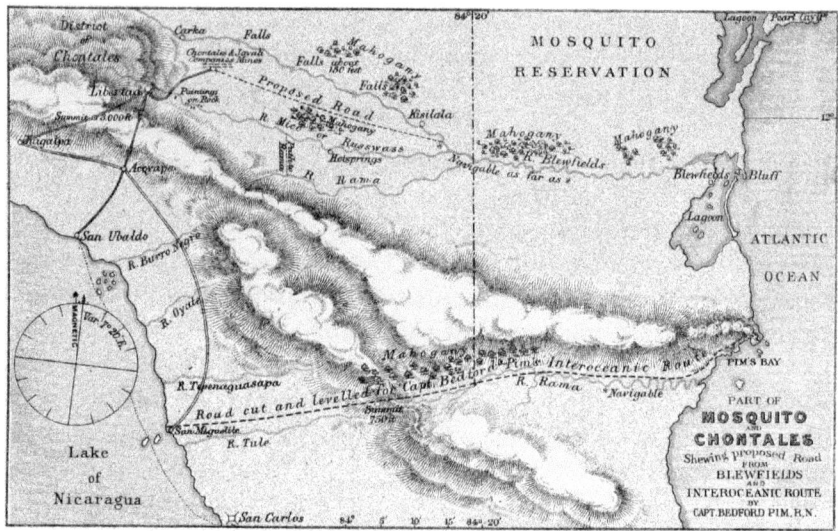

FIGURE 7.1 Bedford Pim's proposed railroad. Source: Bedford Pim and Berthold Seemann, *Dottings on the Roadside, in Panama, Nicaragua and Mosquito* (London: Chapman and Hall, 1869). Digitized by the British Library.

Bedford Pim was a Royal Navy officer who became a major landowner in the Caribbean. He had obtained a land grant from the Miskitu king, and he proposed to build a railroad to connect the Atlantic and Pacific Oceans via the Nicaraguan isthmus. In March 1863, Pim undertook an expedition through the dense forests of Nicaragua and confirmed the practicability of his proposal.[16] On April 8, 1865, he obtained a railway concession from the government of Nicaragua to establish a transit from Monkey Point on the Atlantic coast to Corinto or the Gulf of Fonseca on the Pacific. The terms of the concession held out that this transit could be constructed as a continuous railroad or partly by railroad and partly by steamers through Lake Nicaragua (see Figure 7.1).[17] For Pim, the Nicaragua route presented the only practicable interoceanic route (see Figure 7.2 for Pim's view of the Nicaragua route), and he declared, "Look at Nicaragua! Her geographical position fits her for the commerce of the universe; she is in reality the centre of the New World. Mosquito, to say nothing of its intrinsic worth, offers an Atlantic port; an easy means of reaching this vast wealth, besides being on the highway to all our interests

---

[16] Bedford Pim and Berthold Seemann, *Dottings on the Roadside, in Panama, Nicaragua and Mosquito* (London: Chapman and Hall, 1869), 360.
[17] Ibid., 437.

Nicaragua and the Transit Route 191

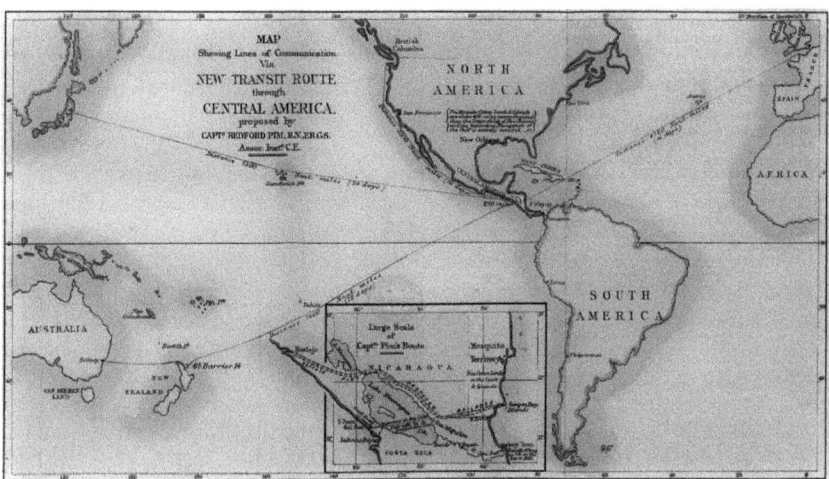

FIGURE 7.2 Nicaragua as the center of world commerce. Source: Bedford Pim, *The Gate of the Pacific* (London: Lovell Reeve & Co., 1863). Digitized by the British Library.

to the westward."[18] John Collinson, a civil engineer who had been employed by Pim to survey the route, pointed out that, considering the expected traffic through the route, the railway would give a dividend of more than 20 percent per annum. "It is self-evident," he wrote, "that this undertaking holds out to its shareholders a certainty of very large returns."[19]

The estimated cost of constructing the railroad, however, was much in excess of the funds available to the Central American Transit Company, which would have to execute it. The 101 miles between Monkey Point and Lake Nicaragua alone was estimated to cost $8,300,000, a sum that was considered by the company to be well beyond its means, causing Pim to return to England "thoroughly discouraged."[20] As with Pim's railroad route, throughout the 1860s, Nicaragua would toy with different plans for the transit route – none of which would ultimately transpire.

Controlling the transit route through plans for constructing a canal or railroad was only one part of Nicaragua's efforts to extend its

---

[18] Bedford Pim, *The Gate of the Pacific* (London: Lovell Reeve & Co., 1863), 395.
[19] John Collinson, *Descriptive Account of Captain Bedford Pim's Project for an International Atlantic and Pacific Junction Railway across Nicaragua: Report and Estimate of Cost* (London: Taylor & Co., 1866), 26.
[20] Folkman, *The Nicaragua Route*, 118.

geographical influence into the Mosquito Coast. A more contentious issue grew around Nicaragua's attempts to take economic control of Greytown. The Treaty of Managua had constituted Greytown as a free port, stipulating in Article VII that:

> No duties or charges shall be imposed upon vessels arriving in, or departing from the free port of Greytown, other than such as may be sufficient for the due maintenance and safety of the navigation, for providing lights and beacons, and for defraying the expense of the police of the port; neither shall any duties or charges be levied on the free port on goods arriving therein, in transit from sea to sea. But nothing contained in this Article shall be construed to prevent the Republic of Nicaragua from levying the usual duties on goods destined for consumption within the territory of the Republic.

Problems would arise over the Nicaraguan interpretation of this article, which would be at variance with both the Miskitu and British understanding of the treaty. On December 1, 1863, the Nicaraguan government fixed the import dues payable by merchants in Greytown at 10 percent instead of the usual 5 percent.[21] In addition, a tax of 15 cents a ton was levied on vessels arriving at the port. Besides, other taxes levied were: land tax, house tax, taxes for horses, hotel tax, tax for selling merchandise and liquor, and tax for lighting oil lamps.[22] On October 4, 1864, Nicaragua issued a decree mandating that maritime importation of foreign goods into the Mosquito Reserve must be through the port of Greytown, subject to the duties of that port.[23] Greytown merchants lamented that goods from Europe or the United States were charged a duty of 40 percent, thus restricting trade.[24] The decree also claimed that the islands and cays in the region were part of the Republic of Nicaragua and would be subject to its fiscal laws. The decree of October 1864 was followed by additional decrees imposing duties on the importation of tobacco: "Customs on imported tobacco will be collected on the 1st January next, in advance, the augmentation of 50% on that which is now derived whether it be leaf or manufactured tobacco."[25] By 1867, the government prohibited the

---

[21] "Decree Establishing the 10 Per Cent Duties on the Total Amount of the Invoices of Goods Imported at San Juan del Norte," Inclosure 7 in Consul Green to Earl Russell, January 13, 1864, FO 881/4013.
[22] Merchants of San Juan del Norte to Lord Stanley, November 4, 1868, FO 56/22.
[23] Squier Cottrell to William H. Seward, December 7, 1864, *Despatches*, roll 4.
[24] Merchants of San Juan del Norte to Lord Stanley, November 4, 1868, FO 56/22.
[25] See enclosures in Squier Cottrell to William H. Seward, January 20, 1865, *Despatches*, roll 4.

import of strong liquor from foreign countries.[26] Earlier in July 1864, the government also mandated a tax of 1 percent on all Indian rubber exported through the port.[27]

This immediately elicited protests from Greytown merchants, who had assumed that they would be exempt from duties by the terms set in the Treaty of Managua. The Nicaraguan government consistently justified its measures by arguing that the revenue generated through these duties would be used for the upkeep of the harbor of Greytown. However, the merchants argued that none of the improvements in the harbor promised had been brought to fruition. In November 1868, the merchants and property holders of Greytown presented a petition to the British government highlighting the unjust fiscal measures instituted in Greytown by the Nicaraguan government. They claimed that "instead of any portion of the large revenue derived from the numerous taxes being devoted to the erection of public schools and hospital, the maintenance of teachers and physicians, the erection of a Light-house and the general improvement, the large surplus funds have been diverged from their legitimate channel and expended for the special use of the State government."[28]

The merchants further claimed that the people of Greytown, who were the taxpayers, were not consulted with regard to the use of the money generated; rather, "the entire control of the treasure funds, is assumed by the Governor intendant, without the people who pay them having any voice."[29] The petitioners also lamented that although they had paid taxes for the repairs and beautification of a Catholic church as well as to support a priest, the Nicaraguan government had not allocated any money for the repair and support of the Protestant church in Greytown. They also complained that despite the predominant use of the English language in Greytown, there was not a single interpreter to facilitate communication between the Nicaraguan officials and foreigners.[30] The Nicaraguan government maintained that it was following the treaty provisions of the Managua Treaty, which allowed for duties and charges to be imposed to defray the cost of maintenance and safety of the harbor and for providing lights, beacons, and the expense of the police. As we will see, this would be just one of several of the treaty provisions that

---

[26] See enclosures in Squier Cottrell to William H. Seward, February 19, 1867, *Despatches*, roll 4.
[27] Squier Cottrell to William H. Seward, July 25, 1864, *Despatches*, roll 4.
[28] Merchants of San Juan del Norte to Lord Stanley, November 4, 1868, FO 56/22.
[29] Ibid.   [30] Ibid.

would become points of contention between the Nicaraguan government on the one hand and the Greytown merchants and the Mosquito Reserve on the other.

7.3 MISKITU AUTONOMY AND RESISTANCE

Following the Treaty of Managua and under the advice of the British Consul James Green, on September 12, 1861, Miskitu Chief George Augustus called a meeting of Miskitu headmen and the multiracial population of the Reserve, where he formed a council of state to govern and represent the interests of the Mosquito Reserve. Headmen from various parts of the Miskitu territory – including Sandy Bay, Pearl Lagoon, Rama Cay, Corn Islands, Wounta, Bluefields, Pearl Cays, Awastara, Duckwarra, Great River, and Hillwawa River – attended the meeting at Bluefields. However, according to Olien, only eleven of the fifty-one headmen and representatives present appeared to be Miskitu, and there was no representative from Greytown. During this meeting, the Miskitu chief appointed a general council of forty-three members comprised of representatives from Corn Islands, Pearl Lagoon, Wounta, Great River, Rama Cay, Bluefields, and Pearl Cays. The council elected its officers, comprising the Miskitu chief as the president of the council, Henry Patterson of Pearl Lagoon as vice-president, and John Herbert Hooker of Bluefields as secretary. The duties of the general council were: "To make, form, and adopt a Constitution, enact and pass Laws and Regulations necessary and lawful for the Municipal Authority of the Mosquito Reserve." The general council elected an eighteen-member executive council, comprised of representatives from Rama Cay, Bluefields, Pearl Lagoon, Wounta, Hillwawa River, and Great River.[31]

One of the first actions taken by the general council was to declare the ports and rivers within the Mosquito Reserve to be free ports and rivers, insomuch as it affected the Reserve and its municipal authority. In addition, it approved an annuity of $1,500 to the hereditary chief on an annual basis. The general council instituted a personal tax of $1 to be paid by every male person of the age between eighteen and sixty to the government of the Reserve. The executive council appointed a treasurer to superintend the finances and revenues of the Reserve and a chief justice

---

[31] "Address of George Augustus Fredrick, Hereditary Chief of Mosquito," September 12, 1861, *Historical Documents*, 318–326.

to superintend the administration of justice, the public instruction and schools, and the public offices of the Reserve. The council enumerated an exhaustive list of regulations for the maintenance of public order in the Reserve, including conduct of judicial proceedings, control of vagrants and "disorderly persons," and offences committed by juveniles.[32]

George Augustus' actions propelled the Mosquito Reserve on a trajectory that would ultimately lead to open conflict with Nicaragua. The death of the Miskitu chief in 1864 was followed by the succession of his nephew, William Henry Clarence, since the old chief died without leaving any son "deemed suitable to become his successor as their mother was not of pure Indian stock." According to Olien, during the reign of George Augustus, there was a significant shift in the values of the Miskitu leadership, where a pure Indigenous descent was seen as a necessary prerequisite for leadership as chief or king. This shift may have resulted from the efforts of the Miskitu to differentiate themselves from the increasing number of black migrants from Jamaica, who were arriving and settling in the Mosquito territory.[33] Thus, the child from the marriage of George's sister Victoria with a Miskitu Indigenous was considered to be the legitimate choice for succession. This emphasis on the "Indian-ness" of the new Chief William Henry Clarence, however, would paradoxically be challenged by the Nicaraguan government on the grounds that the Miskitu government was not "Indian" enough.

Moravian missionaries began to play an important role in the lives of the Miskitu chiefs beginning in the reign of George Augustus, when they established a mission in Bluefields in 1849. When the center of British operations on the shore shifted to Greytown, James Green rented his house to the superintendent of the Moravian mission, H. G. Pfeiffer, on the condition that he educate and take care of George Augustus and the other royal children.[34] Later, when British Consul William Dougal Christie shifted British headquarters to Greytown, Pfeiffer accompanied him and preached the gospel to a large congregation in Greytown, including Americans who were on their way to California. At Christie's request, Pfeiffer took charge of the three sisters of King George Augustus and provided them with a home and education. Another missionary, Brother Lundberg, provided daily instruction to the Miskitu king. During meetings between the missionaries and the Indigenous Miskitus, George

---

[32] "Regulations for the Maintenance of Public Order," *Historical Documents*, 333–335.
[33] Olien, "Miskito Kings and the Line of Succession," 231–232.
[34] Offen and Rugeley, *The Awakening Coast*, 25.

Augustus often acted as an interpreter. An attendee at the Mission's Sunday School, the Miskitu king also directed his subjects to assist the missionaries in various sundry works, including clearing the land for the construction of the chapel and mission house.[35] The Bluefields Sunday School became an important center of Moravian activities and by 1854 boasted 107 enrolled students.[36] By 1866, the mission had six stations in the Mosquito Coast, each with a church and schoolhouse.[37]

At his birth, William Henry Clarence was baptized by the Moravian missionaries.[38] His accession in 1866 came just a year after a devastating hurricane that damaged much of Bluefields and adjoining areas, including the Moravian mission buildings.[39] It is possible that in the aftermath of the hurricane, the Moravian missionaries managed to fulfill an important nurturing role in the Reserve, which added to their legitimacy among the Miskitus. After his accession to the Miskitu chiefdom, the Moravian missionaries continued to occupy an important role in the lives of the Miskitu leadership. At the time of the death of George Augustus, Clarence was living in the mission house in Bluefields. The election of Clarence on May 23, 1866, was accompanied by a twenty-one-gun salute. Johann Eugene Lundberg, a cofounder of the Moravian mission at Bluefields, offered his prayer during the election, "beseeching the Lord God to make the new king a Christian king, and keep him in the paths of virtue and peace." In the evening, the children of the Bluefields school, under the care of Brother Pinnock, marched in procession before assembling in the mission house to sing "God Save Prince William Our King." Clarence, who was only ten years old at the time of his accession, was to be under the guardianship of another missionary, Brother Hoch.[40] While James Green was not part of the Miskitu council, he was still hugely influential in the workings of the council and so, presumably, would have had a role in the election of William Henry Clarence to the Miskitu chieftainship.[41]

The new chief traveled to Jamaica for his education, returning to Bluefields in September 1874. It is likely that in his absence, the Miskitu government was run by the council led by Henry Patterson. Clarence's

---

[35] "Extract of a Letter from H. G. Pfeiffer," *The Awakening Coast*, 41–43.
[36] "Extract from the Diary of Bluefields, 1854," *The Awakening Coast*, 47.
[37] Consul Green to Lord Stanley, November 26, 1866, FO 881/4013.
[38] "Certificate," Inclosure in the Mosquito Chief to Earl Granville, December 20, 1871, FO 881/4013.
[39] See *The Awakening Coast*, 102–109, for Moravian reactions to the 1865 hurricane.
[40] "Election of Chief William Henry Clarence," *Historical Documents*, 158.
[41] Olien, "Miskito Kings," 232.

return was marked by considerable fanfare, much of which was led by the missionaries. Upon landing at the pier, he was greeted by cannon fire. J. E. Lundberg's account of this occasion highlights the role missionaries played on this occasion: "Br. Herzog and myself, with the schoolchildren, had taken up our position in the verandah of the mission-house, and when the king arrived, the children sang to the air of 'God Save the Queen,' a song specially composed for the occasion, commencing with the following words: 'Welcome, thrice, welcome be, Chief, to thy native shore.'" In his speech to the assembled council on September 22, 1874, Clarence did not fail to mention his vision of the role of the Moravian church in the lives of his subjects: "It is also my desire that the government should protect and assist the Moravian Missionaries in the furtherance of the Gospel among the inhabitants of this country; in taking a retrospective view it can truly be said, that they have done much good to yourselves and your children."[42] Clarence's printed proclamation of September 1874 also gives us an insight into the ways in which the missionaries may have mediated politically on behalf of the young chief. Clarence declared that "The Rev. D. J. East and Rev. J. S. Roberts have spared nothing to guide me and to advance the interests of Mosquito, and through their influence I have had frequent and pleasant interviews with the Governor and officials of Jamaica." It was also clear that Clarence intended to continue this relationship with the Moravian church during his tenure as chief. He proclaimed:

When we remember how necessary is His blessing by whom Kings reign and Princes decree justice, how can we, honourable gentlemen, express the obligations, personal and nation, we owe to the Board of the Missions of the United Brethren for their continued interest, and to the Minister and leaders sent into our midst? Let us then cherish the mission with the chapels and schools, and seek to increase them for I am convinced that the religious education of our people is indispensable.[43]

Indeed, one of the first acts enacted by Clarence was the enforcement of compulsory education within the Mosquito Reserve.[44] Since the schools in most cases were run by the missionaries, this also ensured the continuance of missionary work.

From the very inception of the Mosquito Reserve, the Nicaraguan interpretation of the Managua Treaty challenged Indigenous autonomy

---

[42] "Chief William Henry Clarence Assumes His Office," *Historical Documents*, 166–168.
[43] "Printed Proclamation of the Chief (1874)," *Historical Documents*, 337–338.
[44] "Legislation under William Henry Clarence," *Historical Documents*, 341.

in the Reserve. In a meeting between then Consul James Green and the Nicaraguan Governor of San Juan del Norte Ramon Saenz, the latter "expressed his own views of the interpretation the IIIrd Article of the Treaty in relation to the sovereign rights of Nicaragua would admit of, viz., that Nicaragua alone has the right to give privileges for collecting of the native products of the reserved territory, such as cutting timbers, collecting India-rubber, cocoa-nuts, and other natural products."[45] While the British metropolitan government assumed a stance of neutrality on the Mosquito question, Consul Green did not shy away from taking a firm stand in support of the Miskitu claims, maintaining that the Treaty of Managua guaranteed the rights of the Miskitu to the "exclusive use of the lands by occupation and the sole use of the productions thereof" in the territory of the Reserve.[46]

Nicaragua was one of the first countries to begin the export of India rubber and experienced a boom in rubber exports in the second half of the nineteenth century. Most of this rubber was collected in the form of latex from the Mosquito Coast and shipped through Greytown.[47] Bedford Pim noted the importance of India rubber to the commerce of Greytown, remarking that, "as sugar is to the West Indies, so is India rubber to Greytown."[48] According to English naturalist Thomas Belt, "the exports of rubber through the port of Greytown increased from 401,475 lbs., valued at 112,413 dollars, in 1867, to 754,886 lbs., valued at 226,465 dollars in 1871."[49] Belt also pointed to the apparently unregulated way in which the forests on the Nicaraguan Caribbean coast were being exploited for this export commodity: "The Government attempts no supervision of the forests, anyone may cut the trees, and great destruction is going on amongst them."[50] Describing the activity of Nicaraguan rubber traders in Castillo on the San Juan River, Belt wrote: "Parties of men are here fitted out with canoes and provisions, and proceed up the rivers, far into the uninhabitable forests of the Atlantic slope. They remain for several months away, and are expected to bring the rubber they obtain to the merchants who have fitted them out."[51] There was also evidence that intruders from Nicaragua were involved in the exploitation of the India rubber native to the Reserve. Thus, for instance, the residents of the

---

[45] James Green to Lord J. Russell, July 22, 1861, FO 881/4013.
[46] Consul Green to Earl Russell, November 16, 1861, FO 881/4013.
[47] Dozier, *Nicaragua's Mosquito Shore*, 116.
[48] Pim and Seemann, *Dottings on the Roadside*, 347.
[49] Thomas Belt, *The Naturalist in Nicaragua* (London: John Murray, 1874), 33.
[50] Ibid., 34.   [51] Ibid., 32–33.

Reserve complained in autumn of 1877 of unauthorized people from the Republic of Nicaragua who entered the Reserve to extract India rubber and committed outrages and violence upon the inhabitants of the Reserve.[52]

While unjust duties and unauthorized incursion and extraction of resources were important points of contention between the Nicaraguan government and the Mosquito authorities, perhaps the biggest bone of contention was regarding the issue of Miskitu succession of William Henry Clarence (see Figure 7.3) to the chiefdom of the Reserve government. Immediately after the ten-year-old boy succeeded his uncle as the Miskitu chief in 1866, the Nicaraguan government objected to the succession on the grounds that the officials involved in the election were non-Indigenous. Thus, Nicaraguan Minister of Foreign Affairs Rosalío Cortéz wrote, "According to the information received, the election, designation, or appointment of this youth is the result of the suffrages of a meeting of foreigners resident in the Mosquito Reserve, without the intervention in that election, designation or appointment, either of the Indians in general or of the headmen."[53] A memorandum issued by the Nicaraguan government condemned this election as a contravention of the Treaty of Managua. In the memorandum, the Nicaraguan government claimed that foreigners and adventurers had "fallen like a plague on the Mosquito Indians" and that "on the death of the last Mosquito Chief, they managed by their artifices and intrigues to lodge the supreme authority in the hands of a child 11 years old, constituting themselves guardians of that infant, arbiters of the internal government, and an apple of discord between the Government of the Republic and the Diplomatic and Consular Agents of Great Britain."[54] In the aftermath of the filibuster wars, such an accusation of Miskitu complicity with foreign usurpers had particular resonance, adding a veneer of legitimacy to Nicaraguan encroachments on the Reserve.

This point of dispute was also used by Nicaragua to support its decision to withhold payment of a subvention to the Mosquito Reserve fixed at $5,000 per year by the Treaty of Managua.[55] On July 18, 1866, Ramon Saenz issued a declaration de-recognizing the election of the young chief, emphasizing that the election had been disowned by the

---

[52] Acting Consul Thomas to the Marquis of Salisbury, June 15, 1878, FO 881/4015.
[53] Rosalío Cortéz to Mr. Wallis, November 29, 1866, Inclosure 1 in Mr. Wallis to Lord Stanley, December 22, 1866, FO 881/4013.
[54] Memorandum communicated by Señor Martínez, August 19, 1867, FO 881/4013.
[55] "Memoria Presentada por el Sr. Ministro de Relaciones Exteriores Dr. D. Rosalío Cortéz al Soberano Congreso de 1867" (Managua: Imprenta de Gobierno, 1867), 3–7.

FIGURE 7.3 Young Chief William Henry Clarence. Source: Enclosure in Henry Patterson to Earl Granville, September 4, 1872, FO 56/22. Courtesy of the National Archives, Kew.

government of the Nicaraguan Republic.[56] Thus, in its memorandum of 1867, the Nicaraguan government maintained that it was prepared to pay the subvention as long as the government of the Reserve was truly composed of Indians:

> Let those who direct the Government and the Administration of the Mosquitos be real Indians and natives of the country; but let them not be foreigners or aliens to it, nor come to establish themselves on the coast ... It is clear to the President of the Republic that the recent election of the Chief of the Mosquitos was not carried out by them, but by the aforementioned adventurers, who, under certain deceitful appearances, intentionally placed the reins of the administration in the hands of a youth, knowing that not he, but they themselves, under the name of guardians, would be the owners and arbiters of the results of the Convention.[57]

The Nicaraguan envoy, Marshal Martínez, clarified that the Nicaraguan government had never defaulted on the payment of the subsidy to the Reserve during the tenure of the previous Miskitu chief but that the Republic refused to make the payment to William Henry Clarence, who, the Nicaraguan government maintained, had been elected by foreigners and not by the Indigenous population.[58]

Correspondence of the U.S. commercial agent Squier Cottrell underlines the racial undertone of the Nicaraguan objection to the succession of the young chief. Describing an interview with Ramon Saenz, Cottrell wrote:

> The Governor stated that he had been and continued to be greatly annoyed by the importunities of the British Vice Consul ... who had a short time since returned from Blewfields where he had been to enact the farce, as the Governor termed it, of culling together certain foreigners and travellers whom he had met there, and electing a young black boy (niño negro) King of the Mosquito Indians, as the lawful successor of the late King of the tribe.[59]

Saenz requested Cottrell to "receive on deposit the funds appropriate for the Mosquito Indians, until such time as a lawful chief should be chosen as themselves."[60] In Saenz's words and the justification used for withholding the subvention, we can also find the language of race and, particularly the issue of "Indian-ness" again rearing its head as a notable point of contention between the Nicaraguan government and the Mosquito authorities. Nicaraguan efforts to question the legitimacy of

---

[56] See enclosures in Squier Cottrell to William H. Seward, July 21, 1866, *Despatches*, roll 4.
[57] Memorandum Communicated by Señor Martínez, August 19, 1867, FO 881/4013.
[58] Memorandum Communicated by Señor Martínez, August 19, 1867, FO 881/4013.
[59] Squier Cottrell to William H. Seward, July 21, 1866, *Despatches*, roll 4.   [60] Ibid.

the Mosquito Reserve government on racial lines point to the ways in which the Nicaraguan national project of geographical unification was entangled with the deployment of the divisive language of race.

William Henry Clarence (or rather his guardians) responded to Nicaraguan allegations by petitioning the British government against the "unjust conduct and bad faith" exhibited to the Reserve government by the Nicaraguan Republic. Clarence, acting on the advice of his guardian, Henry Patterson, also nominated George Paton (nephew of James Green) as his attorney to recover the pending sum of money from the Nicaraguan government. To prove his Indigenous heritage, the petition also enclosed the marriage certificate of his parents, Joseph John and Princess Victoria. A birth certificate of Henry Clarence was also enclosed, which clearly mentioned that Clarence was the son of "Joseph and Victoria, Mosquito Indians."[61] A letter from Lundberg, the superintendent of the Moravian mission, further clarified that the accession of William Clarence had been done through the consent of all the Indigenous persons, when "it was plainly shown that the children of the late King, being illegal, had no right to the place of the Chief."[62]

While the British government deliberated on the matter, the Nicaraguan government presented a proposal for the amalgamation of the Reserve into the Republic as a solution to the problem. On August 17, 1872, Nicaraguan Minister for Foreign Affairs Anselmo H. Rivas implied that by allowing their chief to be elected by foreigners the authorities of the Reserve had violated the rights of the Indigenous residents in the Reserve and declared the Republic's intention to put the matter right: "My government, therefore, proposes to adopt measures to the end that the Indians being accustomed to respect the sovereignty of Nicaragua, may be gradually amalgamated with the other citizens, until that their complete incorporated in the Republic may be established in conformity with the spirit of the above-mentioned [Managua] Convention."[63] Rivas' letter immediately gave rise to criticism from the British officials, with British consul general to the Central American Republics, Edwin Corbett, expressing to British foreign secretary, Earl Granville, that the Nicaraguan position was simply a delaying tactic to save itself from paying the amount of the subvention and follow the clauses of the

---

[61] "Certificate," Inclosure in the Mosquito Chief to Earl Granville, December 20, 1871, FO 881/4013.

[62] J. E. Lundberg to George Paton, July 25, 1866, Inclosure in Mosquito Chief to Earl Granville, FO 881/4013.

[63] Señor Rivas to Mr. Corbett, August 17, 1872, Inclosure 1 in Mr. Corbett to Earl Granville, September 6, 1872, FO 881/4013.

Managua Treaty.[64] Corbett responded to Rivas by urging him to "strictly carry out" the stipulations of the treaty."[65]

The year 1874 was a climactic moment when the pressures on the Reserve seemed to boil over. In October 1874, John Thomas, a resident of Pearl Lagoon, reported that Nicaraguan subjects had been "pouring into this country, and have committed great outrages against some natives as well as foreigners."[66] In 1874, a group of Nicaraguans attacked a young Belgian man, resident in the Reserve, with knives and machetes and after murdering him, decapitated him. In this case, the authorities of the Reserve took matters into their own hands and captured and tried the suspected murderers according to the laws and customs of Mosquitia. The summary execution of the suspect – a Nicaraguan and Honduran subject – by the authorities of the Reserve without any consultation with the government of the Republic heightened tensions.[67] The British warship *Eclipse* had to make an emergency stop at the Mosquito Coast at the request of British subjects in the aftermath of the execution, as they were worried about their safety and the repercussions of the Mosquito actions.[68] Not only residents of the Reserve but also the Moravian mission faced threats following this incident. In October 1874, the Moravian missionary J. E. Lundberg pointed to the disquiet in the Reserve, following the murder of the Belgian and expressed his fear that the lives of the missionaries were consequently in danger. The steady-state tension between Nicaragua and the Reserve was palpable for the rest of the decade of the 1870s. By June 1878, Acting Consul Thomas reported ill-feeling in Gracias a Dios, where the Indigenous residents faced ill-treatment at the hands of the Nicaraguan comandante. While the Miskitu chief managed to convince the residents of Gracias a Dios to refrain from retaliation, documents indicate that by September 1877, the residents of the Reserve were "in a state of defence."[69]

---

[64] Mr. Corbett to Earl Granville, October 29, 1872, FO 881/4013.
[65] Mr. Corbett to Señor Rivas, October 29, 1872, FO 881/4013.
[66] Mr. Thomas to Commodore de Horsey, October 23, 1874, FO 420/28.
[67] "Memoria que El Señor Ministro de Relaciones Esteriores, Instrucción Pública, Agricultura y Comercio, Don Anselmo Rivas presenta al Soberano Congreso en las Sesiones Ordinarias de su IX Periodo Consititucional de los Actos del Ejecutivo Verificados durante su Receso 1875" (Managua: Imprenta de "El Centro Americano," 1875), iv.
[68] "Notes from an Historical Report from Her Majesty's Consul at Greytown to the Foreign Office, Dated September 1, 1875," Inclosure in Mr. Locock to the Earl of Derby, April 20, 1877, FO 420/28.
[69] "Notice" by Joaquín Elizondo, 3 September 1877, Inclosure in Acting Consul Thomas to the Marquis of Salisbury, June 15, 1878, FO 881/4015.

While the Mosquito Reserve faced the threat of Nicaraguan advances, actions of the Reserve government also undermined its local support base and precipitated conflict with Nicaragua. One of the decisions of Chief William Clarence was to relocate to Pearl Key Lagoon, another important Moravian missionary site. Captain Erskine of HMS *Eclipse*, visiting Bluefields in December 1874, observed that "jealousies have ... arisen between Bluefields and Pearl Cay Lagoon, with reference to which shall be considered the residence of the Chief."[70] On another trip to Bluefields, British Consul Gollan was met by the inhabitants of the town who expressed their dissatisfaction with the chief and their belief that he was uninterested in their welfare since he was so frequently absent from Bluefields, the principal town in the Mosquito territory.[71] The decision of the chief's advisers in trying to cover up the execution of the Nicaraguan and Honduran subject for the murder of a Belgian resident of the Reserve was also seen as an example of the new Miskitu leadership's lack of foresight and tact.[72] Erskine noted that the Mosquito government was in the hands of a few Creoles, who instead of trying to keep on good terms with Nicaragua, used every opportunity to "foster feelings of enmity."[73] Writing in December 1876, Consul Gollan concluded that the young chief was unsuited as the leader of the Mosquito Reserve, pointing to his "lazy, dissipated style of life" and disinterest in the administration of the affairs of the Reserve.[74] In late 1874, the Nicaraguan government alleged that the Miskitu chief had made a proclamation in which he declared himself and the other Miskitus to be independent of Nicaragua. The Nicaraguan officials also maintained that the proclamation had been made with the complicity of British officers on board a British man-of-war. Although William Clarence denied this allegation, it appeared to spark off another spate of tension between Nicaragua and the Reserve and a growing sense among Nicaraguan officials of the importance of subduing the rebellious chief. By December 1874, the residents of the Reserve were forming military companies to counter Nicaraguan encroachments and aggression. The British denied that the proclamation was issued from a British vessel but appeared to corroborate the fact that such a proclamation had indeed

---

[70] "Memorandum by Captain Erskine" (undated), *Historical Documents*, 340.
[71] Consul Gollan to the Earl of Derby, December 13, 1876, FO 420/28.
[72] "Memorandum by Captain Erskine" (undated), *Historical Documents*, 340.
[73] Ibid., 339.
[74] Consul Gollan to Earl of Derby, December 13, 1876, *Historical Documents*, 343.

been made. In a letter to Rivas, British consul in Guatemala, Sidney Locock, admitted, "It was from his own residence in Bluefields, and not from on board a British man-of-war, that the young Chief issued the proclamation which naturally and justly gave offence to the Nicaraguan government."[75] Clarence appeared to admit his mistake himself when he wrote to the Nicaraguan minister of the interior on February 5, 1875, recanting his proclamation and asserting that the Reserve would always respect Nicaraguan sovereignty.[76]

On January 6, 1875, Nicaragua issued a decree intended to extend its jurisdiction over the Reserve. Justifying the measures on the grounds that the Miskitu chief "pretends to assume a character which does not belong to him and is not permitted by laws," the decree authorized the governor of San Juan del Norte to be a watchdog to ensure that the sovereignty of Nicaragua was respected in the Reserve and allowed him jurisdiction over the Reserve. The governor was also authorized to ensure that no foreign authority was admitted in the local administration of the Reserve and that foreign consuls who came to the Reserve first obtain permission from the government of the Republic.[77]

By December 1876, Consul Gollan expressed his apprehension about rumors that the Nicaraguan government intended to induce the Miskitu chief to cede his rights and those of the Miskitu Indigenous residents of the Reserve to the Republic.[78] On September 3, 1877, the governor of Greytown, Joaquín Elizondo, sent a letter to the Miskitu chief in which he proposed the incorporation of the Reserve within the Republic with the promise to pay the outstanding subvention as per the Treaty of Managua and to name William Henry Clarence as governor on the same terms as employees of the same rank in the Republic. Elizondo stressed that such an act of incorporation would benefit all the residents of the Reserve. He wrote that "the Indians and Creoles will not experience any difference unfavourable to them in their mode of being, but will rather enjoy greater securities and will reach a grade of prosperity not attainable by the present state of their population." The letter also promised to encourage foreign immigration and to protect the religious beliefs of the inhabitants.[79] It is

---

[75] Mr. Locock to Señor Rivas, April 5, 1877, Inclosure 1 in Mr. Locock to the Earl of Derby, April 5, 1877, FO 420/28.
[76] Mr. Locock to the Earl of Derby, August 22, 1877, FO 420/28.
[77] "Decree," January 6, 1875, Inclosure 3 in Consul Gollan to Earl of Derby, September 1, 1875, FO 420/28.
[78] Consul Gollan to Earl of Derby, December 13, 1876, FO 420/28.
[79] Señor Elizondo to the Chief of Mosquito, September 3, 1877, FO 420/28.

important to note that the conciliatory tone in the letter, which contrasted with the previous Nicaraguan position and may have resulted from the British position that had been supportive of the Reserve's autonomy. In a meeting with Nicaraguan minister Adán Cárdenas on August 22, 1877, Mr. Locock had emphasized that the differences between the Republic and the Reserve over the terms of the Treaty of Managua could only be resolved by "gentle measures. The chief should be made to understand that he has a friend in the Nicaraguan government. This will be the surest path to that incorporation which the Government of Nicaragua desires."[80] Miskitu Chief William Clarence immediately objected to the proposal for reincorporation by Nicaragua and urged British intervention on behalf of the Reserve.[81]

From the moment the Treaty of Managua was ratified, the British position on the Mosquito Shore was to assume neutrality and desist from intervention in the internal matters of the region. Local British consular agents on the ground, like James Green and Alex Gollan, however, continued to press for a stronger metropolitan stance in favor of the Reserve. On July 26, 1861, Consul Green wrote to then British Foreign Secretary John Russell expressing his apprehension of Nicaraguan intentions regarding Article III of the Managua Treaty, following a conversation with Ramon Saenz, where the latter expressed that Nicaragua alone had the privilege of the extraction of native products in the Reserve. In response, Russell was careful to point out to Green that the Foreign Office would not intervene in matters, which may have simply arisen as a result of a misunderstanding: "It does not seem to Her Majesty's Government that any particular case has occurred requiring a decision ... the British Protectorate has ceased under the 1st Article of the Treaty, and the Indians have not made any complaint or representation whatsoever to Her Majesty's Government in relation to the question raised."[82] Similarly in October 1864, when Green again complained about the failure of Nicaragua to pay the annuity, Russell wrote: "I have only to add ... that as regards matters of this nature, it is the desire of Her Majesty's Government to restrict their interference within the limits of the obligations which they have contracted by the existing treaties."[83] During the tenure of Gollan as British consul, we can also identify the impulse on the part of the Foreign Office to settle differences between the Reserve and

---

[80] Sidney Locock to Earl of Derby, August 22, 1877, FO 420/28.
[81] The Chief of Mosquito to the Earl of Derby, December 6, 1877, 881/4015.
[82] Earl Russell to Consul Green, March 12, 1862, FO 881/4013.
[83] Earl Russell to Consul Green, October 3, 1864, FO 881/4013.

the Republic by counselling both sides rather than direct intervention. Thus, following tensions with Nicaragua because of Clarence's proclamation declaring the Reserve as independent of Nicaragua, Sidney Locock suggested to Gollan to use "his good offices with the Chief to obtain from him some fresh satisfactory admission of the sovereignty of the Republic."[84]

Gollan's actions as consul clearly reveal the gulf that separated the British metropolitan government and its agents on the ground. While the British government had so far espoused a "wait-and-see" approach, matters would force Gollan to seek intervention. Thus, when Nicaragua continued to levy export duties on Greytown despite protests from the merchant community of Greytown and Gollan's own attempts to reason with the Nicaraguan governor at Greytown, Gollan wrote to the British secretary of state for foreign affairs, Earl of Derby, that

The main point that appears to call for your Lordship's authoritative decision is whether this Government [i.e. Nicaragua] with their somewhat lax views as to international engagements, are to have the sole right of interpreting a Treaty to which Great Britain is also a party. If, as I believe, this pretension cannot be tolerated, it will be for your Lordship to decide as to how the present arbitrary proceedings of Nicaragua are to be met.[85]

Gollan's fiery letter had the desired effect. His missive to the Earl of Derby was followed by Locock's stern letter to Rivas, admonishing the Nicaraguan government for the discourtesy shown to Gollan and protesting against Nicaraguan assumption of the "right to interpret, in accordance with its own views and without communication with Her Majesty's Government, the terms of a Treaty to which Great Britain is a party."[86] With Great Britain thus entering the thorny question of the interpretation of the Managua Treaty and Nicaragua showing no signs of backing down, the road was now open towards a settlement by international arbitration.[87]

Great Britain communicated that it would only proceed to arbitration if every question arising out of the Treaty of Managua was included in the reference and the Nicaraguan government suspended its levy of duties at

---

[84] Mr. Locock to Consul Gollan, September 20, 1877, FO 420/28.
[85] Alex Gollan to Earl of Derby, November 18, 1877, FO 881/4015.
[86] Mr. Locock to Señor Rivas, March 19, 1878, FO 881/4015.
[87] "Memoria que el Señor Ministro de Relaciones Exteriores, Justicia e Instrucción Pública Don Anselmo H. Rivas presenta al soberano Congreso en las sesiones ordinarias de su periodo constitucional 1879" (Managua: Imp. de "El Centro-Americano," 1879), xix–xxii.

Greytown until the resolution of the arbitration, terms which the Nicaraguan government accepted shortly thereafter.[88] The choice of the arbitrator finally fell on Austria, as a European government without any stake or interest in the region and mutually acceptable to both Great Britain and Nicaragua.[89] There still remained one point of contention between Nicaragua and Great Britain over the conduct of the arbitration and that revolved around the role of the Mosquito Reserve in the proceedings of the arbitration. The British officials recognized that any attempt to make the Miskitu chief a party to the arbitration would draw Nicaraguan resistance and might delay the proceedings by months. Because the Treaty of Managua had been drawn up without consultation with the Miskitu chief or people, it appeared to the British to be reasonable to proceed to arbitration without their involvement. At the same time, Locock recognized that having an agent of the Mosquito government on hand would be helpful should any queries arise about old laws and customs of the Indigenous people or their present condition and attitudes.[90] In the end, despite Nicaraguan resistance on the ground that the Mosquito was not an "organized nation but an assemblage of men possessing no representation of any kind and whom by the letter and spirit of the Treaty are under the sovereignty of Nicaragua," the matter was resolved by agreeing to the inclusion of a statement by the Miskitu chief as an annexure to the documents to be submitted to the arbitrator, since the Mosquito claims formed one of the questions arising out of the treaty that the arbitrator would have to take a decision on.[91]

7.4 REVIVAL OF CANAL DREAMS

While Nicaragua–Reserve tensions reached a tipping point, halfway around the world, the completion of the Suez Canal in November 1869 all at once brought the question of the interoceanic canal through the isthmus of Central America back into the spotlight. The completion of the Suez Canal demonstrated that the imagination of a canal could really transform into an actual physical infrastructure. The interoceanic canal,

---

[88] Marquis of Salisbury to Mr. Locock, May 4, 1878, FO 881/4015.
[89] Sir Julian Pauncefote to Mr. Lingen, March 31, 1879, FO 881/4015.
[90] Memorandum by Mr. Locock on the Question of the Arbitration on the Treaty of Managua, June 13, 1878, FO 881/4015.
[91] J. R. Graham to Señor Rivas, February 10, 1879, Inclosure 4 in Mr. Graham to the Marquis of Salisbury, February 10, 1879, FO 881/4015, 65; Sir H. Elliot to Count Andrassy, April 19, 1879, FO 881/4015.

which had so far been a wishful dream, suddenly loomed ahead like a certain destiny. Newspapers both in the United States and in Great Britain were quick to make this connection, printing news stories that suggested that the success of the French in Egypt could be replicated in the Americas. The *New York Times* on December 1, 1869, barely a fortnight after the opening of the Suez Canal, opined: "To-day seems the time, in the affairs of an Isthmian Canal, 'which taken at its flood,' may lead on to the increased fortune of the American people. Nothing of equal importance with the inauguration of the Suez thoroughfare has occurred in the modern history of maritime Europe."[92] *The New York Weekly Journal of Commerce* wrote that: "That a ship canal will some time be dug, connecting the Atlantic and Pacific oceans, is not a very daring prophecy. The accomplished fact of the Suez Canal has proved the mechanical practicability of a similar enterprise on the isthmus that unites the American continents."[93] The completion of the transcontinental railroad in 1869 provided a new overland route westward, but aspirations for a canal through Nicaragua persisted.

In 1862, Nicaragua permitted the Central American Transit Company to operate in the transport of passengers through the canal route. In 1867, however, Nicaragua cancelled its contract with the company and in 1869, following the success of the French-led Suez Canal, authorized a canal concession to the French engineer Michel Chevalier.[94] Of course, Chevalier was not the first Frenchman to show interest in developing the Nicaragua Canal. Napoléon III (1840s) and Félix Belly (1850s) had both flirted with the idea of a canal through Nicaragua. Chevalier's success was short-lived, however, and the beginning of the Franco-Prussian War in the following year and the death of the French emperor brought an end to Nicaraguan efforts to secure French backing for its canal.[95] Nicaragua's efforts to gain support for its canal project was characterized by vacillation and rapid change in terms of patrons and collaborators in this decade. Historian Kinloch Tijerino attributes this to the political doubts regarding the viability of Nicaragua as an independent nation, following the period of filibusterism of the 1850s and the

---

[92] *The Sheffield Daily Telegraph*, December 14, 1869.
[93] *Mercury Published as the New York Weekly Journal of Commerce*, March 24, 1870.
[94] "Decreto de 15 marzo, ratificando el contrato de Canal maritime, celebrando en Paris por el Ministro de Relaciones Esteriores Lcdo. Don Tomas Ayon I el Sr. Miguel Chevalier, súbdito frances," *Sesto Periodo Constitucional del Congreso de la República*, 1869, IHNCA.
[95] Tijerino, *El imaginario del canal y la nación cosmopolita*, 326.

impulses towards consolidation with Central America, which also expressed itself in the vacillation over the best way of harnessing its geography.[96]

Nicaragua, however, was not alone in imagining a new Suez Canal through its Central American isthmus. Indeed, it was a propitious moment for an American bid for the canal. In the same year as the opening of the Suez Canal, the inauguration of Ulysses S. Grant as the president of the United States returned the great power again to the center of Nicaragua Canal politics. Grant's interest in a transisthmian canal began in the 1850s when more than 100 of his men of the 4th United States West India Regiment lost their lives crossing the isthmus of Panama. After disappointing expeditions to survey the Darién route in early 1870, Grant began to seriously consider the prospect of a transisthmian canal through Nicaragua. In January 1870, the *Huddersfield Chronicle* reported that

> For the present American opinion seems to favour quite another route – one farther north – for the proposed Canal. This preferred line lies by the channel of the San Juan River, and through the southern part of Lake Nicaragua ... The probability is that, after all, the way by San Juan and Nicaragua will be the one determined on in preference to all others.[97]

The president of Nicaragua, Vicente Cuadra, wanted U.S. – and not European – interests to build the canal and so was anxious for a U.S. survey of the canal route.[98] News of the imminent arrival of the American exploration party in March 1872 was followed by a great deal of excitement in Nicaragua.[99] On April 7, 1872, the U.S. expedition finally arrived in Greytown. The expedition began on a tragic note with the accidental death of its leader, Commander Crossman. The leadership then fell upon Commander Chester Hatfield. He and his men examined four routes between Lake Nicaragua and the Pacific. A second expedition under Commander Edward Lull resumed surveying in December 1872, and he reported to the U.S. Navy that he had located a practicable canal route.[100] The Lull survey proposed to take Lake Nicaragua as the summit level of the canal and connect it to the Pacific Ocean by way of a canal and with the Caribbean Sea by a combination of canal and slack-water navigation,

---

[96] Ibid.   [97] *The Huddersfield Chronicle*, January 8, 1870.
[98] Jackson Crowell, "The United States and a Central American Canal, 1869–1877," *Hispanic American Historical Review* 49:1 (1969), 29.
[99] Ibid., 30.   [100] Ibid., 31.

a total distance of about 181 miles.[101] Lull noted that "The whole region [of Central America] has been very carefully explored, and I am fully persuaded that nowhere is there so favorable a combination of advantageous conditions as in the line through Nicaragua."[102] On March 15, 1872, the Interoceanic Canal Commission was established to study all the survey reports of various possible canal routes through Latin America and recommend the most suitable.[103] In 1874, the Interoceanic Canal Commission failed to reach a conclusive decision and sent out further expeditions to examine the routes through Nicaragua, Darién, and Panama. By February 1876, having compared the data gathered, the commission now presented its final recommendation to President Grant: the Nicaragua route, running from San Juan del Norte to Lake Nicaragua, from the lake to the mouth of the Río del Medio, from which point the canal would connect to the port of Brito on the Pacific Ocean.[104] On September 26, 1876, the *Edinburgh Evening News* reported that "although the Suez Canal will always have the preference for the transit of the European trade with the East, the Nicaraguan route completed, such a canal would certainly engross all or the greater part of the American traffic, both with the East and West."[105] Nicaragua promptly dispatched its special envoy, Adán Cárdenas, to Washington, DC, to negotiate a canal treaty with the United States.[106]

The Nicaragua route was suddenly on the horizon and teeming with possibilities. For a brief moment, Grant toyed with the idea of throwing off the shackles of the Clayton–Bulwer Treaty and taking exclusive control of the proposed canal. The Lull report indicated not just a viable interoceanic route but also a fecund, virgin territory, ripe and awaiting American enterprise:

Nicaragua is full of undeveloped sources of wealth; some of these have been experimented with in a limited degree, but nothing to a beginning of its full

---

[101] "Report upon the Survey for an Interoceanic Ship-Canal through Nicaragua, by Edward P. Lull, A. M. Commander, United States Navy, 1 December 1873," in *Reports of Explorations and Surveys for the Location of a Ship Canal between the Atlantic and Pacific Oceans through Nicaragua, 1872–73* (Washington, DC: GPO, 1874), 63.
[102] Ibid., 70.   [103] Crowell, "The United States and a Central American Canal," 32.
[104] Ibid., 37.   [105] *The Edinburgh Evening News*, September 26, 1876.
[106] A. H. Rivas to Secretarios del Congreso, May 31, 1877, in "Memoria que el Señor Ministro de Relaciones Exteriores, Justicia e Instrucción Pública Don Anselmo H. Rivas presenta al soberano Congreso en las sesiones ordinarias de su periodo constitucional 1879" (Managua: Imp. de "El Centro-Americano," 1879), 237–266. See also Crowell, "The United States and a Central American Canal."

capacity ... Nicaragua is capable of producing all the subsistence required by the operatives in the event of the canal's being built. In addition to those products already mentioned are raised Indian corn, rice, beans, yams, cassava-root, quiquisque (a superior sort of yam), plantains, bananas, tomatoes, oranges, limes, pine-apples, cocoa-nuts, mangoes, watermelons, cantaloupes, jocotes (a species of plum), nisperas, and numerous other fruits and vegetables. In the valley of San Juan, below the mouth of the Sarapiquí, the delicious bread-fruit flourishes.[107]

In many ways, this geographical imagination mirrored the Nicaraguan state's understanding of the resources that lay in the Mosquito Reserve. In 1853, Juan Francisco Irias described the Mosquito Coast in idyllic terms, holding out the promise that the region "could attain to prosperity and riches upon its virgin soil, in cultivating its numerous valuable native fruits, and in consequence of its proximity to the Cape and the great Antilles, thus affording easy means of exportation and a market."[108] Seven years later, Bedford Pim, who had gained a concession for building a railway by the Nicaraguan government, had poetically described the untapped forests of rubber, mahogany, and dyewood that were seemingly waiting to be harvested. Nicaragua's efforts to consolidate the Mosquito Reserve within its Republic stemmed as much from its dry calculations of profit as they did from these lush images of a utopia within reach. And it was again this image of fecundity that the engineers of the Lull survey chose to highlight alongside pages of extensive engineering calculations of the dimensions of the proposed canal.

Even as the Nicaragua route appeared to be having its moment in the limelight, the conditions on the ground in Greytown had been steadily deteriorating. The Lull report described the harbor of Greytown: "A commodious and excellent harbor once existed at Greytown. The strip of sand which formed its outer limits now extended across what was the entrance and has converted the harbour into a lagoon."[109] The silting of the harbor was so extreme that Lull and his party proposed to "cut off the Lower San Juan, and send all the water of the San Juan and its lower tributaries through the Colorado mouth, admitting to the harbor only the waters which come through the canal and through the San Juanillo, which will be perfectly clean."[110] Any plan henceforth to incorporate Greytown as the entry point of the canal would have to make a sizable investment in

---

[107] "Report of Commander Edward P. Lull," *Reports of Explorations and Surveys for the Location of a Ship-Canal between the Atlantic and Pacific Oceans through Nicaragua, 1872–73*, 67–68.
[108] "Rio Wanks and the Mosco Indians," 163.
[109] "Report of Commander Edward P. Lull," 60.   [110] Ibid., 61.

the dredging and restoration of the harbor. Not only so, but Greytown, which had once been a competitor to Chagres due to its comparatively healthy surroundings, was now "decidedly the most unhealthy place on the [Nicaragua] route."[111] It was a depressing turn of fate for a harbor that had once been regarded as a trophy among competing canal interests.

The year 1881 appeared to bring into focus all the myriad tensions and promises of the two decades since the signing of the Treaty of Managua. In 1879, William Henry Clarence died of poisoning under mysterious circumstances and was succeeded by George William Albert Hendy, the son of King George Augustus. In May 1881, a Creole man attempted a coup on Bluefields with the connivance of several Nicaraguans and Creoles. He intended to take possession of the government house and the Moravian church with the intention of ending the rampage by firing on worshippers and setting fire to the town. The ringleader hoped to depose Hendy and put in his place the illegitimate son of a former chief and appoint himself as the governor of Bluefields.[112] The Moravian missionary, Brother Ziock, attributed the failure of the coup to "the vigor and resistance of the revivalists in Bluefields."[113] Rugeley and Offen suggest that the outcome of the coup may have been related to the arbitration ruling published in July 1881 that decided in favor of the Miskitu interests and may have ensured the "vigor" of the missionaries in fighting off the coup, which was probably supported by Nicaragua.[114] Indeed, fears of a negative arbitration decision in early 1881 may have been instrumental in setting off the revivalist missionary movement of the Great Awakening that would characterize the Moravian activities from 1881 onwards. And yet as the tensions over beliefs, rights, and claims within and over the Mosquito Reserve continued to percolate, the year 1881 also saw the U.S. President Ulysses Grant endorsing the results of the reports of the Interoceanic Canal Commission. Expressing that the Nicaragua Canal estimated at $75,000,000 easily out-beat the Panama Canal, whose construction cost Grant himself concluded would amount to $400,000,000, he declared: "We need no longer question the value of an interoceanic canal on the Western continent, as we have long since abandoned all doubt of the value of the Suez Canal to the commerce of the nations of the East."[115] What had been so far an imagined canal now seemed to race closer to becoming a reality.

---

[111] Ibid., 119.   [112] Offen and Rugeley, *The Awakening Coast*, 150.   [113] Ibid., 149.
[114] Ibid., 39, 149.
[115] General U. S. Grant, "The Nicaragua Canal," in *The North American Review*, February 1881 (New York: D. Appleton and Company, 1881), 109–112.

7.5 CONCLUSION: THE QUESTION OF CENTRAL AMERICAN UNION

Throughout the two decades following the *guerra nacional*, the question of the Central American Union continued to simmer. Following on the heels of the *guerra*, the Nicaraguan President Tomás Martínez was a staunch advocate of the ideal of the Central American federation, attributing Nicaragua's humiliation at the hands of William Walker to its isolation from the rest of Central America.[116] At the same time, Nicaragua's long-standing preoccupation with the canal influenced its political and economic trajectory. While other Central American republics experienced cycles of Liberal revolution and economic restructuring in the late nineteenth century, Nicaragua remained under a stable Conservative government. However, Nicaraguan Conservatives, like their Liberal counterparts elsewhere, also pursued policies of economic modernization.[117] Even as Nicaragua's political path diverged in some ways from its neighbors, it continued to regard its dream of an interoceanic canal as a unifying force – a "lazo de unión" that could bind the five Central American republics together.[118] Following the Lull survey, Nicaragua succeeded in gaining public support for its canal from all the republics with the exception of Costa Rica, with whom there was a revival of boundary disputes.[119] However, the unequivocal recommendation of the Interoceanic Canal Commission for the Nicaragua Canal in 1876 suddenly shifted the dynamics with President Pedro Joaquín Chamorro swiftly reclaiming the Nicaragua route from Costa Rica and espousing a new independent attitude that "each one [republic] possesses exclusively what is given to it by nature or acquired by industry; and the only inheritance that we Central Americans could claim from each other, is that of an emancipated fraternity, with no other rights than those we

---

[116] Tomas Martínez to T. C. de Mosquera, November 28, 1866, "Memoria Presentado por el Sr. Ministro de Relaciones Exteriores, Dr. D. Rosalío Cortéz al Soberano Congreso de 1867" (Imprenta del Gobierno: Managua, 1867), 17, *Nicaragua, Ministerio de Relaciones Exteriores, Memoria*, Library of Congress, roll 1.

[117] Gobat, *Confronting the American Dream*, 49.

[118] "Memoria que el Señor Ministro de Relaciones Esteriores, Instrucción Pública, Agricultura i comercio, Don Anselmo H. Rivas presenta al soberano congreso de las sesiones ordinarias de su IX periodo constitucional de los actos del ejecutivo verificados durante su receso, 1875" (Imprenta de "El Centro Americano: Managua, 1875), xiii, *Nicaragua, Ministerio de Relaciones Exteriores, Memoria*, Library of Congress, roll 1.

[119] Crowell, "The United States and a Central American Canal," 42.

reciprocally want to grant ourselves."[120] This new philosophy brought Nicaragua into tension with Central America, particularly Guatemala, whose President Justo Rufino Barrios sought to forcibly incorporate Nicaragua into a Central American Union partly inspired by hopes that all the republics might share in the prospective benefits of the Canal. Barrios' threat galvanized Nicaragua into seeking a swift treaty with the United States for the canal construction. Meanwhile, Nicaragua's negotiations with the United States stalled when the Frelinghuysen–Zavala Treaty failed, amidst concerns that it might conflict with the Clayton–Bulwer Treaty and provoke British objection. By 1885, as the threat of an invasion led by Guatemala loomed over the horizon, and Barrios issued a decree signaling the Central American Union,[121] and Nicaragua released its own manifesto against Barrios' dictatorship.[122] Thus, even as the Lull survey and the subsequent recommendations of the Interoceanic Canal Commission made the dream of the Nicaragua Canal seem finally within reach, the ideal of union that had nourished Nicaragua's relationship with the rest of Central America since the Mexican–American War showed signs of fracturing.

[120] Quoted in Tijerino, *El imaginario del canal y la nación cosmopolita*, 327.
[121] Mr. Whitehouse to Mr. Bayard, March 9, 1885, in Doc. 51 of *Papers Relating To the Foreign Relations of The United States, Transmitted to Congress, with the Annual Message of the President*, December 8, 1885.
[122] "Manifiesto que el Soberano Congreso de la República de Nicaragua dirige a sus comitentes y a los demás pueblos de Centro-América, *Diario Oficial*, San Salvador, April 1, 1885.

8

Canal Dreams and the Fate of the Mosquito Reserve

Six miles from downtown Chicago, twenty-eight million people would throng the sprawling grounds of Jackson Park between May and October of 1893. They were promised marvels from around the world, the very best tokens of modernity and human culture. It was the Columbian World's Exposition of 1893, also known as the World's Fair of Chicago. Meant to commemorate the 400th anniversary of Columbus' "discovery" of America, the Fair housed fourteen "Great Buildings" occupying a total floor space of 63 million square feet and 200 additional buildings.[1] It drew 3,000 visitors every weekday and 10,000 on Sundays, setting a world record for outdoor event attendance on October 9, 1893, when it drew 750,000 people on a single day. Housed in the Transportation Building, a relief model of the Nicaragua Canal aroused considerable public interest.[2] The relief map was a diorama, which covered about 100 square feet and was constructed on a vertical scale of 1:2,000 and a horizontal scale of 1:30,000. Lead pipes were molded into the groundwork, and real water flowed through the lakes and rivers, as well as the proposed channel for the canal (see Figure 8.1). The relief model allowed the viewer to see the engineering details of the canal, including its system of locks, excavations, and dams. In the model, a dam constructed midway between the reservoir and the Atlantic allowed the waters of the river San Juan to be raised to the level of Lake

---

[1] Norman Bolotin and Christine Laing, *The World's Columbian Exposition: The Chicago World's Fair of 1893* (Chicago: University of Illinois Press, 2002), 20.

[2] Benjamin Cummings Truman, *History of World's Fair: Being a Complete and Authentic Description of the Columbian Exposition* (New York: Mammoth Pub. Co., 1893), 340.

FIGURE 8.1 Nicaragua Canal relief model at the Transportation Building of the Columbian World's Fair at Chicago, 1893. Source: Herbert Huwe Bancroft, *The Book of the Fair*, blue cover ed. (Chicago: Bancroft Company, 1893).

Nicaragua. A wooden ship representing a vessel floated from the Pacific to the Atlantic through the miniature canal route.[3] The points on the canal route where work had begun in Nicaragua or was projected to begin were shown by patches of red. "A Record of the Transportation Exhibits," published in 1894, noted that the "excellent model ... did not fail to become very popular."[4]

Nicaragua itself spent over $30,000 to put up its own exhibits, which included Indigenous antiquities, useful and ornamental woods, and a rich collection of mineral resources. One of the Nicaraguan exhibits featured a coconut with a carving on its shell of a portrait of James G. Blaine between the flags of the United States and Nicaragua, with a facsimile of the route of the Nicaragua Canal at the foot of the engraving.[5] The Expo also featured Indigenous culture not only from the United States but also from Latin America. The Miskitu surgeon general, Roland Kuehn,

---

[3] Herbert Huwe Bancroft, *The Book of the Fair*, blue cover ed. (Chicago: Bancroft Company, 1893), 588.
[4] James Dredge, *A Record of the Transportation Exhibits at the World's Columbian Exposition of 1893* (New York: John Wiley & Sons, 1894), 68.
[5] J. B. Campbell, *The World's Columbian Exposition Illustrated* (Chicago, 1893), 324.

was prepared to bear the expense himself for an exhibit featuring Miskitu Indigenous people but lamented that "Nicaragua will not invite us." In the end, while the Nicaragua Canal basked in the halls of the Transportation Building and the Nicaragua exhibit, the Miskitu Indigenous people were "thwarted in their efforts to attend the fair and establish their own exhibit."[6]

The Nicaragua Canal exhibit at the World's Fair reflected the revival of interest in the interoceanic canal through Nicaragua by the late 1880s and early 1890s. The parallel exhibits of the relief map in the Transportation Building and the engraving of the route on a coconut in the Nicaragua exhibit show the ways in which both the United States and Nicaragua sought to represent their role in the fruition of the ambitious Nicaragua Canal project. At the same time, the beautiful three-dimensional model that drew visitors to the Transportation Building belied the violent conflict underway in the very same period in the Mosquito Reserve.

In the 1880s, there was a growing interest in duplicating the success of the Suez Canal in Central America. As the French under Lesseps' leadership championed the Panama Canal, the United States had its eyes set on constructing a canal through Nicaragua. For the Nicaraguan Republic, the proposed canal promised to fulfill its destiny as the center of the American continent and a catalyst for progress and modernization. Through the 1880s and early 1890s, Nicaragua would attempt to extend its jurisdiction over the Mosquito Reserve, whose importance as the Atlantic doorway to Nicaragua and a significant exporter of tropical fruits and wood made it increasingly seen as essential to Nicaragua's "geographical destiny" and integral to control over the Nicaragua canal route. Espousing ideals of liberal nation-making, Nicaragua sought to assimilate the Miskitu by attempting to annex the Reserve to the Republic in 1894.

The absence of the Miskitu exhibit side by side with the prominence of the Nicaragua Canal at the World's Fair is symbolic of how the narrative of modernity centered around the canal was predicated on making invisible the fate of the Mosquito Reserve. What the diorama also hid was the violence, both in terms of actual conflict between Nicaragua and the Reserve on the ground and Anglo-American military and imperial ambitions in the canal route. As Nicaragua sought to fulfill its vision of unbroken sovereignty through an attempt at "re"-incorporation of the

---

[6] David Beck, *Unfair Labor: American Indians and the 1893 World's Columbian Exposition in Chicago* (Lincoln: University of Nebraska Press, 2019), 177.

Mosquito Reserve in 1894, for the first time since the *Cyane* bombardment, the gloves were off on all sides. Yet the crisis was also an internal one within the Mosquito Kingdom, pitting Reserve "Indians" against non-Reserve Miskitus and reviving again the question of racial legitimacy of the Mosquito Reserve government. This chapter delves into this thorny crisis – also known as the incorporation of the Mosquito Reserve – to illuminate the violence that lay behind the dream of the interoceanic Nicaragua Canal and to show the centrality of the canal to geopolitical identity – both of the Republic of Nicaragua and post-Civil War United States.

8.1 RENEWED EFFORTS FOR THE NICARAGUA CANAL

The successful completion of the Suez Canal had important consequences for the plans for a transisthmian canal through Central America. Ferdinand de Lesseps, who had been a key figure in the Suez Canal, was a regular visitor to the Société de Géographie de Paris as had been Humboldt before him. As McCullough writes, "Geography ... had become something of a national cause [in France]. Among men of position it had also become extremely fashionable."[7] In the Société's international congress held in 1875, de Lesseps declared his interest in an interoceanic canal and argued that it should be a sea-level canal without locks. De Lesseps' success in Suez had given him celebrity status in France and strongly veered the Paris society towards a sea-level canal. As discussed in Chapter 7, in 1872, the U.S. President Ulysses Grant established the Interoceanic Canal Commission to find the best possible route for the canal. In the winter of 1875, shortly after the Paris conference, the Commission submitted its report, which unanimously declared Nicaragua to be the best and most feasible route for the interoceanic canal. Almost immediately, the Société reacted by announcing a grand international congress focusing on various proposed projects for the interoceanic canal through Central America, stating that "American efforts had been insufficient."[8]

The Congrès International d'Études du Canal Interocéanique – informally known as the 1879 Paris Congress – convened on May 15, 1879, with 136 delegates from 22 countries. The American delegation included Rear Admiral Daniel Ammen and civil engineer Aniceto Menocal. Other

---

[7] McCullough, *Path between the Seas*, 58.   [8] Ibid., 59.

members of the U.S. delegation included representatives from the American Geographical Society, the National Academy of Sciences, the U.S. Board of Trade, and the City of San Francisco.[9] Besides delegates from various countries, the Congress was also attended by speculators and politicians, many of whom looked up to de Lesseps for the final word on the transisthmian canal.

It soon became evident to the American delegates that the Congress was skewed towards the Panama route since this was the route suggested by de Lesseps. Ultimately, the majority of the members of the Congress decided upon the Panama route, pointing to the fact that although the Nicaragua route was technologically sound, the volcanic nature of the country surrounding it, the condition of the harbor of Greytown, and the length of the canal all militated against it.[10] The frustration of the U.S. delegates clearly comes out through Ammen's report to the U.S. Secretary of State William Evarts. Ammen wrote: "The able engineers were generally in favor of the Nicaragua route, and that nearly, if not all, of the French delegates other than the engineers, were in favor of the Panama route."[11] Menocal found that the subcommittees tasked with various aspects of the canal under the Congress were also not free of prejudice. Writing about a subcommittee on locks, Menocal observed that the committee was inclined to increase the number of locks in the plan of the Nicaragua Canal so as to increase its cost estimate and make it appear inferior to the Panama route.[12] The U.S. delegation noted that several of the engineers from other countries who gave their opinions had never been to Panama or Nicaragua and had no ground-level knowledge of the various canal routes. "The only reliable and well-digested plans presented had been those from the United States, and I was sorry to see that they were weighed on the same scale with imaginary projects traced on imperfect maps of the Isthmus, some of them the result of one night's inspiration."[13] J. Lawrence Smith, a member of the American Academy of

---

[9] Ibid., 71.
[10] J. Lawrence Smith, "Inter-oceanic Canal: Practicality of Different Routes" (Louisville: Bradley & Gilbert, 1880); J. Lawrence Smith, *Panama Canal Pamphlets, 1879–1900*, History of Science Collection at the Linda Hall Library (hereafter *Panama Canal Pamphlets, 1879–1900*), 11.
[11] Admiral Ammen to Mr. Evarts, June 21, 1879, *Instructions to Rear Admiral Daniel Ammen and Chief Engineer A. G. Menocal, U.S. Navy, Delegates on the Part of the United States to the Interoceanic Canal Congress, Held at Paris, May 1879 and Reports of the Proceedings of the Congress* (Washington, DC: GPO 1879), 8.
[12] Ibid., 16.   [13] Ibid., 20.

Sciences, who also attended the Congress, reported that the battle of the routes between advocates of the various routes was fought in the Committee on Technology with the main contest being between the Nicaragua and Panama routes and noted that "when it did come to what seemed to be positive selection of a route, it appeared that at least one-half the affirmative vote was based on a mere sentiment not to oppose an enterprise so earnestly pressed by that most remarkable man, M. Lesseps."[14]

Despite the setback at the Paris Congress, the U.S. delegates, such as Ammen and Menocal, continued to advocate for the Nicaragua route. On December 16, 1879, the U.S. House of Representatives passed a resolution to appoint a select committee of eleven members to deliberate on the selection of a suitable route for the transisthmian canal through Central America.[15] The committee interviewed key personnel, including Ammen and Menocal. The transcript of these interviews allows us to see the reasons why the United States at that point favored the Nicaragua route. In his interview with the committee, Ammen maintained that the Nicaragua Canal could be built at half the cost of the Panama Canal. Moreover, because of favorable winds along the Nicaragua Canal route, not just steam vessels but also sailing vessels would find it easy to gain passage through the canal.[16] "Looking at it economically," Ammen declared, "the Panama Canal has no merit in comparison with the Nicaragua Canal."[17] Menocal, in his interview with the committee, emphasized that a complete and accurate survey of the entire canal line had been accomplished, and that it was on the basis of this ground-level knowledge that it was possible to ascertain the superiority of the Nicaragua Canal to the Panama Canal. He was also quick to assert that his views on the canal question were based wholly on the "facts."[18] Other interviewees also supported the Nicaragua Canal. Lieutenant Frederic Collinson, of the U.S. Navy, asserted that the route through Nicaragua

---

[14] Smith, "Inter-oceanic Canal," *Panama Canal Pamphlets, 1879–1900*, 6.
[15] "Interoceanic Ship Canal: Testimony Taken before the Select Committee on Interoceanic Ship Canal in Regard to the Selection of a Suitable Route ... across the American Isthmus" (GPO, msc.doc. #16, 1881), *Panama Canal Pamphlets, 1879–1900*, 1.
[16] "Statement of Admiral Ammen Continued," February 7, 1880, "Interoceanic Ship Canal: Testimony Taken before the Select Committee," *Panama Canal Pamphlets, 1879–1900*, 9.
[17] Ibid., 11.
[18] "Statement of Mr. A. G. Menocal," February 20, 1880, "Interoceanic Ship Canal: Testimony Taken before the Select Committee," *Panama Canal Pamphlets, 1879–1900*, 37.

was at least 2,000 miles shorter from the Pacific Coast than the Panama Canal. Moreover, Panama, being on the equatorial belt, was subject to doldrums. Collinson recalled that "on one occasion the British admiralty wishing to send one of their sailing vessels into the Arctic Ocean from Panama in time to save the season, had her towed by a steamer through this calm belt and carried 700 miles out to sea before she could find a breeze."[19] Nicaragua on the other hand, had the "advantage in winds, terminal, ports and climate."[20]

Meanwhile, in Panama, de Lesseps pressed on with his project for a sea-level canal, a proposal that had been endorsed by the 1879 Paris Congress. In Panama, de Lesseps aimed to duplicate his success with the sea-level canal at Suez. However, he was completely unprepared for the ground-level conditions, where flooding of the Chagres River in the rainy season, the prevalence of debilitating diseases, such as yellow fever and malaria, and the problem of landslides at Culebra were like solid walls against efforts to excavate the canal. Mortality rates among the labor force rose steeply: by 1885, the official (conservative) death rate reported was 100 a month.[21] Although de Lesseps still clung to the belief that his project in Panama would be realized, by December 1888, the sea-level canal project crashed. By the time bankruptcy was declared, the sea-level project had cost over $200 million and claimed innumerable deaths of workers.[22] The failure of de Lesseps' sea-level canal at Panama provided a new impetus to American efforts to build the canal through Nicaragua.

The 1880s also concomitantly saw a revival in economic and commercial interests in the Mosquito Coast region, particularly in the growth of industries connected with the export of tropical fruit such as bananas. This interest in the Nicaragua Canal route as a means of extraction of natural products can be seen as early as the Lull survey, where, amidst engineering calculations, the survey reports also emphasized the natural bounty and fecundity of the region around the proposed canal. One of the factors favoring Nicaragua over the Panama route had been the apparent salubriousness of the former route. In 1880, Ammen noted that "It is

---

[19] "Statement of Lieut. Frederic Collins, United States Navy," February 28, 1880, "Interoceanic Ship Canal: Testimony Taken before the Select Committee," *Panama Canal Pamphlets, 1879–1900*, 41.
[20] Ibid.
[21] Matthew Parker, *Panama Fever: The Epic Story of One of the Greatest Human Achievements of All Time* (New York: Doubleday, 2007), 167.
[22] Ralph Avery, *America's Triumph in Panama* (Chicago: L.W. Walter Company, 1913), 59.

rather a remarkable fact that, in the different explorations that have been made through Central America, no officer or man has died there from disease, though hundreds have been there at a time."[23] Later, the Maritime Canal Company would praise the salubriousness and fecundity of the route, pointing out the region's richness in tropical fruits: "All tropical fruits grow in abundance, and the rich banks of the rivers of the eastern slopes will yield almost incalculable harvests of plantains, bananas, oranges, pineapples and limes."[24] In 1890, the *California Banker's Magazine* also highlighted that the Nicaragua Canal would allow the quick export of California fruits and garden products to Europe.[25] As Walter LaFeber has shown, Latin American markets increasingly appeared as the solution to the U.S. economic downturn of the 1870s and 1880s.[26] In addition, the emphasis on the export of fruits and tropical products dovetailed neatly with the increasing efforts of U.S. companies to enter the trade for tropical fruits, which would culminate in the establishment of the United Fruit Company in 1899. The growing interest in tropical fruits grown in the Mosquito Coast region would cause a revival in trade in Greytown by the 1880s and in many ways would contribute to Nicaraguan interest in incorporating the Reserve by the 1890s.

Actual ground-level work on the construction of the canal began in the 1880s and 1890s. On April 25, 1887, Nicaragua granted a concession to a private association of U.S. citizens for the right to construct the canal. A similar concession was made to the association from the Republic of Costa Rica. In November 1887, a team under the United States Army Corps of Engineers was organized for a survey and axial location of the Nicaragua Canal.[27] In 1889, an act of the U.S. Congress, with the objective of constructing a transoceanic canal through Nicaragua, incorporated this association under the name of the Maritime Canal Company, and A. G. Menocal was named as its chief engineer. The terms of the

---

[23] "Statement of Rear Admiral Ammen," February 6, 1880, "Interoceanic Ship Canal: Testimony Taken before the Select Committee," *Panama Canal Pamphlets, 1879–1900*, 5.
[24] "The Maritime Ship Canal of Nicaragua, 1890," H. C. Taylor, *Panama Canal Pamphlets, 1885–1900*, History of Science Collection at the Linda Hall Library (hereafter *Panama Canal Pamphlets, 1885–1900*).
[25] William L. Merry, "The Nicaragua Canal" (reprinted from the California Banker's Magazine, October 1890), *Panama Canal Pamphlets, 1885–1900*.
[26] LaFeber, *The New Empire*.
[27] "The Proposed Nicaragua Canal," *Scientific American*, November 26, 1887.

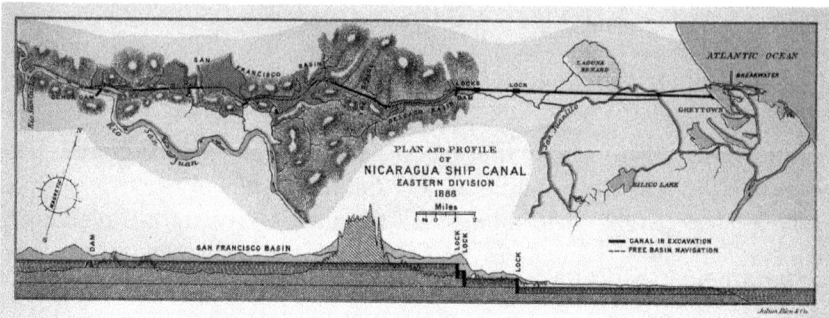

FIGURE 8.2 Eastern division of the canal route. Source: "Plan and profile" (col.) dated 1888, in *Panama Canal Pamphlets, 1885–1890*. Courtesy of the Linda Hall Library of Science, Engineering and Technology.

concessions allowed the company the right to construct the canal, sell its stocks and bonds to raise funds, and seek foreign monetary assistance.[28] By the spring of 1889, the company had completed axial and detailed surveys of the canal route, including locks and harbors, and had begun preparatory work on constructing living quarters, storehouses, wharves, etc. Preliminary work on the canal commenced in June 1889, and it was formally inaugurated on October 8 of the same year.[29]

The company's proposed route for the canal extended from Greytown on the Atlantic coast to Brito on the Pacific as the respective termini. The total distance port to port was 169.448 miles, of which 26.783 miles would be excavated, and the remaining 142.659 miles would be free navigation by Lake Nicaragua, the San Juan River, and through basins in the valley of the streams Deseado, San Francisco, and Tola. Lake Nicaragua was taken as the summit level of the canal at 110 feet elevation. The sea level on each side of the canal would be reached by three locks, which were located as close as possible to the edges of the canal (see Figures 8.2 and 8.3).

---

[28] Senator John Sherman, "The Nicaragua Canal" (printed from the *Forum*, 1891), Joseph Nimmo, *Panama Canal Pamphlets, 1880–1900*, History of Science Collection at the Linda Hall Library History of Science Collection at the Linda Hall Library (hereafter *Panama Canal Pamphlets, 1880–1900*).

[29] "Letter from the Secretary of the Interior, Transmitting the Original Report of the Maritime Canal Company of Nicaragua," December 5, 1892, *Nicaragua Canal: Reports of the Committee on Foreign Relations of the Senate in the 51st–53rd Congresses with Subject Index* (Washington, DC: GPO, 1894), reprinted in *Panama Canal Pamphlets, 1880–1900*.

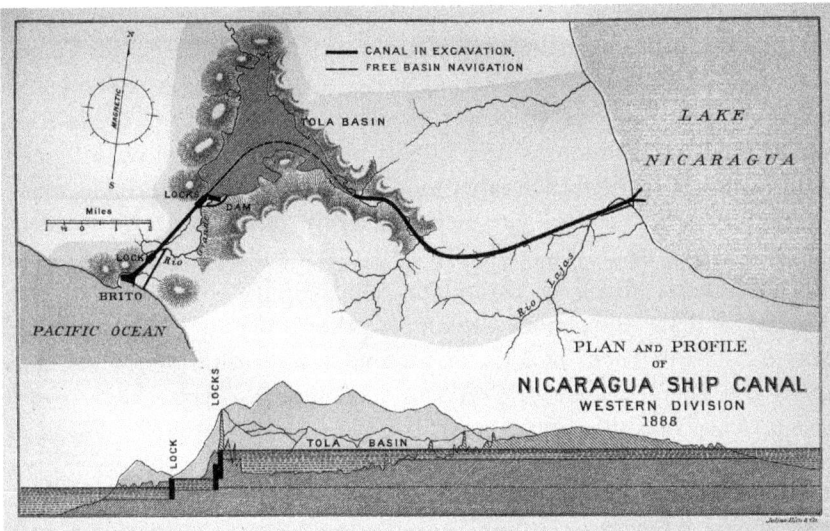

FIGURE 8.3 Western division of the canal route. Source: "Plan and profile" (col.) dated 1888, in *Panama Canal Pamphlets, 1885–1890*. Courtesy of the Linda Hall Library of Science, Engineering and Technology.

The company under Menocal's guidance first began work on the harbor of Greytown as it was critical for landing supplies and machinery. The company initiated work on the construction of a breakwater and made a contract for dredging the entrance and inner bay to a depth of 20 feet. By 1890, Menocal could proudly assert that, "It is expected, therefore, that within the next five months vessels drawing 15 or 20 feet may be able to enter the bay and discharge their freight directly on the wharves of the company."[30] The company had also made headway on numerous other aspects of the construction, including erecting hospitals, quarters, shops, and storehouses, clearing streams of obstructions, making several miles of the route ready for dredging, and building 10 miles of broad-gauge railroad and 70 miles of telegraph and telephone lines.

8.2 NICARAGUA–RESERVE TENSIONS

The revival of interest in the Nicaragua Canal coincided with a period of Nicaraguan history, which also saw a new impetus towards liberal

---

[30] A.G. Menocal, "Nicaragua Canal: Its Design, Final Location and Work Accomplished," Appendix A, *Nicaragua Canal*, reprinted in *Panama Canal Pamphlets, 1880–1900*.

nation-making through assimilation of Indigenous groups and efforts to fulfill a vision of unbroken sovereignty from the Atlantic to the Pacific coasts. As Frances Kinloch Tijerino writes: "Surrounded by liberal governments that had come to power by force of arms, both in Costa Rica and Guatemala, Honduras and El Salvador, the conservative administrations that succeeded each other in Nicaragua during this decade, made vigorous efforts to consolidate their hegemony and make their providential 'geographic destiny' a reality."[31] The 1880s and 1890s saw a series of official policies aimed at assimilating Indigenous populations, which resulted in an Indigenous revolt in the town of Matagalpa in March 1881.[32] These policies of forcible assimilation gained strength under the liberal regime of President José Santos Zelaya (1893–1909) and provide an important context to understand Nicaraguan efforts to annex the Mosquito Reserve in this period.

While the Arbitration Award of 1881 had clearly benefited the interests of the Mosquito Reserve, it also arguably heightened tensions between the Republic of Nicaragua and the Reserve government. Nicaragua maintained that the Arbitration Award did not construe any impingement on the sovereignty of Nicaragua over the Reserve and therefore, allowed for Nicaragua to take measures it deemed necessary for the safety and security of the Republic from any threats arising on the Atlantic coast. Moreover, the Nicaraguan government maintained that the assumption behind the clause of self-government of the Miskitu Indigenous population granted by the Treaty of Managua no longer applied as the government of the Reserve was not in the hands of the Indigenous community but foreigners. Additionally, the Nicaraguan government increasingly viewed the separate Reserve as an obstacle to national growth. Thus the Nicaraguan minister, Adán Cárdenas wrote, "As long as it is governed in this manner, the Reserve, which covers a considerable extent of the Atlantic coast of Nicaragua, will be a continual obstacle to the industrial and administrative development of the neighboring part of the Republic which would naturally communicate with the Atlantic by means of the great rivers which flow through it."[33] With the Nicaragua Canal construction about to commence, Cárdenas expressed his worries that the increasing movement of foreigners into the territory

---

[31] Tijerino, *El imaginario del canal y la nación cosmopolita*, 331.
[32] Ibid., 337. See also Jeffrey Gould, *To Die in This Way: Nicaraguan Indians and the Myth of Mestizaje, 1880–1965* (Durham: Duke University Press, 1998).
[33] Señnor Cárdenas to the Marquis of Salisbury, January 17, 1889, FO 420/96.

would threaten the peace of the Republic if the Reserve remained in its "anomalous position" with respect to Nicaragua.[34]

Immediately following the Arbitration Award, the Nicaraguan government began to make efforts to map the limits of the Reserve and by 1884 had dispatched an engineer to accomplish this task.[35] By the 1860 Treaty of Managua, the limits of the Reserve were delineated as:

> Such district shall be comprised in a line which shall begin at the mouth of the River Rama, in the Caribbean sea; thence it shall run up the midcourse of that river to its source, and from such source proceed in a line due west to the meridian of 84°15' longitude west from Greenwich; thence due north up the said meridian until it strikes the River Hueso, and down the mid-course of that river to its mouth in the sea, as laid down in Baily's map, at about latitude from 14° and 15° north, and longitude 83° west from the meridian of Greenwich.

In October 1887, the Nicaraguan government issued an ordinance that provided for the appointment of a commissioner for the Reserve and "constituting that region as a district under the name of District of Siquia."[36] Commissioner Ysidro Utrecho then proceeded to mark off the limits of the new district. In fixing the boundaries of the new district, the Nicaraguan government employed an engineer, Señor Climie, to provide scientific and technical knowledge in the demarcation of the territory. The Mosquito chief protested that in demarcating the new district, Nicaragua had encroached on the Mosquito Reserve, while the Nicaraguan commissioner maintained that it had only occupied the territories at the confluence of the Rama and Siquia Rivers west of 84°15' longitude, which it had every right to do by the Treaty of Managua.

Already by the winter of 1887, Nicaragua had begun to station police and soldiers at the mouth of the Rama, enforcing regulations on passing vessels.[37] The Mosquito government was further enraged by the Nicaraguan establishment of a post office in Bluefields and the perceived incursion of the Nicaraguan soldiers into the Reserve territory.[38] In August 1889, in response to a threat from Colombia to take possession of the Corn Islands, Nicaragua sent troops to the islands. However, by March 1889, the Mosquito chief, apprehensive of Nicaraguan intentions,

---

[34] Ibid.
[35] Chief Hendy to Inspector General of Cape Gracias, April 18, 1884, FO 53/61.
[36] Señor Cárdenas to the Marquis of Salisbury, January 17, 1889, FO 420/96.
[37] Consul Brown to Secretary of State, November 23, 1887, *Despatches*, roll 8.
[38] Mr. Bayard to Mr. Phelps, November 23, 1888, FO 420/96.

demanded that the troops be withdrawn.[39] In May 1889, the vice-president of the Mosquito territory forwarded a protest to Acting British Consul General Sadler against the appointment of a magistrate for Cookra Oola at the entrance to Pearl Lagoon on the grounds that the area was within the reservation and that by appointing a magistrate in that area, the Nicaraguan government had contravened the Treaty of Managua.[40] What the Reserve government and residents feared was that Nicaragua was attempting to encroach on these territories with a view to annexation. Central American newspapers fed the grist through their premature congratulatory articles. The *Diario de Centro América* of Guatemala, for instance, announced on April 16, 1889, "that most rich portion of territory [i.e. Mosquitia] is to form part of the Nicaraguan republic."[41]

By the summer of 1889, the Nicaraguan government also indicated its desire to effect an abrogation of Article VII of the Treaty of Managua, which constituted Greytown as a free port. There can be little doubt that this move was a reaction to the commencement of the construction work of the canal, which now made the completion of the canal – and thus, the revival of Greytown's fortunes – appear as an inevitable result. By June 1889, already about seventy engineers and around a 100 laborers were at work on the route, laying the lines for telegraph and railroad.[42] By March 1890, Nicaragua was ready to take bolder steps and on March 23 issued decrees assuming jurisdiction over the islands off the coast of the Mosquito Reserve, which had up until that point been administered as part of the Reserve. Thus, Nicaragua extended its jurisdiction over the Corn Islands and made Las Dos Bocas, at the confluence of the Rama and Siquia, a free port.[43] The prevalent sentiment among British officials was that "the annexation of the entire Mosquito Reserve ... is only a question of time."[44] The Mosquito chief, Jonathan Charles Frederic, protested the new decrees, comparing the Nicaraguan Republic to an "adopted mother" who appeared to have "a greater desire to administer the lash of harassing than to tender to the inhabitants of this territory the comforts of her love."[45]

---

[39] J. Sadler to Marquis of Salisbury, November 11, 1889, FO 53/63.
[40] Foreign Office to Acting Consul Sadler, May 1, 1889, FO 420/96.
[41] Extract from the *Diario de Centro América* of Guatemala, April 16, 1889, FO 420/96.
[42] Acting Consul D'Souza to Foreign Office, June 1, 1889, FO 420/96.
[43] Arthur Chapman to the Marquis of Salisbury, April 22, 1890, FO 53/64.
[44] Julian Baker to Commodore Lloyd, May 7, 1890, FO 53/64.
[45] Jonathan C. Frederic to Ysidro Urtecho, Commissioner, March 24, 1890, FO 420/111.

Nicaraguan actions gave rise to resentment but also resistance. On April 19, 1890, in an act of rebellion against Nicaragua, the ex-magistrate of the Corn Islands hoisted the flag of the island against the express orders of the Nicaraguan Commissioner Ysidro Utrecho.[46] On June 20, the Indigenous communities and residents of the Corn Islands presented a memorial to the Mosquito chief protesting against the forcible takeover by Nicaraguan soldiers and pointing to the soldiers' violence and encroachment on private property.[47] In September 1891, Mosquito Chief Robert Henry Clarence appealed to the British government to intervene in the matter of Nicaraguan encroachment on the Mosquito Reserve, declaring that, "The proceedings of the Government of Nicaragua in striving to make her sovereignty absolute is grievous to myself and to my people and shortly we will have to take to the swamps through her encroachment."[48] The Treaty of Managua did not mention the Corn Islands and the Foreign Office on its part maintained the provisions of the Treaty of Managua did not give Great Britain "any right of interference or remonstrance as regards the Corn Islands."[49] On the matter of Greytown, the British government felt that the abrogation of Article VII would be economically detrimental to British interests and the British Board of Trade in London advised the Foreign Office that "no treaty which in any way abrogated Article VII of the existing Treaty should in the interests of this country be conceded."[50]

With it looking increasingly difficult to abrogate Article VII, therefore, the Nicaraguan government now turned its attention towards bypassing Greytown altogether and established a new town, aptly named "América," which could serve as the eastern terminus of the canal route and be "exclusively localized in Nicaragua jurisdiction."[51] Ciudad América was founded on January 1, 1890, with the Nicaraguan flag hoisted at a point northwest of the delimited port of Greytown (see Figure 8.4). The naming and founding of this city expressed Nicaraguan hopes for becoming a central locale for the American continent by serving as the location of the interoceanic canal route. On January 31, the Nicaraguan government approved the new port and city as the mouth of the canal on the Atlantic side and approved the creation of a municipal

---

[46] Ysidro Utrecho to the Commissioner of the Mosquito Reserve, April 26, 1890, FO 53/64.
[47] Memorial to Jonathan Charles Frederic, June 20, 1890, FO 53/64.
[48] Robert Henry Clarence to Marquis of Salisbury, September 15, 1891, FO 53/64.
[49] Foreign Office to Mr. Chapman, August 13, 1890, FO 420/111.
[50] Board of Trade to Foreign Office, August 8, 1889, FO 420/96.
[51] Consul Sadler to the Marquis of Salisbury, March 14, 1890, FO 420/111.

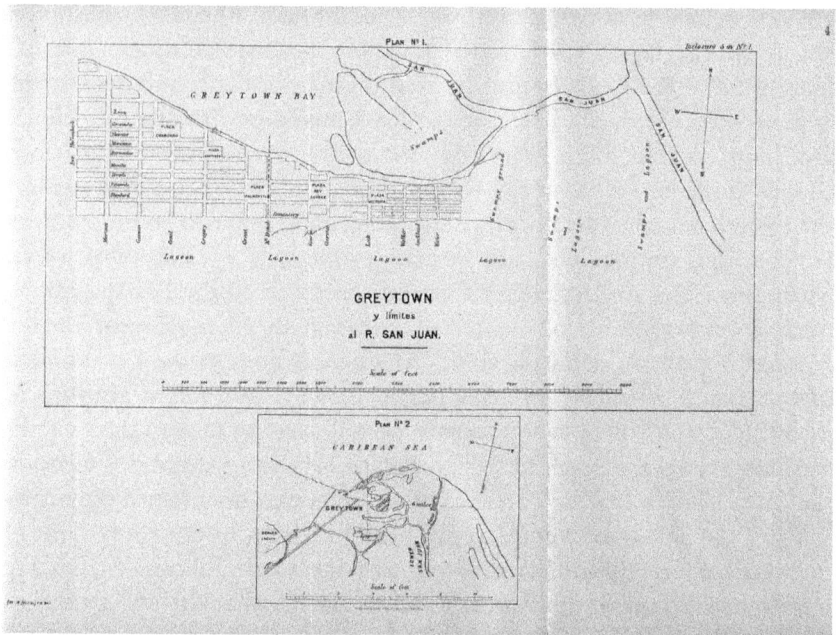

FIGURE 8.4 Ciudad América. By the Nicaraguan decree of November 18, 1889, the jurisdiction of Greytown was bounded on the west by the western limit of the cemetery and extended on the east to 6 miles from Plaza Victoria. The new town of América would comprise the whole bay westward of the cemetery, including the entrance to the bay. Source: "Plans Nos. 1, 2, and 3, showing Limits of the Free Town of Greytown," Enclosure 5 in No. 1, Consul Sadler to the Marquis of Salisbury, March 14, 1890, FO 420/111. Courtesy of the National Archives, Kew.

government for the new port. The buildings of the Canal Company were located in this town. The U.S. consul at San Juan del Norte pointed to the immediate needs of the new town: "But just now the chief need of America is a supply of people to populate it, leaving out of the count the employees of the Canal company there are not twenty persons who reside in America, Nicaragua."[52]

While the prospect of the canal certainly provided one spur to Nicaraguan actions towards the Mosquito Reserve, another equally important reason stemmed from the growth of an export economy based on tropical fruit production. The 1880s coincided with the growth of the banana industry in Nicaragua, with the Mosquito Coast region proving to be an ideal location for banana plantations. By 1882, the banks of the

---

[52] Consul Brown to Assistant Secretary of State, February 15, 1890, *Despatches*, roll 9.

Bluefields River on both sides were lined by banana plantations, which stretched for over 40 miles from Las Bocas.[53] By 1883, exports of bananas had risen to 30,000 bunches per year from this region, and the report on trade of Nicaragua in 1887 mentioned that the export of bananas was on the rise.[54] The growth of the banana industry attracted business, with twenty small companies involved in the banana production in the Mosquito Coast. Since the main market for bananas from the Shore was in New Orleans, the industry depended a great deal on the steamship services – such as that of the Bluefields Steamship Company, which would later become a subsidiary of the United Fruit Company[55] – that allowed for the export of this fruit. As Eduardo Pérez Valle writes about the Bluefields banana trade, "The frequency of shipments and the quantities of cargo attested to the prosperity of the Reserve's business."[56] Between 1883 and 1886, the value of shipments of bananas from Greytown to New Orleans amounted to $86,000.[57] Most of the commercial enterprises in the Bluefields region were North American, and the investment in the banana industry amounted to about $10 million.[58] According to a U.S. consular agent at Bluefields, Mr. B. B. Seat, "the majority of the large plantations have been projected by the aim of American capital, and are now held and operated by Americans under leases from the Mosquito government."[59] Describing the topography and rich natural bounty of the Mosquito Reserve, the Managua-based newspaper *El País* wrote on May 16, 1888, that it was the "most prized property of the Nicaraguan people."[60]

The town of Bluefields itself went through a transformation as a result of the banana trade, with wooden houses replacing traditional thatched huts and the main streets boasting shops and even a printing press.[61] The

[53] H.M.S. *Buzzard* Reporting Proceedings, May 7, 1890, FO 53/64; Eduardo Pérez-Valle, *Expediente de campos azules: Historia de Bluefields en sus documentos* (Managua: 1978), 138.
[54] Pérez-Valle, Expediente de campos azules, 138; Report for the Year 1887 on the Trade of Nicaragua, Inclosure 2 in No. 38, Board of Trade to Foreign Office, August 8, 1889, FO 420/96.
[55] Lester D. Langley and Thomas Schoonover, *The Banana Men: American Mercenaries and Entrepreneurs in Central America, 1880–1930* (Lexington: University Press of Kentucky, 1995).
[56] Pérez-Valle, *Expediente de campos azules*, 138.
[57] Consul Brown to Assistant Secretary of State, November 16, 1886, *Despatches*, roll 8.
[58] Pérez-Valle, *Expediente de campos azules*, 139.
[59] B. B. Seat to Mr. Brown, June 18, 1887, *Despatches*, roll 8.
[60] *El País*, May 16, 1888, El IHNCA en el Exilio.
[61] Pérez-Valle, *Expediente de campos azules*, 139.

demand for bananas also served as an impetus to establish plantations in other parts of the Shore, including Pearl Lagoon, the Great River area, and the Corn Islands.[62] Apart from bananas, the other lucrative tropical fruit was coconuts, whose value of shipments between 1883 and 1896 was $37,000.[63] The increase in demand for bananas led to a concomitant change in the demographics of Bluefields as well. The majority of the 3,500 people living in Bluefields in 1893 were black Jamaican and African American migrants from the Southern United States. Thus, the U.S. Consul Brown wrote that "nearly every steamer coming from New Orleans during that period [1886–1887] has brought to Bluefields plantations one to three colored laborers from that port."[64] The other main natural resource of the region lay in its export of wood, especially mahogany. The Reserve government attempted to protect its interests by passing a series of laws between 1883 and 1892. According to Eduardo Pérez Valle, these laws were influenced by North American interests and were to the detriment of Indigenous groups. Thus, he writes that by a law in 1885, the construction of thatched huts used by Indigenous residents was prohibited in Bluefields and Pearl Lagoon. Pérez-Valle wrote: "After 1889, a law was enacted annually to protect the status of the Reserve, called the 'Ley of Protection of the Mosquito Reserve.' The Law for the Protection of the Reserve was undoubtedly in order to make it clear to the outsiders, especially Nicaraguans, that they could not interfere with the status quo on the Coast."[65]

Nicaraguan actions – even in their efforts to map and delimit the Reserve territory – were often motivated by a desire to control these resources. The commander of H.M.S. *Buzzard*, thus commented in a report on the Mosquito Coast, "if anything valuable like mahogany was observed coming down a creek by the Nicaraguan authorities, a notice was immediately posted up at the spot declaring it Nicaraguan territory, as it was westward of the limit."[66] In addition, Nicaragua sometimes seized fruit vessels plying the Bluefields River at the mouth of the Rama.[67] The other important export commodity produced in this region was India rubber, but by the late 1880s this industry was in decline. The link between this burgeoning trade in tropical commodities and Nicaragua's

[62] Consul Brown to Assistant Secretary of State, November 16, 1886, *Despatches*, roll 8.
[63] Ibid.
[64] Consul Brown to Assistant Secretary of State, April 17, 1887, *Despatches*, roll 8.
[65] Pérez-Valle, *Expediente de campos azules*, 142.
[66] H.M.S. *Buzzard* Reporting Proceedings, May 7, 1890, FO 53/64.
[67] Consul Brown to Assistant Secretary of State, November 22, 1887, *Despatches*, roll 8.

increasingly hostile stance towards the Reserve and desire to regulate the territory through mapping, delimitation and extending jurisdiction can be seen through Señor Cárdenas' correspondence, where he wrote:

> Until the year 1886 the Nicaraguan government abstained from taking any measures in regard to the territory of the Republic adjacent to the Reserve ... But, in view of the development, during recent years, of agriculture and of the banana trade, which attracts a considerable number of natives and foreigners to the valleys and rivers of Nicaragua, as well as a number of steamers which carry the produce to the United States, the government of the Republic took the measures necessary for causing its right to be respected, for putting an end to the abuses referred to, and for securing order and guarantees in that territory.[68]

In November 1894, when tensions between the Nicaraguan government and the Reserve were at their peak, the *Diario de Nicaragua* ran near daily columns detailing the cartographic and geographic surveys of the Mosquito Coast by the state-commissioned engineer José Vitta, scientific work that arguably lent empirical grounding to the state's territorial ambitions.[69]

The period following the Award of Arbitration saw an escalation of tensions between the Republic of Nicaragua and the Reserve, spurred on by the newfangled prospects connected to both the canal route and extractive commerce. As Nicaraguan Commissar Rigoberto Cabezas observed, the Mosquito Coast was "the arteries of the [Nicaraguan] republic."[70] The coming of a Liberal government under José Santos Zelaya in 1893, after three decades of conservative rule, was characterized by an impetus towards consolidating the nation through securing the canal route.[71] Things would finally come to a head in 1894, a year of unprecedented conflict which would finally end with Nicaragua's formal annexation of the Mosquito Reserve in a process that the Nicaraguan government termed "reincorporation."

8.3 THE 1894 CRISIS

By the end of January 1894, reports of hostilities between the Republic of Nicaragua and Honduras (whose government suspected Zelaya of aiding

---

[68] Senor Cáardenas to the Marquis of Salisbury, January 17, 1889, *Selection*, FO 420/96, 12.
[69] See November 4 to November 27, 1894, issues of *Diario de Nicaragua*, *EL IHNCA en el Exilio*.
[70] *Diario de Nicaragua*, November 3, 1894, *EL IHNCA en el Exilio*.
[71] Tijerino, *El imaginario del canal y la nación cosmopolita*, 341.

liberal dissenters in Honduras[72]) and the rumor of a Honduran attack on the town of Cape Gracias a Dios spread alarm within the Reserve and attracted attention across the Atlantic, motivating the British admiralty to dispatch its warship H.M.S. *Cleopatra* to Greytown and spurring the U.S. consular agent at Bluefields, Mr. B. B. Seat, to appeal for an American man-of-war to be sent to Bluefields to protect American interests.[73] Nicaragua on its part justified sending armed troops into the Reserve on the grounds that it had to protect its territory from Honduran aggression. These movements of Nicaraguan troops in the Reserve elicited alarm and consternation among the residents and the authorities of the Reserve. The Mosquito government immediately protested against the mobilization of troops in the Reserve, arguing that the actions of the Republic were an infraction of the rights of the Reserve under the Treaty of Managua. Mosquito officials demanded that Nicaraguan Commissioner General Lacayo withdraw the troops or surrender their arms to the municipal authorities of the town of Bluefields. On January 10, a signed protest by the Mosquito chief to Commissioner Lacayo threatened to raise a protest to the British government if the request for withdrawal and disarming of troops was not complied with.[74] Lacayo responded with his own counter-threat, characterizing the Mosquito attitude as rebellious and declaring that "any attempt of whatever nature that is made against the sovereignty, such acts would be a violation of the Treaty of Managua, and it would demonstrate that we have in the Reserve an enemy allied to those who are at war against us and are on our frontier."[75] A detachment of 126 troops arrived in Bluefields on February 5, followed by another detachment under General Cabezas on February 8,[76] with Lacayo warning the Mosquito chief that any action taken against the troops by

---

[72] Mr. Baker to Mr. Gresham, December 6, 1893, and Mr. Baker to Mr. Gresham, December 26, 1893, Documents 439 and 441, *Papers Relating to the Foreign Relations of the United States, 1894, with the Annual Message of the President, Transmitted to Congress, December 3, 1894* (Washington, DC: GPO, 1895).

[73] Vice-Admiral Sir J. Hopkins to Admiralty, February 10, 1894, FO 420/149; Mr. Seat to Mr. Gresham, January 25, 1894, *Executive Documents of the House of Representatives for the Third Session of the Fifty-Third Session Congress, 1894–95* (Washington, DC: GPO, 1895), 235.

[74] The Chief of the Mosquito Indians to General Lacayo, January 10, 1894, enclosed in Mr. Gosling to the Earl of Kimberley, March 21, 1894, FO 420/149.

[75] General Lacayo to the Chief of the Mosquito Indians, January 12, 1894, enclosed in Mr. Gosling to the Earl of Kimberley, March 21, 1894, FO 420/149.

[76] "Memorandum Respecting the Affairs of the Mosquito Reserve," October 2, 1894, FO 420/151.

the authorities and residents of the Reserve would be taken as an offense against the Nicaraguan forces.[77] Tensions escalated on February 11, as the Nicaraguan troops proceeded to take possession of government buildings in Bluefields, freeing prisoners and arresting a British subject.[78] While the Mosquito chief appealed to the British government for help, the next day, the Nicaraguan Intendente-General of the Atlantic Coast Rigoberto Cabezas issued a proclamation announcing a state of siege in Bluefields and declaring martial law.[79] In a letter to British Consul Bingham, Lacayo justified Nicaraguan actions on the grounds that the Mosquito authorities had challenged the sovereignty of the Republic during a time of war and had treated the Nicaraguan soldiers who had arrived in the Reserve to protect it from foreign invasion as enemies.[80]

While Lacayo denounced the actions of the Mosquito authorities as "scandalous and wicked," he simultaneously resurrected the question of the racial legitimacy of the Mosquito authorities. Writing to British Consul Bingham, Lacayo averred that the Treaty of Managua and the Arbitration Award no longer had any meaning since the Miskitus had been suppressed and their "tribal rule supplanted by a negro oligarchy."[81] Justifying the institution of martial law, Lacayo declared that

Nicaragua holds that it has a right to the military protection of this territory, and a right to punish any attempt at rebellion there, and now particularly, in view of recent events, the reason is made abundantly clear which supports us in claiming our right of military occupation of the Reserve. Indeed, how could we leave our frontiers at the mercy of a foreign enemy?[82]

On the ground in Bluefields, British Vice-Consul Hatch reported the alarm and fear among the Indigenous communities and residents of the town. "The people are going away," he reported to Bingham, "and closing up the houses afraid of the Spaniards. They have gone to the Bush with children and all they could carry from their homes. Everything

---

[77] General Lacayo to the Chief of the Mosquito Indians, February 8, 1894, enclosed in Mr. Gosling to the Earl of Kimberley, March 21, 1894, FO 420/149.
[78] The Chief of the Mosquito Indians to General Lacayo, February 12, 1894, enclosed in Mr. Gosling to the Earl of Kimberley, March 21, 1894, FO 420/149.
[79] Rigoberto Cabezas, Proclamation, February 12, 1894, enclosed in Mr. Gosling to the Earl of Kimberley, March 21, 1894, FO 420/149.
[80] General Lacayo to Consul Bingham, February 16, 1894, enclosed in Mr. Gosling to the Earl of Kimberley, March 21, 1894, FO 420/149.
[81] General Lacayo to Consul Bingham, February 16, 1894, enclosed in Mr. Gosling to the Earl of Kimberley, March 21, 1894, FO 420/149.
[82] Ibid.

is quiet, but at any moment the slightest thing may cause collision."[83] Hatch also informed Bingham that under the pretense of searching for arms, Nicaraguan soldiers had assaulted men, insulted women, and committed robberies. Hatch's wife had herself been indecently propositioned by a Nicaraguan soldier.[84] The Mosquito Chief himself had retreated to Pearl Lagoon.[85] Bingham subsequently met with Lacayo and demanded an apology from the Nicaraguan troops and asserted that Lacayo's actions had contravened the Treaty of Managua.[86] Despite Lacayo's efforts to justify Nicaraguan actions, the British government was sufficiently concerned by the news of the situation in Bluefields and also of reports of conscription of British subjects in the Corn Islands to send its ship H.M.S. *Cleopatra* to Bluefields – in response to Bingham's request for a ship of war – which arrived in Bluefields on February 25 (see Figure 8.5).[87]

Captain Curzon-Howe of H.M.S. *Cleopatra* immediately attempted to defuse the Nicaraguan military buildup in Bluefields. On March 2, 1894, Curzon-Howe landed a force of fifty armed soldiers in Bluefields and compelled the Nicaraguan government to raise the siege on Bluefields. Curzon-Howe, on his part, signed a provisional agreement with Lacayo, which promised that the commissioner would organize a police force for the safety and security of Bluefields, organize a municipal council, withdraw military forces from the Reserve, and abide by the international agreements between Nicaragua and Great Britain. On March 6, Curzon-Howe conveyed the majority of Nicaraguan troops to Greytown on the *Cleopatra*, removing them from the Reserve territory. However, during *Cleopatra*'s absence, a riot broke out in Bluefields between some of the Nicaraguan police and some "coloured men." At around 3 p.m. on March 6, a black Jamaican, thought to be the servant of Lacayo, walked down the main street of Bluefields with a revolver, firing shots at crowds of people passing by. In retaliation, some passersby assaulted the Jamaican. This led to a tense situation in Bluefields, with the black

---

[83] Pro-consul Hatch to Consul Bingham, February 15, 1894, enclosed in Mr. Gosling to the Earl of Kimberley, March 21, 1894, FO 420/149.

[84] Consul Ham to Mr. Gosling, March 7, 1894, enclosed in Mr. Gosling to the Earl of Kimberley, March 31, 1894, FO 420/149.

[85] Pro-consul Hatch to Consul Bingham, February 13, 1894, enclosed in Mr. Gosling to the Earl of Kimberley, March 21, 1894, FO 420/149.

[86] Consul Bingham to Mr. Gosling, March 7, 1894, FO 420/149.

[87] "Memorandum Respecting the Affairs of the Mosquito Reserve," October 2, 1894, FO 420/151.

FIGURE 8.5 British seamen from H.M.S. *Cleopatra* with Consul Bingham in a white shirt at the back. Source: CUR/8 © National Maritime Museum, Greenwich, London.

population being reportedly "intensely excited over this occurrence." After several gunshots in the night, fired in the upper end of the town, and the death of two policemen, both Vice-Consul Hatch and Commissioner Lacayo requested British marines to be landed as quickly as possible to prevent riot and bloodshed.[88] The landing of British marines under Curzon-Howe from H.M.S. *Cleopatra* appeared to finally bring the situation under control. Even Mr. B. B. Seat, the U.S. consular agent, acknowledged the effectiveness of the British marines: "The request [for landing British marines] was promptly responded to, and this morning we are feeling secure in the presence of her Britannic Majesty's hardy, brave-looking marines."[89] With a British warship now clearly in control

---

[88] Mr. Seat to Mr. Braida, March 6, 1894, Inclosure 1 in Mr. Braida to Mr. Uhl, March 7, 1894, *The Executive Documents of the House of Representatives for the Third Session of the Fifty-Third Congress* (Washington, DC: 1895), 241.
[89] Ibid.

of the situation, the U.S. legate in Managua, Mr. Baker, sent a telegram to Mr. Gresham of the U.S. Department of State, urging him to send an American warship.[90]

Curzon-Howe made it clear to Lacayo that his actions had been motivated only by his desire to bring order to Bluefields and did not imply a condonation of Nicaraguan actions. Curzon-Howe was keen that a provisional council assume administrative power and ensure order in Bluefields. However, the Mosquito chief and his council refused to resume their posts unless a British ship remained to guard them, asserting that they would not remain alive even for one hour if the British forces left.[91] Similar fear of Nicaraguan retaliation prompted Curzon-Howe to request Lacayo to hand him the arms and ammunition that were stored in the courthouse in Bluefields, and he proceeded with 5 stands of rifles and 30,000 rounds of ammunition to Greytown, where he handed them over to the governor for safekeeping. "My reason for this," explained Curzon-Howe, "is that every time I have left that place a disturbance has been provoked, and the supposed number of twenty-nine troops has been suddenly swelled to 100 (with power to add to this number). It therefore was a considerable source of danger to my officers and men in the case of a concerted surprise and attack."[92] Consul Braida, who arrived in Bluefields on March 13, reported that the town was occupied by British marines and soldiers and appeared to be peaceful and orderly.[93] However, the formation of a council in Bluefields remained elusive due to Nicaraguan opposition and the increasing demands of the United States' citizens. On March 16, the *Cleopatra* was relieved by the *Canada* under Captain Wilson, who soon realized that as long as the British forces remained in Bluefields, the provisional government would not be formed "for there was no inducement to set up a government to which taxes would have to be paid when the work was being done for nothing by British sailors."[94] Consequently, he withdrew the guard, and by the end of March, British seamen had left Bluefields.

---

[90] Mr. Baker to Mr. Gresham, March 6, 1894, *Executive Documents*, 239.
[91] Minutes of Meeting of Executive Council of the Mosquito Reserve, March 8, 1894, enclosed in Admiralty to Foreign Office, April 12, 1892, FO 420/149.
[92] Captain Curzon-Howe to Vice-Admiral Sir J. Hopkins, enclosed in Admiralty to Foreign Office, April 12, 1892, *Further Correspondence*, FO 420/149.
[93] Mr. Braida to Mr. Uhl, March 17, 1894, *Executive Documents*, 253.
[94] "Memorandum Respecting the Affairs of the Mosquito Reserve," October 2, 1894, FO 420/151.

While a provisional government soon took charge of Bluefields, the Nicaraguan government withdrew the exequatur of Bingham's commission as the British consul in Greytown on the grounds that he had exceeded his authority and fomented "a spirit of disobedience" to Nicaraguan laws. In mid-April, Captain Clarke, upon arriving at Bluefields on H.M.S. *Magicienne*, found armed Nicaraguan troops in the town, and he felt that the Nicaraguans had no intention of leaving the Reserve.[95] Captain Clarke and the captain of the U.S. warship *San Francisco*, which had arrived in Bluefields on April 24, came to an arrangement that either a U.S. or a British warship would be constantly present until the crisis subsided.[96] On May 10, Clarke brought Chief Robert Henry Clarence to Bluefields, leaving him in Lacayo's protection as he feared that the chief would be murdered if he remained at Pearl Lagoon. On June 3, the *Magicienne* left Bluefields for Jamaica, while the U.S. ship *New York* remained in Bluefields.

The presence of Nicaraguan troops in the Reserve and the lack of legal status of the provisional council, however, added to the misgivings of the residents of the Reserve so that by June 10, the British Minister Gosling reported that "the Mosquitos and the United States' residents in the Reserve are determined to create an insurrection should any project be put forward for setting aside the Treaty of Managua." A petition by the American citizens of the Reserve requested that the Nicaraguan troops stationed in the Bluff be removed.[97] Around mid-June, nine Jamaican policemen were discharged by the Nicaraguan commissioner. When the discharged men insisted on being paid for their services, General Cabezas ordered his soldiers to charge at them with bayonets. In the midst of this, three Americans barged into the Government House in support of the Jamaican policemen. This incident caused feelings to run high in the town among all classes of residents, and in the evening of July 5, a large mob gathered outside the Government House armed with rifles. Firing soon started and showed no signs of abating until morning. Two Nicaraguan soldiers were killed, and a British subject was injured. Around 10 p.m., the American citizens fired rockets to signal to the U.S.S. *Marblehead* for help. However, the bar being too rough, Captain O'Neil sent a message that he would land a party of marines in the morning. During the night, the Nicaraguan flag was hauled down. At the request of the merchants and other inhabitants of the Reserve, the Mosquito chief and his council

---

[95] Ibid.   [96] Ibid.   [97] Mr. Gosling to the Earl Kimberley, June 10, 1894, FO 420/150.

resumed their previous position and issued a proclamation. Captain O'Neil landed the men from *Marblehead* on the morning of the 6th, and things began to heat up with the rumor that "the Nicaraguans intend to lay the 'niggers' low," and the prospect of an uprising seemed imminent.[98] On the night of the 6th, a skirmish followed between Cabezas' troops and the American citizens of Bluefields. On the 7th, Cabezas, fearing for his life, agreed to give up the archives, books, and papers belonging to the Mosquito government as long as his life and those of his men were spared. Cabezas left that afternoon for Rama on a steamer with sixty soldiers, leaving the Mosquito chief and his old council in charge of Bluefields. By mid-July, martial law was in force in the Corn Islands, following a fight between resident British subjects and a detachment of Nicaraguan troops. Following the latter's defeat, the locals restored the governor of the Corn Islands and instituted martial law.[99]

On July 21, Commander Stuart of H.M.S. *Mohawk* arrived at Bluefields. He found the town quiet but felt apprehensive since the Nicaraguan commissioner had still not returned and the Mosquito chief had no real authority. There did not appear to be a police force to maintain order in the town. Stuart felt that the Jamaicans were the main source of trouble in Bluefields, and he issued them a notice declaring that he would not tolerate mob law. Instructions from the Foreign Office cautioned Stuart to abstain from any direct interference in the local affairs, except to protect British lives and property and prevent conflict. On July 26, Stuart returned to Bluefields and was immediately faced with rumors that Cabezas was about to return with an army to occupy the town. He then took matters into his own hands and landed his men from the *Mohawk* at Bluefields and offered asylum on board the *Mohawk* to any British subject who had been involved in the July 5–6 incidents.

In a letter to Stuart, Cabezas indicated that he intended to reestablish order in Bluefields and punish the rebels. Stuart, who was heading to Limón for further instructions, requested Cabezas to refrain from occupying Bluefields until his return from Limón. British subjects, meantime, were camped near the courthouse under the protection of the officers of the *Mohawk*. On August 3, Cabezas returned to Bluefields with his troops, informing Stuart of his intention to form a government, punish

---

[98] Bulletin, Inclosure 26 in No. 109, Mr. Gosling to the Earl of Kimberley, August 22, 1894, FO 420/150.
[99] "Strategic Importance of the Corn Islands – Recent Disturbances Here," in Enclosure 13 in No. 85, Admiralty to Foreign Office, August 31, 1894, FO 420/150.

rebels and emphasizing that he would not allow Jamaicans to be members of the council. Stuart informed Cabezas that these actions would amount to a contravention of the Treaty of Managua and the Arbitration Award of the Emperor of Austria. Soon after, more Nicaraguan troops arrived in Bluefields under the leadership of Lacayo and Señor Madriz. Stuart now attempted to evacuate British subjects and on August 7 left for Limón with 140 British subjects and the Mosquito chief.[100]

By the orders of Madriz, Hatch and thirteen other men, including some British subjects, were arrested, marched through the streets of Greytown in great indignity with a band playing before them, and then sent to Managua to face charges. The British government reacted by demanding an explanation from Nicaragua of its actions in the arrest and imprisonment of British subjects and warned that it would hold Nicaragua responsible for any illegal or unjust treatment of British subjects. On August 29, Hatch and the other prisoners were expelled by decree without a trial. By November, the Nicaraguan government had named a new chief of the Mosquito, Andrew Hendy, whose election appeared to be carried out behind closed doors at night in the presence of Indigenous groups who lived outside the Reserve. John Tayler, a resident of Bluefields, describing the election, wrote, "this man is Chief in name only, for he has no power over anything, merely a picture on the wall. There is no flag, and no one was ever invited to the appointment, for it can hardly be called an election, – the business was carried on in the night."[101] On November 20, Nicaragua issued a Decree of Reincorporation announcing that the constitution and laws of Nicaragua would be "obeyed by the Mosquito peoples, they being under the protection of the flag of the Republic." The Mosquito Reserve was renamed the Department of Zelaya.[102] Bingham alerted Gosling about the suspicious nature of the proceeding, reporting to him that "the vote of the Indians for their incorporation with Nicaragua was obtained by means of intimidation and threats."[103] The Nicaragua government would maintain that the "reincorporation" had been voluntary on the part of the Miskitus.[104] While contention over the manner in which the incorporation had taken

---

[100] "Memorandum Respecting the Affairs of the Mosquito Reserve," October 2, 1894, FO 420/151.
[101] Mr. Newstead to the Earl of Kimberley, December 10, 1894, FO 420/150.
[102] Decree of Reincorporation, Inclosure 1, in No. 21, Señor Barrios to the Earl of Kimberley, January 16, 1895, FO 420/159.
[103] Mr. Gosling to the Earl of Kimberley, December 12, 1894, FO 420/150.
[104] *Diario de Nicaragua*, February 21, 1895, *El IHNCA en el Exilio*.

place would continue well into 1895, there would be no turning back again. The Miskitu had finally been conquered.

8.4 BLACKNESS, INDIGENEITY, AND THE FATE OF THE RESERVE

In the aftermath of the 1894 events, the Nicaraguan government took pains to recoup its image by placing the blame for the violent events on the machinations of the "foreign" elements in charge of the Reserve government. In November 1894, the *Diario de Nicaragua* ran a column that reproduced the report of the commissioner in Mosquitia, Don José Madriz, and which served to communicate the Nicaraguan version of events. Through this report, Nicaragua maintained that its own actions had been prompted by the hostilities perpetrated by the Reserve government against the sovereignty of the Republic. The report also suggested that it had been the Reserve government and not the Republic that had engaged in senseless violence. "No habia sido posible al adversario llamar noche al día! Los cadáveres de nuestros soldados en el Bluff y Corn Island, no daban lugar a equivocación."[105] [It has not been possible for our adversary to call the day night. The bodies of our soldiers at the Bluff and at Corn Island allow no room for equivocation.[106]] Asserting that its own efforts to bring order to the Reserve had been opposed by its foreign element, the report stated that: "The measures for the reestablishment of authority of Nicaragua were, in fact, insupportable to people who from time immemorial had done as they chose in this rich territory, masters of the government and of tribes of unhappy Indians whom they exploited, submitting them to the yoke of eternal slavery."[107] In this way, the Nicaraguan government distinguished between the "foreign" government and the "true" Indigenous residents, who had been forced to subservience and whom Nicaraguan incorporation would deliver from "slavery."

Placing the blame for the violent turn of events on the "foreign" – especially Creole and West Indian migrants – allowed the Nicaraguan government to adhere to its vision of nation-making that saw black populations as irremediable obstacles to progress and Indigenous populations as assimilable. One of the main allegations against Hatch, for

---

[105] *Diario de Nicaragua*, November 2, 1894, *El IHNCA en el Exilio*.
[106] My translation.
[107] "Report of the Nicaraguan Commissary," August 10, 1894, FO 420/150.

instance, was that "the blacks continued to receive inspiration from him."[108] As Frazier writes:

> The speeches and writings of government officials and the testimonies of Nicaraguan citizens made it clear that these Negroes were a threatening and unwelcome element and stood as an obstacle to Nicaraguan sovereignty. These same sources, however, present the indigenous population of the coast as backward and oppressed, but as assimilable into the Nicaraguan nation. The differentiation between the indigenous and Afro-descendent peoples of the coast was not just expressed in government rhetoric. It also manifested itself in the enforcement of the regulations that the Nicaraguan government imposed along the coast.[109]

Indeed, throughout the difficult year of 1894 and in the wake of the annexation, the Nicaraguan government maintained that it had only attempted to supplant a "negro oligarchy."[110]

While the Nicaraguan government sought to shift blame away by characterizing the Mosquito Reserve government as "black" and a "circle of foreigners," the British Foreign Office consistently portrayed the actions of British officers on the ground as pragmatic, rational, and cool-headed, emphasizing the role of British troops in bringing order to the chaos on the ground. Nowhere is this clearer than in the correspondence concerning the captain of H.M.S. *Cleopatra*, Commander Curzon-Howe. Following the landing of the *Cleopatra* in March 1894 in response to a riot in Bluefields, a memorandum of the British Foreign Office reported that "the mere presence of a British party, who were not under the necessity of firing a single shot, was sufficient to restore order immediately." The Foreign Office also transmitted a petition to Queen Victoria from Chief Robert Henry Clarence and the other Indigenous residents and inhabitants of the Reserve that underlined the indispensability of British soldiers in bringing a modicum of peace to the Reserve,

> The petitioners at present are feeling safe under the great vigilance of your Majesty's marines, who are now in charge of the town ... if your Majesty withdraw from the situation, our lives – the lives of men, women, and children – will be nothing in the hands of these vengeful invaders, as we have affirmed assurances that vengeance will be taken as soon as opportunity offers, and that without mercy.[111]

---

[108] *Diario de Nicaragua*, November 30, 1894, *El IHNCA en el Exilio*.
[109] Samuel Frazier, "Ethnicity, Empire, and Exclusion: The Incorporation of a Caribbean Borderland, 1893–1909," ILASSA 27 (2007).
[110] Carlos Alberto Lacayo to the British Consul, March 3, 1894. Quoted in Pedro Joaquín Cuadra Chamorro, *La reincorporación de la Mosquitia* (Granada: El Centro-Americano, 1944), 14–15.
[111] Robert Henry Clarence, Petition, March 8, 1894, enclosed in Consul Bingham to the Earl of Rosebery, March 24, 1894, FO 420/149.

FIGURE 8.6 Robert Henry Clarence and Consul Bingham with officers of H.M.S. *Cleopatra*. Source: CUR/8 © National Maritime Museum, Greenwich, London.

An archival photograph suggests Clarence personally interacted with officers of H.M.S. *Cleopatra* (see Figure 8.6). Similarly, the actions of Commander Stuart of H.M.S. *Mohawk* were presented as those of a pragmatic officer with considerable presence of mind whose quick-wittedness saved the lives of several British subjects. Indeed, the British Foreign Office consistently maintained – despite the visibility of British naval power in the way the 1894 events unfolded – that its main intention throughout had been to bring order to chaos. The imperial hubris that only British pluck could finally save the situation is apparent in the pages of Foreign Office correspondence.

Like the British, the U.S. naval and state correspondence also highlighted the role of American warships in the maintenance of peace and the protection of American subjects. Thus, the landing of the U.S.S. warship *Atlanta* in May 1893 was justified by the U.S. Consul Braida on the grounds that the troops had arrived at the express request of U.S. citizens to protect the canal works. Thus, consul Braida wrote: "The troops

(4 officers 37 blue-jackets-one gattling gun) landed on the afternoon of May 25th at the La Fe dock in the City of American and occupied the store house of the Nicaragua Canal Construction Co. maintaining a strictly neutral attitude."[112] Similarly, the dispatches of the U.S. consuls emphasized that the naval commanders had repeatedly urged American citizens to remain neutral and not to take part in hostilities.[113] Instead, Consular Agent B. B. Seat emphasized the efforts of U.S. naval commanders such as Ensign Hill of U.S.S. *Columbia* to attempt to negotiate with Nicaraguan authorities on the ground to bring order.[114]

Despite both British and U.S. efforts to defuse the situation created by Nicaraguan actions on the ground and their joint criticism of the high-handed actions of Nicaraguan troops, particularly in their treatment of British and American citizens in the Reserve, both British and U.S. views regarding the source of trouble in the Reserve were eerily similar to those espoused by the Nicaraguan government. Thus, just as the Nicaraguan government maintained that it was attempting to overthrow a "negro oligarchy," both the British and U.S. officers believed that the true reason for hostilities was the preponderance of black residents among the Reserve population. This can be seen, for instance, in Commander Stuart's efforts to deport Jamaican immigrants from Bluefields as a way of mitigating riots. Similarly, the naval commander of U.S.S. *Marblehead* agreed with the Nicaraguan authorities in attributing the hostilities in Bluefields "to the negros."[115] Thus, despite their various stances on the Mosquito Question, Nicaraguan, British, and American officials converged in their racial interpretation of the events of 1894 through their vilification of the Afro-descended element of the Reserve and, thus paradoxically, fed into the Nicaraguan national rhetoric of assimilation of the Miskitu Indigenous base.

Yet what the documents also reveal is that instead of assimilation, what was happening on the ground among the Indigenous communities was a deepening internal fragmentation. A report written by the Moravian missionary Heinrich Ziock in 1892 suggests that there may have been a heightening of Zambo–Tawira conflict in the last years of the Reserve. His account suggests that the election of Robert Henry Clarence, who was a Tawira from his father's side, antagonized the Zambo

---

[112] Mr. Braida to the Department of State, May 28, 1893, *Despatches*, roll 10.
[113] Mr. Seat to Mr. Braida, August 20, 1894, *Despatches*, roll 11.
[114] B. B. Seat to Mr. Braida, August 20, 1894, *Despatches*, roll 11.
[115] Mr. Gresham to Mr. Baker, August 4, 1894, *Executive Documents*, 320.

Indigenous groups. According to the account, the latter, with the complicity of Nicaraguan authorities, elected an "anti-king" for the Mosquito territory. Heinrich recalled, "Many of our own people joined the resistance movement, refused to pay taxes, and sided with the anti-king. Thus, in the Spring of 1892, it seemed that the peace was seriously jeopardized, that a civil war loomed, and indeed, that the existence of the Moskito nation was seriously threatened."[116] Accounts of erosion of the Miskitu Indigenous base can also be gleaned from British and American correspondence in this period.

Just as the Nicaraguan government pointed to "internal" reasons within the Reserve as the true reason for the events of 1894, so too did British and American officials. For Curzon-Howe, it was a combination of the Reserve government's ineptitude and Nicaraguan desire for the rich Atlantic region that gave rise to the hostilities of 1894. Describing the Mosquito chief as "very ignorant," he wrote:

> The country under the Treaty [of Managua] has been ruled by the Chief and Council, who have paid themselves out of the 5 per cent duties sometimes levied; but I fail to see that anything has been done for the country, either religious, educational, or material. It is, of course a state of affairs most agreeable to all the merchants as they paid only as much duty as they liked, and had an entirely free hand everywhere. The increased business in fruit and mahogany, which trades have been enormously developed, has been long a source of envy, naturally to Nicaragua, who covets these sources of revenue, which are being lost to it; hence the situation.

British and U.S. officials pointed to signs of a rift between the Reserve government and the Indigenous base. Writing in January 1894, shortly before the beginning of the tumultuous events leading up to incorporation, U.S. Consul Mr. B. B. Seat wrote:

> As a matter of fact the Mosquito Indians proper know but little of the Government as it exists; and according to well authenticated reports have become dissatisfied and have recently developed considerable opposition to this local regime. They claim that they are not the beneficiaries of anything that is done; that their country is being alienated and its wealth squandered for the enrichment of their rulers, while they as a people are left destitute and poor.[117]

A memo from the British Foreign Office in March 1889 pointed to the "complaint of certain Indians that the Government at Bluefields is Negro

---

[116] "The Sambo and Tawira Miskitu, 1892," from Heinrich Ziock, *Missions-Blatt aus der Brüdergemeine* (1894), reprinted in Offen and Rugeley, eds., The Awakening Coast, 256.

[117] Mr. Seat to Mr. Braida, January 22, 1894, *Historical Documents*, 366.

and not Indian, and does not represent the real Indians."[118] The report of the commander of the *Mohawk* pointed to a rift between the Reserve government and the Miskitu, at least those living outside the Reserve: "It will be seen that the Indians collected for the Convention by General Cabezas were, for the most part, from the district of Cape Gracias, outside the Mosquito Reserve. They, after some persuasion, elected a Chief named Hendy, also from the same district, outside the Reserve."[119] Distancing himself from the preceding line of Miskitu rulers, the new chief emphasized that he was part of the "Hendy family" that had "always been a friend of Nicaragua."[120]

Taken together, these documents suggest a fracturing of the Reserve from both outside and within. While Nicaraguan aggression shattered the autonomy of the Reserve from without, the internal stresses within Miskitu Indigenous society, some segments of which were increasingly separated from the Reserve government, splintered it from the inside.

8.5 THE CANAL IN THE AMERICAN GEOPOLITICAL VISION

Even though the United States maintained that its intervention in Nicaragua had been strictly of a neutral character, the military involvement of U.S. warships and the evidence of rivalry with British warships deployed in the Mosquito Coast point to the fact that behind the rhetoric of peace-making and neutrality lay the threat of flexing naval muscles. Not since the *Cyane* bombardment had the gloves been off to this extent. Several different warships intervened in the 1894 hostilities at different times – including U.S.S. *Columbia*, *San Francisco*, *Marblehead*, and *Zulu*.

The American rivalry with their British counterparts comes through clearly in the correspondence of both the U.S. consuls and the U.S. Department of State. As early as May 1893, following the landing of the U.S.S. *Atlanta*, Consul Braida posited the U.S. position on the situation in the Mosquito Coast that "the ascendancy of British influence could never be permitted."[121] On the landing of British marines at Bluefields in March 1894, the U.S. Department of State immediately wrote to the consul at Bluefields, Mr. Baker: "Did Great Britain land

---

[118] Memorandum by Mr. Bertie, No. 21, March 22, 1889, FO 420/96.
[119] Commander Stuart to Admiralty, December 5, 1894, FO 420/159.
[120] A. Hendy to Jose Santos Zelaya, March 30, 1895, reprinted *Diario de Nicaragua*, April 26, 1895, *El IHNCA en el Exilio*.
[121] Mr. Braida to the Department of State, May 28, 1893, *Despatches*, roll 10.

troops under asserted right of sovereignty or only for protection? Prompt answer desired."[122] Consul Braida was critical of Captain Howe's efforts to persuade Nicaraguan officials to form a provisional government in the Reserve, describing it as a "suspicious arrangement" to "form a provisional government upon a basis which we considered un-American."[123] Echoing these sentiments, Mr. Gresham wrote: "I am unable to see that this joint assumption of authority by British and Nicaraguan agents is compatible with the stipulations of the treaty of Managua. By that treaty Great Britain renounced all sovereignty over the Reserve."[124] Baker, the U.S. legate in Bluefields, went a step further, describing the provisional government as imposed jointly by the Nicaraguan authorities and the British Consul Bingham as a "bold usurpation" that "does not rest upon the consent of 1 per cent of the people governed by it."[125]

Arguably, at the root of this rivalry was the respective positions of U.S. and British naval and defensive powers at the end of the nineteenth century. While "Britannia ruled the waves," the United States still remained a peripheral naval power. Moreover, it was still recovering from the hardships and turbulence of the Civil War period. At this juncture, as the postwar United States attempted to carve out a position of leadership and rebuild its image as a global leader, the Nicaragua Canal appeared to be the answer it had been searching for. Unlike Great Britain, the United States did not envision having a large navy but rather, in the words of Captain George Scriven of the U.S. Army, "a small fleet of swift and powerful ships which shall carry her flag with honor upon every sea."[126] At the end of the nineteenth century, the U.S. Navy ranked seventh in the world behind Great Britain, France, Italy, Russia, Germany, and Spain. In this circumstance, American control over the Nicaragua Canal was seen as a possible game changer. Scriven wrote:

So, no doubt it will be the fortune of our navy to be always small in numbers, but with no distant colonies to defend, and without vessels at the alarm of war gathered, so far as may be wise, upon our own threatened coasts; we may obtain

---

[122] Mr. Gresham to Mr. Baker, March 14, 1894, *Executive Documents*, 250.
[123] Mr. Braida to Mr. Baker, March 21, 1894, *Executive Documents*, 257.
[124] Mr. Gresham to Mr. Bayard, April 30, 1894, *Executive Documents*, 272.
[125] Mr. Baker to Mr. Gresham, May 10, 1894, *Executive Documents*, 289–290.
[126] Capt. George P. Scriven, "Nicaragua Canal, Letter from the Acting Secretary of War in Response to the Senate Resolution of March 29, 1894, Transmitting a Report on the Nicaragua Canal in Its Military Aspects" (Washington, DC: GPO, 1894), *Panama Canal Pamphlets, 1880–1900*.

the preponderance on either seaboard if we have but a short cut across the Isthmus.[127]

Both for commercial and military reasons, the United States increasingly viewed the Nicaragua Canal as an answer to its need – especially following the devastating Civil War – to regain its economic and strategic position as a global leader. In 1887, Commander H. C. Taylor in his treatise, *The Control of the Pacific*, illustrated the role of U.S. control over a transisthmian canal through Central America to achieve its ambitions of controlling the Pacific. He wrote: "To the question, 'Do we control the Pacific?' our statistics answer decidedly, 'No'; but to the question, 'Shall we control the Pacific?' the inauguration of a Central American canal would give loud affirmative response that would be understood throughout the world."[128] Pointing to the failure of the Panama sea-level canal, Taylor opined that "M. De Lesseps has already convinced the world that nature does not contemplate a canal at Panama, and that man cannot in this case overcome nature's obstacles. No one can see without regret the financial disaster now overhanging the French people."[129] For Taylor, the Nicaragua Canal was a touchstone to achieving U.S. naval supremacy over the Pacific coast and to provide an impetus to U.S. shipping and commerce in tropical products, as well as the guano trade from South America.

For Taylor, the topography of the Nicaragua Canal route was particularly well suited for the transportation of naval vessels in wartime. Lake Nicaragua, which formed the center of the canal route, as a large freshwater lake, offered a significant advantage for sojourning naval vessels in contrast to a saline sea environment, which was often injurious to health. Taylor wrote:

Hence may issue squadrons in the height of vigor and discipline striking rapid and effective blows in both the oceans, and returning to refit in this sheltered stronghold, and to draw from it nourishment and fresh strength for a renewal of hostilities. There cannot be imagined a more potent factor in deciding threatened difficulties or in securing honorable peace with a powerful enemy than the presence in this healthy and capacious water-fortress of a strong fleet, prepared, at a telegraphic sign from the home government, to issue fully equipped from either entrance for instant service in the Atlantic or Pacific.[130]

---

[127] Ibid.
[128] Commander H. C. Taylor, *The Control of the Pacific* (reprinted from the Forum for June 1887), *Panama Canal Pamphlets, 1885–1890*.
[129] Ibid.   [130] Ibid.

In another tract, Taylor argued that the Nicaragua Canal route would serve as a base for not only control over the Atlantic and Pacific coasts of the United States but also the islands in the West Indies. Thus, Taylor asserted that Nicaragua as a naval base was "without parallel in history."[131]

No less than Alfred Thayer Mahan, possibly the most influential proponent of U.S. sea power in the nineteenth century, advocated for the Nicaragua Canal route as the answer to American naval strategic needs and ambitions. In 1893, in an essay entitled *Hawaii and Our Future Sea Power*, Mahan wrote:

Whether the canal of the Central American isthmus be eventually at Panama or at Nicaragua matters little to the question now in hand, although, in common with most Americans who have thought upon the subject, I believe it surely will be at the latter point. Whichever it be, the convergence there of so many ships from the Atlantic and the Pacific will constitute a centre of commerce, interoceanic, and inferior to few, if to any, in the world; one whose approaches will be watched jealously, and whose relations to the other centres of the Pacific by the lines joining it to them must be examined carefully ... the Isthmian Canal is an inevitable part in the future of the United States.[132]

Echoing Mahan's views on the isthmian canal, in the early 1890s, reports submitted to the U.S. Congress also emphasized the military advantage of the Nicaragua Canal, particularly in the control of Hawaii and the Bering Sea.[133] In December 1892, Mr. Sherman from the Committee on Foreign Relations presented his report to the Senate, which also highlighted the military potential of the canal.[134] In March 1894 – around the same time as the Nicaraguan government had begun its attempts to forcibly seize the Mosquito Reserve – the Senate transmitted a report by Capt. George P. Scriven, of the Signal Corps., entitled *Nicaragua Canal in Its Military Aspects*. Scriven wrote:

We have fought the great war of modern times, we have had millions of men under arms in the field, our military power on land is without limit, therefore we

---

[131] H. C. Taylor, Commander, U.S. Navy, "The Nicaragua Canal" (no place, publisher, or date), *Panama Canal Pamphlets, 1885–1900*.

[132] Alfred Thayer Mahan, "Hawaii and Our Future Sea Power," first published in *The Forum*, 1893; reprinted in Captain A. T. Mahan, *The Interest of America in Sea Power, Present and Future* (Boston: Little, Brown and Co., 1917), 44–52.

[133] *Nicaragua Canal: Reports of the Committee on Foreign Relations of the Senate in the 51st–53rd Congresses with Subject Index* (Washington, DC: GPO, 1894), *Panama Canal Pamphlets, 1880–1900*.

[134] Ibid., 35.

are unconquerable – such is the reasoning. But we forget that the United States is by nature and by neglect one of the most vulnerable nations of the world, and that no great power has so vast an extent of frontier exposed to the attack of an enemy.

Thus, Scriven presented the Nicaragua Canal as an answer to the United States' new vision of its own position as a global power in the aftermath of the bitter Civil War period. In these writings of U.S. naval officers, we can also detect a rivalry with Great Britain, which was the most celebrated naval power of the time. Commenting on British naval bases in the Caribbean, Scriven averred that "England seems to have placed her more powerful works nearer to the vitals of the United States." Highlighting the fact that even the Suez Canal had not been free from British military interests, Scriven wrote, "behind the mild assurance of exemption of the Suez Canal stood the guns of the British fleet and the land defense on the route to India."[135] This view of the Nicaragua Canal as a possible naval base arguably played a role in the U.S. government's desire to control the canal and serves to provide a useful backdrop to the Anglo-American rivalry during Nicaragua's 1894 attempt at annexation. In fact, arguably the U.S. efforts with regard to the Nicaragua Canal always had a military aspect to it, which is evident in the role played in surveys and expeditions by prominent naval and military officers, such as Daniel Ammen and A.G. Menocal. The United States' ambitions with regard to the Nicaragua Canal may also have encouraged a tacit approval of Nicaraguan efforts at annexation of the Reserve. As Charles Hale writes: "Secretary of State Walter Q. Gresham ignored these demands [for local self-government in Bluefields], having already determined that the annexation would advance the broader objective of securing rights to a canal passage through Nicaraguan territory."[136]

Besides the military aspect, the Nicaragua Canal was also seen to be a commercially important venture, particularly for U.S. trade and commerce. A *New York Evening Post* article from March 1888 tried to calculate the earning potential of the Nicaragua Canal. The latter was seen as a possible avenue for rerouting several existing trading routes: trade across Central America, trade between Atlantic ports of the United States and countries west of Cape Horn, trade between Pacific ports and

---

[135] Capt. George P. Scriven, "Nicaragua Canal. Letter from the Acting Secretary of War in Response to the Senate Resolution of March 29, 1894, Transmitting a Report on the Nicaragua Canal in Its Military Aspects" (Washington, DC: GPO, 1894), *Panama Canal Pamphlets, 1880–1900*.

[136] Hale, Resistance and Contradiction, Kindle e-book location 616.

countries east of Cape Horn, trade between Europe and countries on the Pacific, and trade of British Columbia with Europe. An estimated shipping of 4,507,044 tons passed through these routes combined in a single year. The article declared that:

> In six years, of all the classes of trade within the zone of attraction of the canal, and the fair probability of additions from the European traffic by sail, with Japan, New Zealand, Fiji, and the South Pacific groups, should render it safe to predict a total tonnage of six to six and a half millions for the Nicaragua Canal in 1894. If the cost of constructing the canal should prove to be double the estimate of the engineers, the financial adventure would still be safe and profitable. The commerce which exists to-day assures so much. Half of that commerce is our own.[137]

H. C. Taylor would give a more conservative estimate of 5 million tons of shipping per year through the Nicaragua Canal route.[138] According to Taylor, even the earnings generated from 5 million tons of shipping would be enough to offset the cost of construction of the canal and generate considerable revenue. Since sailing vessels found it difficult to navigate the Suez Canal, there was also the possibility of such vessels plying through the Nicaragua Canal because of favorable winds. In July 1894, the Committee on Interstate and Foreign Commerce presented a report to the U.S. Senate that outlined the necessity of the Nicaragua Canal. The report pointed to the distances saved because of the canal through Nicaragua and the concomitant potential for an increase in trade. The Committee argued that the opening of the Suez Canal had benefited European trade while not having any similar impact on the commerce of the United States. The Committee argued that to maintain competitiveness with European trade, the Nicaragua Canal was essential: "We are now confronted with the ugly fact that in the field of endeavor here referred to our relative position will continue subordinate and conspicuously impotent, unless we place ourselves on an equality with our competitors by opening a shorter and cheaper avenue to the trade of that part of the world."[139] The report concluded that "the success of the Suez Canal has made the Nicaragua Canal a necessity." The naval ambitions of the United States in the Nicaragua Canal can also

---

[137] "The Nicaragua Canal: Its Expected Earnings and Its Effect on Ocean Routes" (Unidentified author, article reprinted from the *New York Post*, March 24, 1888), *Panama Canal Pamphlets, 1885–1900*.
[138] H. C. Taylor, Commander, U.S. Navy, "The Nicaragua Canal."
[139] 53rd Cong., 2nd Sess., House of Representatives, Maritime Canal Company of Nicaragua (Washington, DC: GPO, 1894; report no. 1201), *Panama Canal Pamphlets, 1880–1900*.

be seen through the unratified Frelinghuysen–Zavala Treaty of 1884. As Francis Kinloch Tijerino notes, the unratified 1884 treaty between Nicaragua and the United States over the construction of the Nicaragua Canal implicitly reserved the canal for U.S. military use: "Pursuant to Article VII, Nicaragua reserved the exercise of civil jurisdiction over the canal belt "in time of peace"; clause that, by omission, left that strategic territory in the hands of the United States in time of war."[140]

8.6 CONCLUSION

That the twists and turns of 1894 – including Nicaraguan aggression and British and American naval involvement – were, in the end, an expression of the struggle over control of the Nicaragua Canal was evident even to contemporaries on the ground. The *Bluefields Messenger* of March 30, 1894, opined:

the landing of a British force in the Mosquito territory of Nicaragua recalls a great international question which was thought to have been finally disposed of 34 years ago. The struggle between Great Britain and the U.S. for the hegemony of the projected Nicaragua Canal raged for years in this arid reservation which Patterson indicated, nearly two centuries ago, as holding the key of the commerce of the world.[141]

For both Nicaragua and the United States, the Nicaragua Canal held the possibility of a unifying vision of modernity that neatly converged both of their racial and geographical ideals of progress. Both nations regarded their Indigenous populations as obstacles to progress. In the context of Westward expansion, the United States' view of "Indians" coincided with the Nicaraguan impetus towards assimilating the Reserve Indigenous population within a view of Nicaraguan nationhood that was predicated on whitening and *mestizaje*. As Daniel Immerwahr writes, "What getting the Greater United States in view reveals is that race has been even more central to U.S. history than is usually supposed."[142] The same was true for Nicaragua in the nineteenth century. For both Nicaragua and the United States, the canal was key to securing "geographical destiny." For Nicaragua, possession of the Mosquito territory and the canal route presented the promise of unbroken sovereignty from the Atlantic to its Pacific coast. Similarly, for the post-Civil War United States, the control

---

[140] Tijerino, *El imaginario del canal y la nación cosmopolita*, 334.
[141] *Bluefields Messenger*, March 30, 1894, *Despatches*, roll 11.
[142] Immerwahr, *How to Hide an Empire*.

over the canal route was seen as the key to being a continental nation with an ease of connection between its Atlantic and Pacific coasts and providing essential defensive capabilities to its exposed coastlines on the west.

The dual exhibits of the Nicaragua relief map in the Transportation Building and the engraved coconut shell with a facsimile of the canal route in the Nicaragua Building of the 1893 exposition point to the centrality of the canal both to Nicaraguan and U.S. visions of geopolitical identity at the eve of the twentieth century. Yet, just as the Miskitu were absent from the grand event, so too the Mosquito story of incorporation is harder to tell. Nicaraguan rhetoric suggests that the incorporation of the Reserve was accomplished by the co-optation of the disaffected Indigenous base. At the same time, we have evidence of rebellions and flight from Reserve towns. In the aftermath of the incorporation, many Reserve towns, including Bluefields, became depopulated. According to Charles Hale, the Nicaraguan rhetoric of "reincorporation" shaped the subsequent "nationalist discourse towards the Coast, which ever since has tended to portray Coast people's identities and demands as legitimate only if they did not threaten the national project."[143] The Mosquito question and the Nicaragua Canal question had been intertwined ever since the first glimmer of the possibility of a transisthmian canal. What the events of 1894 proved beyond a doubt was that the pursuit of the canal was predicated on the dismantling of Mosquito autonomy. Ultimately, the vision of an interoceanic connection was steeped in the logic of racial exclusion.

---

[143] Hale, *Resistance and Contradiction*, Kindle e-book, location 659.

9

Conclusion

The Turn towards Panama

In May 1902, the eruption of Mt. Pelée on the island of Martinique forcefully brought to the American public the dangers of volcanic eruption in the Caribbean. One of the deadliest volcanic eruptions in history, the disaster wiped out an entire town with a death toll of 35,000 people in the town of Saint-Pierre, which lay 10 km south of the summit of the volcano. News of the unprecedented eruption filled the front pages of newspapers across the United States and underscored the deadly and fragile nature of the topography in the Caribbean and Central America. Following the eruption, the public became more vigilant about active volcanoes. The periodic spewing of ashes and smoke by volcanoes that had previously been regarded as harmless was now reported with alarm. Even as late as February 1902, the Nicaragua Canal appeared before the American public as the natural choice for a transisthmian canal that had the potential to spur American commerce and catapult the United States to global leadership. Even at this time, the presence of active volcanoes in Nicaragua had been seen as part of the picturesque and tantalizing landscape of the country, which was imagined to be the location of the transoceanic canal. Thus, the *San Francisco Call* of February 9, 1902, had described the village of Momotombo as "a village at the northwest end of Lake Managua, snug at the foot of the volcano Momotombo, the smoke of whose torment ascends forever and ever."[1] Right after the news of the eruption of Mt. Pelée, however, the exotic Momotombo assumed a much more threatening visage. Today, the role of the Nicaragua postage stamp

---

[1] *San Francisco Call*, February 9, 1902.

depicting Momotombo spewing smoke and ashes in finally convincing the United States to abandon the Nicaragua route has assumed mythical qualities.

While the Spanish–American War and how it altered the way news was consumed in the United States have been explored,[2] what is less well understood are the way the Central American isthmus came to be viewed both politically and militarily by the United States. The sensationalism that dominated the American press following the Spanish–American War was reflected in the rhetorical shift of the Panama Canal Lobby, which now moved from arguing for the technical and engineering superiority of the Panama Canal to a fearmongering rhetoric that centered on volcanic dangers on the Nicaragua route. The natural landscape of Nicaragua, which had previously been described in survey reports as fertile and "Edenic," was now transformed into a threatening space. The canal had been lauded as both the United States' and Nicaragua's geographical destiny. Now that same landscape, that same topography had turned against the project.

Thus, the apparent abruptness of the decision to build the canal in Panama in 1902 belied the steady buildup of a new American way of looking at the world that was heavily informed by the American press. While by the early twentieth century the engineering advantages of Panama were becoming more evident, the convergence of statesmen, lobbyists, scientists, and the American public around the threat of volcanic eruption along the Nicaragua route revealed that the question of where to locate the canal had always been as much about politics, perception, and power as about engineering and technology.

9.1 LEGACIES OF THE SPANISH–AMERICAN WAR OF 1898

The Spanish–American War (1898), or what historians such as Daniel Immerwahr more accurately term the Spanish–Cuban–Puerto Rican–Philippine–American War, was a turning point in the United States' relationship with Latin America and the Caribbean. Following the Treaty of Paris (1898), the United States effectively established a

---

[2] See, for instance, Charles Brown, *The Correspondents' War: Journalists in the Spanish–American War* (New York: Scribner, 1976); W. Joseph Campbell, *The Spanish–American War: American Wars and the Media in Primary Documents* (Westport: Greenwood Press, 2005); Marcus M. Wilkerson, *Public Opinion and the Spanish–American War: A Study in War Propaganda* (New York: Russell and Russell, 1967).

protectorate over Cuba, a form of imperial intervention that would later be replicated in other parts of the Caribbean, including Panama and Nicaragua. With the end of frontier wars in the nineteenth century and the consolidation of the United States as a continental nation, the United States had run into a natural end to its domestic expansion. The Spanish–American War, which for the first time allowed the United States to expand territorially beyond its own continental borders, marked a turning point where Latin America now presented newer possibilities of U.S. imperial expansion. The spoils of war, including a sphere of influence in Cuba, annexation of Hawaii, and territorial gains in the Philippines and Puerto Rico, radically transformed how the United States viewed its own destiny. As Daniel Immerwahr points out, the war allowed for the United States to view itself as *America* with maps, political speeches, and ordinary parlance adapting to the notion of a Greater United States – a view of the United States as an expanding global power unfettered by its own continental borders.[3]

This transformation had profound implications for the fate of the Nicaragua Canal. During the Spanish–American War, the question of the Nicaragua Canal appeared most forcefully in the context of the U.S.S. *Oregon*. In March 1898, following the sinking of the battleship *Maine* in Havana Harbor, there was a growing fear of a Spanish attack on the East Coast of the United States. Amidst calls for the U.S. Atlantic fleet to protect the vulnerable East Coast, the *Oregon*, which at the time was stationed in the Pacific, was instructed to join the Atlantic fleet, necessitating a long and arduous trip for the battleship around Cape Horn in a journey from the Pacific to the Atlantic. The voyage itself was challenging, with the ship encountering storms and being compelled to stop repeatedly for coaling. The dramatic journey of the *Oregon* – which was costly as well as perilous – took sixty-six days to complete the transit between the Atlantic and the Pacific and underscored the vital importance of an isthmian canal during military emergencies.

Although there is a common belief that following the *Oregon* episode, there was a growing impetus to the construction of the Panama Canal, the examination of newspaper reports of the time indicates that it was the *Nicaragua* Canal that was seen as the solution to the problem of ensuring quick and easy transit between the oceans. The *Portland Oregonian* declared: "That 13,000-mile trip of the Oregon in response to an

---

[3] Immerwahr, *How to Hide an Empire*, 73.

emergency call is an argument for the building of the Nicaragua canal that even cheeseparing statesmanship cannot ignore."[4] The *New York Times* of May 22, 1898, published the views of Lyman Coolie, "a well known engineer" who averred that:

> if the Oregon is at Barbados, sixty-two days would be required by her in reaching that point from San Francisco via Cape Horn. With the Nicaragua Canal complete forty-four days' time would have been saved over one existing route and thirty-four days over the other. The journey from San Francisco to New York could be made in eighteen days by a slow vessel or in ten or twelve by a swift one. Would not this be of value to the Government when so much depends on the rapidity with which our vessels must be moved from point to point? Possessing the Nicaragua Canal, we could prevent any navy in the world from traversing the Horn for the purpose of attacking us east or west.[5]

Similar sentiments were expressed across the Atlantic in Latin America. The Chilean periodical *El Mercurio de Valparaíso* noted that "one of the most important results of the short war between Spain and this country [the United States] has been the universal demand for the immediate construction of the Nicaragua Canal. The voyage of the Oregon ... has been an object lesson for the nation."[6] In Nicaragua, the newspaper *El Comercio* argued that the Spanish–American War had benefited Nicaragua as it had shown the vital importance of the Nicaragua Canal and would now inevitably lead to the construction of the canal. *El Comercio* eloquently added: "Nicaragua, above all, is destined to undergo a marvelous transformation ... we will be indebted to this war for the beginning of our true prosperity."[7]

At the topmost political offices, the Spanish–American War made the isthmian canal appear to be a necessity that must be constructed at all costs. Mahan's doctrine of naval power had its first practical application in the theater of the Spanish–American War, which convincingly showed the American public the vital need for the United States to transform into a naval power. Theodore Roosevelt, then assistant secretary of the Navy, was a vocal proponent of Mahan's ideology and was closely involved in the Spanish–American War. Accepting the rank of lieutenant colonel in a volunteer cavalry regiment, Roosevelt led a successful charge in San Juan Heights, Cuba, which was followed closely by the U.S. siege of Santiago de Cuba and the eventual surrender of Cuba by Spanish forces. Both as an

---

[4] *Portland Oregonian*, May 29, 1898. [5] *The New York Times*, May 22, 1898.
[6] *El Mercurio de Valparaíso*, October 4, 1898.
[7] *El Comercio* (Nicaragua), June 5, 1898.

assistant secretary of the Navy and, later, as the U.S. president, Teddy Roosevelt would view the future of the United States as one dependent on the expansion of naval power, and his experience of the Spanish–American War is perhaps one explanation for his championship of the isthmian canal whose construction became something of his pet project during his own term as president of the United States. Following the Spanish–American War, the United States adopted a more interventionist attitude towards Latin America, and the canal was an integral part of the vision of a new, expanding *America*.

The Spanish–American War witnessed a new, sensationalized coverage in newspapers and is widely considered the beginning of the notorious "yellow journalism" in the U.S. press.[8] This new kind of journalism was characterized by bold headlines, full-page illustrations, and a focus on sensationalism. The yellow press fed into an atmosphere of warmongering and mustered public support for American involvement in the Spanish–American War (see Figure 9.1). The rivalry among newspapers of Boston, New York, Chicago, and San Francisco led to an increasingly reckless coverage of the War to gain more newspaper circulation among American readers. The most notorious rivalry was between William Randolph Hearst, the owner of *The New York Journal* and Joseph Pulitzer of the *New York World*. The popularity of the yellow press can be seen in the huge increase in circulation figures of newspapers in this period. As Wilkerson points out,

At the beginning of 1895, the circulation of Pulitzer's paper was less than 400,000; by April, 1896, the combined circulation of the *Morning World* and *Evening World* had reached 742,673 a day; and early in 1898, it totaled 822,804. At the time the *Evening Journal* was started in connection with the *Morning Journal*, Sept. 28, 1896, Hearst claimed a circulation of 407,000, making it the largest morning paper in the country. In early November of the same year, the *Journal* stated that its combined circulation was 1,506,634, but this figure evidently included the circulation of the *Sunday Journal*, which then probably exceeded 600,000.[9]

These high circulation figures also reflect the growing awareness and readership among ordinary Americans who could now remain abreast

---

[8] Brett Griffin, *Yellow Journalism, Sensationalism, and Circulation Wars* (New York: Cavendish Square, 2019); David Ralph Spencer, *The Yellow Journalism: The Press and America's Emergence as a World Power* (Evanston: Northwestern University Press, 2007); W. Joseph Campbell, *Yellow Journalism: Puncturing the Myths, Defining the Legacies* (Westport: Praeger, 2003).
[9] Marcus Wilkerson, "The Press and the Spanish–American War," *Journalism Quarterly* 9:2 (June 1932), 147–148.

FIGURE 9.1 Crowd gathered outside the *New York Journal* Building on Park Row to read the latest news of the Spanish–American War displayed on bulletin boards. Source: George E. Stonebridge Photograph Collection, 1897–1918 (bulk 1899–1904), the New York Historical, nyhs_PR066_484. ©The New York Historical.

of events transpiring around the world at the cost of a single cent.[10] While there is a debate over the exact nature of influence the yellow press had over the course of the Spanish–American War, there can be no doubt that the coverage in these newspapers shaped public opinion on the War and in many cases prompted the U.S. government to take notice of events in the War. Writing about the sensationalized case of Evangelina Cisneros, a young woman who was imprisoned during the Cuban War of Independence, Carol Wilcox writes:

The US Press influenced the agenda of President William McKinley and his cabinet. When the story of Evangelina Cisneros first came to light, and, as it

[10] Hearst's *Journal*, for instance, became a one-cent paper in 1896, reaching a circulation of 150,000, prompting Pulitzer to lower the cost of the *World* to one cent as well. Wilkerson, *Public Opinion and Spanish–American War*, 8.

was repeated and embellished and spread to other newspapers in the United States and abroad, the US government could not help but take notice. On October 12, 1897, McKinley's cabinet discussed the Cisneros Affair. The event had raised the government's consciousness about what was transpiring in Cuba four months before the sinking of the *Maine* on February 15, 1898.[11]

In many ways, the Spanish–American War heralded a new American way of looking at the world that was strongly influenced by the press.

9.2 THE TRIUMPH OF LOBBYING

From 1897 to 1901, successive canal commissions and surveys of the canal routes initiated by the United States repeatedly returned the same recommendation: that the Nicaragua route was preferable to the Panama route for the construction of the isthmian canal. On November 16, 1901, the Isthmian Canal Commission, headed by Rear Admiral H. J. Walker, concluded that: "This Commission is of the opinion that 'the most practicable and feasible route' for an isthmian canal, to be 'under the control, management, and ownership of the United States,' is that known as the Nicaragua route."[12]

The failure of de Lesseps' sea-level canal at Panama led to the French New Panama Canal Company assuming the responsibility for completion of the Panama Canal in 1894. Despite its final recommendation of the Nicaragua route, the Isthmian Canal Commission report was ambiguous regarding the competing merits of the Nicaragua and Panama routes. In fact, the report pointed to the technical superiority of the Panama Canal on various aspects of a transisthmian canal but had finally settled on the Nicaragua route due to the failure to obtain an acceptable offer of sale from the New Panama Canal Company. Thus, the report noted:

There are certain physical advantages, such as a shorter canal line [about 49 miles for Panama versus 184 miles for Nicaragua], a more complete knowledge of the country through which it passes, and lower cost of maintenance and operation in favor of the Panama route, but the price fixed by the Panama Canal Company for a sale of its property and franchises is so unreasonable that its acceptance can not be recommended by this Commission.[13]

---

[11] Carol Wilcox, "Cuba's 'Hot Little Rebel' and Spain's 'Criminal Fugitive': The Prison Escape of Evangelina Cisneros in 1897," in *Sensationalism: Murder, Mayhem, Mudslinging, Scandals and Disasters in 19th-Century Reporting*, eds. David Sachsman and David Bulla, 235 (London: Routledge, 2017).

[12] *Report of the Isthmian Canal Commission 1899–1901* (Washington, DC: GPO, 1901), 263.

[13] *Report of the Isthmian Canal Commission 1899–1901*, 263.

Following the publication of the Isthmian Canal Commission report, two individuals in particular, the New York attorney William Nelson Cromwell and the Frenchman Philippe Bunau-Varilla, whom newspapers described as the "Panama Canal Lobby," attempted to mobilize public opinion in favor of the Panama Canal route and to persuade the U.S. government to choose the Panama route as the location for the transisthmian canal. In 1896, Cromwell was hired by the New Panama Canal Company because of his connections at the highest levels in the United States. As McCullough writes, "it is clear that his [Cromwell's] fundamental objective was to sell the French company to the United States government, or that failing, to some other government or combination of foreign capital. And for such efforts he expected to be well paid. His fee for services rendered when finally submitted to the Compagnie Nouvelle would be for $80,000."[14] Bunau-Varilla had previously served as an engineer at Panama for de Lesseps, and his zeal for the Panama Canal was derived both from his desire to "vindicate French genius" and to protect his investments in the French company. The supporters of the Panama Canal route had based their arguments on technical grounds. This was most apparent in the Paris Congress of 1879 but is also visible in the writings of proponents of the Panama Canal, such as the American engineer Henry Abbot, who leveraged his own technical knowledge to make a case for the Panama Canal from 1898 to 1902. After the report of the Isthmian Canal Commission, however, which had chosen Nicaragua not on technical grounds but more for convenience, the Panama Canal Lobby – in particular, Philippe Bunau-Varilla – would choose to focus not so much on the technical superiority of the Panama Canal but on the more sensational details of Nicaragua's volcanic threats.

Travel narratives to Nicaragua written prior to the eruption of Mt. Pelée depicted the country's volcanoes not as threatening or dangerous but rather as part and parcel of what made Nicaragua a unique and picturesque location for the construction of a transisthmian canal. In his travelogue entitled *In and out of Central America*, published in 1890, Frank Vincent noted: "One day, at León, the largest city in Nicaragua, I counted fourteen volcanoes in sight from the cathedral roof. Several of these are continuously active, their steep and smooth purple cones, with spirals of fleecy smoke curling lazily upward, giving always a unique and pleasing character to the landscape."[15] Similarly, in his *Notes on the*

---

[14] McCullough, *The Path between the Seas*, 273.
[15] Frank Vincent, *In and out of Central America: And Other Sketches and Studies of Travel* (New York: D. Appleton & Co., 1890), 10.

Nicaragua Canal, published in 1897, Henry Sheldon wrote: "The lake [Lake Managua] is extremely picturesque, various mountains are in sight, and the views when approaching the town mountain Momotombo and the small mountain Momotombito, the Little Momotombo, are delightful."[16] Likewise, William Simmons in his *The Nicaragua Canal*, published in 1900, described the landscape of Nicaragua thus: "Its majestic mountains and smouldering volcanoes, with their canopies of smoke, lift one's thoughts to the plane of sublimity."[17]

Similarly, in official surveys and reports, the presence of volcanoes in Nicaragua had not been completely ignored, but reports had downplayed the importance of the volcanoes for the prospect of building a canal through Nicaragua. The Nicaragua Canal Commission (1897–1899) had reported that the volcanic activity in Nicaragua did not pose any imminent danger to the proposed canal route. The report had observed that: "While the Nicaraguan depression is occupied to a considerable extent by volcanic rocks, these belong in large measure to a former geological period, and the activity to which they owe their origin has long since entirely ceased." Where there were signs of volcanic activity, the report noted that such activity "was on the wane."[18] The Isthmian Canal Commission, similarly, had noted the role of volcanic activity in precipitating earthquakes but had concluded that it was hard to "justify a comparison between the Nicaragua and Panama routes as to the number of earthquakes or their severity. They are precisely on the same footing historically as they are geographically."[19]

Starting on January 16, 1901, with a speech at the Cincinnati Commercial Club, however, Bunau-Varilla made the volcanic dangers in Nicaragua the centerpiece of his arguments in favor of the Panama Canal. In his pamphlet entitled *Panama or Nicaragua* – of which he had 13,000 copies mailed out – Bunau-Varilla emphatically wrote:

To the people who think I am exaggerating this capital point I will say: Open any dictionary of geography, any encyclopedia, and read the article titled "Nicaragua." I will say also: look at the coat of arms of the Republic of Nicaragua, look at the Nicaraguan postage stamps. Young nations like to put

---

[16] Henry Sheldon, *Notes on the Nicaragua Canal* (Chicago: A. C. McClurg & Co., 1897), 196.
[17] William Simmons, *The Nicaragua Canal* (New York: Harper & Brothers Publishers, 1900), 303.
[18] *Report of the Nicaragua Canal Commission, 1897–1899* (Baltimore: The Lord Baltimore Press, 1999), 132–133.
[19] *Report of the Isthmian Canal Commission, 1899–1901*, 168.

on their coat of arms what best symbolizes their moral domain or characteristics of soil. What have the Nicaraguans chosen to characterize their country on their coat of arms, on their postage stamps? Volcanoes![20]

Meanwhile, on January 4, 1902, the New Panama Canal Company slashed its asking price from $109 million to $40 million, prompting the Isthmian Canal Commission to issue a *Supplementary Report* on January 18, unanimously endorsing the Panama route.[21] As if on cue, in May 1902, Mt. Pelée erupted, and the American press immediately connected this eruption to the presence of smoking volcanoes on the Nicaragua Canal route. Mirroring the sensationalist coverage of the Spanish–American War, newspapers reported on the eruption of Mt. Pelée on front pages with bold headlines and detailed illustrations (see Figure 9.2).

Newspapers were quick to point out that Nicaragua was replete with active volcanoes including Momotombo, which seemed to be perennially "smoking" and had a history of eruptions (see Figure 9.3).[22] The volcanoes of Nicaragua, which had previously been characterized as unique and picturesque, were immediately transformed by the American press into a threatening feature that undermined the Nicaragua Canal route.

Even as the coverage of Mt. Pelée in the U.S. press steered public opinion against the Nicaragua Canal, there was an increasing convergence both in the political and scientific spheres about the prudence of abandoning the Nicaragua route due to the threat of volcanic eruptions. The first eruption of Mt. Pelée on May 8 wiped out the entire city of Saint-Pierre. On May 20, Mt. Pelée erupted again, followed by the eruption of another volcano in nearby Saint Vincent. More frighteningly, came news of the eruption of Mt. Momotombo, which lay 100 miles from the Nicaragua Canal route.[23] The idea of abandoning the Nicaragua route gained traction, not least in the scientific community where the *Scientific American* of May 24, 1902, opined: "We do not doubt that the former advocates of a canal at Nicaragua will decide, in the presence of this awful cataclysm at St. Pierre, that the location of the canal in such a center of

---

[20] Philippe Bunau-Varilla, *Nicaragua or Panama* (New York: Knickerbocker Press, 1901), *Panama Canal Pamphlets, 1885–1913*, History of Science Collection at the Linda Hall Library.

[21] "Supplementary Report of the Isthmian Canal Commission," Senate Document no. 123, 57th Cong., 1st Sess., John G. Walker, Report of the Isthmian Canal Commission, 1899–1902, c. 1, vol. 1, (Washington, DC: GPO, 1904), 675–681.

[22] *Barbour County Index*, June 25, 1902.

[23] McCullough, *The Path between the Seas*, 318.

FIGURE 9.2 The front page of the *San Francisco Call*, May 10, 1902.

volcanic action as Nicaragua is simply out of the question."[24] In an article entitled "Volcanic Veto on the Nicaragua Canal" the *Minneapolis Journal* of May 17, 1902, tried to portray this convergence of political,

---

[24] *Scientific American*, n.s.v. 86 (1902), May 24, 1902.

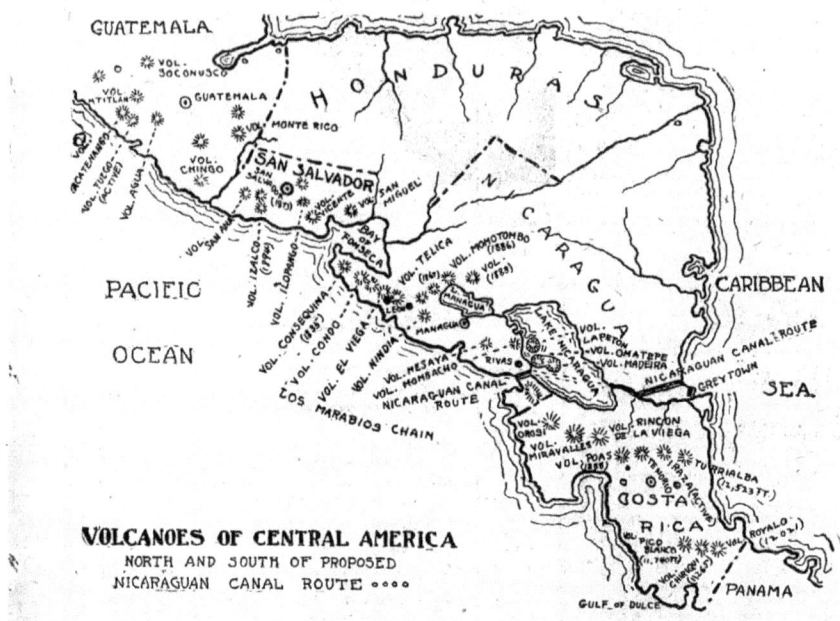

FIGURE 9.3 Illustration of volcanoes around the Nicaragua Canal route. Source: *The Minneapolis Journal*, May 17, 1902.

economic, and scientific opinion on the Nicaragua Canal by quoting at length words of a senator, a geologist, and a railway magnate – all sharing the same view that Nicaragua was too dangerous to build a canal through. The article quoted James J. Hill, the railroad tycoon's opinion that

> Nicaragua is a dangerous and unfit place for any great works of a public character, and most of all for a vast canal system built of concrete and masonry to which any earthquake or volcanic disturbance would be fatal. It is a nasty, crooked route, anyway, curving and dodging about among the volcanic peaks. It is not a safe place to put any big vessel.[25]

Bunau-Varilla greeted these developments enthusiastically. He wrote:

> What an unexpected turn of the wheel of fortune! ... If not the strongest of my arguments against Nicaragua, at least the most easily comprehensible of them was thus made a hundred times more striking owing to the prodigious emotion aroused by the catastrophe. I waited a few days, ready to turn against Nicaragua the terror which the disaster of Mont Pelee had produced.[26]

---

[25] "The Volcanic Veto on the Nicaragua Canal," *The Minneapolis Journal*, May 17, 1902.
[26] Philippe Bunau-Varilla, *Panama: The Creation, Destruction and Resurrection* (New York: McBride, Nast & Co., 1914), 228.

In a final bid to turn the tide against the Nicaragua Canal, Bunau-Varilla purchased ninety one-centavo Nicaraguan stamps that depicted Momotombo in eruption and sent them to every member of the Senate. While the myth surrounding the postage stamp suggests that it was this genius move by Bunau-Varilla that was the final blow to the Nicaragua cause, a longer view of history suggests that the role of the U.S. press in steadily directing public attention to the dangers of the Nicaragua route created the fertile ground needed for the stamp to take its intended impact. The convergence of public sentiment, lobbying theatrics, scientific warnings, and growing congressional support created the political momentum for a turn to Panama. On June 19, 1902, the Panama Canal Bill was passed in the Senate to a final vote of "67 yeas and 6 nays."[27] The Spooner Act of June 28, 1902, authorized the purchase of the New Panama Canal Company for $40 million – a significant reduction from its earlier asking price – making the Panama route a financially desirable option for the United States. The turn towards Panama was a triumph of lobbying but also reflected a new American geopolitical imagination, one that was heavily shaped by the U.S. press.

9.3 THE FATE OF THE CENTRAL AMERICAN UNION

Throughout his presidency, José Santos Zelaya remained a staunch supporter of the Central American Union. Moreover, he instinctively understood that the dream of the Nicaragua Canal and the vision of the Union were inextricably linked: building the canal promised not just national regeneration but also regional unity. He enshrined his faith in the Union in the constitution of 1893, whose first article declared: "Nicaragua is a disintegrated section of the Republic from Central America. Consequently, it recognizes as a primary need to return to the Union with the other sections of the dissolved Republic."[28] On the first anniversary of his accession to power in July 1894, Zelaya consciously linked the tasks of building the canal and achieving a Central American Union: "Two great works are stirring at this moment in the sphere of the possible, and seem ready to be resolved: the Nicaragua canal and the union of Central America. The first has to make our country an emporia; and the second will make her worthy of being among the nations."[29] Nicaraguan

---

[27] *New York Times*, June 20, 1902.
[28] *Constitución Política*, December 10, 1893, Emilio Alvarez, *Ensayo histórico sobre el derecho constitucional de Nicaragua* (Managua: Tip. La Prensa, 1936), 236.
[29] Tijerino, *El imaginario del canal y la nación cosmopolita*, 341.

historiography generally attributed the United States' final choice of Panama to Zelaya's intransigence over allowing American sovereignty over the canal route.[30] However, according to Michel Gobat, until the United States' turn towards Panama, Zelaya was the "most pro-U.S. president in Nicaraguan history" and made "unparalleled efforts" to convince the United States to build the interoceanic canal through Nicaragua.[31] Moreover, the dream of the canal successfully tempered Zelaya's regional ambitions for a time and prompted him to maintain cordial relations even with regional rivals such as Costa Rica.[32]

Relations between the United States and Nicaragua deteriorated after 1902, as their competing canal ambitions clashed.[33] Once the United States shifted its focus to Panama, a desperate Zelaya sought out European and Japanese investors, a move that brought him into conflict with the United States, which was determined to eliminate any competition to the Panama route. Zelaya's ambitions regarding the Central American Union similarly unnerved the United States. Zelaya became progressively more militaristic in his ambitions for the Union, and the American press reported worriedly of Nicaraguan armed interventions into its Central American neighbors. As in the Spanish–American War, newspapers across the United States vilified Zelaya and his regime in a classic case of "yellow journalism."[34] Echoing the topographic narrative that had secured the turn towards Panama, American newspapers compared the situation in Central America to a boiling "political volcano"[35] and published newspaper reports that portrayed Zelaya as morally and sexually depraved.[36]

Symbolic of the role that the Mosquito Coast would play in the U.S.–Nicaraguan relations for the rest of the century, the Nicaraguan Governor of the Atlantic coast Juan José Estrada rose in revolt against the Zelaya government's taxation and economic policies, reportedly supported by arms and men from New Orleans.[37] The incident provided the entry point for U.S. intervention, with the Taft administration dispatching a force to the rebel stronghold of Bluefields. With regional stability now at a premium to ensure the successful construction of the Panama Canal and the

---

[30] Ibid. [31] Gobat, *Confronting the American Dream*, 67.
[32] Vincent Peloso, "The Politics of Federation in Central America, 1885–1921," PhD thesis, University of Arizona, 1970, 43.
[33] Ibid., 98. [34] Bermann, *Under the Big Stick*, 143.
[35] *The San Francisco Call*, March 20, 1909.
[36] See, for instance, *The Spokane Press*, December 10, 1909.
[37] Bermann, *Under the Big Stick*, 144–145.

realization that a Central American Union under Zelaya's control would irrevocably undermine U.S. regional hegemony, the United States publicly lent its support to the Estrada movement and played a key role in the ouster of the Nicaraguan strongman. It was a turning point.

9.4 ERASURE

With the ouster of Zelaya, dreams of a unified Central America would eventually peter out by the early twentieth century – though not before the United States briefly imagined one under its own influence (see Figure 9.4) – and Nicaraguan relations with the United States entered a new phase of U.S. interventionism. Using a combination of dollar and gunboat diplomacy, the United States would eventually replace British influence in the region, marking a decisive shift in the history of Anglo-American quest for the Nicaragua Canal. The Hay–Pauncefote Treaty (1901) formalized this transition, with Britain conceding its role in favor of U.S. leadership in canal-building efforts in the isthmus. This consolidation of American power in the region set the stage for the Roosevelt Corollary (1904) to the Monroe Doctrine, ushering in a new phase of U.S. interventionism in Latin America.[38]

Finally, and perhaps not surprisingly, the turn towards Panama occurred without any consideration of the Mosquito question. While Nicaragua continued to witness internal disturbances and the Miskitu continued their appeal to the British government to reverse the "incorporation" and reestablish British protection over them, with the decisive shift towards the Panama Canal, the Mosquito Coast temporarily ceased to be a great power concern.[39] In April 1905, the Harrison–Altamirano Treaty between Great Britain and Nicaragua annulled the Treaty of Managua, recognizing Nicaraguan sovereignty over the Mosquito Coast in exchange for certain concessions to the Indigenous Miskitus. The complete absence of any consideration of the Mosquito question in the deliberations of 1902 regarding the location of the canal underscored the irrelevance of local culture to the American imperial vision of a transisthmian canal. The imperial logic that had guided canal politics

---

[38] For a comprehensive account of the evolution of the Monroe Doctrine and its extensions, including the Roosevelt Corollary, see Jay Sexton, *The Monroe Doctrine*.
[39] See Baracco, "The Last Days of the Mosquito Reserve"; Hale, *Resistance and Contradiction*.

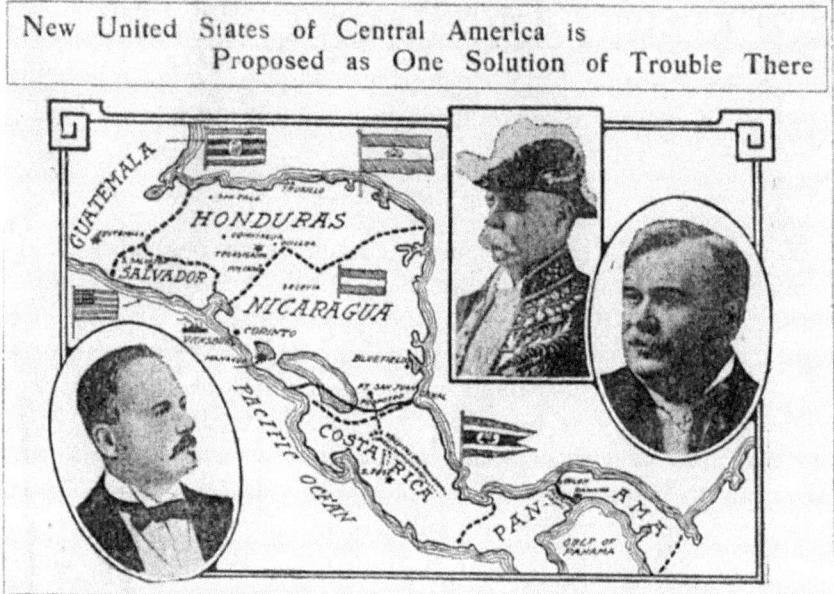

FIGURE 9.4 "New United States of Central America." Source: *Ouitumwa Tri-Weekly Courier*, December 21, 1909.

throughout the nineteenth century was most starkly expressed in what it chose to forget and abandon.

Ultimately, the failure of the Nicaragua Canal laid bare the central contradiction of the imperial age: that dreams of connection, modernity, and progress were built on – and undone by – fractured foundations of rivalry, division, and exclusion.

Index

Aberdeen, Lord, 36, 41–45, 48, 55, 63
Accessory Transit Company
  conflict with Greytown, 21, 136
  creation of, 123
  internal differences, 161
  role in filibustering, 154, 157, 160–163, 166
  split, 165
  U.S. citizens, 120, 126
Adam, Charles, 34
African American immigrants, 150, 152–153, 232
Agnes (sister to Miskitu chief George Augustus), 64, 72, 86, 92
Aguán River, 68
American Atlantic and Pacific Ship Canal Company, 104, 123, 128–129, 163, 188
American Geographical Society, 220
Ammen, Daniel, 219–221, 251
Aspinwall, William, 100
Assollant, Alfred, 168
Austen, Francis, 70

Baily, John, 36, 40, 45–46, 227
Baker, Lewis, 238, 247–248
Balboa, Vasco Núñez de, 7
Baldwin, Roger, 97–98
Baldwin, Thomas, 138
Barclay, Herring & Richardson, 25
Barrios, Justo Rufino, 215
Belize
  administrators, 27, 31, 36
  during Caste War, 83
  merchants, 27
  relations with Mosquito Coast, 9–10, 27–29, 37, 42, 44–45, 72
  timber economy, 26–27, 29, 82
Bell, George, 57
Bell, James Stanislaus, 38–39, 42, 52, 54, 57, 71, 181
Belly, Félix, 150, 158, 177–178, 209
Belt, Thomas, 198
Bescher, Mr., 128
Bidlack Treaty, 50, 100
Bingham, Herbert, 235–236, 239, 241, 248
Bishop, Joseph Bucklin, 3–4, 57
Blaine, James G., 217
Bluefields
  1894 crisis, 234–236, 238, 240, 243
  banana economy, 231
  government, 54, 56, 64
  population, 232
  Prussian settlement, 72
  religion, 58
  slavery, 32
  strategic importance, 57
  survey, 56
Bluefields Messenger, 253
Bluefields River, 34–35
Bluefields Steamship Company, 231
Bocas del Toro, 81
  condition of harbor, 34
  conflict with New Granada, 41
  isthmian route, 81
  land grants, 53
  revenue, 28

271

Bocas del Toro (cont.)
    slavery, 32
    visit of H.M.S. *Tweed*, 32, 34, 37
Boletín Oficial (León), 103
Boletín Oficial de Costa Rica, 175–176
Bonaparte, Louis Napoléon, 47, 49
Bonilla, Juan, 48
Boone, Mr., 139
Borland, Solon, 140–141
Braida, S. C., 238, 244, 247–248
British Columbia, 252
British Honduras. *See* Belize
Brito, 147, 224
Brown, George, 53
Buitrago, Pablo, 67
Bulwer, Henry Lytton, 111–112, 127
Bunau-Varilla, Philippe, 262–263, 266–267

Cabezas, Rigoberto, 233–234, 239–240
Cadogan, William Hodgson, 52
Calero, Alonso, 7
California
    filibustering, 156, 161
    fruit production, 223
    Mexican–American War, 120
    residents on board U.S.S. *Prometheus*, 133
    transit route, 130
California Banker's Magazine, 223
Cañas–Jerez Treaty, 177
Canty, George, 167–168
Cape Gracias a Dios, 54, 56, 58, 187, 203, 234
Cárdenas, Adán, 211, 226
Caribs, 64
Carmichael, John, 82
Caste War of Yucatán, 83
Castellón, Francisco, 47, 61, 75–76, 79, 81, 147
Cayman Islands, 56
cedar, 55
Central America
    Anglo-Spanish rivalry, 9
    bombardment of Greytown, 141
    as canal location, 5–6, 15, 208, 210, 218–219, 221, 249–251
    canal rhetoric, 26
    Clayton–Bulwer Treaty, 113, 127
    dispute with Mosquito Kingdom, 20, 28–29, 31–32, 37, 42, 48, 91
    efforts towards canal, 40
    guerra nacional. *See* Central America: during the period of filibustering
    identity, 176
    impact of Nicaragua Canal, 5
    patriotism, 32
    during the period of filibustering, 151, 153, 162–163, 167, 171, 173–175, 177–178
    relations with Europe, 46, 150, 177–178
    relations with Great Britain, 11, 26, 39–40, 46, 49–50, 53, 62, 67, 73, 75, 79, 83, 91, 179
    relations with Nicaragua, 22, 186, 215
    relations with United States, 14, 35, 46, 66, 83, 100, 102–103, 133, 178
    Seaway Proposal, 16
    topography, 25, 47, 255
Central America Land and Mining Company, 154
Central American (newspaper), 156
Central American Transit Company, 188–189, 191, 209
Central American unity
    breakdown of Federation, 15, 20, 28, 45, 109
    against British threat, 60
    early twentieth century, 269
    efforts of Justo Rufino Barrios, 215
    efforts under José Santos Zelaya, 267–269
    failure of, 148
    Federation, 25, 40
    during the filibustering era, 175–177, 214
    impulse towards, 210
    after turn to Panama, 22
    U.S. encouragement of, 105, 117
Chagres, 81, 97–98, 100–101, 121, 133–134, 213, 222
Chamorro, Fruto, 148–149
Chamorro, Pedro Joaquín, 214
Chatfield, Frederick
    as British consul, 40
    diplomacy in Central America, 50
    involvement in Mosquito Coast affairs, 82, 91, 128
    land grants, 54
    recall of, 135
    rivalry with E. G. Squier, 109–112
    territorial claims, 50, 68
    Tigre Island, 110–111
    view of canal route, 49
Chevalier, Michel, 209

Childs, Orville, 101, 123–124, 147
Christie, William Dougal, 134
   appointment as consul general, 65, 69, 73
   in Bluefields, 83–84
   domestic policies, 101
   end of tenure as consul general, 94
   narrative of Miskitu savagery, 73
   perception of King George Augustus, 85, 87–88
   shift to Greytown, 69, 73, 84–86, 88–89, 122–123, 195
   visit to Costa Rica, 69, 73–77, 79–81, 109
   visit to Jamaica, 85, 122
   visit to Nicaragua, 80
Clark, Francis J., 50
Clarke, Arthur, 239
Clayton–Bulwer Treaty, 14
   British perception of, 126
   diplomatic effect, 113, 135
   failure to resolve Mosquito question, 99, 112, 121, 123, 127, 143
   neutrality, 112–113
   terms, 127, 129, 157
   U.S. perceptions of, 127, 211
   violation of, 134, 215
Clayton, John, 104–105, 110–111
Clementi (Miskitu chief), 37
Climie (Nicaraguan engineer), 227
Collinson, Frederic, 221
Collinson, John, 191
Colombia, 227
Congrès International d'Études du Canal Interocéanique, 219
Coolie, Lyman, 258
Corbett, Edwin, 202–203
Corn Islands, 229
   1894 crisis, 236, 240, 242
   conflict with New Granada, 37, 42–45, 227
   fruit production, 232
   Miskitu coronation, 45
   Nicaraguan claims, 228–229
   relationship to Mosquito Kingdom, 37, 44–45, 187
   relationship to Mosquito Reserve, 194
   sea island cotton, 28
   slavery, 32, 42–43
   territorial dispute, 29, 32
Corps of United States Topographical Engineers, 124

Correo del Istmo, 103, 117–118, 146
Cortes of Cádiz, 39
Cortéz, Rosalío, 199
Costa Rica
   border with Nicaragua, 27, 147, 176
   canal route, 50, 74, 147, 214, 223
   claims on Mosquito Coast, 28–29, 81
   domestic politics, 74
   government, 226
   in the *guerra nacional*, 163–168, 171–173, 177, 179
   navigation of San Juan River, 147
   relations with Great Britain, 59, 77, 117, 127
   territorial claims, 41, 58, 75, 80, 147
   trade, 59, 70, 74, 84
Cottrell, Squire, 157–158, 165, 167–168, 189, 201
Cox, William, 53
Crampton, John, 106, 138
Crane, Smith, 130
Crimean War, 146, 179
Cromwell, William Nelson, 262
Crossman, Commander, 210
Cuadra, Vicente, 210
Cuba, 145, 257–258, 261
Curzon-Howe, Captain, 236, 238, 243, 246, 248

Daily Union, 101
Dallas, George M., 50
Daly, J. M., 86, 88, 128
Darley, Arthur, 34
Dávila, Gil Gonzales, 47
de Cerda, Manuel, 47
de la Rocha, Pedro Francisco, 119
de Lesseps, Ferdinand
   Panama Canal, 218, 220–221, 262
   Panama sea-level canal, 219, 222, 249, 261
   Suez Canal, 219
de Marcoleta, José, 142, 156
Diario de Avisos, 156
Diario de Nicaragua, 233, 242
Dimitry, Alexander, 178
Dixon, John, 52, 61
dyewood, 212

Earl of Derby, 207
East, D. J., 197
Edinburgh Evening News, 211

El Comercio, 258
El Costaricense, 76
El Mercurio de Valparaíso, 258
El Nicaraguense, 159, 174
El Salvador, 34, 66, 102, 109, 147–148, 165, 173, 226
Elgin, Lord, 44
Elizondo, Joaquín, 205
Erskine, John, 166–167, 204
Escalona, Antonio, 42–43
Estrada, Juan José, 268–269
Evarts, William, 220
Everett, Edward, 138, 140
Expo. *See* Panama–Pacific International Exposition

Fabens, Joseph, 120, 140–142, 154, 157
Fancourt, St. John, 36, 38–39, 44
Farmer's Cabinet, 110
Fayssoux, Callender, 166
Fletcher, Crawford, 141
Foote, Consul, 138
Foster, John, 75
Fox-Strangeways, Thomas, 52
Franco-Prussian War, 209
Frederick Douglass' Paper, 153
Frelinghuysen–Zavala Treaty, 215, 253

Gaceta de Guatemala, 141, 175
Galindo, Juan, 25, 40
Gálvez, Mariano, 45–46
Garrison, Cornelius, 161
Geddes, James, 157
George Augustus Frederic
  accession, 41–42, 44
  agency, 92
  in Bluefields, 69
  Council of State, 52, 194
  death of, 195–196
  expedition to San Juan del Norte (Greytown), 59, 61
  minority, 49, 54, 85
  Miskitu values, 195
  Moravian mission, 143, 195–196
  proclamation, 143
  relations with Nicaragua, 195
  residence in Bluefields, 93
  tour of Mosquito Coast, 92
  visit to Corn Islands, 45
  visit to Jamaica, 72
  visit to Miskitu settlements, 186

George Frederic, 10, 36–38
George William Albert Hendy, 213
Gold Rush
  discovery of gold, 97
  as maritime venture, 98
  Nicaragua route, 21, 98
  Oregon Trail, 97
  transit routes, 114
  U.S. expansionism, 12, 99–100, 123, 160
Gollan, Alexander, 185, 204–207
Gordon's Passenger Line, 97
Gosling, Audley, 239, 241
Granada (Nicaragua), 50, 80, 97, 119, 146, 243
Grant, Ulysses S., 210, 219
Granville, Earl, 134
Great Britain
  eighteenth-century Mosquito protectorate, 9, 27
  naval might, 247–248
  neutrality, 22, 32, 206
  nineteenth-century Mosquito protectorate, 26, 34, 41, 46, 52, 56, 88, 91, 105, 114, 123, 127, 131, 133, 179, 186, 206
  relations with Spain, 9
  relations with Costa Rica, 73–74
  Royal Navy, 9, 38, 43, 189
Great Exhibition of 1851, 14, 93
Green, James, 93–94, 131
  administration of Greytown, 131–132, 136
  appointment as vice-consul, 73
  on Bluefields, 72
  defense of Greytown, 128
  developments in Greytown, 86, 126, 128
  election of William Henry Clarence, 196
  and King George Augustus, 71–72, 93, 186, 194
  member of Council of State, 52
  on Miskitu autonomy, 198
  Moravian mission, 195
  relations with British Foreign Office, 71, 133–134, 136
  on territorial disputes of the Mosquito Kingdom, 71
  on Treaty of Managua, 185, 187, 198, 206
  and William Dougal Christie, 85, 87, 129, 139
Gresham, Walter Q., 238, 248, 251
Grey, Charles, 62, 69–70, 73, 82–83

Greytown
  1894 crisis, 234, 236, 238, 241
  administration, 131–132, 136, 152, 156
  aftermath of bombardment, 151
  aftermath of filibustering, 165, 168, 171, 179
  as base for filibusters, 150, 153, 155–159, 165, 167–168, 172, 181
  bombardment, 21, 120–122, 141–143, 145, 149–150, 154–156, 219
  British perception of, 126–127, 179
  canal route, 6, 21, 74, 124, 153, 160, 177, 224–225, 228
  and Central American Transit Company, 189
  Ciudad América, 229
  climate, 73
  condition of harbor, 186, 212, 220
  conflict with Accessory Transit Company, 135, 137–138, 140
  conflict with Nicaragua, 21, 127
  decline, 142
  defense, 131
  earthquake of 1863, 178
  as free port, 129, 180, 186, 192, 228–229
  law and order, 73
  naming of, 69
  Orville Childs' survey, 124
  population, 85, 89, 125–126, 144, 152–153
  port duties, 77, 129, 133–134, 187, 192–193, 207–208
  Punta Arenas, 130–131, 135–138
  strategic location, 72
  territorial dispute, 123
  trade, 198, 223, 231
  transformation after Gold Rush, 21, 122–123, 125–126
  transit route, 135, 153
  Tweed mission, 32
  U.S. citizens, 134, 136, 140–141, 151–152
  U.S. perception of, 106, 131, 139, 141
  U.S.S. *Prometheus*, 132–133
guano trade, 249
Guatemala
  Central American Union, 109, 186, 215
  diplomatic efforts, 34
  government, 226
  guerra nacional, 165, 173
  relations with Mosquito Kingdom, 68
  relations with United States, 46, 102
Gulf of Fonseca, 50

Haly, Stanislaus Thomas, 26, 28, 53–54, 57
Harrison–Altamirano Treaty, 269
Hatch, Edwin, 235–237, 241–242
Hatfield, Chester, 210
Hawaii, 250, 257
Hay–Pauncefote Treaty, 269
Hearst, William Randolph, 259
Hendy, Andrew, 241, 247
Hill, James J., 266
Hine, Marquis L., 163
Hise, Elijah, 101–102, 112
Hise–Selva Treaty, 102
H.M.S. *Tweed*, 32, 37–38, 41, 43
Hoch, Brother, 196
Hodgson Jr., Robert, 35, 56
Hodgson, Alexander, 52
Hodgson, George, 52, 61–63
Hollins, George, 120, 138–139, 141–142, 144
Honduras
  boundary disputes with Mosquito Kingdom, 27, 69
  Central American union, 147–148
  conflict with Nicaragua, 233
  government, 226
  guerra nacional, 173
  Legislative Chamber, 34
  relations with Great Britain, 66, 179, 186
  response to *Tweed* mission, 34
  timber economy, 27
Huddersfield Chronicle, 210
Humboldt, Alexander von, 1, 219
Hunter, Judy, 42–44

India, 251
informal empire, 11
Ingram, William, 52
Institution of Civil Engineers, London, 47
Interoceanic Canal Commission, 211, 214–215
Irias, Juan Francisco, 185, 212
Isthmian Canal Commission, 3, 261–263

Jackson, Andrew, 46
Jamaica
  aftermath of Greytown bombardment, 141
  canal route, 70
  government, 36
  immigrants, 56, 69, 84, 89, 123, 126, 195, 232, 236, 239, 245
  relations with Mosquito Kingdom, 59
Jerez, Máximo, 176
Johnson, Colonel, 39

Jolly, W. D., 121
Jonathan Charles Frederic, 228
Jones, William Carey, 150
Joseph John (Miskitu chief), 202

Kerr, John Bozman, 148
King Jeremy, 66
Kinney, Henry
  and Accessory Transit Company, 154
  arrest of, 154, 172
  canal route, 21, 150, 154
  early life, 154
  as governor of Greytown, 155
  in Greytown, 153, 157–158
  land grants, 154–155
  Miskitu support, 153, 155–156, 181
  problems over election, 156–157
  resignation from post of governor, 157
  return to Greytown, 171
  U.S. expansionism, 168
  and William Walker, 157–159
Kuehn, Roland, 218

Lacayo, C. A., 234–239
Lamar, Mirabeau, 178
Latin America
  identity, 175–176
  independence, 39
Law, George, 134
Lawes, Nicholas, 66
León (Nicaragua), 147, 262
Letts, John M., 114
Little, Commander, 61–63
Loch, Granville, 67, 70–71
Lockridge, Samuel, 166
Locock, Sidney, 205–207
Lull survey, 210–212, 214–215
Lull, Edward, 210
Lundberg, Johann Eugene, 196–197, 202–203
Lyons, Richard, 179

MacDonald, Alexander, 26
  alliance with Robert Charles Frederic, 27–29, 31
  as Belizean administrator, 20, 27, 36
  on Costa Rica, 59
  departure from Mosquito Coast, 54
  economic motives, 27–29
  governance of Mosquito Kingdom, 31–32, 38–39, 41, 52–53
  relations with Central America, 34
  Tweed mission, 26, 32, 34, 37, 43, 48, 51
Machuca de Suazo, Diego, 7
Madriz, José, 241–242
Mahan, Alfred Thayer, 250, 258
mahogany, 27, 29, 55, 57, 71, 82, 84, 129, 212, 232, 246
Malmesbury, Earl, 179
Marcy, William, 140, 148, 158
Maritime Canal Company, 223, 225
Martínez, Marshal, 201
Martínez, Tomás, 176, 189, 214
Marure, Alejandro, 34, 47
Matina, 28–29, 77, 81
Maximilian I, 188
McKinley, William, 260–261
Menocal, Aniceto, 219–221, 223–224, 251
Messrs. A. Mathé and Co., 82
Messrs. Brown and Cox, 54
Metcalfe, Charles, 32, 36
Mexican–American War, 46, 116
Minneapolis Journal, 265
Miskitu
  agency of, 36, 69, 93, 143
  British perception of, 63–65, 86–91, 94
  chieftainship in the nineteenth century, 20, 26
  eighteenth-century polity, 28
  erosion of loyalty to chief, 64, 86, 88, 92
  ethnic identity, 11
  in the *guerra nacional*, 181
  impact of canal politics, 5–6, 11
  impact of Greytown bombardment, 142
  internal conflict, 22, 68, 219, 245
  Nicaraguan perception of, 91, 108, 199
  patron–client relations, 56
  relations with other Indigenous communities, 38, 64, 87, 93
  relations with British officials in the nineteenth century, 21, 27, 29, 44, 59, 86
  relations with Great Britain in the eighteenth century, 9–10, 27, 66
  relations with Nicaragua, 22, 205, 218, 241
  role in British administration, 52, 56, 58, 69
  role of Moravian mission, 195–196
  Zambo–Tawira conflict, 9, 37, 245
  territorial claims, 26
  Treaty of Managua, 180, 186, 192, 226, 235
  U.S. perception of, 99, 105

Molina, Felipe, 75, 81
Molina, Luis, 161, 173
Mora, Juan Rafael, 163, 165–166, 178
Moravian mission, 58, 86, 93, 143, 196, 203, 213, 245
Morazán, Francisco, 40, 45
Morgan, Charles, 165
Mosquito Coast
  British informal empire, 11
  canal route, 6, 11
  geographical survey, 233
  Nicaraguan view of, 228
  Sandy Bay, 39, 92, 194
  topography, 188, 212
  tropical fruit production, 218, 222–223, 230–232
  twentieth-century canal plans, 19
  twentieth-century developments, 268–269
Mosquito Kingdom
  Anglican Church, 58
  boundaries, 26, 29, 51, 68, 77, 82
  citizenship, 53
  Civil War (1791), 37
  comparison to Aztecs, 67
  comparison to Maya, 67
  flag, 29, 45, 62
  as Indigenous polity, 6
  internal politics, 28, 36
  legitimacy, 21, 49, 58, 60–61, 66–67
  Nicaraguan perception of, 81, 84, 91
  as regional power, 9
  relations with Great Britain, 20, 127
  relations with Spain, 7
  slavery, 27, 43
  strategic value of, 70
  territorial claims, 42, 59, 61, 77, 81, 125
  timber extraction, 55
  U.S. perception of, 101, 106, 114, 131
  use of English law, 38
Mosquito Reserve
  annexation to Nicaragua, 21–22, 202, 205, 219, 223, 233–234, 236, 238–242, 250–251, 254
  Arbitration Award of 1881, 226–227, 233, 241
  arbitration, 208, 213
  boundaries, 228
  British support of, 206, 243
  conflict with Nicaragua, 186, 198–199, 203–205, 218, 227–228

coup attempt, 213
Decree of Reincorporation, 241
internal frictions, 245–247
laws, 232
Moravian mission, 185, 203
natural resources, 212, 231
population, 194, 245
production of rubber, 198
subvention, 199, 201
Treaty of Managua, 180, 185–186, 199, 202, 205, 227, 234, 239
Mt. Momotombo, 255–256, 263–264, 267
Muñoz, José Trinidad, 131
Murphy, W. S., 35

Napoléon III, 209
National Academy of Science, 220
Navarro, Luis, 68
Nelson, Horatio, 9
Netherlands, 46
New Granada
  canal negotiations, 46, 50
  disputes with Mosquito Kingdom, 28–29, 31–32, 41, 43, 58–59, 77, 81
  Viceroyalty of Santa Fé de Bogotá, 28
New Holland, 31
New Orleans, 145, 158, 167, 231–232, 268
New Orleans Delta, 145
New Panama Canal Company, 4, 261–262, 267
New York City, 46
New York Commercial Advertiser, 101
New York Courier and Enquirer, 107–108
New York Evening Post, 251
New York Herald, 106, 131, 136, 143, 158, 169
The New York Journal, 259
New York Times, 209
New York World, 259
New Zealand, 31
Newport, Matthew, 52–53
Nicaragua
  affinity for United States, 117, 119, 178
  anti-British sentiments, 62
  boundary disputes, 69, 75, 147
  civil war, 119, 153
  decline as site of canal, 22
  divergence from Central America, 99, 118
  early support for canal, 39
  education system, 119
  instability, 148

Nicaragua (cont.)
  lack of profit from transit route, 146, 159
  laws, 34, 239
  León–Granada rivalry, 60–61, 80, 131, 146, 149–150, 176, 185, 187
  as preferred location for canal, 1, 3
  relations with Mosquito Reserve. *See* Mosquito Reserve
  relations with France, 62
  territorial disputes with Mosquito Kingdom, 41
  view of Mosquito Coast, 231
  vision of modernization, 188, 226
  volcanoes, 255, 262–264, 267
  weakness of government, 122, 148
Nicaragua Canal
  in Anglo-American rivalry, 50
  as Central American enterprise, 47
  Chinese interest, 14, 18–19
  effect of *guerra nacional*, 151
  erasure of narrative, 3–5
  French interest, 47
  Ortega, Daniel, 18
  Russian interests, 19
  twentieth-century plans, 19
  U.S. efforts, 35, 46, 50, 99, 102, 169, 210, 219, 223
  vision of, 1, 45–47, 99, 119, 185, 267
Nicaragua route
  Anglo-Spanish rivalry, 9
  comparison with Panama route, 4, 18, 40, 98–99, 101, 122–123, 130, 134, 169, 178, 213, 220–222, 261, 263
  early explorations, 7
  surveys, 40, 101, 210–211, 224, 251, 261, 263
  topography, 249
Nolloth, Captain, 128

O' Leary, Daniel, 43
O'Neil, Charles, 240

Pact of Chinandega, 109, 131
Pact of Nacaome, 60, 66
Palenque, 67
Palmerston, Viscount, 112
  on boundary disputes, 77, 83
  involvement in Mosquito Coast affairs, 65, 73, 86
  on relations with Costa Rica, 74
  on relations with United States, 106, 127
  resignation, 135
  on the role of Britain in Central America, 75, 81, 83, 89, 91
  view of Greytown, 51, 127, 129
Panama Canal
  climate change, 14, 18
  construction of, 268–269
  Lobby, 256, 262
  Oregon episode, 257
  racial dimensions, 17
  triumphalist narrative, 1–6, 18
Panama Railway Company, 172
Panama–Pacific International Exposition, 17–19
Parker, Harold, 136
Paton, George, 202
Patterson, Henry, 194, 196, 202
Pearl Key Lagoon, 32, 56, 58
Pfeiffer, H. G., 86, 89, 93, 143, 195
Philippines, 257
Pierce, Franklin, 122, 144–145, 154, 162
Pim, Bedford, 189–191, 198, 212
Polk, James, 100
Porter, James, 52
Portland Oregonian, 257
Prince Philippe, 47
Princess Victoria (Miskitu princess), 202
Providence Island, 8
Prowett, John, 35
Puerto Rico, 257
Puig, Salvador Martí, 118
Pulitzer, Joseph, 259

Quijano, Manuel, 26, 32

railway, 26
Rama (ethnic group), 38, 63–64, 93
Realejo, 50, 97
refugees, 57
Registro Oficial (Nicaragua), 117
Richmond Enquirer, 50
Rivas, Anselmo H., 202–203
Rivas, Patricio, 61, 157, 162–164
Robert Charles Frederic
  affinity for Britain, 38
  Anglican Church, 58
  antislavery, 36–37
  commission, 53
  death of, 38, 41, 49, 54, 87
  English laws, 55
  land grants, 53, 55, 57, 154

political acts, 31, 37
relations with Belize, 27
territorial claims, 27–28, 36–37
Tweed mission, 26
visit to Jamaica, 10
will, 54
Robert Henry Clarence, 229, 234–235, 239–241, 243, 245
Roberts, J. S., 197
Roberts, Orlando, 37–38
Robinson, Lowrie, 39, 54, 64
Rockwell, John, 100
Roosevelt, Theodore, 258–259
Royal Geographical Society, 25, 40
rubber, 193, 198–199, 212, 232
Russell, John, 36, 206

Sadler, James, 228
Saenz, Ramon, 188, 201, 206
Salas, Colonel, 62
Salem Gazette, 110
Salinas (Costa Rica), 147
Salinas, Sebastián, 91
Salt Creek, 28–29, 34, 39, 41, 77
Sambolyer (Carib chief), 64
San Andres, 42
San Francisco, 17, 97–98, 100, 130, 159, 161, 224, 258–259
San Francisco Call, 255
San Juan del Norte. *See* Greytown
San Juan River
  bungo men, 140
  Colorado branch, 124
  description of, 130
  early explorations, 7
  El Castillo, 7, 9, 128
  Fort San Carlos, 127–128, 158
  in Anglo-Spanish rivalry, 7, 9
  rapids, 40, 124, 131
  role in filibustering, 161, 163
  role in *guerra nacional*, 166–168, 171
  Sarapiquí route, 59, 61–62, 70, 74–75, 77, 163–166, 212
  trade, 79
Savage, Henry, 35
Scientific American, 264
Scriven, George, 248, 250–251
Seat, B. B., 231, 234, 237, 245
Sharpe, Robert, 43
Shepherd brothers, 53, 56, 155
Shepherd, Peter, 27, 54, 74, 154

Shepherd, Samuel, 27, 29, 54, 154
Sherman, John, 250
Silva, Buenaventura, 102
slave flight, 57
Smith, Lawrence, 220
Société de Géographie de Paris, 219
Spanish Royal Order of 1803, 28
Spanish-American War, 256
Sparks, Major, 70–74, 80–81
Spencer, Sylvanus, 165
Spooner Act, 267
Squier, Ephraim George, 84
  appointment to Nicaragua, 102–103
  Central American Union, 117
  in León, 103–104, 118
  representations of Miskitu, 114, 116
  as scholar, 102–103
  treaties, 105–106, 111, 113
  view of Mosquito government, 105, 113
St. John's Church, Bluefields, 44
Stephen, James, 31
Stephens, John Lloyd, 46–47, 103
Stevenson, Henry, 138–140
Stewart, H., 172
Stuart, Commander, 240–241, 244
Suez Canal, 21–22, 186, 208–210, 213, 218–219, 251–252

Tarleton, John, 156–158
Tayler, John, 241
Taylor, H. C., 249–250, 252
Taylor, Henry, 31
Taylor, Zachary, 102, 105, 111
Tehuantepec route, 50, 100–101, 170, 215
Texas, 46, 49, 107, 116, 154, 168
Thomas, John, 203
Tracy, Henry, 98
Treaty of Managua
  annulment, 269
  arbitration clause, 207–208
  contravention, 199, 228, 234, 236, 241
  status of Greytown, 192–193, 228
  terms, 186–187, 198, 206, 229
Treaty of Paris (1898), 256

U.S. Board of Trade, 220
U.S. Senate, 46
U.S.S. *Cyane*. *See* Greytown: bombardment
U.S.S. *Prometheus*, 125, 130, 132–136
U.S.S. *Saranac*, 136
United States Army Corps of Engineers, 223

United States – ideology and expansion
  American Revolution, 9
  Anglo-Saxon alliance, 109, 111
  control of the Pacific, 104, 249
  dollar diplomacy, 269
  Greater United States, 257
  gunboat diplomacy, 122, 146, 269
  Kansas–Nebraska Act, 144
  Lewis and Clark Expedition, 25
  Manifest Destiny, 106–107, 109
  Mexican–American War, 50, 99–100, 116–117, 120, 145, 154, 186, 215
  Missouri Compromise, 144
  Monroe Doctrine, 13, 269
  naval ambitions, 22, 248, 250–251, 253, 257–258
  neutrality, 22, 123
  Ostend Manifesto, 145
  post-Civil War, 21–22, 219, 248, 253
  post-Cold War order, 19
  Roosevelt Corollary, 269
  slavery, 116, 144–145
  Southern expansionism, 145, 168
  Spanish–American War, 257–261, 264, 268
  Taft administration, 268
  Transcontinental Railroad, 209
  U.S. press, 101, 106–107, 110, 143, 209
  view of Central America, 256
  view of filibustering, 150–151, 162
  view of Greytown, 126, 144
  War of 1812, 106
  West India Regiment, 210
  Westward expansion, 15, 107–109, 253
  yellow journalism, 259–261, 264, 268
Utrecho, Ysidro, 227, 229

Valientes (ethnic group), 87
Van Diemen's Island, 27
Vanderbilt, Cornelius
  competition from Panama route, 130
  conflict with Greytown authorities, 21, 128, 130, 132–133
  conflict with William Walker, 162–163
  efforts towards canal, 123–124, 131
  transit route, 146
  transit services, 125, 130–131, 135, 146, 159
Victoria (sister to Miskitu chief George Augustus), 72
Vitta, José, 233

Wainwright, Captain, 172
Walker, H. J., 261
Walker, Patrick, 31, 134
  administration of Mosquito Shore, 39, 49, 52, 55–57, 59, 63, 65, 71, 84
  antislavery, 42–44
  appointment as consul, 20, 26, 41, 48, 63
  on boundaries, 48
  death, 62, 69
  knighthood, 44
  land grants, 54, 57
  move to Bluefields, 57
  occupation of San Juan del Norte, 101, 104
  as part of Alexander MacDonald's Commission, 53
  quest for San Juan del Norte, 51, 58–59, 61–62, 64
  relations with George Augustus, 42, 44–45, 86
  visit to Jamaica, 59–60, 64, 66–67
Walker, William
  Central American unity, 173–174
  evacuation of filibusters, 167–168
  fame, 153
  in Granada, 153, 157–158, 160–161
  importance of Greytown, 153, 165–166
  importance of Nicaragua Canal, 21, 150–151, 159, 171
  Nicaragua transit route, 159–162, 169, 171
  return to Greytown, 169
  slavery, 173
  Southern expansionism, 168
  support among African Americans, 152–153
  territorial claims, 158
Walsh, William, 53
War of Jenkins' Ear, 9
Webster, Daniel, 35
Webster–Crampton Treaty, 147
Weekly Herald, 101
Wellington (Miskitu chief), 39, 54
Welsh, James, 82
West Indies
  British regiments, 44, 70
  immigrants, 17, 242
  merchants, 27
White, James, 158
White, Joseph L., 104, 129, 133
William Clarence (Miskitu prince), 38–39, 86

William Henry Clarence
   appeals to Great Britain, 202, 206
   death of, 213
   education, 196
   election, 196, 199, 201–202
   ethnicity, 195
   Moravian mission, 196–197
   proclamation, 204–205, 207
   relations with Nicaragua, 205
   relocation to Pearl Lagoon, 204
Wilson, Captain, 238
Wolff, Mr., 171
Wood, Alexander, 120
Wood, Samuel Smith, 136
Woolva (ethnic group), 63–64, 93
World War I, 17
World's Fair of Chicago, 216–218

Young, Thomas, 38

Zelaya, José Santos, 226, 267–269
Zeledón–Wyke Treaty, 180, *See* Treaty of Managua
Ziock, Heinrich, 213, 245–246

For EU product safety concerns, contact us at Calle de José Abascal, 56–1°, 28003 Madrid, Spain or eugpsr@cambridge.org.